Ryland Clenton

THE
CLENDONS

Five Hundred Years of the
Clendon Family
An Illustrated History

RYLAND CLENDON

First published in Great Britain 1997 by
Harold Martin & Redman Ltd.
The Wells House, Holywell Road, Malvern Wells,
Worcestershire WR14 4LH

British Library Cataloguing in Publication Data

A catalogue record for this book is available
from the British Library

ISBN   1 901394 09 3

Printed and Bound in Great Britain

*All profits accrued by the author from
the sale of this book will be
donated to the Cancer Research Campaign.*

CONTENTS

LIST OF ILLUSTRATIONS

It is perfectly possible to read and enjoy 'The Clendons' without more than a glance at the tables. However, they provide a wealth of information for those interested in digging it out.

In Parts 1, 2 and 3, the tables are relatively easy to follow. They are mostly incorporated within the text, and drawn up in families.

In Part 4 James Reddy Clendon's descendants are listed generation by generation. To assist in the identification of family relationships, and the construction of family trees, a numerical system is used. This is illustrated below:

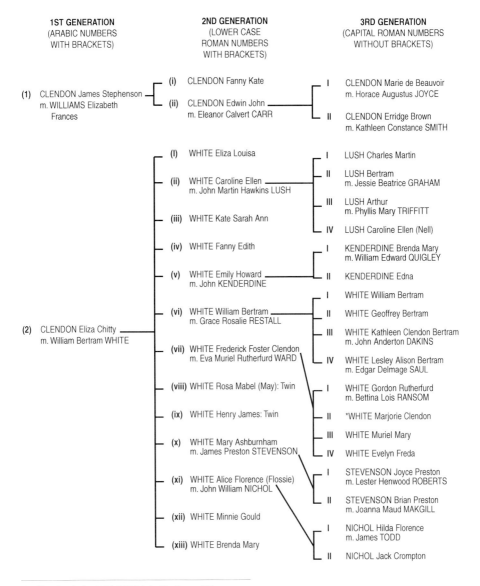

1ST GENERATION (ARABIC NUMBERS WITH BRACKETS)	2ND GENERATION (LOWER CASE ROMAN NUMBERS WITH BRACKETS)	3RD GENERATION (CAPITAL ROMAN NUMBERS WITHOUT BRACKETS)

(1) CLENDON James Stephenson
m. WILLIAMS Elizabeth Frances

(i) CLENDON Fanny Kate
(ii) CLENDON Edwin John
m. Eleanor Calvert CARR

I CLENDON Marie de Beauvoir
m. Horace Augustus JOYCE
II CLENDON Erridge Brown
m. Kathleen Constance SMITH

(2) CLENDON Eliza Chitty
m. William Bertram WHITE

(I) WHITE Eliza Louisa
(ii) WHITE Caroline Ellen
m. John Martin Hawkins LUSH
(iii) WHITE Kate Sarah Ann
(iv) WHITE Fanny Edith
(v) WHITE Emily Howard
m. John KENDERDINE
(vi) WHITE William Bertram
m. Grace Rosalie RESTALL
(vii) WHITE Frederick Foster Clendon
m. Eva Muriel Rutherfurd WARD
(viii) WHITE Rosa Mabel (May): Twin
(ix) WHITE Henry James: Twin
(x) WHITE Mary Ashburnham
m. James Preston STEVENSON
(xi) WHITE Alice Florence (Flossie)
m. John William NICHOL
(xii) WHITE Minnie Gould
(xiii) WHITE Brenda Mary

I LUSH Charles Martin
II LUSH Bertram
m. Jessie Beatrice GRAHAM
III LUSH Arthur
m. Phyllis Mary TRIFFITT
IV LUSH Caroline Ellen (Nell)

I KENDERDINE Brenda Mary
m. William Edward QUIGLEY
II KENDERDINE Edna

I WHITE William Bertram
II WHITE Geoffrey Bertram
III WHITE Kathleen Clendon Bertram
m. John Anderton DAKINS
IV WHITE Lesley Alison Bertram
m. Edgar Delmage SAUL

I WHITE Gordon Rutherfurd
m. Bettina Lois RANSOM
II *WHITE Marjorie Clendon
III WHITE Muriel Mary
IV WHITE Evelyn Freda

I STEVENSON Joyce Preston
m. Lester Henwood ROBERTS
II STEVENSON Brian Preston
m. Joanna Maud MAKGILL

I NICHOL Hilda Florence
m. James TODD
II NICHOL Jack Crompton

---

* Therefore the key to WHITE Majorie Clendon would be:
3 (generation number) (2) (grandparent) (vii) (mother) II (2nd child born): 3(2)(vii)II

Many people have helped me in producing
this book, but two deserve special thanks
above all the others:

Tom – for your inspiration and enthusiasm which encouraged
me to attempt this project in the first place. Your constant
support and advice throughout has made the book a far better
product than I could have achieved on my own;

Sue – for living with my moods, my
obsession about the Clendon family history,
for surviving, and for sustaining me.
I dedicate this book to you:

SUE

Remember this
Oh woman true
It does not matter
What you do.

My love is constant
Never ends
You are the best
Of all my friends.

Whate'er the future
Or the past
My love for you
Will always last.

Remember this
Sweet woman do
I know thee well
Yet still love you.

INTRODUCTION

The earliest reference to the name Clendon is a Northamptonshire village recorded in the Domesday Book. This book starts there. It traces the story of the present family from their medieval roots in Northamptonshire, through a period in Kent in the 18th century, to migrations to USA and New Zealand in Victorian times – and for my great grandfather's branch – to the present day.

This book is based on the original genealogical research carried out by Erik Chitty, Douglas Clendon, and Bette Edwards on the Chitty and Clendon Families.

The two families have been linked since 1777 when Gideon Chitty and George Clendon bought a common vault in the churchyard at St. George's, Deal. The families intermarried three times, and in 1847 a party from both families, led by my great-great grandfather emigrated to the USA, and settled in Glens Falls, New York.

Bette Edwards is descended from one of the Chittys in this party. An American, she lives in Massachusetts and has two Clendon/Chitty marriages in her pedigree. She is the only one of the three original family genealogists still living. She has an enormous knowledge and interest in the history of both families, has a large collection of archives, and contributed greatly to the research on the American and Argentinean branches for the 1974 edition.

Erik Chitty was an actor by profession, but his time consuming hobby from his undergraduate days was genealogy. He became recognised as an eminent genealogist, and was a Fellow of the Society of Genealogists.

Douglas Clendon was my father. As a child I can remember him studying wills and old records at home, piecing together the evidence, trying to work out who was related to whom in medieval times. When in my teens one of our summer family holidays was spent in Northamptonshire visiting libraries, villages such as Glendon, and Mears Ashby, and searching through old records for clues about our ancestors.

Erik and Douglas started their collaboration in the 1940's. The first description of the Clendon family was compiled by Erik Chitty in 1949. It is a document of about 30 pages long and three copies were produced: one for the Society of Genealogists, one for Douglas Clendon, and one for the compiler. In 1994 my son Tom and I found it in the library at the Society of Genealogists, and took three further copies.

Erik, assisted by Douglas and Bette published two further definitive genealogical records of the Chitty and Clendon families. The first was in 1954 and consisted of around 130 pages of quarto. About half are devoted to the Clendon family. Enough copies were produced to send to all known relatives who were interested – for a charge of 5/- plus postage. A substantial number went to USA and New Zealand.

The second was in 1974. This was much fuller with many pages of genealogical records of descendants and living relatives. The volume comprised just over 200 pages of A4, about half of which relate to the Clendon family. 500 copies were produced, and the charge was, I think, £2 per copy. All 500 have been sold, but photocopies can be provided by arrangement.

Genealogy is a never ending hobby. My father continued to work at it, on and off, until he died in 1970. I had no enthusiasm for it until twenty years later when we were selling the house where he and my mother had lived all their married life. I had to sort out all his papers. I decided to keep those connected with genealogy and family history. What I discovered excited my interest, and that of my younger son Tom.

There was an enormous amount of descriptive material – old wills, letters, documents and photographs – which gave us a much more vivid and exciting picture of our ancestors than the bare bones of the genealogical records, and the family tree!

We decided to find out as much as we could about the life and times of our ancestors. How they lived, where they lived, why they moved from one part of the country to another, why they emigrated to USA, and New Zealand – and the effect of these decisions on their lives.

This took me and my wife, Sue, to all the places where they had lived – in England to the Northamptonshire villages, to Kent, and to Birmingham, in North Wales to Cwmrhaidr, near Machynlleth, and Dolgellau.

We went to the USA and met Bette and Bob Edwards. They took us to Glens Falls, New York, where the Clendon and Chitty families settled in the nineteenth century, and where my grandfather was born. Sue later returned with Tom to visit Bob and Bette who have since helped with further research.

We went to New Zealand for six weeks. We visited the historic places in the Bay of Islands and Rawene associated with James Reddy Clendon, the most illustrious New Zealand member of the Clendon family. Ross Clendon, a New Zealand cousin at present living in Manila, has contributed a magnificent account of the exploits of James Reddy Clendon for inclusion in this book – probably the most authoritative account yet to be published.

We met Philippa Holmes, a descendant of James Reddy Clendon, and stayed with her in Tauranga. She has a large collection of Clendon archives. Her list of the descendants of James Reddy Clendon included in this book contains over 1,000 names! We went to Akatarawa where my great grandfather Thomas Clendon attempted to develop a prosperous farm out of bushland. We stayed for some time in Lower Hutt with Nancy Walker, one of his grandchildren, whom we had known since 1970. We met many other descendants of Thomas Clendon, many of whom live in Lower Hutt or nearby around the Bay of Wellington. While there we were told much about the life and times of Thomas and his family in their early settlement days. For this, and for many other items of genealogical information provided by my New Zealand relatives for inclusion in this book, I am extremely grateful.

This book differs from earlier editions. It does not cover the Chitty family, and it omits much of the genealogical data recorded in the 1974 edition.

The aim is to provide a narrative account of the lives of our Clendon ancestors, with illustrations, extracts from wills, letters and other documents – and also a selection of relevant family tree diagrams and genealogical tables updated to the present day.

Abbreviations

b.	born		d.	died
c.	christined		i.	interred
m.	married		Prob.	Probate
unm.	unmarried		pr.	proved
d.f.r.	de facto relationship		dtd.	dated
	(living together as man		lib.	book
	and wife but not married)		fol.	page or section
fl.	alive		Adm	letters of administration
dvp.	alive in father's lifetime		mi	memorial inscription

Part 1

EARLY HISTORY

THE DE CLENDON FAMILY TREE

The descent of the memorial land at Clendon and its eventual passage by marriage to the Newbottle family is shown by the numbers in this pedigree:

(1) Henry de Clendon

(2) Richard (time of King John)

(3) William de Clendon (time of King Edward I)

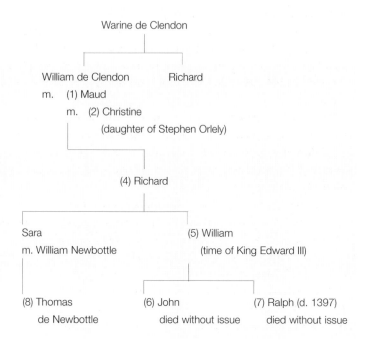

Warine de Clendon

William de Clendon   Richard

m.   (1) Maud

    m.   (2) Christine

          (daughter of Stephen Orlely)

(4) Richard

Sara   (5) William

m. William Newbottle   (time of King Edward III)

(8) Thomas   (6) John   (7) Ralph (d. 1397)

    de Newbottle   died without issue   died without issue

CHAPTER 1
CLENDON ORIGINS (1086-1460)

Where does the name Clendon come from? How far back can we go in our history of the Clendon family? These are questions that I am often asked by people when they hear that I am studying our family history. This chapter sets out to provide the answers.

There is a story that our family name originates from a Norman called de Clendon who came over from France to England with William the Conqueror in 1066, and was granted land in Northamptonshire. However there is no evidence to support this theory. My brother David, while at Emmanuel College, Cambridge, researched this at the University library. He discovered that there were very few families whose pedigrees can be traced back to times before 1066. Despite the fact that England has one of the largest and oldest collections of public records in the world, insufficient information has survived to trace more than a few families back that far. According to the Oxford Guide to Family History [The Oxford Guide to Family History. David Hey. Oxford University Press. 1993.] only the Ardens and Berkeleys can prove a descent from a pre-Conquest Englishman. A few more families can prove their descent beyond the Conquest into Normandy, but de Clendon is not listed among them!

When trying to trace our family name to its origin, there are three basic problems. The first, which I have already mentioned, is the lack of records available – due to the fact that in early times very few people could read or write, few things were written down, and not much of what was written has survived.

The second problem is that even if records are available for us to inspect, and they have been traced, surnames and place names were often spelt differently on different occasions. Clendon was spelt Clendone in the Domesday book, Clendar in a university document in 1659, and was commonly written as Glendon.

The third problem – and the most fundamental – is that our earliest ancestors did not have surnames! They were simply known by their personal names (eg William). Sometimes the father's name, (eg son of John), was added. Sometimes there was a by-name, or nickname, (eg Broad head). But such additional names were not surnames, nor were they hereditary.

The Oxford Guide states that in 1066, hereditary surnames were used only by a few of the great land owning families, and it was William I's barons with such names as William de Warenne from Varrenes near Dieppe, and Ilbert de Laci from Lassy, south of Bayeux, who introduced the idea of stable surnames in England. During the two centuries following the conquest most major land owning families and knights came to adopt hereditary surnames, especially if they lived in the south of England. Fashion played some part in this, but the need for landowners to ensure continuity of their property was the driving force in those uncertain times. This explains why, at that time, most surnames were taken from the place where the family lived, and owned property. It was only in later centuries, as the practice of taking a surname spread lower down the social scale, that other origins of surnames became more widely used. A popular origin was the holder's occupation eg Sawyer, Taylor, Smith, and Weaver; another origin was the father's personal name eg Williamson, Johnson, and Richardson. However the adoption of surnames was a slow process, particularly among the unskilled labourers in towns, and countrymen living in the north. During the fifteenth century surnames were prevalent almost everywhere, but the process was not complete until the sixteenth century.

It is remarkable, therefore, that we can identify a family with the name de Clendon living in the 12th century. Although the story at the start of this chapter is untrue, it probably came about because this family existed – and the use of the prefix de could easily have been misunderstood to mean that the name was of Norman origin.

The earliest recorded member of this family was called Henry de Clendone. He was alive during the reign of King John (1199-1216). He was living in a place called Clendon, where he owned the manorial land. He (or his ancestor) would have taken his name from that place, ie de Clendon means of Clendon. French words were used in England then in that way, after the fashion set by the Norman barons. As explained later, our family could have been related to these de Clendons or could have taken their name independently from the same place – Clendon.

The Concise Oxford Dictionary of Place Names states that the place name of Clendon has its origin in the Old English words claenan dune, meaning '(at) the clean hill' and 'clean' refers to freedom from growth of thornbushes and the like.

Clendon is in Northamptonshire, situated about two miles west-north-west of Kettering. Today it is called Glendon, but it was known as Clendon for over 600 years from the 11th to the 18th century. It is Clendon, the place, that provides the earliest known reference to our family name. It is mentioned in the Domesday Book, published in 1086. This book records the findings of the "general survey" of all property throughout the country which King William I initiated soon after he had conquered England. The survey identified property in Clendon (there spelt Clendone) that was owned by the crown.

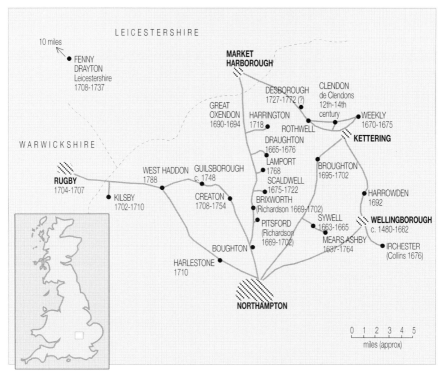

Map 1: Part of Northamptonshire where the early Clendons lived.

The following extract is from Bridges History of Northamptonshire (Vol. II, P.15), which was published in 1791. It first describes Clendon as it was in the late 18th century, and then provides the reference to the property recorded in the "general survey", and published in the Domesday Book.

> *Clendon, corruptly called Glendon, is a small inclosed lordship lying to the south of Thorp-Malsover*, containing now only two or three houses, of which the principal is the seat of Ralph Lane Esq; lord of the manor, but formerly several more. In the gallery of Mr Lane's house are various coats of arms and family portraits; and amongst other pictures, a full length of Queen Catherine Par, in a rich habit of the times, for which the family was offered an hundred pounds.*
>
> *At the time of the general survey, half an hide† and a third part of an hide in Clendone, pertaining to the manor of Rothwell, were in the hands of the crown . . .*

---

*   Thorp-Malsover, now known as Thorpe Malsor, is actually a mile south of Glendon.
†   "hide", in old English law, is a variable unit of area of land enough for a household.

A hundred years later the parish was known legitimately, (no longer corruptly!), as Glendon. There was no church, but there was a railway line. The signal box, at the junction of the Nottingham and Leicester lines, bore the name Glendon Junction. I saw it frequently on train journeys from Derbyshire when going to work in London, until a few years ago when it was demolished.

Kelly's Directory of Northamptonshire (1914) describes Glendon as it was nearly a hundred years ago as follows:

> *Glendon is a parish on the main line of the Midland Railway, forming the junction for the branch lines to Nottingham and Leicester . . . .Messrs James Pain Ltd have ironstone quarries here. There was once a church here dedicated to St Helen, but it has longsince disappeared. The living is a rectory net yearly value £88 in the gift of Mrs Booth, and held since 1902 by the Rev Charles Maunsell Weatherall MA of Emmanuel College Cambridge, who is also rector of and resides at Rushton. Glendon Hall, a fine mansion, in a park of about 400 acres, is the property and residence of Mrs Booth who is the lady of the manor and sole landowner. The soil is red shale and ironstone and the land is chiefly arable. The area is 791 acres; rateable value, £4,635; the population in 1911 was 48. Letters received through Kettering . . . Wall letter box Glendon Hall cleared 6 pm; Sundays 11.15 am. The children of this place attend school at Rushton . . .*

I have visited the place twice. The first time was with my parents and my brother when I was a schoolboy. Glendon Hall was owned and occupied then by a family in whose hands it had been for many generations. The second time was recently with my wife, Sue and son, Tom, doing research for this book.

Glendon Hall and its grounds had been sold and the house divided into apartments. The owner of one of them welcomed us in. Her entrance was the original front door of the house, and her apartment contained the old front hall, part of which had now been converted into a kitchen. She gave us a print of Glendon Hall in 1830 to include in this book.

Most road maps no longer mark Glendon although there are a few sign posts to it at the junctions of nearby lanes. There are some other houses there but the Ordnance Survey road map of England now marks it up as Glendon Hall. The children from the place still attend the primary school at Rushton.

For over 200 years the de Clendon

Glendon Hall, 1830.

family owned the manorial land at Clendon. In 1397 when there was no male heir, the property passed by marriage into the Newbottle family.

The following extract from Bridge's History of Northamptonshire tells the story of the de Clendons, and the manorial land, in more detail.

By inquisition taken in the twenty fourth of Edward I (1296) William de Clendon was found to hold nine virgates* of land in Clendon of the Earl of Gloucester, who held them in capite of the King. This was that part of the lordship which at the time of the domesday survey pertained to Rothwell manor. William de Clendon appears to have been the descendant of Richard son to Henry de Clendone, who in the reign of King John gave his two virgates of land here to St James's Abbey near Northampton.

His successor in these nine virgates was Richard the grandson of Warine de Clendon, who by inquisition taken in the eighth year of Edward II (1315) after the decease of Gilbert de Clare, Earl of Gloucester and Hertford, was found to hold in Clendon a sixth part of one knight's fee.

William de Clendon his son was seized of them in the seventh of Edward III (1334) and left them to John his son, upon whose death without issue this estate devolved on Ralph de Clendon his younger brother, which Ralph by

---

*   "virgate" is an old land measure, commonly 30 acres.

inquisition taken in the thirty sixth year of Edward III was certified to have been an idiot from his birth.

On which account this manor in Clendon was seized into the hands of the crown, and granted with the custody of the said Ralph for his life-time to Hugh Wake. Upon the decease of this Ralph, in the eighteenth of Richard II, (1397), Thomas de Newbottle the son of Sara, daughter to Richard de Clendon the grandfather of the said Ralph de Clendon, was declared to be his heir, and had livery* of this inheritance . . .

From 1397, when Ralph de Clendon died, there is a period of only about 70 years before William Clendon, our ancestor, was born. He lived only 10 miles from the village of Clendon. On the face of it, it seems that it might not be too difficult to establish a link between the two families.

However, my father spent many years seeking out old records, and searching for clues as to the names and whereabouts of any more Clendons in Northamptonshire during that period, in order to find a connection between our family and the de Clendons – but without success.

The only surviving records from that time are those giving information about the people who were involved in the ownership of the land. Other records such as births, marriages and deaths were not kept then. It is reasonable to assume that there were other brothers and sisters in the de Clendon family who married and had families, but who were unable to inherit the land because they were too distantly related, and whose names were not recorded. It is possible that we could be descended from such a branch of the manorial family, living in the same vicinity, but there is no documentary evidence to prove it.

Thus the answers to the questions posed at the beginning of the chapter are as follows. The name Clendon comes from a place of that name in Northamptonshire, now called Glendon. The de Clendon family lived there, owned the manorial land, and can be traced back to 1200. We may be descended from a branch of that family. Alternatively our forefathers may have taken their name independently from the same place of origin, Clendon. The earliest ancestor that we can trace lived ten miles from there and was born sometime around 1460 to 1480.

---

*   "livery" is an obsolete word meaning "handing over"

CHAPTER 2
EIGHT GENERATIONS IN NORTHAMPTONSHIRE
(1460 – 1708)

WILLIAM CLENDON *(Will 1524)*

Our earliest traceable ancestor, William Clendon, was the first of the eight generations of Northamptonshire Clendons. He was a tanner, and lived in Wellingborough. He and his wife Alice both wrote wills. This is all I know of them.

Looking at their wills, and the family tree diagram, you can identify the names William, Alice, Agnes and Elizabeth Clendon as the names of their grandchildren, the children of their son Henry. Thus by 1524 William Clendon was a grandfather several times over. I have assumed that he was then born around 1460 to 1480. These are the dates to which it is possible to trace our first known ancestor.

The following are the wills of William and Alice Clendon:

The Will of WILLIAM CLENDON of Wellingborough dated 1524, proved -?-. To be buried at All Hallows. My best good to be my mortuary after the manner & custom of the town. To the mother church of Lincoln 12d. To the High Altar of Wellingborough for tithes forgotten 16d. To Corpus Christi Guild 2/-. To the high rood 12d. To St Katherine's Guild 12d. To the sepulchre light 8d. To the torches 12d. To the bells 12d. To Stapuls Bridge 16d. To the building of the church house 12d. To Henry & Laurans BURGE each 6/8. To Alys WELCH 12d. To (?grandson) WILLIAM CLENDON two couples of ewes. To (?granddaughter) ALYS CLENDON an ewe and a lamb. To my son HENRY CLENDON all my tanned leather and all manner of instruments that belong to my occupation. To my wife ALYS the residue, she and my son HENRY to be executors. Witnesses: Sir John PARNELL curate, John BRABONE, John WELCH, Wm PATRYKE, Rechard MAUNCELL.

Northampton Archdeaconry Court Book B 1520-26 folio 170

The Will of ALICE CLENDON of Wellingborough dated 1532 Dec 3, proved -
?-. To be buried in All Hallows Churchyard. For my mortuary as the law
allows. To mother church of Lincoln 12d. To (?high altar) of parish church for
tithes forgotten 16d. To rood loft 12d. To Corpus Christi Guild . . .? . . . To Our
Lady's Guild 12d . . . Various legacies to church etc . . . To the poor for a dirge
at my burial £3. For (?mass) for husband and me 4 marke. To Laurence
BURGE a cup, 6/8, a possnet & a board cloth. To Agnes SYLVERSTON kirtle,
petticoat, apron & smock. To Lucy PAGE best hat, two pails, a sheet. To Mary
BORTEN sheet & towel. To ELIZ'TH YEDYE kerchief & apron. To Alice ? green
gown, 3 wysshins, 3 best sheets, pan, two pots . . . (and various other items)
. . . To (?grandchildren) AGNES CLENDON . . . candlestick & kerchief, JOHN
CLENDON . . .THOMAS CLENDON, platter & sheet, WILLIAM CLENDON
. . . pan, blankets, pair of sheets, bason, candlestick, board cloth, table . . . to
him & ALICE each 20/- if it may conveniently be performed, to ALICE
CLENDON coverlet, great kettle, board cloth, folding table, stool, charger, spit etc.
Residue to son HENRY my executor. Witnesses: Sir John PARNELL, Wm
GWYN, Thos SAMEWELL.
> *Northampton Archdeaconry Court Book E 1531-38 fol 4*

It is interesting to note from the wills that Wellingborough was at that time
in the Diocese of Lincoln, and this couple made legacies to the cathedral
there, as well as to other charities and the church locally. Also they seem
only to have had one child, a son, Henry, our ancestor.

HENRY CLENDON *(Will 1557)*

Our second generation of Northamptonshire ancestors, Henry also lived in
Wellingborough. He owned a shop in the market place, as well as some
land. He was dead by 1558. He had seven children, but the name of his wife
is not known. He wrote a will (see below).

HENRY CLENDON had issue seven children;

1	**WILLIAM CLENDON**	will 1560/66
	of Wellingborough	
	Yeoman	
	m. KATHERINE -?-	
2	**GEORGE CLENDON**	alive 1558
	1st m. ELIZABETH -?-	alive 1623
	2nd m. -?- BURTON	

     George Clendon had issue four children (see family tree diagram)

3	**ALICE CLENDON**	died in her father's lifetime

4	**AGNES CLENDON**	alive 1558
5	**ELIZABETH CLENDON**	alive 1558
6	**JOHN CLENDON**	died in his father's lifetime
7*	**THOMAS CLENDON** of Wellingborough husbandman	will 1601
	m. MARGARET -?-	

Thomas and Margaret Clendon had issue three sons – see next table.

Looking at Henry's will below it appears that his wife died before him, since she is not named, and that the oldest son William is charged with bringing up two of the daughters. William had the lion's share of the inheritance. Our ancestor Thomas had to be content with £26. 13s. 4d. and two silver spoons! The will is as follows:

The Will of HENRY CLENDON of Wellingborough dated 1557 Feb 1 pr 1558 Apr 30 (Prerogative Court of Canterbury F.7 Noodes) To son WILLIAM house that I dwell in, shop in market place & all my land, he to bring up my daughters ANNIES & ELIZABETH until their marriages. To daughters AGNES & ELIZABETH each £20 besides the gift their mother gave them. To sons GEORGE & THOMAS each £26.13.4 and to GEORGE, THOMAS, AGNES & ELISABETH each two silver spoons. Residue to son WILLIAM, exor. Supervisor: Robert WOOTON clerk, parson of Hardwicke. Witnesses: John JEW, clerk, John VINCENT, alderman, Henry HARRIATT.

Our ancestor from the third generation of Northamptonshire Clendons was:

THOMAS CLENDON *(Will 1601)*

Thomas also lived in Wellingborough. He was a husbandman – the equivalent nowadays of a farmer. His wife's name was Margaret. He enjoyed, it seems from his will, see below, a good standard of life.

He employed a resident maid servant, and provided for his family and for his wife's creature comforts in a practical way . . . "MARGARET also to have competent meat and drink and fire to warm and comfort her . . . "

---

*   denotes an ancestor

THOMAS and MARGARET CLENDON had issue three sons:

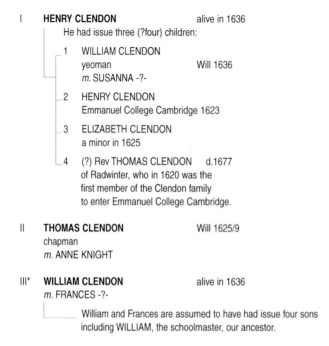

I   **HENRY CLENDON**   alive in 1636
       He had issue three (?four) children:

       1   WILLIAM CLENDON
            yeoman   Will 1636
            m. SUSANNA -?-

       2   HENRY CLENDON
            Emmanuel College Cambridge 1623

       3   ELIZABETH CLENDON
            a minor in 1625

       4   (?) Rev THOMAS CLENDON   d.1677
            of Radwinter, who in 1620 was the
            first member of the Clendon family
            to enter Emmanuel College Cambridge.

II   **THOMAS CLENDON**   Will 1625/9
       chapman
       m. ANNE KNIGHT

III*   **WILLIAM CLENDON**   alive in 1636
       m. FRANCES -?-

            William and Frances are assumed to have had issue four sons
            including WILLIAM, the schoolmaster, our ancestor.

Thomas could afford to be a little more generous with his younger sons
than his father was. Our ancestor William gets £20, a cow bullock of two
years old, the best brass pan, a bed, mattress, and bolster. The will reads as
follows:

> *The Will of THOMAS CLENDON of Wellingborough husbandman dtd 1601
> Aug 23, pr 1601/2 Feb 25. To wife MARGARET 10 ewes and lambs, 10 gist
> sheep, with the wool growing on them this year, to be kept for her by executor,
> she to have profits from them during her life. Executor shall also pay her £6
> yearly and shall pay to the Lord of Manor rents from one yard of copy-
> hold land of which he shall enjoy the use. MARGARET also to have competent
> meat and drink and fire to warm and comfort her, also the moeavles &
> furniture except one bed wherein my maid servant doth lie, also two hives of bees,
> one fourth of the fruit in the orchard, six platters, four pewter dishes, two
> porringers, two candlesticks, best brass pot, four silver spoons, square table in the
> hall with two buffet stools and the chair in the hall chimney. Executor to have
> the second brass pot and to share with her residue of brazen vessels. To son
> WILLIAM £20, a cow bullock of two years old, best brass pan, bed, mattress,
> bolster.*

To son THOMAS featherbed, second spit, two hives with bees, and to his wife ANNE brown bullock and two sheep, or 10/- in lieu of the sheep. To (grandson) WILLIAM son of kinsman JOHN CLENDON one sheep or 5/-, and the like to kinsfolk John BAGGOT, Elizabeth HUNT and Thomas son of Peter CLEY. To other children whose baptism I was a witness each 12d. To repair of church 10/- and of bridge 6/8. To Thos HOLE best russet coat, flaxen doublet & russet hose. To Benjamin HIPWELL second russet coat, flaxen doublet, & russet hose, shirt & pair of shoes. To kinswoman Dorothy SMITH one strike of barley three years. To kinsman Peter CLEY for making this my last will and testament 10/-. Residue to son HENRY CLENDON, executor. Overseers: brother GEORGE CLENDON and Peter CLEY. Witnesses Hen. ASPINALL & Peter CLEY the writer hereof. Inventory in total £93.15.0.

Northampton Archdeaconry Court Book W 1596-1602 folio 276

WILLIAM CLENDON (alive 1636)

Very little indeed is known for certain about our fourth generation Northamptonshire ancestor other than that he was called William, and he was alive in 1636 when his nephew William wrote a will, and referred to him as "Uncle William". I have been unable to find the evidence that his wife's name was Frances, but Erik Chitty entered her on the family tree diagram in the 1974 edition, which I assume is valid.

William is, however, important from the genealogical point of view because there is so little information available about him in the available records. Indeed there is no absolute proof that he had any issue, although Erik Chitty came to the conclusion that he did, and that among them was William Clendon, Master of Wellingborough School, our ancestor.

The evidence to support this conclusion is complicated. It is not easy to follow. It indicates that four men called Clendon, who were living at the same time and in the same locality, were brothers, and that their father was William Clendon (alive 1636). It takes into account events that took place many years later over several generations in three different Clendon families. Since the events and persons concerned occur in subsequent generations, an explanation of how they illuminate the ancestry of William the schoolmaster is given after they have been introduced in the text and pedigree charts. This explanation can be found in a separate section entitled "The Ancestry of William the Schoolmaster" later on in this chapter.

Here is the genealogical table based on the above conclusions:

WILLIAM and FRANCES CLENDON had issue four sons:

I   **JOHN CLENDON**   Will 1665,
    of London
    m. ELIZABETH -?-

        They had issue seven children:

        1   -?- CLENDON   d 1663

        2   THOMAS CLENDON   d 1650

        3   JOHN CLENDON of Inner   b 1634
            Temple & Great Harriden   d ?1719
            London
            m. ELEANOR -?-
                They had issue six children, (see family tree diagram).
                [Two of their sons, Rev JOHN CLENDON 1676-1756, curate at Scaldwell from 1699-
                ?1710, and THOMAS CLENDON d 1750/1 of Mears Ashby, feature in the evidence
                to be discussed later concerning the ancestry of WILLIAM CLENDON the
                Schoolmaster]

        4   ELIZABETH CLENDON
            m. -?- ORFETT

        5   HANNAH CLENDON
            m. THOMAS STAGG

        6   SARAH CLENDON
            m. -?- KING

        7   MARTHA CLENDON   a minor in 1665

II **JAMES CLENDON**   alive in 1665
    ? of Reading   ?Adm 1694

III **THOMAS CLENDON**   alive in 1625
    built Mears Ashby Hall

IV* **WILLIAM CLENDON**   b
    Master of Wellingborough School   d   ?1664
    m. -?- ELIZABETH KNIGHT   m ?1635 Feb 21   St Martins in the Fields,
                                                                     London

        They had issue a son, our ancestor:

        1* Rev WILLIAM CLENDON   b ?1640
            of Scaldwell   d 1722 Sep 4
                                                  i Sep 14   Scaldwell

            m . MARY -?-   b
                                                  i 1704 Sep 4   Scaldwell

                They had issue five children.

---

*   denotes an ancestor

The fifth generation Northamptonshire ancestor is:

WILLIAM CLENDON *Master of Wellingborough School*

Not much is known about this William. My grandfather found his name originally in Cambridge University records. Although William did not go to Cambridge, his son William did and is entered in the records as: "son of the Master of Wellingborough School". In this context "Master" means "Headmaster".

His name is in the list of headmasters as "William Glendon" in a book about the school called "Four Centuries" which was published by the Wellingborough School in 1988. The date of his headship is given as 1662 – 1664, two years later than the dates quoted in the 1974 edition. It is not known why his tenure was so short. Perhaps he died in 1664.

His signature as headmaster of the school, which some have suggested is written "Glendon" is held at the Northamptonshire County Record Office. It is illustrated here as the earliest artefact of the family.

William Clendon

His name has not been found in Northamptonshire parish registers. A search of London registers revealed, however, that his assumed brother John's son John was christened on 8 March 1634 at St Martins in the Fields – and also that a William Clendon, possibly the schoolmaster, was married to "Eliz. Knight" on 21 February 1635, also at St Martins in the Fields.

At this point I would like to pause from pursuing our direct ancestors down the line to draw attention to some wider issues which become apparent at about this stage of the family history.

The first is that a glance at the family tree chart reveals that there are a lot more Clendons appearing on it. It has broadened sideways, and has become more complicated to follow, particularly as so many of the Clendons of the time had the same names. William, Henry, Thomas and John appear again and again. This illustrates the puzzles that genealogists have to try to solve. I remember that my father, who discovered most of these people, spent many hours over the years trying to work out who was who, and the relationships between them. And even now they are not all fitted in. The 1974 edition contains much more information than is given here. There are eight closely typed pages under the following headings: Abstracts of Clendon Wills and administrations before 1800, University Clendons, Apprentices, Parish register extracts, and Miscellaneous references. A photocopy of these pages is available on request.

The second point is that we have now come across Mears Ashby, a village two or three miles west of Wellingborough, and ten miles due south of Glendon Hall.

Mears Ashby Hall is the most impressive private house in England to be associated with the Clendon family. It was built by a Thomas Clendon in 1637. This fact is recorded in the Victoria County History of Northamptonshire Vol IV page 129, and also see Northants Notes & Queries New Series Volume 2 p.144. This Thomas Clendon was the brother of William Clendon, the Master of Wellingborough School.

The Hall is a picturesque Jacobean gable house (see illustration). It has the initials TC inscribed in the stonework over the porch. These initials are also to be found, with the date 1637, embossed on the original rainwater heads.

The Hall was in the family for four generations. When Thomas Clendon died it passed into the ownership of his great nephew Thomas Clendon who married Anne Wilkes. This nephew was extremely well off. In addition to Mears Ashby Hall he owned other land there, and in Bermondsey, eight houses in central London, three farms in Hunts and Northants, land elsewhere in Northants and in Essex! He died in 1751 and was buried in the church at Mears Ashby. His grave stone is there in the floor of the centre aisle. The house passed on his death firstly to his nephew William Clendon, who died in 1764 at Mears Ashby. As there was no heir, the house and all the estate passed in accordance with the will of Thomas Clendon (d. 1751) to another of his nephews, Owen Manning.

Many of the Clendon family from England, America and New Zealand have visited Mears Ashby Hall. Sue, Tom and I did so in the early 1990's. A

Mears Ashby Hall, Northamptonshire.

year or so later, in April 1994, the house was put on the market for £650,000. Tom has the sale brochure. One interesting visit was by Bette Edwards, over from the USA in 1975. Her description of the house, and the hospitality she received, is given in an extract from a letter below. She has named her own house in Lenox , Mears Ashby.

Mears Ashby
Schermerhorn Park
PO Box 1732   *14th January 1991*
Lenox
Mass 01240
USA

Dear Tom, Jenny and Charlie

. . . Here I am and ready to tell you about our visit to Mears Ashby. To begin with, I'd heard and read about Mears Ashby Hall but did not know who owned the Hall but we so badly wanted to have a glimpse of it. In truly American fashion (something cousin Erik never would have done) I wrote a letter addressed to "The owners of Mears Ashby Hall, Mears Ashby, Northants, England" and in 10 to 14 days, I think, I received a reply. I had stated that I was a Clendon descendant and relative of the Thomas Clendon who built and had owned the Hall and of our wish to have a fleeting glimpse of it when we were to be in the Cambridge or Ely area travelling by train. The letter I received from Col. Stockdale was enthusiastic and one of the most cordial letters I've ever received! They invited Carol and me to spend the weekend with them or at least overnight if we couldn't manage a weekend as I had told him of our fully planned schedule. He said he and Mrs Stockdale would be honoured to receive us and if I'd phone when we arrived at the train station, Mrs S. would go to fetch us and take us to Mears Ashby and what a lovely thing it would be to meet a blood relative of the builder and first owner of the Hall. We already felt a warm welcome awaited us and we were so delighted we were going to actually spend time within the Hall which our ancestor had built . . . the Hall had been in the Stockdale family for many generations. He was known as Minshall Stockdale though a few initials preceded the Minshall but of course we called him Colonel Stockdale and she Mrs (but I think her name was Margaret Violet – called Peggy) They had 4 children, all grown and with children of their own, 2 sons and 2 daughters, I think – one son lived on the road beyond the Hall . . .

I phoned and soon Mrs S arrived to meet us. She was a complete aristocrat through and through and one realised it immediately in her speech and manner but not by her appearance which is often the case,. She didn't put on any false "airs" but was so natural and easy to meet . . .

They had a duck pond near the Hall on the property and loved their ducks and animals, horses, dogs, cows, calves etc. We arrived at 2.25 pm 29 September 1975 (referring to my diary now) . . .

The Hall, of course, is very beautiful and Carol and I kept imagining it in Thomas Clendon's day. On the rain heads on either side of the doorway – a T, and on the other side a C. The gardens and grounds were gorgeously kept by the many gardeners, a beautiful dove cot for I have forgotten how many pigeons and doves . . .

The Stockdales were most interested to see our genealogy, and read all about Thomas Clendon . . . I slept in a luxurious bedroom in the centre of the house over the large entrance hall in the oldest part of the house and had the strangest feeling sleeping in a room where I knew an ancestor had frequented! . . . In the a.m. a maid came and knocked and came in to open the draperies and to bring early morning tea . . .

Mears Ashby Hall had fabulous paintings and antiques, furnished in the period of the Hall. From an inner vestibule, one entered the main hall (long and wide) and with fireplace at one end – on one side after that to the left was a wing, I think they said had been added, but done beautifully to exactly match the interior architecture and exterior of the house. It was their informal sitting room, oak panelled with heavy and well polished brass knobs on all the doors, a lovely fire place, leather chairs and leather sofa, a long table behind the sofa where we sat for our cocktails before dinner in the evening. Col. Stockdale knew we'd named our house Mears Ashby after the original as he teased us by calling it (our house) "Mears Ashby Junior" . . .

The butler came to announce that dinner was served and at first I thought he was an arriving guest as he too was dressed in evening dress so I just said "Good evening", then realised he was the butler! Butler and maids stood around the large and elegant dining room as we were served and ate our dinner. At one point Col. Stockdale said in a low voice to me "We don't talk about anything personal in front of the servants so be guarded!" . . .

Mrs S., the afternoon we arrived, showed us through the whole Hall even to the servant quarters, kitchens and pantries and the bell system for ringing for service in various rooms. . . .

Then in 1976 Bob and I were invited back again but will have to tell you about that another time.

Much love
　　　　Bette –
　　　　and Bob too"

The third point to mention now is the connection with Emmanuel College Cambridge. The College was founded in 1584 by Sir Walter Mildmay, who came from Northamptonshire. He was Chancellor of the Exchequer in Queen Elizabeth's reign. The first Clendon to go to the College was Rev

Thomas Clendon of Radwinter who entered in 1620.

There have been members of the family at Emmanuel in each century since then, and at various times the College has helped with research into the family history. A description of our links with Emmanuel can be found in Part 5.

Seven Clendons in a direct ancestral line to (and including) my brother and myself went to Emmanuel College. The first of these was the Rev William Clendon of Scaldwell, and he comes next in our story.

Rev WILLIAM CLENDON (?1640-1722)

Rev William Clendon of Scaldwell was the sixth generation of our ancestors in Northamptonshire, and the first of a line of parsons. He was born about 1640. Because of his occupation his career is on records that are easy to find, and much more is known about him than the previous generations. All the villages listed below where he held office were within ten miles of Clendon (see map).

Described in the Cambridge University records as son of the Master of Wellingborough School, he was admitted as a sizar* at Clare Hall, Cambridge on December 1st 1658. When he matriculated† in 1659 his name was entered in the records as Clendar.

He migrated to Emmanuel College on January 18th 1659/60††. The entry in the admissions book for that date reads:

			£	s	d
Jan 18 William Clendon	*North-*	*{from }*	*00.*	*02.*	*06*
	-ampt	*{Clare Hall }*			
		{2d year }			

William graduated with a BA in 1662, and took his MA in 1666.

A year after graduation he was licensed for performance of duty at Sywell on June 14th 1663. William Cley had been the incumbent there since

---

*   a "sizar" was a class of entry to a Cambridge College for students from families who were not well off. Their fee was reduced in return for undertaking college duties;

†   "matriculation" is the formal process of being registered as having satisfied the academic requirements for entry to the University;

††   "Jan 18th 1659/60" is an old style date. These existed before 1752, when Britain adopted the present day Gregorian Calendar. Under the old style, dates for the first quarter of each year showed two years, the second of which is our post-1752 new style year.

The church of
St Peter and
St Paul, Scaldwell

August 29th 1633 and was replaced on August 6th 1663, a few months after William had arrived, by William Hutton. On March 1st 1664/65 William was licensed to preach.

He became Rector of Draughton, Northants, on 19th April 1665 where he stayed for five years. On 29th November 1670 he moved to Weekly where he was Vicar for a further five years.

His final incumbency was as Rector of Scaldwell from March 31st 1675 for 47 years until the year of his death. Rev John Clendon, 1676-1756, (see pedigree diagram) was his assistant curate there from September 25th 1699 to possibly 1710. This Rev John Clendon's son Thomas was the last Clendon to own Mears Ashby Hall.

William died in 1722 on September 4th, and was buried at Scaldwell on September 14th. He was about 82 years of age.

His wife Mary had died eighteen years before, and was buried at Scaldwell in 1704 also on September 4th.

Administration of Mary's estate was granted to her husband; the record of this, and of William's will reads as follows:

Administration of the goods etc of MARY CLENDON granted 1706 Apr 25 (Northamt. Arch. Ct.) to her husband Rev WILLIAM CLENDON Rector of Scaldwell. Surety: Geo RAYSON of Northampton, gent. Inventory £32, taken 1706 Aug 3 (sic); Notes re agreement with Rev Rich. RICHARDSON clerk deceased and £7 from her late daughter Mrs FRANCES RICHARDSON deceased. Exhibited 1706 May 25.

The Will of WILLIAM CLENDON of Scaldwell, clerk, dated 1718/19 Feb 16, pr 1722 Sep 12 (Northamt. Arch Ct Liber Sept fol 297). To ANNE wife of my son WILLIAM of Creaton Clerk, £20. To my son THOMAS, JANE his wife, my son-in-law John ANDREWS and his wife my daughter ANNA, each 1/-. To my granddaughter MARY HUMPHRIES' eldest son 5/-. To the poor of Scaldwell 40/-. Residue to my son WILLIAM, executor. Witnesses: Edward & Stephen RANDELL, John MOFFAT.

This time our ancestor, Thomas, inherited only 1/-.

The Rev WILLIAM CLENDON and his wife MARY had issue five children:

I*	**The Rev THOMAS CLENDON**	c 1665 Mch 27	Draughton, Northants
	of Fenny Drayton	i 1737 Sep 6	Fenny Drayton, Leics
	m. JANE CLEIPOLE	m 1692	Weastcheap, Northants
		i 1727 Aug 9	Fenny Drayton, Leics

    The Rev Thomas Clendon and his wife Jane Cleipole had issue ten children
    – see next genealogical table.

II	**ANNE CLENDON**	c 1667/8 Jan 3	Draughton
	m. JOHN ANDREWS	both were living in 1718	

III	**ELIZABETH CLENDON**	c 1669 Dec 9	Draughton
		not named in 1718	

IV	**The Rev WILLIAM CLENDON**	b 1671?	?Weekley
		i 1754 Jan 4	Creaton

sizar Emmanuel College Cambridge, 1689/90 Mch 5, matric.1691, BA 1693/4, deacon Peterborough 1696 Jun, clerk at Scaldwell 1696 Jun 6 to his father, and at Boughton, priest 1699 Jun 3, Rector of Creaton, Northants 1708 Aug, to 1754. [Will, available]

	m. ANNE RICHARDSON	m 1718 Aug 7	Harrington
	of Pitsford	i 1767 Feb 18	Creaton.

    They had issue four children:

	1	MARY CLENDON	b 1720 Aug 6,	
			c. Sep 19	Scaldwell

	2	WILLIAM CLENDON	b 1721/2 Jan 15,	
			c Jan 22	Creaton
			d 1768?	

apprenticed 1735 Jan 19 to Robt KING of Northampton, woollen draper, for consideration of £80; but a yeoman of Lamport in his Will, [available] m 17

	m. ELIZABETH	living 1768

    They had issue two children:

		i	JOHN CLENDON

    of West Haddon, Northants, yeoman, assumed administration of father's estate, 1788; named in 1806 Poll for Knights of the Shire.

		ii	MARY CLENDON	a minor in 1768

	3	The Rev JOHN CLENDON	b 1723/4 Jan 22,	
		of Brompton Regis	c Feb 3	Creaton
			d 1802?	

Guilsborough School; sizar Emmanuel College Cantab, matric 1740/1 Jan 22, BA 1744/5, deacon 1746 Dec Norwich, MA & priest 1748, Vicar of Brompton Regis Somerset 1751-1802. Renounced as executor of his brother's will.

	4	SAMUEL CLENDON	b 1725 Dec 3	
			c Dec 13	Creaton

---

*   It can be seen from the above genealogical table that each succeeding generation has a different form of number notation (eg V, or 4, or ii).

        Also the names and numbers are indented so that all members of the same generation have the same style of number, and position, on the page.

V	**FRANCES CLENDON**	b 167-	
		i 1703/4 Jan 31	Brixworth
	The Rev ADRIAN RICHARDSON,	m 1699/1700 Jan 16	Brixworth
	of Brixworth	b 1664	Brixworth
		d 1703	

son of the Rev RICHARD RICHARDSON & his wife MARY. Curate Oxendon 1688, Vicar of Brixworth 1700-1703; left land to his brother-in-law WILLIAM CLENDON.

They had issue two children:

1	RICHARD RICHARDSON	b 1700	
		d 1701	?Brixworth
2	SAMUEL RICHARDSON	b 1702	
		d 1703?	?Brixworth

ANCESTRY OF WILLIAM THE SCHOOLMASTER

By referring to the family tree diagram of the early Clendons it can be seen that there is a firm line between William (alive 1636) and his son Thomas (alive 1625). This relationship is established in the will written in 1625 by Thomas Clendon, the chapman, brother of William, as follows:

> . . . To Thomas Clendon my servant son of William £40, my Bible, all my chandinge things as furvise etc . . .

The diagram shows a ?? on the line between William the Schoolmaster and the above Thomas Clendon. If it were possible to prove that they were brothers it would follow that William Clendon (alive 1636) was the father of William the Schoolmaster.

However there is no direct evidence in the form of a written record to make that brotherly link between Thomas and William. It has to be inferred by two pieces of circumstantial evidence that links both Thomas and William so closely to the family of John Clendon, who married Elizabeth and wrote a will in 1665, that it can be concluded that they were each his brother. John's name, with that of another brother James, can be found to the left of Thomas and William on the same line. Note that there is a firm line between John and James, which indicates that it is absolutely certain that they are brothers. The evidence for this is to be found in John's will dated August 8th 1665 where John refers to his "brother James Clendon".

The first piece of circumstantial evidence rests in the ownership of Mears Ashby Hall. This large manor house was built by Thomas in 1637, and when he died without an heir the ownership passed to grandson of John Clendon (Will 1665), also called Thomas Clendon. This is the Thomas who married Anne Wilkes and died 1751?, to be found on the left of the chart two generations later. It is considered virtually certain that, at that time and in these circumstances, the property would have passed within the immediate family – and that therefore John (Will 1665) and Thomas (alive 1625) were brothers.

The second piece of circumstantial evidence links John (Will 1665) with William the Schoolmaster. Rev John Clendon (1676-1756) was another grandson of John (Will 1665) and his name can also be found on the left side of the chart. He was an assistant curate from 1699-?1710 to the Rector of Scaldwell, who was Rev William Clendon, the son of William the schoolmaster. This implies a family relationship and that William the Schoolmaster and John were brothers.

If the above assumptions are valid, and Erik Chitty considered them to be so, these four Clendons – John, James, Thomas, and William the School-master – were four brothers, and were the sons of William (alive 1636).

Rev THOMAS CLENDON (1665-1737)

The seventh of our Northamptonshire ancestors was another parson, the Reverend Thomas Clendon of Fenny Drayton. His early life was also spent within ten miles of Clendon. His son also called Thomas, the last of our Northamptonshire ancestors, was actually born only four miles from Clendon.

The Rev Thomas Clendon was christened on March 27th 1665 at Draughton Northants, three weeks before his father became the Rector there. He followed in his father's footsteps to Emmanuel College Cambridge, entering as a sizar on July 19th 1681 at the age of 16. He matriculated in 1683 at age 18, and gained his BA in 1685/6 and MA in 1689.

July 10th Thomas Clendon Northamp: 0 — 2 – 6

He was ordained a priest at Lincoln Cathedral on March 11th of 1687/88, and was a curate and schoolmaster at Oxendon, Northants from 1690 to 1694, (licensed on April 11 1693), perhaps in succession to his brother-in-law Adrian Richardson.

In 1692 he married Jane Cleipole at St Peter's Church, Draughton, Northants, by licence of the Bishop of London.

He was curate of Broughton, Northants from 1695 to 1702 when he became the Vicar of Kilsby, Northants. He was Vicar of Kilsby from May 20th 1702 until 1710, (the next incumbent was presented on November 2nd 1710); although in 1704 and 1707, when his sons entered Rugby School, he was named in the school records as the Rev Mr Clendon "of Rugby".

His death has been erroneously dated as 1710 when he left Kilsby, but in fact he was Rector of Fenny Drayton, Leicestershire, from 1708 until 1737. He was buried there on September 6th 1737. His wife, Jane, had died ten years before him, and was buried on August 9th 1727 at Fenny Drayton.

Their wills have not been traced.

The Rev THOMAS CLENDON* and his wife JANE CLEIPOLE had issue ten children:

1   **WILLIAM CLENDON**
    entered Rugby School 1704

2   **ELIZABETH CLENDON**   c 1693 Aug 28   Scaldwell

3* **The Rev THOMAS CLENDON**   c 1695 Nov 7   Broughton
                                    i 1757 Aug 5   Sturry
    Thomas also entered Rugby School in 1704.
    [Details of his marriages and children are given in Chapter 3]

4   **LEBBEUS CLENDON**   c 1696/7 Feb 13   Broughton
                                    i 1711 May 29   Fenny Drayton
     Third son to enter Rugby School in 1704

5   **MARY CLENDON**   c 1698 May 2   Broughton
                                    dead by 1709

6   **The Rev JOHN CLENDON**   c 1699 Apr 22   Broughton
                                    d 1772 (by Oct 28)
    Entered Rugby School 1707, Trinity College Oxford matric 1717 "age 16", BA 1721, deacon 1722,
    priest 1724, Vicar of Desborough, Northants 1727/8 March 6. Apparently father of:

    └── i   BEVERIDGE CLENDON   b 1737?   Boxley, Kent (not in published register)
            St Pauls School 1749 aged 12, pensioner Emmanuel College Cambridge as Pauline Exhibitioner
            1757, left 1760.

7   **JANE CLENDON**   c 1700 Jul 30   Broughton
    m. NATHANIEL BRYAN   m 1731 Sep 11   Fenny Drayton
    of Ticknal, Derbyshire.

8   **ANNE CLENDON**   c 1701 Oct 30   Broughton
                                    i 1737 Jun 5   Fenny Drayton

9   **MARY CLENDON**   c 1709 Apr 28   Fenny Drayton
                                    i 1709 Jun 5   Fenny Drayton

10 **JOSEPH CLENDON**   c 1710 Oct 28   Fenny Drayton
                                    i 1710 Dec 27   Fenny Drayton

Rev THOMAS CLENDON (1695-1757)

Rev Thomas Clendon of Sturry and Reculver, was the eighth and last of our direct ancestors to be born in Northamptonshire. He departed as a boy in

1702 when his father became Rector of Fenny Drayton in Leicestershire.

Educated at Rugby School, he followed his father and grandfather to Emmanuel College, Cambridge, and then became curate to his father. He eventually settled near Canterbury in Kent where he held the livings of Sturry and Reculver.

The story of his life, his wives, and his family, opens up a completely new phase in the history and fortunes of the Clendon family, which is revealed in Chapter 3.

Historical Table

This table relates the events in the history of the Clendon Family covered in Chapters 1 and 2 to the Royal reigns and chief happenings during that period.

Date

1066	William I	Norman Conquest	
		Castles built	Land at Clendon in Northamptonshire
		1086 Domesday Book completed	is described in Domesday Book
1087	William II	Manors, churches monasteries built	
1100	Henry I		
1135	Stephen		
1154	Henry II	Thomas a Becket	
1189	Richard I	Crusades	
1199	John	Magna Carta	Henry de Clendon gave two virgates
		Robin Hood	of land at Clendon to St James' Abbey
1216	Henry III	Barons Wars	Richard de Clendon son of Henry lived
		First Parliament	
1272	Edward I	Conqueror of Wales	1296 William de Clendon
		Hammer of the Scots	held nine virgates of land at
			Clendon Manor
1307	Edward II	Bannockburn	1315 Richard de Clendon
	Robert Bruce		had inherited the land
1327	Edward III	French Wars	1334 William de Clendon,
		Black Prince	son of Richard, had
		The Black Death	inherited the land
			John de Clendon son
			of William inherited the land
			1346 Ralph de Clendon brother of
			John certified an idiot from
birth,			
			and custody granted to Hugh Wake
1377	Richard II	Peasants Revolt	
		Chaucer	1397 Ralph died intestate and Clendon
			Manor was passed by marriage to the

			Newbottle family
1399	Henry IV		
1413	Henry V	100 years war Agincourt	
1461	Edward IV	William Caxton	William Clendon, tanner
1483	Edward V	12 yrs old murdered in the Tower	of Wellingborough, born about 1460 – 1480
1483	Richard III		
1485	Henry VII	The first of the Tudors	
1509	Henry VIII	dissolved Monasteries built a strong Navy, made himself Head of the Church of England	William Clendon, tanner of Wellingborough, alive Will dtd 1524
1547	Edward VI	a boy-king, died age 16	Henry Clendon of Wellingborough alive
1553	Mary	Roman Catholic, married Philip of Spain	Will dtd 1557/58
1558	Elizabeth I	Spanish Armada 1588 Shakespeare	Thomas Clendon the husbandman of Wellingborough alive. Will 1601
1603	James I (1st Stuart)	Gunpowder plot Pilgrim Fathers set sail for America	William Clendon of Wellingborough alive 1636
1625	Charles I	Civil War Executed 1649	William Clendon Schoolmaster of
1649	Common- wealth & Protectorate	Cromwell ruled strict Puritanism	Wellingborough m 1635? d 1662?
1660	Charles II	Plague Fire of London	Rev William Clendon Rector of Scaldwell
1685	James II	attempted to bring back Catholicism	?1640-1722
1689	William & Mary		Rev Thomas Clendon of Fenny Drayton 1665-1737
1702	Anne	Last of Stuarts	Rev Thomas Clendon of Sturry & Reculver born 1695

PART 2

MIGRATION TO KENT

18th CENTURY

1695, the year of birth of the second Rev Thomas Clendon, marks the start of a century of change in the history of the family. In the 18th century the family migrated from Northamptonshire, to Leicestershire, Chichester and Kent.

The conventional and respectable middle class family household in the parsonage was left behind, to be replaced by a generation of poverty and drunkenness. This concludes with a child who ran away to sea and eventually established himself in a secure and prosperous way of life.

CHAPTER 3
TO CANTERBURY

Rev THOMAS CLENDON *(1695-1757) OF STURRY & RECULVER*

Thomas was born in the autumn of 1695 into a family that was rooted in the life of a small group of Northamptonshire villages and the nearby town of Wellingborough. His forefathers had lived in that area for over two hundred years. Indeed, as already explained, the family had probably lived there continuously since the time of King John in 1200, which would be five hundred years in the same locality.

Thomas's early childhood followed a similar pattern to that of his ancestors. He was born the son of a local clergyman in a village called Broughton about six miles from Wellingborough, and five miles from Scaldwell where his grandfather had been the Rector for 20 years – and was to remain there for a further 27 years. His father, another Rev Thomas Clendon, was Curate to the Rector of Broughton. Young Thomas was the third child in a family that was eventually to number ten. His older sister Elizabeth had been christened over at nearby Scaldwell, possibly by her grandfather. Thomas was christened at Broughton, on November 7th 1695.

Thomas lived in Broughton until he was six and a half years of age. At that time it was a small community of about 300 people, mostly engaged in farming. The Rector's name was Nathaniel Whalley. Today is it a fair sized town. It is only three miles from Clendon Hall.

At that time I imagine that the family must have been a closely knit one. Young Thomas's Uncle William, for example, like father and grandfather, was a parson. A graduate of Emmanuel College Cambridge also, Uncle William, was a Curate at Scaldwell to his own father, young Thomas's grandfather. This Uncle William remained living in the neighbourhood for the rest of his life as Rector of Creaton, another local village – as did his children and grandchildren.

Young Thomas's aunt Fanny married a parson called Adrian Richardson at nearby Brixworth when Thomas was four. Adrian had been a school teacher at Oxendon as had Thomas's father, so they had known each other for some years. He was Vicar of Brixworth. Brixworth is only a mile away from Scaldwell where Grandfather was Rector and Uncle William was Curate, and only six miles from young Thomas's home in Broughton.

On that wedding day in the Winter of 1699/70, January 16th, there must have been a large gathering of the clan, including the local Clendon Clergy, their wives and families. Thomas's mother Jane was five month's pregnant at the time, carrying her sixth son John. Perhaps she was there, and if so she might have taken Thomas, then a child of four.

When Thomas was eight, four years later in January 1703/04, the bride and groom and their two infant children were all dead. Frances Clendon, the bride, was the last to die. Her funeral was on January 31st. What a contrast to the wedding only four years before. However, even though Thomas was older, he was less likely to have been taken to his Aunt's funeral than to her wedding, because two years before she died his family moved some distance away.

On May 20th 1702 his father had become Vicar of Kilsby. Although still in Northamptonshire, Kilsby is on the northwest edge of the county, about 21 miles from Wellingborough and 12 from Scaldwell. So it was more difficult for a young boy to keep in touch with his relations. None of them were now living within a reasonable walking or riding distance. Furthermore Kilsby was located just beyond Watling Street, the Roman Road which bisects Northamptonshire, and which divided the land into two distinct kingdoms in Anglo Saxon times. The west side of Northamptonshire was still regarded by the inhabitants as distinctly different from the east where the Clendons came from.

Kilsby is only 5 miles from Rugby in Warwickshire where Thomas and two of his brothers were sent to school in 1704. (The third followed in 1707). Thomas and his brothers were probably the first out of their family to attend school outside the county of Northamptonshire. Rugby School was a famous boarding school with a national reputation and an intake from a wide catchment area. As a result Thomas was exposed to far wider range of influences in his formative years at school than his predecessors had experienced.

By moving to Kilsby Thomas's father had removed the family from the immediate environment of past generations, but his transfer to Fenny Drayton in 1710 took them finally right out of the home territory altogether. Fenny Drayton is some 25 miles or so further north up Watling Street from Kilsby – and is about 50 miles from Wellingborough. 50 miles was a long journey not easily or often undertaken in the days of horse drawn transport.

Thomas meanwhile remained at Rugby School, I presume, until he proceeded like his father and grandfather before him to Emmanuel College Cambridge, at the age of 18. There was however one difference. He was entered as a "pensioner", whereas his ancestors had each entered as a "sizar". A "sizar" was a student who performed college duties such as waiting at high table to help pay his way through University. Thomas's father must have been better off financially than his predecessors because as a "pensioner" all Thomas's expenses were paid from outside the College – presumably by his father.

Perhaps Kilsby and Fenny Drayton were better paid livings than the Northampton villages around Wellingborough. This could be a reason why Thomas's father moved away. He certainly appeared to be better off financially than his father and grandfather whose sons were sizars at Emmanuel.

Thomas's career at Cambridge and as a Curate followed the usual family pattern. He was entered at Emmanuel on June 25th 1713 and gained his BA in 1716/17 and his MA in 1720. He was ordained a Deacon at Lincoln Cathedral (as was his father) in 1717. He then became Curate to his father at Fenny Drayton in 1717 and was ordained a Priest at London on March 13th 1717/18. What he did subsequently is somewhat unclear.

His next recorded appointment was on October 24th 1729 when he became Rector of Reculver, a village on the Kent coast not far from Canterbury. On 27th June 1734 he also became the Vicar of Sturry, with a Chapel at Hoath. Sturry is near to Reculver, and is about three miles from Canterbury.

A curacy to his father of over eleven years seemed to me to be far too long a time. I wondered whether he could have been working elsewhere, possibly in Canterbury, before being appointed to the living in Reculver in 1729.

When I started to look into it I discovered that Erik Chitty had come to the same conclusion. His papers show that he was still actively looking in 1975 for evidence to shed light on this period. Erik wrote to Peter Clendon Joyce, a New Zealander and descendant of James Reddy Clendon about this matter on 5th February 1975. This extract from his letter displays Erik's appraisal of the problem:

> The trouble is that the Rev Thomas CLENDON was curate at Fenny Drayton, Leics, from 1717, and acquired two livings in Kent in 1729/34. But there is no record of when he left Fenny D. or where he went before 1729. During this time he certainly married a wife Elizabeth and fathered your ancestor Thomas. But family tradition seems to be that, before Elizabeth, he had married Agnes or Marie (DE) BEAUVOIR, mother of Thomas . . .

This family tradition is expressed in many places in the archives, and originates chiefly from George Clendon II (1798-1887), his great grandson, who wrote and spoke a lot about his ancestors. This George Clendon (see family tree diagram) was my great great grandfather who emigrated to America, and is usually referred to in this book as George II, or George the Chemist, to distinguish him easily from the other George Clendons alive around that time. George II wrote letters home to his sister Sarah Ann Clendon (1807-1902), who lived in Great Yarmouth in Norfolk, and to New Zealand to his nephew James Stephenson Clendon (1827-1899) who was the oldest son of his brother James Reddy Clendon (1800-1872). Some of these letters written in the 1880's have survived. My father saw many of the originals when he visited New Zealand in 1968, and I have his longhand copies. Typewritten copies were also sent to me by Bette Edwards in USA which I think originate from Philippa Holmes in New Zealand. I do not know the present whereabouts of the originals; in 1968 they were in the possession of Bowen Clendon, a solicitor in Auckland NZ.

Sarah Ann Clendon also wrote a 'Commonplace Book' which was studied by Erik Chitty and furnished many clues to the Clendon genealogy covered in this chapter. Efforts are still being made to trace the whereabouts of this book, which may be in the hands of the Chitty family. Much of the subsequent material in this chapter is derived from these accounts of George Clendon II and his sister Sarah Ann.

Since they were the great grandchildren of the Rev Thomas Clendon, their knowledge of him and his marriages was derived from stories and accounts handed down by mouth over three generations. They would have learnt most of it from their own father George Clendon I (1760/1-1839), the Cinque Port Pilot. Some errors and exaggerations will undoubtedly have been introduced in the telling and remembering. Especially as 160 years had elapsed from when Rev Thomas would have married his french "Beauvoir" bride in the 1720's to the time when George II wrote about it in the 1880's. Nevertheless there is a clear thread running through the documents, as can be seen from the extracts which follow.

When he was an old man George II lived with his son Benjamin Clendon in Buckner's County, Virginia, USA. Benjamin questioned his father George about his ancestors. Benjamin related the replies in a letter dated 7th October 1887 to his cousin James Stephenson Clendon at Whangerei, New Zealand, as follows:

> . . . I regret to say that my father's health [George CLENDON II 1798-1887] is failing and I doubt about his being able to get out about again . . . Before he commenced failing in health I questioned him in regard to Rev Thomas CLENDON & he gives the following.
>
> Thos. CLENDON in his younger days was attached to Canterbury Cathedral, had what is termed a Prebendary Stall there & that he married a wife BEAUVOIR (pronounced BOOWAR) that wife was a French girl of Huguenot parents great numbers of whom settled in Canterbury on being expelled from France at the time of the edict of Nantes. The Canterbury people treated them with great kindness. The Crypt of the Cathedral was given up to their use in a part of

which they had their own chapel & could worship in their own language. Thos
CLENDON became afterwards Vicar of Sturry & Reculver (adjoining parishes in
Kent). One son was born to them named Thomas. The wife died . . . I regret that
my father does not know the christian name of miss BEAUVOIR . . .

George Clendon II's sister Sarah Ann Clendon was also writing to James S
Clendon (her nephew) at that time about their ancestors. The following is
an extract from her letter to him dated 27th October 1884:

. . . I am afraid I can give you little information as far as our ancestors are
concerned, for we never troubled much about them. I have been told they came
from Kettering in Northamptonshire & most of them were in the church – I have
copied the tablet in Sturry Church which I think must have been put up by Mrs
CADMAN – you will perceive she was the daughter of the second wife of my
great grandfather. [Rev Thomas Clendon]. I believe the first wife was named
BEAUVOIR, for I have heard my father say his Uncle Dr BEAUVOIR was at
one time headmaster of the Kings School at Canterbury . . . If there is anything
more you should like to know from me & I am spared to answer the questions I
shall be pleased to answer them.
*   With love etc Yr affect. Aunt – S. A. CLENDON*

In 1931, Benjamin's daughter Ellen Clendon, by then called Mrs Lewis H
Cowles, of Cleveland Ohio USA, was in correspondence with her first
cousin Arthur Clendon of Birmingham (my grandfather) on the same
subject. In her letter of February 18th 1931 she writes:

My dear cousin Arthur . . . .Yesterday I visited the Historical Society in search
of the marriage of The Rev Thomas to AGNES BEAUVOIR also the birth of
Thomas but could not find anything but the closing bell rang when I was in the
middle of some Kent parish registers. I shall go again. Our parish registers have
no indexes which means glancing over page after page – It takes time. I hope you
and cousin Elsie are well – With much love Ellen.

No records were ever found, but the story has been reiterated so many
times that it has become a well established belief that the Beauvoir marriage
actually did take place. Philippa Holmes, a New Zealand descendant of
James Reddy Clendon, possesses a large collection of family records relating
to him, his forebears and descendants, among which is a letter from her
great aunt, Emily Kenderdine, saying:

. . . The Rev Thomas Clendon married Countess Marie de Beauvoir, one of a
Huguenot family who took refuge in England . . .

Bette Edwards, one of the original three family researchers, upholds this view very strongly. She states that Rev Thomas married a Huguenot lady from the french nobility called Marie de Beauvoir. She argues that merely because an official record of the marriage has yet to be found, it is wrong to conclude that the marriage did not exist. She is convinced that the strength of the oral history and family tradition is sufficient proof, and that the marriage record could be found if only we knew where to look for it.

There is one further interesting aspect to the mystery. Rev Thomas would certainly have known the Rev Dr Osmond Beauvoir (1720-1789). He was the distinguished head of King's School Canterbury who came of a Guernsey family. Fuller details of Dr Beauvoir's life are among our archives. Dr Beauvoir was 25 years younger than Rev Thomas. There is no evidence that he was he a blood-related Uncle of Rev Thomas's grandchild, George I. Why then should he be referred to as "his Uncle" by George I (see letter from SA Clendon above). Is it because Rev Thomas married a sister of Dr Beauvoir?

Dr Beauvoir was the third son of Rev William Beauvoir, Chaplain to the Embassy in Paris. It is possible that he could have had an older sister. Also it could be possible that Rev Thomas had gone to Paris, after he was curate to his father, to be an assistant to the Rev William Beauvoir at the Embassy. There he could have met and married Rev William Beauvoir's daughter. If this were true, it would explain the absence in English records of a job during this period, and of his marriage to a lady by the name of Beauvoir. This romantic possibility was suggested to me recently by Kim McIntosh of Sturry, and has been researched by Bob Edwards but he has found no evidence to support it. Kim has micro-fiche records of the Sturry parish registers written by Rev Thomas in his own hand, and she also told me that regular services for Huguenots, in French, are still held in the Crypt of Canterbury Cathedral.

Whether the Beauvoir marriage took place or not still remains a mystery. Erik Chitty remained thoroughly sceptical throughout the debate which ranged across three continents, as expressed in an extract from his letter of 5th February 1975 to Peter Clendon Joyce in New Zealand:

> *Dear Mr Joyce – or should I say "Cousin Peter"?*
>
> *. . . I had also hoped that Eridge Bowen CLENDON – or YOU? – might also know more than most about the "DE BEAUVOIR" legend, as his sister, your mother, seems to be the only CLENDON given that name . . . [Marie de Beauvoir CLENDON]*
>
> *A curious point that makes me rather query the "Huguenot" tradition is that two members of the Guernsey, Channel Islands, BEAUVOIR family were schoolmasters at Canterbury, and probably knew the CLENDONs there. But*

neither of them seems to have left a surviving son; so it is a further mystery why
certain CLENDON girls, living at Dover and Deal in the early 19th century, used
to visit a gentleman at Canterbury whom they called "Uncle BEAUVOIR" ! (The
Guernsey family would not rate as "Huguenots".)

 But you see, my researches and those of the late Dr Douglas CLENDON
have failed to find the slightest evidence of a CLENDON/BEAUVOIR
connection . . .

 Looking forward to hearing from you again
 Yours sincerely
 Erik Chitty "

Whatever conclusion you may draw about the Beauvoir mystery, one thing
is certain – Rev Thomas Clendon's family life continued in a way that was
less settled than his predecessors in Northamptonshire. He had three further
wives, and fell out with his two oldest children who left home. Sadly of his
remaining six children there was only one, Mary, who survived beyond
childhood.

He continued as Rector of Sturry and Vicar of Reculver until 1757 when
he died. He was buried at Sturry on August 5th 1757. His age was given as
52, but he was actually in his 62nd year. His will reads as follows:

The Will of THOMAS CLENDON, clerk, vicar of Sturry & Reculver with the
Chapel of Hoath, Kent, dtd 1757 Jul 21, pr 1758 Apr 4 (Canterbury Arcd.
Court Vol 95 fol 386). To be buried in Sturry Church near to my pew door where
I have two children already buried. From the ill usage I have received from my
children THOMAS and SARAH by a former wife . . . to them 1/- each.
(Residue) to MARY my present dearly beloved wife with her son GOODFELLOW
and her daughter MARY or if there should be any other by me – she the sole
executrix. Witnesses: Bartholomew SPAIN, Barnett John BARNETT.

This will provides the evidence of the serious rift in the family.

Our ancestor, Thomas, and his sister Sarah had incurred the wrath of
their father, and were cut off with the proverbial shilling!

If family tradition is correct, Rev Thomas Clendon was married four
times. What is known of these marriages, and of his issue, is given in the
genealogical table below.

Looking at the table, it appears that Thomas had a connection with
Canterbury Cathedral from 1732 to 1737/8. No mention is made in the 1974
edition of him holding office there, although it had been said by George
Clendon II that Rev Thomas Clendon was attached to the Cathedral and had
a Prebendary stall – see letter above from Benjamin Clendon, dated 7th
October 1877.

NEAR THIS CHANCEL

LIES THE BODY OF

THE REV.^D THOMAS CLENDON,

LATE VICAR OF THIS PARISH

AND OF RECULVER:

HE DIED 1757, AGED 52.

AND MARY HIS WIFE,

WHO DIED NOV.^R 26. 1807,

AGED 87.

A plaque at
St Nicholas
Church, Sturry

To settle the matter, I checked this point with the Cathedral Archivist, but she could not find any evidence that Rev Thomas Clendon had held office at the Cathedral.

Perhaps it was his wife, Elizabeth, who had the connection. It was her children that were christened and buried in the cloisters, and it was she who was buried there.

The Rev THOMAS CLENDON   c   1695 Nov 7   Broughton, Northants
of Sturry and Reculver   i   1757 Aug 5   Sturry

m. (1st)
AGNES (or MARIE DE) BEAUVOIR

m. (2nd)   m   (before 1732 Oct)
ELIZABETH -?-   i   1737/8 Jan 17   Canterbury Cathedral Cloisters

m. (3rd)   m   1738/9 Feb 22   Sturry, by Licence of Feb 19
MARY KENDALL widow née YOUNG
(previously 2nd wife of WILLIAM KENDALL
of Sturry, married 1716)   d   1743 Sep 15

m. (4th)   m   (before 1752 Mch)
MARY -?-   d   1807 Nov 26, aged 87
    an inmate of Bromley   i   1807   Sturry
    College 1776, resigned 1803

The Rev THOMAS CLENDON (1695-1757) had issue by his several wives:

*i	**THOMAS CLENDON**	b	1728?	(family tradition)
		i	1820 Mch 4	St. Bartholomew's, Chichester

ii	**SARAH BEDINGFIELD CLENDON**			
		c	1731 Jul 7	Sturry, living 1757

iii	**HARRIOT CLENDON**	c	1732 Oct 12	Canterbury Cathedral
		i	1737 Dec 10	Canterbury Cathedral, Cloister Yard

iv	**MARY CLENDON**	c	1733 Nov 23	Canterbury Cathedral
		i	1733 Jan 19	Canterbury Cathedral, Cloister Yard

v	**WILLIAM REMNANT CLENDON**			
		c	1735 Dec 23	Canterbury Cathedral
		i	1738 Dec 22	Sturry
vi	**GOODFELLOW CLENDON**	c	1752 Mch 3	Sturry
		i	1761 Jul 2	Sturry

vii	**WILLIAM CLENDON**	c	1753 Mch 29	Sturry
		i	1753 Apr	Sturry

viii	**MARY CLENDON**	c	1754 Oct 8	
	(eventual beneficiary			
	of her father's	d	1842? aged 86"	(family tradition)
	Will – see above)	m	17??	
	m. GEORGE CADMAN			

(Commander RN 1782 Jun 24, Captain 1809 Oct 25, in the Navy List 1822, but not 1842.)

CHAPTER 4
POVERTY, ADVENTURE, RICHES

THOMAS CLENDON – OF CHATHAM & CHICHESTER

Our next ancestor was another Thomas Clendon! He did not start off well at home. He had several stepmothers, had a serious row with his father, and left home never to return. He ended up in various rather menial jobs, drank too much, and was unable to cope with the upbringing of his own children.

There are several accounts of Thomas, all derived from memories and writings of George Clendon II, his grandson, who said he knew him well.

First there is a document "Abstract of my family history" written by George Clendon II and dated December 31st 1884. It was copied by his granddaughter Ellen in 1931, and sent then to her first cousin Arthur Clendon (see earlier) in England. The relevant extract from this version of our family history is:

> *My great Grandfather . . . was vicar of the two parishes of Sturry and Reculver. His son THOMAS became impoverished and was porter of the gate of Chatham Dockyard. He removed shortly after to the City of Chichester where he lived till his death in 1820 in his ninety second year . . .*

To accompany this document Ellen wrote notes entitled "A few remarks" which included:

> *. . . Grandfather also omitted to say that his grandfather THOMAS was a drunkard and always occupied menial positions – but what could you expect with this succession of step mothers! . . .*

A more revealing commentary arises in the letter dated 7th October 1887 from Ellen's father, Benjamin Clendon, in USA to his cousin James Stephenson Clendon in New Zealand:

> *. . . One son was born to them named THOMAS. The wife died and when THOMAS was a big boy or young man, his father married again (do not know whom) & on bringing his wife home there was a scene which ended by the son dashing the keys upon the floor & leaving the paternal roof to return no more. There were several children by the 2nd marriage but of these father knows but*

little. The unfilial conduct of THOMAS towards the second wife caused a coolness and separation between the 2 branches of the family so that we now know little of each other. As to the headstrong THOMAS my father says "he never amounted to much" but lived as the Yankees say "in a chronic state of shortness" all his life. He became a horse jockey, afterwards a porter at Chatham dockyard, where he married, probably a Chatham girl, & here our Grandfather Clendon [George I, the Pilot] was born. THOS afterward was exciseman at the salt works at Sandwich about midway between Deal and Ramsgate. My father remembers him well. He died at the age of 93 . . . " [Thomas died when George II was 22]

According to Miss Sarah Ann Clendon, Thomas was married twice – George, our ancestor, being the only child of the 1st marriage. The remainder were born to the 2nd wife, who must presumably have been Jane, mother of Ann Clendon (see E below).

Thus the genealogical record is as follows:

THOMAS CLENDON of Chatham	b	1728?	(family tradition)
			& Chichester
	i	1820 Mch 4	St Bartholomew's, Chichester
(1st) m.	m	1759 May 1	St. Mary's Chatham
ANN WRIGHT			
(2nd) m	m	1764 or before	
JANE -?-			

THOMAS CLENDON had issue (according to Miss SARAH ANN CLENDON)

*A	**GEORGE CLENDON I**	b	1760/1 (family tradition)	
	Pilot of the Cinque Ports	c	1761 Feb 20	St Mary's Chatham
		d	1839 Oct 31	Deal
	(1st) m.	m	1782 Dec 26	St Mary, Dover (by Licence)
	SUSANNA EARLE		*[not TEMPLE as stated by SARAH ANN CLENDON]*	
	spinster of that parish, minor,			
	daughter of THOMAS EARLE	i	1791 Feb 27	St Mary, Dover
	(2nd) m.	m	1795 Jan 22	Deal (by Licence)
	ELIZABETH CHITTY	c	1773 Aug 13	Deal
		d	1858 Apr 11	Greenwich
B	**WILLIAM CLENDON**	b	1764/5	
		i	1827 Oct 27	St Mary, Dover, aged 62:
		m	1787 Jun 2	St Mary, Dover
	MARGARET CROUCHLEY			
	of St Mary, Spinster	i	1809 Feb 12	St Mary, Dover

C   **ROBERT CLENDON**   i   1800 Apr 24   St Mary, Dover (died young)

D & E Two daughters – who afterwards became **Mrs SILVERLOCK & Mrs HALE**

E   **ANN CLENDON**
                                c   1781 Oct 25   Chichester Sub-Deanery.
     She seems to have become Mrs Silverlock.
     Two SILVERLOCK children were baptised at Chichester Sub-Deanery:

          i   ANN ELIZABETH dau. of HENRY & ANN
                                c   1808 Sep 16
          ii   HENRY   son   c   1808 Sep 16
                                c   1811 Mch 28

GEORGE CLENDON I (1760/1-1839)

Our next ancestor was the oldest son of Thomas Clendon of Chatham and Chichester. He was the first of three Georges, known as George Clendon I, or George the Pilot.

He came from very poor beginnings. He had very little schooling and was sent as a child to work on a farm. He ran away to sea. He was taken prisoner of war by the French and learnt navigation while in captivity. He eventually became a Cinque Port Pilot and held a Trinity House Licence. This was a substantial position and he became very prosperous. We learn later how he financed his son James Reddy Clendon's venture to New Zealand as a ship's captain and merchant. So it seems highly likely that he also assisted others of his children to set themselves up in their careers. Many of them travelled widely and were successful in business and professions. Purely by his own efforts, he overcame the circumstances of his birth and early childhood and reached a position in society equal if not higher than that of his forefathers.

There are a number of descriptions of his early life in family records. Most of them date from the time I have already mentioned when George Clendon II (1798-1887) was getting on in years and went to live with his youngest son Benjamin on a farm in Buckner's Station, Louisa County, Virginia, USA.

---

*   SARAH ANN CLENDON recorded that Uncle SILVERLOCK died aged 86 and indicated connections among other families mainly in New Zealand, (see 1974 edition for further details).
     MARTHA SILVERLOCK & EDWARD TITCHENOR witnessed a MARGARET CLENDON's marriage in 1846.
     The descendants of B WILLIAM CLENDON, above, are not recorded in the 1974 edition but are to be found in some copies of the 1954 edition at revised page 134a, (photocopy can be supplied on request).

George II's oldest son George Clendon III (1827-1909) also lived at Buckner's Station on a nearby farm. He wrote a succinct version of his grandfather's life in his letter of Oct 21 1885 to his cousin James Stephenson Clendon in New Zealand:

> . . . Our Great great grandfather must have had interest and power behind him. He had two parishes, Sturry & Reculver. His son THOMAS was of no account in a Yankee sense, but his son our grandfather [GEORGE I (1760-1839)] was a man. He & his brother WILLIAM ran away to sea at the mature ages of 8 & 10. Our grandfather was taken prisoner in after years by the French & learned navigation in jail. When he came out he rose in his profession & did well . . .

A more measured summary occurs in the "Abstract of my family history" written in 1884 by George Clendon II:

> . . . My father GEORGE CLENDON was born in Chatham in the year 1760 and removed with his father the above named Thomas of Chichester where at the age of ten years he was sent to do boy's work on a farm in the neighbourhood. From this farm he soon ran away and strolling towards Portsmouth he saw some men employed doing something to a boat, he went and asked them if they wanted a boy. They did so he went with them and became a sailor. During a war with France he was taken prisoner and while a prisoner he acquired a useful education and among other things he studied navigation, in which he became so proficient that when he was old enough he was made a pilot . . .

In 1885 George Clendon II was being pressed from New Zealand for information about his father George by James Stephenson Clendon. With his father dead, James was turning to his elderly Uncle George II in the USA as a source of knowledge about earlier generations in England.

As a result George II wrote a long letter to James Stephenson Clendon. When in 1968 my father saw the original (then in the possession of Bowen Clendon, James Stephenson Clendon's grandson) he wrote on his longhand copy: *"in a very shaky but good script"*.

George II gives a graphic and interesting description of the early life of his father, George I, as can be seen below:

> Buckner's Station – Dec 4th 1885
> My dear nephew James,
>   Your letter of 29th September was duly received but has not yet been acknowledged. I had a confused notion that my son George had written but learned yesterday that he had not. My granddaughter Clara seeing the concern I felt about it, & knowing that I am more infirm than I was when I wrote to you

cheerfully, offered to write for me. The offer put me into quite good spirits & I began at once to think of what I would tell her to write. I am better this morning & can write for myself & without further introduction will write what I intended to tell her to write.

My grandfather was living in Chichester in the year 1770 when he was so poor that he was obliged to send my father (who was then, but 10 years old, & had been to school only about 3 months) to get his own living on a farm. There he and another boy were sent to work in the garden. Instead of working they amused themselves with marbles. The farmer, seeing them laid hold of the other boy & gave him a thrashing. While he was doing this my father made his escape. But where was he to go? How was he to get food?

He dared not go either to his father's or to the farm. And here, as my father told me, God's Providence was his director. Had it not been for this I would have grown up an ignorant ploughman. But he knew nothing of God's designs but wandered disconsolately till he saw some men employed about a boat . . . He went up & asked if they wanted a boy . . . They did; he embarked with them, and became a servant of his majesty, King George the third, for the boat belonged to a King's ship, & he was in it a month before his father knew where he was.

I do not know how many years he remained in the King's service but when he was discharged he got employment in a packet which took passengers from Dover to Calais.

By & by war broke out again (I suppose continuing to go to sea) he was taken prisoner. But one of his Calais friends became security for him & he was allowed his liberty excepting that he had to shew himself at a certain place once a week. He took advantage of this liberty by going to school, where he acquired such a knowledge of the science of navigation that when he returned to England he studied the passage from the Goodwin sands to Gravesend (twenty miles from London) passed an examination & was made a pilot.

Now his wanderings were over he married my mother & was settled. My mother (your grandmother) gave birth to 10 children, who with the exception of one who died in her infancy lived to adult age, but we never met all together but once in our lives. On that occasion, we all happened to be at home excepting the youngest child who was an infant & out to nurse. She was sent for & fastened up in a chair so that she could face the table & we dined together. We parted that evening & never met again . . .

. . . I ought to have told you that my father was married twice. The first wife left one daughter, who lived to be married but after many years died childless.

12th- When the first wife died he took the daughter she left him to the house of Mrs CHITTY, & the child was in her charge when he was absent piloting ships. (I am much troubled to write this morning). The child grew up to be a woman (her name was Susanna) married to Thomas ERRIDGE, was left

a widow and died childless. But my father had then been married nearly 50 years
to the daughter of his landlady, Elizabeth CHITTY & for many years she
continued to live with him and her daughter . . .

Clearly George II was not so lucid when he wrote the last two paragraphs
quoted above. He appears to have re-read his unfinished letter started on
the 4th and realised that he had left out a complete section of his father's
life – but put the letter aside to finish on another day. When he returned to
the task 8 days later on the 12th he wrote a rather confusing account of his
father's first marriage, the children from that marriage, and his father's
relationship with the Chitty family.

However, that story is known to us from other sources.

When George became a Pilot of the Cinque Ports, he first worked at
Dover, one of the actual five ports, and was settled there by 1782. He would
probably have started as a junior Pilot, becoming a senior Pilot later,
perhaps when he moved to Deal.

He was about 21 years of age when he married Susanna Earle on
Boxing Day 1782. She was a local girl, under 21. A baby girl was born to
them four and a half months later in May, but died when only twelve weeks
old. Each May, for the next three years, another child was born. The second
and fourth children also died as babies. The third child, however, named
Susanna after her mother, survived – but was only 5 years of age when her
mother died.

George buried his wife on February 27th 1791, alongside the children
at St Mary's Church, Dover – the church where they were married only eight
years before. But who could now look after his daughter while he was at
sea? Mrs Elizabeth Chitty was to do this for him. She was the widow of a
friend of his – a fellow Pilot of the Cinque Ports – called Gideon Chitty.

George and Gideon had known each other for many years before
Gideon's death three years previously. In fact their association was close
enough in 1777 for them to have a Double Vault, No. 29, in the names of
Gideon Chitty and Mr Clendon in the churchyard at St. George's Deal.
George was about 16 years of age at the time, and Gideon, 37. On the face
of it, it seems curious that George should be so closely associated with
Gideon at that age. Erik Chitty and his cousin Marion Chitty of Glens Falls,
New York State, USA, were both researching this point, and corresponding
about it in 1929. They believed that there must have been an earlier
connection between the families that would explain the joint ownership of
a Double Vault but were never able to trace one. Perhaps as a young
seaman George was apprenticed to Gideon, or Gideon took him "under his
wing" for some reason.

Whatever the explanation for this association between the two families at so early an age in George's life, it helps us to understand why it would be natural for Gideon's widow to offer to look after Susanna for him.

George accepted – moved with Susanna into the Chitty home in Deal – and Mrs Elizabeth Chitty became his landlady.

The Chitty household had been a big one, (see later for full record). They had seven children in all and the older ones had by that time married and left home. But the 6th child, a daughter called Elizabeth after her mother, was 17 years of age. She was at home when George Clendon was widowed. Elizabeth probably helped her mother to care for Susanna, and would have grown closer to George now that he had come to live with the family. Their relationship deepened, and soon after she reached the age of 21, she married George. He was then about 33.

George Clendon (1760-1839)   *Elizabeth Chitty, George Clendon's second wife*

As the Chitty family became so intertwined with the Clendon family, both by marriages and friendships over many generations to this day, it is appropriate at this point to record some details about Elizabeth Chitty's family.

Elizabeth Chitty was a daughter of Gideon Chitty who was born in 1739 on December 19th at Dover. Gideon was christened, as son of Thomas and Susanna Chitty in 1740 March 3rd, also at St Mary's Church. He was married there, on 18th April 1762, to Elizabeth Bayly, who was born in 1741 on May

24 and baptised in 1751 on Jan 25 at Folkestone. It appears that her father Michael Bayly had changed from some Nonconformist sect to the Church of England, as he and his four eldest children were all baptised at the same time!

It is not known how Gideon became a Pilot of the Cinque Ports, but he also went to sea as a boy, and when in Turkey narrowly escaped with his life, as George II relates in his letter of 4th December 1885:

> . . . Gideon Chitty, I do not know much about, except that he went to sea when he was a boy. When the ship was in Turkey he went ashore with the boat's crew; some of the sailors offended a Turkish woman, when some men resented the insult by attacking them with sharp weapons.
>
> What became of the men I do not know but when Gideon was found lying on the ground with his abdomen so ripped up that his bowels protruded & were lying on the ground. He must have been skilfully treated after he was picked up for he became the ancestor of a large family who have lived or are living in New Zealand, the United States & England. He died I think at the age of 48.
>
> His widow, my grandmother was a courageous woman. When she was quite old, happening to go into the kitchen she saw a soldier busily employed in picking up & putting into his pocket whatever he could conveniently steal.
>
> None of the family was in the house but herself & the children, but she laid hold of the man, told one of the children to run out & call for assistance, & though he struggled hard she held him fast till help came, when it was thought best to let him go, after they had taken from him what he had stolen. I must write no more today . . .

Full details of Gideon and Elizabeth Chitty, their ancestors and descendants, can be found in the 1974 edition. However, the genealogical table of their immediate family enables us to see where our ancestors, Elizabeth and George Clendon, fit in.

GIDEON (1739-1788) and ELIZABETH (1741-1827) CHITTY had issue seven children*:

A	**THOMAS CHITTY**	c	1763 Feb 9	St Mary, Dover
	mariner	d	1805?	
		m	1784 Nov 13	Deal
	MARY CURLING	c	1767 Jun 16	Deal
		d	18??	

---

*   All the children of Gideon and Elizabeth Chitty except John Chitty (B) had issue; and it is their posterity that makes up the main part of the Genealogical Record of the Chitty and Clendon families which comprises the 1974 edition.
    Erik Chitty is descended from Richard (E). Bette Edwards is descended from both Michael Chitty (D) and Elizabeth Clendon (F).

B	**JOHN CHITTY**	c	1764 Dec 19	St Mary, Dover
	named in father's Will 1785	d	1785/6	
	but not in aunt REBECCA's 1786 Aug 17			

C	**REBECCA CHITTY**	c	1766 Oct 14	St Mary, Dover
		d	1843 Dec 19	
	m. (1st)	m	1786 Nov 27	Deal (by Licence)
	JAMES REDDY	b	17??	
	Lieut. R.N.	d	1803 Aug 27?	
	m. (2nd)	m	180	
	JOHN PARSON	b	17	
	Capt. of East Indiamen	d	1841 Nov 21	Yarmouth

D	**MICHAEL CHITTY**	c	1768 Oct 14	Deal
	Capt. of East Kent Militia	i	1816 Aug 7	Gorleston
	m. ELIZABETH – ? -	m	17??	
		b	1770/1	
		d	1836	Gt Marlow

E	**RICHARD CHITTY**	c	1771 May 3	Deal
	yeoman, miller, etc	d	1857 Nov 23	Deal
	m. (1st)	m	1791 Dec 31	Deal
	FRANCES WOODRUFF	c	1772 May 3	Deal
		d	1833 Jan 31	Deal
	m. (2nd)	m	1834 Oct 16	Deal
	ELIZABETH STOKES, widow,	b	176	
	formerly BEER	d	1850 May 20	Deal aged 85

F	**ELIZABETH CHITTY**	c	1773 Aug 13	Deal
		d	1858 Apr 11	Greenwich
	m. *GEORGE CLENDON	m	1795 Jan 22	Deal (by Licence)
	Pilot, widower	b	1760/1	
	("30" according to Licence, Jan 20)			
		d	1839 Oct 31	Deal aged 78

G	**SARAH CHITTY**	c	1776 Feb 29	Deal
		d	1833 Aug 12	Deal
	m. LANCELOT HAYMAN	m	1794 Nov 15	Deal
		c	1774 Apr 3	Deal
	upholsterer, dead by 1816	d	18??	

George Clendon
(1760-1839)

After his marriage to Elizabeth Chitty, George Clendon set up his own house in Deal and settled there for the rest of his life. They had ten children.

By 1819 George had changed his status from Pilot of the Cinque Ports to Trinity House Pilot. This occupation was clearly well paid. We do not know the extent to which he engaged in other sea-faring or trading activities. However, by 1832 he had acquired enough wealth to own two thirds of the Schooner "Fortitude", her cargo and stores, – the combined value of which was £2,304 – and to risk sending one of his sons, James, off with it to New Zealand. As will be seen later this risk didn't pay off! Nevertheless this George died a wealthy man.

Through his will he set up a Trust which was in existence until 1902 when it was finally divided up on the death of his last surviving daughter Sarah Ann Clendon – creating correspondence concerning land in New Zealand from English solicitors to Col F J P Chitty in Glens Falls, New York State, USA, and others!

He died, aged 78, on October 31st 1839 at Deal. His death certificate states that he died of "Inflammation of the Lungs". The informant was Susannah Benoy of Lower Street, Deal. She was present at the death, and signed the certificate with an "X" mark.

After he died his widow, Elizabeth, moved to London.

Later she gave her son George II the portraits in oils of herself and her husband which are illustrated in the 1974 edition. These portraits, dated 1811, were in the USA in 1951 in the possession of Gilbert Clendon, (1857-1953), grandson of George II. Their present whereabouts is unknown. The portrait of George (as an older man) is reproduced above.

The death of George and Elizabeth is recorded on a mural tablet in St George's Churchyard, Deal – near Gideon Chitty's tombstone – which reads:

In the Vault beneath
lie the remains of
Lieut. THOMAS CLENDON of the
Indian Navy who died
on the 16th April 1838
aged 35 years.
Also GEORGE CLENDON
father of the above who
Died 31st October 1839
aged 78 years.
ELIZABETH, widow of the above
GEORGE CLENDON
died at Greenwich 11th April 1858
aged 84 years
and was interred in the
Nunhead Cemetery, Peckham, Surrey.

The Will of "George Clendon the elder of Deal, Pilot," was dated 1838 May 26 and proved 1840 Feb 4 at London by the widow and George and John Chitty Clendon, sons. It is a long document, a copy of which I have in the collection of "Clendon Wills". As mentioned earlier it sets up a trust for his daughter Sarah Ann Clendon.

It names his wife Elizabeth, sons and daughters, George Clendon the younger, John Chitty Clendon, Sarah Ann Clendon, Elizabeth wife of Charles Chitty, James Reddy Clendon, Rebecca wife of William Lott Howard, Louisa wife of Joseph Dixon, Mary Parson, wife of William Knowles, Susanna Erridge widow, and grandchildren Thomas William Clendon, Mary Ann Stafford Clendon, and Catherine Sophia Eliza Clendon children of deceased son Thomas Clendon; witnessed by H.West, painter, Deal, and Martin L.Daniel, solicitor, Ramsgate.

His marriages and issue are recorded in the genealogical tables below. From now onwards these tables are consistent with the format used in the 1974 edition. Each person has been recorded using the same notation (by figures and letters) in this book as in 1974. Thus it is easy to refer from one edition to another.

This procedure has created, however, one minor anomaly in the way George Clendon I's issue are numbered in this book. It arises because the main section of the 1974 edition is derived from the issue of Gideon and Elizabeth Chitty. It is thus a Chitty-based, not a Clendon-based system. Therefore the early Clendons (prior to George's marriage into the Chitty family) had to be accommodated in a separate section. George, with his first wife and his four children by her, are in this section. George then reappears in the main section as a widower marrying into the Chitty family. There, his children by his 2nd marriage are tabulated as being those of Elizabeth Chitty – hence her 1st child Elizabeth, (although his 5th), is given the notation (I), (not (V)).

In order to maintain consistency I have also tabulated George's marriages, and their issue, separately below. Thus Elizabeth, the first child of George's second marriage, is also given the notation (I), as in 1974. In a straightforward Clendon genealogical table she would be given a (V), as George's 5th child. Similarly our ancestor George Clendon II should strictly be given a (VI), not a (II).

GEORGE CLENDON (1760/1-1839) had fourteen children – four by his first wife SUSANNA EARLE and ten by his second wife ELIZABETH CHITTY, as follows:

GEORGE AND SUSANNA CLENDON (1st wife) had issue four children:

(I)	**ANN CLENDON**	b	1783 May 2	St Mary, Dover (SAC's note)
		c	1783 May 4	St Mary, Dover (SAC's note)
		i	1783 Jul 30	St Mary, Dover (SAC's note)
(II)	**JANE CLENDON**	b	1784 May 30	St Mary, Dover (SAC's note)
		c	1784 Jun 8	St Mary, Dover (SAC's note)
		i	1784 Jul 25	St Mary, Dover (SAC's note)
(III)	**SUSANNA CLENDON**	b	1785 May 7	St Mary, Dover (SAC's note)
		c	1785 May 8	St Mary, Dover (SAC's note)
	died without issue	d	1844 Sep 22	i. St George, Deal
	m.THOMAS ERRIDGE	m	1805 May 13	Deal
	pilot	b	1776/7	
		d	1837 Jul 17 aged 60	Deal, i. St George Deal
(IV)	**GEORGE CLENDON**	b	1787 May 22	St Mary, Dover
		c	1787 May 23	St Mary, Dover
		i	1787 Jun 13	St Mary, Dove

GEORGE AND ELIZABETH CLENDON (2nd wife) had issue ten children

(I) **ELIZABETH CLENDON**   b 1796 Aug 8   Deal
                              c 1796 Aug26   Deal
                              d 1866 Jan 13   Blackheath Rd. London

     m. CHARLES CHITTY   m 1817 Jun 9   Deal
     Army Officer & Stock-Broker c 1792 Apr 25   Deal
     (her 1st cousin)   d 1865 Dec 26   Poole, Dorset
     Son of Michael Chitty, third son of Gideon Chitty, see Gideon's genealogical table above.
     Bette Edwards is descended from this branch of the family, see 1974 edition pp.50-53.

(II)* **GEORGE CLENDON II**   b 1798 Aug 1   Deal
                              c 1798 Aug 31   Deal
     chemist, emigrated to USA d 1887 Nov 28   Buckners, Louisa Co, Va. USA

     m. MARY ANN DRAPER   m 1826?   Ramsgate? Kent
                              c 1801 Sep 27   Margate, Kent
                              d 1878   Louisa County, Va. USA

(III) **JAMES REDDY CLENDON** b 1800 Oct 1   Deal
                              c 1800 Oct 22   Deal
                              d 1872 Oct 24   Rawene, Hokianga, New Zealand
     pioneer merchant in New Zealand, 1st US consul to NZ, signatory of Treaty of Waitangi, etc.

     m. (1st)   m 1826 Oct 2   St Philip's Sydney, NSW, Australia
     SARAH ISABELLA HILL   b 1803/4
                              d 1855 Aug 11   Russell, NZ
     m. (2nd)   m 1856 Jan 9
     JANE COCHRANE   b 1838 Jul 28   Hokianga, NZ
                              d 1919 May 21   Rawene, Hokianga, NZ

     The exploits of James Reddy Clendon, and table of his descendants, constitute Part Four of this edition.

(IV) **THOMAS CLENDON**   b 1802 Oct 16   Deal
     Lieutenant, Bombay Marine c 1802 Nov 5   Deal
                              d 1838 Apr 16   Deal

     m. FRANCES BOWEN   m 1826 Mch 21   Bedminster
                              b 18
                              d 1835 Nov 18   Colaba, Bombay 33

(V) **REBECCA CLENDON**   b 1804 Nov 27   Deal
     emigrated to NZ   c 1804 Dec 19   Deal
                              d 1899   New Zealand

     m. WILLIAM LOTT HOWARD   m 1829 Oct 29   Deal
     postmaster   b   emigrated to NZ
                              d 1865   New Zealand

(VI)	**SARAH ANN CLENDON**	b	1807 Feb12	Deal
		c	1807 Mch 13	Deal
		d	1902?	Yarmouth

Died, a spinster, at the home of her FELLOWS cousins. A letter from HARRIET CORDER suggests that she was dead by 1901 Oct 13. Her "Commonplace Book" furnished many clues to the CLENDON genealogy.

(VII)	**JOHN CHITTY CLENDON**	b	1809 Dec 16	Deal
	dental surgeon, of London	c	1809 Jan 10	Deal
		d	1870 Oct 1	London
	m. (1st)	m	18??	
	-?- HUGHES	b	18??	
		d	1869 Mch?	
	m. (2nd)	m	18??	
	CHARLOTTE ANNE HEATH	b	1821/2	
		d	1884 Feb 20	Brighton

(VIII)	**MARY JANE CLENDON**	b	1811 Nov 25	Deal
		c	1811 Nov 30	Deal
		d	1812 Feb 10	Deal
		i	1812 Feb 12	Deal

(IX)	**LOUISA CLENDON**	b	1813 May 28	Deal
	emigrated to Australia	c	1813 Jun 24	Deal
		d	1879 Oct 29	Sydney, NSW, Australia
	m. JOSEPH H DIXON	m	183?	
	emigrated to Australia	b	18??	
		d	1863/4	Sydney, NSW, Australia

(X)	**MARY PARSON CLENDON**	b	1815 Aug 6	Deal
	emigrated to USA	c	1815 Aug 27	Deal
		d	1849 Nov 2	Piqua, Ohio, i Homer
	m. WILLIAM KNOWLES	m	1838 Apr 17	Marylebone
		b	1806 Mch 11	Plaxtol, Kent, emigrated to USA
		c	1806 Apr 1	Plaxtol, Kent, emigrated to USA
		d	1899 Apr 28	

PART 3

ENGLAND, USA AND NEW ZEALAND

19th & 20th CENTURY

So far I have referred to the earlier Clendons as "our ancestors" because I am fairly certain that anyone who knows that they are descended from a Clendon will be descended from George Clendon and Elizabeth Chitty. But from now on there is a parting of the ways. George and Elizabeth have, in the 200 years since their marriage in 1795, created a large dynasty. They have many descendants. In the 1974 edition these took up nearly 70 pages of tables. Apart from those in my own branch of the family, I am in touch with only a handful of the other descendants of George and Elizabeth. Hopefully this book might help to rekindle some of these relationships.

Part 3 begins with the children of George I and Elizabeth. It then describes the lives of my ancestors in the George Clendon II/Thomas Clendon branch, and their immediate families. It concludes with full genealogical tables of all the descendants in this branch updated to July 1996.

CHAPTER 5
SEAFARING AND EMIGRATION 1798-1887

This chapter is about the sons and daughters of George Clendon I, the Pilot.

The life of one of them, George Clendon II (my great great grandfather) who emigrated to the USA, is described in as much detail as possible. The remainder are mentioned in summary only.

Another son was James Reddy Clendon. He emigrated to New Zealand where he became the most famous and eminent member of the family. In the 1830's he is said "to have acquired more authority than any other European in New Zealand" (see Readers Digest Guide to New Zealand p.51). He is mentioned briefly in this chapter but Part 4, written by Ross Clendon, is devoted entirely to him.

GEORGE CLENDON II *(1798 – 1887)*

My great great grandfather George Clendon II was born in Deal on August 1st 1798, and christened on August 31st. He is referred to in the 1974 edition as George Clendon Junior. I do not know very much about his early life except that the family soon became scattered – in fact there was only one occasion when he and his brothers and sisters were all together in one room. This was at dinner one day and it is described by him in the previous chapter. This dinner was not in 1820, as stated in the 1974 edition, but earlier, either late 1815 or early 1816 when Mary Parson was a baby – and George was 17. On close examination of the "Abstract of my family history" by George it can be seen that 1820 (which was on a previous page) is the date he uses to show how soon he and the rest of the family became scattered.

Thus the relevant section of his "Abstract of my family history" reads as follows:

In the year 1820 –

Elizabeth	*born in 1796 was in Ireland*
Myself	*born in 1798 was in London*
James	*born in 1800 was in Calcutta*
Thomas	*born in 1802 was in Bombay*
Rebecca	*born in 1804 was in Yarmouth*

> Sarah Ann   born in 1807 was in Walmer
> John   born in 1809 was in Dover
> Louisa   born in 1813) at home
> Mary Parson   born in 1815)

> *The only survivors of the family are Rebecca, Sarah Ann and myself –*
> *December 31st 1884.*

I studied the records to try to find out what the children were doing in 1820 and reached the following conclusions:

Elizabeth, 24, was married to Charles Chitty, then an Army Officer, and was living in Ireland – her 2nd child was born in Shandon, Cork, in June 1819.

George, 22, was in London – but there is nothing to indicate what he was doing there. He might have been apprenticed to, or working for a Chemist in London.

James, 20, seems to have started his seafaring career on a ship in Calcutta, possibly serving under his Uncle John Parson (see below).

Thomas, 18, was in the Bombay Marine and was aboard the ship "Benares".

Rebecca, 16, would be staying with her Aunt Rebecca who lived in Yarmouth.

At this point I think it is worth making a few notes about Aunt Rebecca. She was the oldest daughter of Gideon and Elizabeth Chitty, i.e. she was Rebecca's mother's older sister, and also possibly Rebecca's godmother. She was the widow of Lt. James Reddy (godfather of James Reddy Clendon), and by then married to John Parson. He was a commander of East Indiamen, and master of ships registered in Bombay and Calcutta. Their only daughter was Mary Parson b 1805, (after whom Mary Parson Clendon, below age 5, was presumably named), and she married Henry Fellows. Their son and his wife were the "Fellows cousins" who gave a home to Sarah Ann Clendon, below next, in Yarmouth when in her old age.

Sarah Ann, 13, was at school in Walmer, a suburb of Deal.

John, 11, was at school in Dover.

Louisa, 7 & Mary Parson, 5 were at home.

Clearly the family were encouraged to spread their wings from an early age. As a pilot, their father must have had strong connections with seafarers, ships captains and merchantmen. He would have plenty of opportunity to arrange for any of his sons to sail abroad if they wanted to. In fact by the end of their lives six out of the nine children who survived into adulthood had been overseas, and five had emigrated permanently.

George Clendon II grew up in this environment but did not appear as a young man to be contemplating a career which took him abroad. His writings give no clue at all about his own early life, apart from being in London in 1820.

The first evidence of his occupation emerges in 1826 when he was appointed executor to Thomas Erridge of Deal, pilot, husband of his half-sister Susanna, and was described as a chemist as follows:

Will of THOMAS ERRIDGE of Deal, Pilot, dtd 1826 Apr 19, pr 1837

Sep 18 (Cant'y Archd. Ct) by SUSANNA ERRIDGE & GEO. CLENDON Ramsgate, chemist. SUSANNA'S Will dtd 1844 Feb 19, pr Oct 21 (Cant. Archd.) by STEPHEN MORRIS, pilot.

His marriage to Mary Ann Draper probably took place at Ramsgate in 1826. I know nothing about Mary Ann, or her family. George presumably set up house in Ramsgate with her because their first child, George (known as George Clendon III) was born there on March 27th 1827. I was told by my father that they lived in Ramsgate until they emigrated, and that their son, my great grandfather Thomas, was born there and lived there during his childhood.

A sword-belt was in the possession of George II's descendants in the United States in 1974. It is engraved "Independent Artillery of Ramsgate" in which George II presumably served.

There is nothing to be found in the archives to give a clue as to what sort of life George and his growing family were living in Ramsgate. It was not until George was approaching fifty years of age that evidence appears that he was considering emigrating to the USA. This took the form of a letter sent to him from William Knowles, his brother-in-law, the husband of his youngest sister Mary Parson Clendon. She and William had already emigrated to Piqua, Ohio, USA. after their marriage in 1838. Evidently George had been enquiring about the prospects in USA for his son George III.

William's thoughtful reply provides a valuable insight into the life of a British emigrant in USA at that time. It must have been considered by George and his family when deciding to emigrate to USA a year or so later.

The letter is such a rich source of information on life in the USA at the time when George and his family set sail, that it is reproduced in full as follows:

Piqua, July 1st 1847
My dear Sir:

After much reflection on the subject I proceed to give you my opinion, founded on some experience, respecting your Son's coming to this Country. – If he could enjoy good health and be contented with your business I would advise him to remain at Ramsgate; but if he cannot be happy there I would not check his inclination. The World is before him; he has youth, talent, education, and energy of character; these qualities with a common degree of prudence, your pecuniary aid, and the blessing of God give him peculiar advantages, especially as he "likes work".

The life of a Farmer in the United States is one of incessant toil. I suppose he would not think of settling in a slave State. It requires a larger capital than £400 to become a Planter and own Slaves and no respectable white man could labour there without losing Caste. In the Eastern and Middle States the land (except in a few favoured spots) is much inferior to the West and no good Farms can be bought except at a comparative high rate. In the West there are millions of Acres of fertile soil forming an inexhaustible magazine, sufficient for the support of all the inhabitants of China should they be settled there. To farm this land profitably a man must chop down the timber, build his log house, plough and sow, reap and mow, in a word do all the labor himself or with very little assistance, and then he lives away from society, or is compelled to mingle with men on a fair estimate about on the level with the agricultural labourers of England. The price of Indian corn, Wheat, Oats, etc. is at Piqua about half what it brings in the New York and Philadelphia markets; the charge for transportation would make the difference. Here it is a rare thing to see land manured. If it will not produce a good crop without that expensive operation it is abandoned. There is no room for the exercise of mind or science in the matter; it is all ploughing, sowing, and gathering. The Eastern States farm more after the English fashion, but such immense quantities of produce grown in the West depress the market and render it unprofitable.

We are in the Miami Valley about 90 miles North of Cincinnati; it reminds me of the Valley of the Nile (from its fertility) only instead of the remains of Ancient Cities, obelisks and pillars we have the ruins of the primeval forest, with blackened lofty trunks of giant trees still scattered about the fields. Were I now inclined to farming I would have a grazing Farm, it is not so laborious and I think far more profitable and pleasant than corn growing and one need not always be on the spot.

The romance of living in a Log Hut in the midst of solitude and mud would soon be over, and be succeeded by discontent. There are many opportunities of employing small Capital here in mercantile and manufacturing business which could with difficulty be obtained in England, but a too hasty investment of money had been the utter ruin of a vast number of Emigrants. There is much wisdom in the plan of waiting a year or two before entering into business; and [? "with"] my friends George could easily obtain profitable employment without touching his Capital till he had seen the Country and deliberately made up his mind to remain or return. There are many pleasant and intelligent people in our town but not of course equal to first rate English society. Our State and Town also are amongst the most favored in this particular. Piqua contains about 3,000 people; its population has more than doubled since we have been here and it is increasing fast. Should your Son determine on coming out and will favor us with his company we should be most happy to receive him and make him as comfortable as is in our power.

We are on the Miami Canal extending from the Ohio River to Lake Erie and from this point he can have an easy communication with all the Western Country. I think he had better pay us a visit and even should he return the time spent would not be entirely lost. I am unable to determine whether Canada or the United States would be preferable for settlers on the whole. Probably for Scientific men this Country – as I understand Canada is full of young Englishmen seeking remuneration in the Towns. Farmers I think have an equal chance; but poor remuneration and hot weather wherein to perform their most laborious work. They are on this account I think more exposed to fevers than other people; from Midsummer to Michaelmas both countries are subject to bilious fevers; The remainder of the year is generally healthy. I cannot judge between the relative morality of Canada and Ohio; open vice is discountenanced in both and there are plentiful means of religious instruction. We have 10 churches in this place and are a professing "good sort of people". You ask if I am yet reconciled to free Institutions including slavery? I answer that I am not a Citizen of this Country as they call them but a Briton, a man of Kent, who will "never be or have a slave". The slave question will I have no doubt not many years hence dissolve the Federal Government of this Country and it will be well if it is done peaceably. The struggle will and must come and the conquest of Mexico (should this inglorious war prove in the end successful) will precipitate the event – good men look into the future with apprehension and dismay for where the foundation is rotten the superstructure must fall.

The end of Summer is I think a preferable time to Spring for coming here for there will be more time for acclimation before the sickly season returns. It is unnecessary to encumber himself with much baggage or clothes as they can be purchased here nearly as cheap as in England. I have no idea of returning home at present unless it were in my power to make a visit, which I cannot afford. My Business is getting better and I hope soon to overcome my late losses though I am still far behind. Our little Boy has been very sick but thank God is much

better. Mary and our two girls with myself enjoy excellent health and many
undeserved blessings. I will enclose a list of Seeds, etc. which if your Son should
come out and would take the trouble to procure for me he will confer no small
obligation, as I cannot get them here.

I have one more caution to give to George. Should he meet in this Country
any professing friend who would kindly offer to assist him in the disposal of his
money to beware especially if he is an Englishman, for there are a set of swindlers
of this description, deep, plausible, designing men who on the plea of being fellow
countrymen would if they could get a chance rob of every shilling.

Mary unites with me in kind regards to yourself, Mrs. Clendon, and
family.

Believe me to remain
Yours affectionately,
Wm. Knowles

George decided soon after receiving that letter that he himself would
emigrate to the USA, and take the family with him. The 1974 edition states
that they left "about 1850" but I think it was nearer 1847 for the following
reasons.

The oldest son George III writes in a letter dated 21st October 1885:

. . . I left England when only 20 years old . . .

If this statement is true they must have left before his 21st. birthday, which
was 24th March 1848. Also a note against George III in the Clendon file in
the "A W Miller Collection" at the Glens Falls library states:

. . . came 1847 . . .

Another says:
. . . America 1847, Glens Falls 1848 . . .

What caused George to take this step, is not directly stated in any records
that I have seen. At the age of 50 he would have been well settled and,
judging by his actions in USA, he was a successful businessman and wealthy
enough to continue to enjoy a good standard of living in Ramsgate. It seems
that it could have been partly for the benefit of the younger generation –
his oldest son George III had clearly expressed a desire to emigrate – and
partly to fulfil a desire to set himself up afresh in a new country where there
was more freedom and opportunity.

It has also been handed down within the family to my first cousin
Susan Miller, that George had become fed up with the influence of the

aristocracy and social snobbery in England, and that he wanted to go to USA where all men are equal and he would not have "to doff his cap" to anyone. This attitude of George's is hinted at by his son George III in a letter dated October 21st 1885; when referring to family history he wrote:

> . . . my father took no interest in my researches when a boy, thinking perhaps aristocratic notions would unfit me for trade & I got but little help from him . . .

When George and Mary Ann went to the USA they took their five children with them. If George III was 20, then John would have been 18, Mary 16, Thomas, my great grandfather 11 – and Benjamin 10 years old.

They also took with them two nephews – Chitty brothers. They were sons of George's older sister Elizabeth, who had married her cousin Charles Chitty. They were George Clendon Chitty, then 28 years old, and Frederick John Parson Chitty, aged 23. Bette Edwards is a great grand-daughter of Frederick J P Chitty.

George would have been 51, and his wife 49 years of age, when they settled in Glens Falls, New York State. On June 29th 1850 George Clendon bought 100 square rods of land at the northwest corner of Glen and Pine Streets from Jacob M. and Maria Richards for $800 (Book R of Warren County deeds, page 208). This purchase price led Judge John Austin, a distant relative living in nearby Queensbury, who kindly researched the deeds for us in 1993, to believe that there was already a house on this lot.

A description of the plots of land involved, including the above and subsequent transactions, are to be found in a letter dated January 19th 1993 from John Austin to Mrs Elizabeth Edwards, (Bette), a copy of which is in my archives.

By 1858, there were two houses there. One on the northerly corner of Pine and Glen Streets was occupied by George III. He was then 31 and married to Mary Hunt. By time they had produced six of their nine children, and four had survived.

The other house, the next one to the north, was occupied by George II. It is in this house (see illustration) that my great grandfather Thomas Clendon lived, with his father and mother, even after he had married, and where my grandfather Arthur Clendon was born on August 12th 1868. I can remember my grandfather very clearly, and it is rather amazing to me to think that he was in that house with his grandfather George II – who in turn knew his own grandfather Thomas of Chatham and Chichester so well – and who wrote down events in our family history that reach back into the early 1700's.

To return to the life of George II – there is a note in the records in the

"A W Miller Collection" that George built both these houses. If so he must have paid a good price originally for just the plot of land! It is also recorded that George was the Director of an Insurance company. George was clearly very prosperous.

He set his son George III up in a Chemist's business in Glens Falls – but there is a change of language! In American parlance the Chemist became a "Druggist", and the business was known as the "PHOENIX DRUG STORE".

Before long George II had left the running of the business to George III, referred to now in Glens Falls as George Clendon Jr. But when the Civil War broke out George II came out of his retirement to look after the business while his son, who eventually became a Major, went off to fight. It is not clear what happened to the business after the war.

These events are illustrated by the following newspaper cuttings from the "A W Miller Collection" in Glens Falls library.

Soap Factory cor* Glen & Pine, conducted by Geo Clendon Jr
Hard & soft soap & candles of superior quality
Glens Falls Free Press April 19 1856

--------oo--------

Phoenix Drug Store, Glen St. 4 drs. South of Warren
'Purchased stock of Dr. Jas. Ferguson& added thereto a fresh assortment'
Drugs, chemicals, pat.med., trusses, Perfumery, camphene, Burning Fluid,
Paints & oils, Kerosene
Geo Clendon, Jr. Press. 1/13/60*

--------oo--------

Phoenix Drug Store Geo. Clendon, Jr. Glen St. 4 doors s of Warren
Drugs, Chemicals, Pat.Med., Trusses, Perfumery, Camphene, Burning Fluid"
Press. 5/18/60

--------oo--------

Geo. Clendon, Jr. Phoenix Drug Store Glen St. opposite the G.F.Bank
During my absence with the Army of the Potomac, my business will be under

---

*Note cor = corner
Note. The American notation for dates is: Month/Day/Year.
Hence in the above advert '13th January 1860' is '1/13/60', not '13/1/60'.

the supervision of my father, a Druggist with more than thirty years' experience.
Camphene, Burning Fluid, Kerosene, Paints, Oils and Artists Materials
Geo Clendon Jr.
Advertisement in the Glens Falls Republican Newspaper Sept. 30, 1862.

--------oo--------

Within seven years of this advertisement appearing George and his wife had left Glens Falls. Book 20 of the Deeds shows, on page 251, that on 27th May 1869 George and Mary Ann Clendon of Cleveland Ohio sold for $4,000 the northerly part of their land, (the house occupied by them in 1858), to Theodore S. DeLong of Glens Falls. It is interesting to note that George III's oldest daughter Mary married Cutler DeLong, presumably a relative of Theodore, two years later on July 31st 1871 in Glens Falls.

Also in 1869 George's son Tom (my great grandfather) left Glens Falls for England. He never returned to the USA, nor saw his parents again.

On 22nd March 1871 (Book 24 of Deeds, page 370) George and Mary Ann Clendon of Cleveland, Ohio, "formerly of Glens Falls," conveyed to Walter A. Faxon of Glens Falls for $1,500 the house at Glen and Pine Streets, described as "premises now occupied by" Faxon. In 1871 they moved to a farm at Buckner's Station, Louisa County, Virginia where they lived with

The House at Glen and Pine Streets.

George Clendon
(1798-1887)

their youngest son Benjamin. George was then 73.

It is not known why George and Mary Ann went to Cleveland Ohio, or what they did there for those few years. Perhaps there is a connection between their stay there and the fact that two of Benjamin's daughters (b 1868 & 1877 see later) went to live in Cleveland Ohio as adults.

George and Mary Ann lived with Benjamin at Buckner's Station for the rest of their lives. Mary died in 1878, and George on November 28th 1887. During this time George III also bought a farm nearby, which he called "Thanet Farm", after the area of Kent where he was born.

George clearly enjoyed a happy and peaceful retirement there surrounded by his family. This is reflected throughout the letters he wrote at the time; for example he wrote on 11th March 1884 about his three grandchildren (Benjamin's daughters Clara K, then age 16, Fannie 14, and Nellie (Ellen) age 10) in a letter to his sister Sarah Ann Clendon in Yarmouth, England:

> *. . . She [Nellie] was rather unwilling to go to school. But after a few days she told me she liked the teacher, & after a few more days she advanced from liking the teacher to liking what she was taught, & when she came home in the evening instead of taking up her play things she took her slate & book set herself little sums in addition, & studied her reading & spelling book. She continues to do so & the consequence is, she is making rapid progress & I am happy to say that*

she has a very affectionate disposition. In this she resembles her sisters.

I went into the living room a few days ago & found Clara K sitting in a chair with her arms around & embracing Fannie. It is very pleasant to see such love. Nearly every day I see Nellie seated on her father's knee, & playing with him, & what is better still, the love of the children is not all expended in kissing & embracing, but is shown also in the kind assistance of each other , & to their father & mother & to me . . .

. . . I would like to write much more but my head is too weak. Give my kind regards to Mr & Mrs Fellowes. I have written to New York for a newspaper – The Christian Union – & will send it to you when it arrives. It is a paper I receive weekly & warmly approve of.

Your affectionate brother George

His religious faith comes through in other writings – his own – in a letter dated 24th July 1885 written by him to his nephew J S Clendon

. . . I send my kind love to your wife & daughter. May God bless all of you & grant that when the right time comes we may have a happy meeting in heaven . . .

And after he died – in a letter written by his son George III to J S Clendon, on 21 December 1887

. . . I sent you a paper with a notice of my father's death. He was very weak all summer & gradually faded away retaining his marvellous sweetness of disposition to the last. He was never irritable & disliked giving trouble. Only a night or two before his death he wanted me to lie down by him as sitting up all night would weary me. Dear old father, I cannot say there was ever anyone like him, so good, so unselfish. He is an ornament, an acquisition to heaven itself. Strong language you will say, but it is true.

Fortunately he did not suffer. For some hours before he went to heaven he was unconscious. I knew he was dead only by his ceasing to breathe . . .

Finally, the cutting from the newspaper, mentioned above, which gave "notice of my father's death"

CLENDON – Died at his son's [Benjamin's] home, in Louisa County, Va., November 28th 1887, Mr GEORGE CLENDON.

The burial services were conducted by Rev. L.J.Haley, and attended by a good number of friends, who met to pay their last tribute of respect to a good man.

Mr. CLENDON was born in Kent county, Eng., in 1798, came to the

United States in 1850, and in 1871 removed to Louisa county Va. It has been
the pleasure of the writer to know Mr. Clendon for the past twelve years, and to
bear testimony to his amiability of disposition and purity of character. When in
his presence one would feel lifted above the ordinary sphere of man. He leaves the
assurance of a life of immortality beyond the grave.

   "Blessed are the dead who die in the Lord"
   A FRIEND

George was 89 years of age.

GEORGE II (1798-1887) and MARY ANN (1801-1878) CLENDON had issue five children:

(1) **GEORGE CLENDON III**   b   1827 Mch 24   Ramsgate
    Major in the US Army   d   1909 Jan 5   Glens Falls

    m. MARY HUNT   m   1848 May 24   New York City
    (?Widow of GORDON HUNT,   b   1822 Apr 7   Ramsgate
    née RANSOME?)   d   1908 Jan 10   Glens Falls

        GEORGE III and MARY CLENDON had issue nine children. Their descendants now live
        throughout the USA (see 1974 edition).

(2) **JOHN CLENDON**   b   1829   Ramsgate?
    died without issue   d   1910 Aug 25   Ramsgate, aged 81
    farmed in Glens Falls (Clendon Farm by Clendon Brook still exist), returned to Ramsgate. W ill: of 95
    West Cliff Rd, Ramsgate, gentleman, proved by H K DANIEL, solicitor, effects £8338-4s-10d.

    m. JUDITH GOODISON   m   Ramsgate
                                b   18

(3) **MARY CLENDON**   b   1831   Ramsgate?

    m. (1st)   m   18   Glens Falls
    GEORGE CLENDON CHITTY   b   1819 Jun 21   Shandon, Cork, Ireland
    her cousin, died without issue d 1854 Mch 11   Warrensburg, New York State, USA

    m. (2nd)   m   18
    THOMAS COLLINGS   b   18   Littlehampton, Sussex
    widower

THOMAS and MARY COLLINGS had issue three children and further descendants (see 1974 edition)

(4)* **THOMAS CLENDON**   b   1836 Jan 8   Ramsgate ?
     of USA, Wales, England & NZ d 1921 Jun 17   Lower Hutt, New Zealand

    m. ELIZA KELSEY VYE   m   1861 Apr 9   Ramsgate
                                b   1839 Aug 7   Ramsgate
                                d   1915 Mar 6   Lower Hutt, New Zealand

        The issue and posterity of THOMAS & ELIZA constitute the remainder of Part Three of this edition.

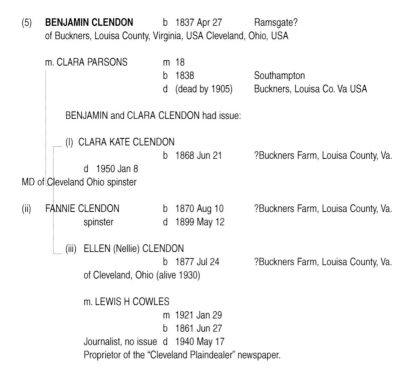

(5) **BENJAMIN CLENDON**   b 1837 Apr 27   Ramsgate?
     of Buckners, Louisa County, Virginia, USA Cleveland, Ohio, USA

     m. CLARA PARSONS   m 18
                             b 1838   Southampton
                             d (dead by 1905)   Buckners, Louisa Co. Va USA

          BENJAMIN and CLARA CLENDON had issue:

          (I) CLARA KATE CLENDON
                             b 1868 Jun 21   ?Buckners Farm, Louisa County, Va.
                  d 1950 Jan 8
MD of Cleveland Ohio spinster

(ii)   FANNIE CLENDON   b 1870 Aug 10   ?Buckners Farm, Louisa County, Va.
          spinster   d 1899 May 12

          (iii) ELLEN (Nellie) CLENDON
                             b 1877 Jul 24   ?Buckners Farm, Louisa County, Va.
          of Cleveland, Ohio (alive 1930)

          m. LEWIS H COWLES
                             m 1921 Jan 29
                             b 1861 Jun 27
          Journalist, no issue d 1940 May 17
          Proprietor of the "Cleveland Plaindealer" newspaper.

POST SCRIPT
A summary of the lives of George II's brothers and sisters

When George died at his son Benjamin's house in Virginia USA, he was far
away from "Kent County, England" where his father, George I, the ship's
pilot – and his mother Elizabeth Chitty, the daughter of a pilot – had
brought him up. He was not the only member of that family to sail overseas
– most of them did.

Starting with George I's family by his first wife Susanna, the only
surviving child was also called Susanna – the rest died in infancy. Susanna
married a ship's pilot, Thomas Erridge, lived in Deal and died there, a
widow, when 59 years of age.

The oldest from the second family, was Elizabeth, called after her
mother, Elizabeth Chitty. She married her mother's brother's son Charles
Chitty. Although his grandfather and father were seafarers, he was not. He
became an Army Officer, rose to the rank of Captain – and then became a
not very successful stockbroker in London, (see pp 52-55 of the 1974 edition
for a fuller description of his life and issue). They had ten children. Two of
them emigrated to Glens Falls USA with George II (their uncle). The older
one was George Clendon Chitty (1819-1854). He went on to marry George

II's daughter Mary Clendon in Glens Falls, but died a few years later without having children. The younger one was Frederick John Parson Chitty (1824-1907). He married a girl from Glens Falls, and after living in Piqua, Ohio for a while returned to Glens Falls, where he lived until he died. In the American Civil War 1861-5 he became a Colonel. He lived at 15 Bay Street, close to the Clendon houses in the centre of Glens Falls, for many years. One of his descendants, Louis Chester Chitty Jr, lives in Glens Falls – close to Clendon Farm, and Clendon Brook. Sue and I visited him and his family there in October 1991 with Bob and Bette Edwards. Bette is Frederick Chitty's great granddaughter.

The second was George II himself, who emigrated to the USA, with two nephews – as described above.

The third was James Reddy Clendon – a most distinguished seafarer – whose story comprises Part Four of this edition.

The fourth was Thomas Clendon. He joined the Bombay Marine when sixteen and a half years old. He saw service as a Lieutenant in Bombay and in England. His wife died in Bombay when his four children were young, and he himself was on a sick certificate in England before he died. He was buried at Deal aged 36.

The fifth was Rebecca. Like her brothers and sisters she was born and christened at Deal – and married there at age 25 to William Lot Howard, also of Deal. They emigrated to New Zealand where he became the Postmaster of the Canterbury District and a prominent figure in the development of New Zealand Postal Services. They had five children. Their daughter, Fanny Clendon Howard, was known as "The Canterbury Belle".

The sixth was Sarah Ann Clendon – still affectionately known in my family as "Aunt Sarah". Although not a traveller she kept in touch with her brothers and their families overseas. Copies of some of her letters are in my possession. She also kept a scrapbook containing numerous press cuttings and copious notes about the family. This "Commonplace Book" was used by Erik Chitty to provide him with clues about early Clendon family members. To date I have not discovered its whereabouts.

Erik Chitty gave my father a beautiful framed picture of Aunt Sarah which hangs in my sitting room today. It has red velvet in the frame, and the photograph is somehow printed on china or porcelain, not on paper or card. It shows an old lady, in lace cap, peering over spectacles, worn very crookedly. She also was an amateur painter, and left some watercolours of Welsh scenes which my father had, (and always referred to them as "Aunt Sarah's paintings"). They are now in the possession of my brother David.

Aunt Sarah lived in later life at the home of her Fellows cousins in Great Yarmouth, Norfolk, England. They were descendants of her Aunt Rebecca by her second husband John Parson, her first being Lt. James

Reddy, who it is presumed was godfather to James Reddy Clendon. When she died in Yarmouth in about 1901, her father's estate was wound up by Messrs Marchant Benwell & Marchant, solicitors, of Deptford. I have papers concerning the final distribution by them in 1902 – and these relate to a man born in 1760/1!.

The seventh was John Chitty Clendon. Not a traveller, he was a dentist of some distinction – with royal connections. He was dentist to the Westminster Hospital, 1844-63, MRCS 1846, Lecturer on Anatomy and Diseases of the Teeth at Westminster Hospital School of Medicine, author of "Observations on the Extraction of Teeth and on the use of Chloroform in Dental Surgery", and a pioneer in the use of anaesthetics and also of differentiated forceps in dental surgery. He is also said to have been dentist to the Dowager Queen Adelaide. In 1852 his address was 28 Albermarle Street London W, and he died in 1870 at 23 Cambridge Gardens, Kensington Park. He married (1st) a Miss Hughes who died about 1869. His second wife was Charlotte Ann Heath who was, according to her nephew Sir Oliver Lodge, a protégé of Queen Adelaide.

The eighth, Mary Jane Clendon died in infancy.

The ninth, Louisa Clendon, emigrated to Australia. Little is known about her except that she died on October 29 1879 in Sydney, New South Wales, having married Joseph H Dixon who died at Sydney about 1863/4. In a letter dated 1866, Frederick Corder (who married Harriet Chitty, sixth daughter of Elizabeth, Louisa's oldest sister) mentioned that Dixon died insolvent, and that his youngest son had to pay for the funeral. Joseph and Louisa Dixon had issue five children, one of whom married a doctor who practised in Richmond NSW, and another was an attorney in Sidney, NSW, Australia.

The tenth was Mary Parson Clendon. At aged 22 she married William Knowles in Marylebone. He came from Plaxtol in Kent and together they emigrated to the USA. In 1847 he wrote the letter to George II from Piqua, Ohio, which is reproduced earlier, describing life in USA. Within two years of that letter Mary had died at age 43. She was described as "a devoted member of the Protestant Episcopalian Church and Treasurer of the Piqua Female Bible Society". William and Mary Parson Knowles had issue six children. Their descendants fill 14 pages of the 1974 edition – about 400 of them spread across the USA, many in Texas, comprising a wide range of academic, professional and other occupations.

CHAPTER 6

A LIFE SPANS THREE CONTINENTS
1836-1921

This chapter is an account of the life story of my great grandparents, Thomas Clendon and Eliza Kelsey Vye.

Thomas was born in Ramsgate on 8th January 1836, the year before Queen Victoria came to the throne. A glimpse of his childhood is provided by his younger brother, Ben, who wrote in about 1888 to his cousin J S Clendon in New Zealand:

> . . . I feel much solicitude for Tom's welfare. The reminiscences of our earlier days are of the pleasantest kind. He is but 15 months my senior; we slept in the same bed, drank of the same cup, enjoyed the same sports & went to the same horrid school. After leaving England in 1850 (I was then 13) we were near each other, Tom in the machine shop & I on the Farm . . .

This extract gives the impression of a happy childhood, despite the horrid school! Tom must also have had pleasant memories of his childhood in Ramsgate because he returned there from USA as a young man, as soon as he could afford to. This letter from Ben also raises the question again of the precise year in which Tom left Ramsgate as a child when his father emigrated to the USA, and settled in Glens Falls, New York State. As discussed in the previous chapter, many references give the date as 1847; one says USA 1847, Glens Falls 1848. If these are true, Tom was only eleven when he left his birthplace. However he was definitely in Glens Falls by the age of 14 – because it was in June 1850 that his father bought the land there.

The only other reference that I can find to Thomas in his youth shows that he sang in the church choir in Glens Falls. Many years later Amy C Green, (daughter of Tom's brother George III), wrote in a letter to my grandfather Arthur Clendon (Tom's son), dated January 28th 1928:

> . . . a fine new Gothic Church – Presbyterian . . .
> Your Father, my Father and Uncle Ben, all sang
> in its choir when they were young men . . .

Tom was one of four sons, George, John, Thomas and Ben. Two of his brothers, John and Ben, went into farming, and the oldest, George, who may also have started in farming for a short time, soon followed in his father's footsteps in the drugstore.

Before I went to the USA in 1991 all I knew about Tom's adult life there was that he was living at his father's house, and working in Glens Falls. I was intrigued by the story my father had always told me that Tom made a fortune in an engineering business as a young man in America – came to England – and spent it all! I wanted to find out how Tom had made his money.

When in the USA, Sue and I were taken for the day to Glens Falls by Bette and Bob Edwards. We learnt a lot of interesting things about the town, and saw some Clendon gravestones, and some references to Clendons in the library. But we failed to come up with anything definite about the work he had done there. Bette and Bob agreed to keep looking.

They returned to Glens Falls themselves in October 1992, and this time they were successful. In the library they discovered an entry in a book called "History of Warren County, Biographical sketches of Prominent Men and Pioneers", edited by H.P. Smith and published 1981 by Heart of The Lakes Publishing Co., Interlaken, NY 14847. The entry read as follows:

> *The oldest manufacturing business now in Glens Falls is the foundry and machine shop of J.L. & S.B.Dix. The business was established about the year 1844 by James Wells. In 1848 Hopkins & Dix bought out Wells, and continued the business until 1854, when Henry M.Lewis came into the firm. In about a year, however another change altered the firm name to Hopkins, Dix & Clendon. In 1856 Hopkins withdrew; in 1869 Hopkins succeeded Clendon . . .*

When at the library Bob and Bette enquired from the Glens Falls historian how prosperous a foundry and machine shop business would have been. They were told that Clendon could certainly have made a lot of money as a partner in an Iron Foundry, especially if there was no competition locally. The historian also said that he thought that the foundry was located down near the river as one enters Glens Falls from the South.

At age 19, therefore, Tom became one of three partners owning a foundry and machine shop business. He must have had to buy his share of the business, and no doubt his father helped him financially. By all accounts his father was by this time very comfortably off. He was the director of an insurance company, he had built a second house for his son George, and his son John had a farm. It seems natural that he would have helped his son Tom to get started in business as well.

A year later when Tom was 20 the senior partner, Hopkins, withdrew from the firm, and it became Dix & Clendon. I assume that Tom was then owner of a half share, having helped to buy out Hopkins. If so, and there was no competition locally, he certainly was in a position to make handsome profits and accumulate considerable wealth. This he appears to have done because only three years later, at age 23, he could afford to return to England for a visit, and while there undertake a grand tour of Europe.

In England, he obtained a British Passport, which I now have. It is a single sheet of thin paper measuring about 14 by 10 inches, with the Royal Coat of Arms at the top, and Lord Russell's crest at the foot. It is signed by Lord Russell and by Thomas Clendon. It is inscribed, in perfect copper plate writing:

Thomas Clendon's passport.

We, Lord John Russell, a Member of Her Brittanic Majesty's Most Honorable
Privy Council, a Member of Parliament, and Her Majesty's Secretary of State for
Foreign Affairs, &c. &c. &c.

Request and require in the Name of Her Majesty all those whom it may
concern, to allow

Mr Thomas Clendon, a British Subject Travelling on the Continent ------

to pass freely without let or hindrance and to afford him every assistance
and protection of which he may stand in need.

Given at the Foreign Office, London, the 9th day of August 1859.

J Russell
Signature of the Bearer
Thomas Clendon

He used the Passport to travel to France and Italy. At various places he had
to attend at Consulates or Embassies to have it endorsed, perhaps an early
form of visa. All are handwritten, signed and stamped. Here are a few
examples:

Vu par nous Agent Vice Consul de France a Douvres
Bon pour se rentre en France
  Douvres Le 9 Aout 1859
   [Dover]   *Vu Debarque a Marseille*
            [date unreadable]

Napoli
per le Signor Tommaso Clendon
Luddo Brittanico
  29 Agosto 1859   *Rome 5 Sept 1859*
           Visit a Consulate Regia Brittanic
           Buono a London

It is worth noting that the passport describes him as a British Subject, and
that it was not valid for his return to the USA. Maybe he had a different
passport for travel to America, or he had dual nationality and one was not
necessary.

While in England he would surely have returned to Ramsgate.
Moreover, because he came back eighteen months later to marry Eliza
Kelsey Vye, I believe that he met her when he was in England in 1859, and
that their courtship began then.

Eliza's father, Jesse Vye, was a grocer in Ramsgate, who lived at 25
Queen Street. His shop could not have been far from the chemists. He and
Tom's father (George Clendon II) were much the same age, Jesse two years

the younger – and both were prosperous businessmen with large families. They were quite likely to have been friends. In all probability their children knew each other and went to the same school. If so, it would have been natural for Tom to look them up – and in doing so to renew his acquaintance with Eliza. She was twenty years of age.

The Vye family was well established in Ramsgate. Jesse had been born there on August 30th 1800, and was baptised at St. Lawrence Church on September 28th 1800, the same church where he was married to Jane Jarman on 10th March 1825. Jesse's parents Charles and Sarah Vye had lived there, and were both buried in that same church. Eliza Kelsey Vye was the seventh out of their family of ten children. A copy of the Vye family tree that was produced about 1920, in my archives, shows that there were a large number of Vyes living in Ramsgate in the 19th century.

Eliza was rather fond of her oldest brother George Vye, who also had a soft spot for her. In one document she is referred to as "George's property". She kept a letter from him written in 1858 (when she was 19) after she had an accident, addressing her as "My Dear Sister Eliza" and including such sentiments as " . . . Cheer up my Dear Girl! you will be well long before Christmas and that is only a month today and then I hope I shall be with you to help you eat your Xmas Pudding. Trusting you are not in much pain, I

Thomas Clendon (1836-1921)

Eliza Kelsey Vye (1839-1915)

send you my love & a kiss, . . . so good bye, Dear Eliza, Your Affectionate Brother, George."

On 7th August 1860, her father gave Eliza a leather bound Bible, with a clasp at the side, for her 21st Birthday present. I feel that the Bible has a special significance. Firstly to Eliza because it was her 21st present from her father Jesse who wrote a poem in it to her; secondly to her son Arthur because she wrote in it "Arthur Clendon, from his Mother, October 1st 1887" and gave it to him when he went to Emmanuel College, Cambridge as a parting gift, shortly before she left for New Zealand, never to see him again; thirdly to my father (Arthur's son) because he wrote about this parting on the back page, and kept it by his bedside during his last illness; and finally to me because in 1990 I found the Bible, by a stroke of good fortune, in that bedroom twenty years later amongst a pile of old books and rubbish that had been discarded – only a few moments before I left it for the last time when the house had been sold.

The poem, although rather melodramatic and Victorian, appealed to me at the time. It still does; knowing now what Eliza suffered in her later years, it turned out to be rather apt:

When in future distant years
Thou shalt look upon this page
Through the crystal vale of tears
That dim our eyes in after age
Think it was a Father's hand
Though his smiles no more should see
Pointing towards that better land
Gave this sacred gift to thee.

To thy Chamber still and lone
Fly, and search this sacred page
When earth's blandishments are gone
Every grief it will assuage
Close thy door against the din
Of worldly folly worldly fear
Only let the radiance in
Of each heavenly promise here.

Lightly thou esteem it now
For thy heart is young and wild
And upon thy Girlhood's brow
Nought but sunny hopes hath smiled
But when disappointments come
And the world begins to steal
All thy spirits early bloom
Then its value thou will feel.

When thy bruised spirit bends
'Neath the weight of sorrows chains
When of all Life's summer friends
Not one flatterer still remains
Lay this unction to the wound
Of thy smitten bleeding breast
There the only balm is found
That can yield the weary rest.

Six months after receiving this she married Tom.

The wedding took place on 9th April 1861 at the Ebenezer Chapel, Ramsgate, according to the rites and ceremonies of the "Independent denomination". Tom's occupation was given as "Engineer". Witnesses were Jesse Vye, Eliza's father, and Ellen Mary Vye, her younger sister. When I was in New Zealand I was told that after the wedding Tom and Eliza went on a grand tour of Europe, but I am not convinced of this. I think this story may have been confused with Tom's 1859 tour. There is no reference to a second tour in the archives, and the fact that their marriage was in 1861 was not well known or recorded in the 1974 edition, whereas the existence of the 1859 passport was common knowledge. It was only recently when, as part of the research for this book, my son obtained a copy of their marriage certificate that the discrepancy in the dates became obvious.

When Tom brought Eliza back with him to Glens Falls, they lived in his father's house there. Their first child, Edith, died in infancy. Their next was a son, Harry. His exact date of birth is not known; the Glens Falls records of that period have been destroyed by fire. However, when he died in September 1935 he was recorded as being aged 71, so he was born in 1863 or 1864. The third child was Arthur, my grandfather, born on August 12 1868. Tom was 32 and Eliza had just turned 29.

Then next year, in 1869, Tom sold up his share of the business, and they returned to Ramsgate. Quite why they did so is not really clear. It is probably a mixture of factors. One may have been that Eliza was homesick. I have heard that said by her grandchildren in New Zealand. But she may not to have been all that unhappy, judging by the inscription, on the back of a photo of George II's Glens Falls house (now in Bette Edward's dining room), which reads: " . . . *One of their five children, Thomas Clendon, returned to England in his twenties and brought back his bride (Eliza Kelsey Vye, of Ramsgate, Kent), where they lived happily with his parents for a number of years in this very house"*.

The fact that Thomas did not set up house on his own as his brothers had done, suggests perhaps that he was not truly settled. From what my father told me his aim was to make as much money he could in America and then to return to England to enjoy life.

When Tom and Eliza returned to England, they went first to Ramsgate. Their next son, Sidney, was born there on 24th May 1870. He was born at home, at The Hope, Elms Park, Ramsgate. This time Tom's occupation was given as "Gentleman". He was 34.

Some time later Tom acquired a large property, called "Cwm Rhaiadr", near Machynlleth in North Wales, and moved there with the family. My father knew where it was, but never took me there. In the papers belonging to Susan Miller, my first cousin, is an extract from the Times newspaper of Friday May 8th 1936, describing the property in "The Estate Market" column as follows:

CWM RHAIADR

North Welsh land, over 1,000 acres, with a modernised stone house, near Machynlleth, takes its name from the famous waterfall, Cwm Rhaiadr . . . Mr. A.G.Bradley in "In Praise of North Wales" says he was on his way to Cwm Rhaiadr House, which he had heard was the most beautifully-placed country house in Wales" . . . Cwm Rhaiadr will be submitted at Shrewsbury on June 16, by Messrs Maple & Co Limited (Tottenham Court Road [London]). The property of 1,011 acres is suitable either for game or sheep grazing. There are two trout streams. The furniture and farming stock are to be taken by the buyer of the freehold. The mountain pastures can carry 1,500 sheep. Cwm Rhaiadr is about 20 miles from Aberystwyth.

Sue and I visited Cwm Rhaiadr in May 1996. The old farmhouse had long since gone. Built in 1652 it had been burnt down in a fire in 1884. It was in such a magnificent setting at the head of a beautiful remote valley, that the then owner, Richard Peyton, replaced it with a large imposing mansion house. This was acquired in 1896 by a relative of the present owner, Mr John Norman, whose grandfather Owen Owen, the famous Victorian draper, was born there in 1848. The estate was withdrawn from the 1936 sale advertised above, and has remained in the same family since 1896. By 1964 the mansion house had fallen into disrepair and was replaced by two modern Colt houses. One is occupied by the tenant farmer, and the other is used by the family.

Tom and Eliza lived in this beautiful place for less than eight years. By 1878 they were in Birmingham, living in Springfield Street on December 1st 1878 when their son Vivian was born. This time Tom's occupation was given as "Farmer".

My father told me that Tom ran short of money living in the style of a Country Gentleman. But why move to Birmingham? Why not Ramsgate? Perhaps because of the good schools, perhaps contrary to the family tradition that "he never worked again after he left USA", he did work in Birmingham as engineer, or at least moved there in the hope of finding some suitable work.

The family lived in Birmingham for about nine years. At least two of the boys, Arthur and Sidney, were educated there at King Edwards School. Also at the school were some of the five sons of Dr James Hickinbotham. They were good friends of the Clendon boys. Ryland Hickinbotham and Sidney Clendon started school on the same day, and went in holding hands. And in his 'teens Arthur Clendon was to fall in love with their older sister, Elsie Hickinbotham. More about the Hickinbothams and Clendons later.

In Autumn 1887 Tom and Eliza left England, with all their children except for their son Arthur, and emigrated to New Zealand. By this time it is said that Tom had either spent, or lost on the Stock Exchange, the best part of his fortune – and he declared "If I am going to be poor, I might as well be poor in one of the colonies". He hoped, I think, that he had sufficient capital to buy some uncultivated land in New Zealand, and turn it fairly quickly, into a prosperous farm. He was 51.

The sailing ship in which their furniture was travelling was shipwrecked in Wellington harbour. Among the items salvaged the following were still in the family when I was in New Zealand in 1992:

- a pair of Victorian button-backed chairs; (the gentleman's chair belonged to Tom's granddaughter Nancy Walker, and the lady's chair to his grandson Tom Clendon);
- a writing box and cast iron figure (belonged to Tom's grandson Arthur Clendon;
- an oil painting (belonged to grandson Jack Clendon).

Tom and Eliza started off by living in Newtown – then called Wadestown – on the outskirts of Wellington.

Tom wrote to his brother Ben in the USA to tell him about his news and whereabouts, but did not make contact with his cousin James Stephenson Clendon, in New Zealand. So it was Ben who wrote to cousin James in a letter as follows:

Buckner's Station
Louisa County. Va
Oct. 8th 1888

My dear Cousin,
A letter came to hand only day before yesterday & I assure you we were all pleased to hear from you again . . . My brother Tom, his wife & 3 sons have settled in Wellington. His second son, Arthur is in Cambridge University. They have no daughter. Tom had an idea of "going into sheep" with his boys I think, but he found the prospect so gloomy that he decided to wait for a time, so two of his sons, Henry & Sydney [sic] are travelling for Mercantile firms. Vivian, the younger goes to school. My brother had not found an opening when he last wrote & he says farming lands have depreciated in value to the extent of one half in the last 10 years . . . My brother's address-
Thos CLENDON
Valley Lodge
Wadestown
WELLINGTON.

I hope you will meet with Tom soon, his sight is much impaired from cataract
partially blind, in fact which I expect has something to do with his not having
seen you.

I am similarly afflicted but not much so, as yet . . . Wife & girls unite in
kind love to you & yours.

Affy yours   B. CLENDON

This letter reveals that things were not going too well for Tom in New
Zealand. He was going blind, and future prospects looked gloomy. Eliza was
also feeling the pinch. In a letter written on 25th January 1889 to Elsie
Hickinbotham it is clear that she had to manage on much less money than
before. She had no servants, and disliked doing her own house work – but
as she says in the letter: "in our altered circumstances I am obliged to do it".
The economic situation was bad – business was at a standstill – and there
was little work to be found. All young men had to rough it and were poor.

Compared with the society she was accustomed to in England she
thought home life was greatly inferior. She observed that children were a
good deal neglected. They ran wild, spoke badly, and had bad manners.
This was due to their mothers being too busy to attend to their children
properly, and not employing nurses or Governesses.

Harry, her oldest son then in his twenties, was not in the best of health
and not doing well financially. Sidney, at age 18, was away from home
"without any fixed address", either working or looking for suitable land for
his father to buy and develop into a farm.

Sidney's memories of his parents (as told to me by his daughter Nancy
Walker) are that they were a devoted couple. He had a pet name for her,
"Bobby" which he called her. He described Eliza as a very prim lady, class
conscious, fond of wearing hats and gloves. Another of her granddaughters
(Hazel Clendon) told me that Eliza used to say "You can tell a lady by her
gloves and her handkerchief".

In Wadestown she made for herself a "charming home, furnished very
prettily," she had friends whom she considered to be very nice, and was beginning to enjoy the social life. She took afternoon teas with other ladies and
enjoyed a day at a Regatta in Wellington harbour. She also enjoyed going to
church, it reminded her of home, and she "liked the Clergyman immensely".

Eliza, however, did not continue to enjoy the social life that she had
found in Wadestown for very long. A year or so later, around 1890, Tom
finally took the plunge and bought land at a remote place in the hills called
Akatarawa. He had been considering an even more remote area, Manawata,
100 miles further away, near Palmerston North. But it was not so handy for
Wellington, so he chose Akatarawa, only a day's journey away. This proved
to be a disastrous mistake, because Manawata was good land, which would

have turned out to be a prosperous farm.

Akatarawa is up the Hutt Valley, on the edge of the Taura Mountain Range, about 40 miles north of Wellington. At first sight the land must have been beautiful. 100 years later, in 1992, Sue and I were taken there by Nancy Walker. It has now been turned over to the public as a Park. You approach it up a long narrow winding lane that goes up and up a narrow valley arising out of the Hutt valley. Even today it is remote and inaccessible. The land is scenic, hilly, with a river running through it. Part of it remains cleared but much has now been overgrown again by the bush, including the site of the house which Tom and Eliza built. The foundations, which until recently were exposed, are now impossible to find.

Originally the site was entirely covered with the dense bush that pervaded New Zealand at that time. It still covers the hilly uncultivated areas. The bush consists of a dense thicketted forest, and is virtually impenetrable. The first thing the early settlers had to do on acquiring land, whether to develop a township or to create a farm, was to embark on bushfalling. A well known NZ architect/designer told me about this when we were staying at his house for Bed & Breakfast. We were discussing the system of laying out towns and streets in "sections" – and the dull uniformity of the housing in and around the Lower Hutt. He said of the early settlers: "They didn't start thinking until they'd cut the trees down".

So it was a gamble for Tom in his mid-50's, and with deteriorating health, to put the last remnants of his capital into a venture that would involve him and his family in hard manual work, before he could reap any reward.

His favourite brother Ben in the USA was clearly worried about the way things were turning out. Ben's letter [written in late 1889 or early 1890] to his cousin James Stephenson Clendon, indicates his anxiety:

Buckner's Station
Louisa County. Va.

My dear cousin
    Your letter of Sept 5th is before me . . . I heartily wish that my brother Tom & family were *nearer you & I think with you it would have been better for him to have settled in the Northern part of the Island . . .
    I am grieved to hear that his health has not been good in your colony & that his eyesight is in such a bad state . . .
    Believe me,
    Yr affectionate cousin,
    B. CLENDON

---

* James Stephenson Clendon was the Resident Magistrate at Whangarei, which is 500 miles north of Wellington.

The venture started off quite well. Tom and the three boys set about clearing the land. Although it was long and hard work, Tom was able to sell the timber. They built a house on the hillside overlooking the farm and the river. They built a bridge over the river and began to clear and develop the land on the other side. About 100 yards to the right of the house the river curved round under the hills and formed a pool which the boys used for swimming.

A long verandah extended along the front of the house, overlooking the farm. Eliza stood on the verandah and rang a handbell, (which her grandson Jack Clendon had in his house when we visited him in 1992), to summon the family when the meal was ready. She made her own bread with yeast made from potato peelings. She was famous for her pigeon pie. The pigeons were easy to catch as they were heavy and did not fly well. Vivian could shoot them without much trouble. Pigeon was also a favourite food of the Maoris who would beat them down with a stick and cook them wrapped in clay in an earthen oven heated by hot stones. When the clay came off – so did the feathers!

It would be wrong though to paint a picture of idyllic and healthy country living – that was far from the truth. Eliza was very unhappy there. Accustomed to a more comfortable way of life with domestic servants, she was faced at 52 years of age with coping on her own. She worked hard cooking, cleaning, and doing the washing. She was lonely, often ill, and cried a lot. And after all that effort to clear the bush, (Nancy Walker told me that "grandfather and the boys spent ages bushfalling"), they realised that the land was no good.

The farm never prospered. Indeed, if Tom's idea was that he would create a large successful farm capable of supporting his boys as young men, and enabling him to live there in retirement with Eliza in passable comfort – the venture was an outright failure. The farm appears merely to have provided the food necessary for a hand to mouth existence. Meat was shared with the neighbouring farms. One farmer killed a sheep one week and it was divided up between about five families, and they took it in turns. They had a garden, grew vegetables, currants, and had an orchard. They kept chickens which roamed free in the orchard. Vivian collected the eggs and took them down to the saw mill to sell. On the other side of the river they kept pigs, and before they built the foot bridge they reached them by stepping stones which the pigs could not walk over so that they would not eat the garden produce. They also had ducks, geese, cows, horses and sheep – and they kept bees.

Vivian could not go to school as there were none available. He worked on the farm and his mother encouraged him to keep diaries*, some of which have survived. Sidney often went off to work elsewhere to bring money into the family. When he did, he gave it all to his father. When Vivian was older he joined Sidney during the winter on survey work parties. They lived in camps, in remote areas, and surveyed the uncharted land.

One by one the boys left. The first to go was Harry on August 8th 1892. He was then about 26. Harry's departure was recorded in Vivian's diary. The following extracts show what it felt like to be a boy of 13 up there in the hills, the kind of life his parents endured, and what happened when his brother Harry was taken away.

*1892

July 27th   Wednesday. Very showery and snowing hard in the morning. In the afternoon I went to Morgans and got the English letters and newspapers

July 28th   Thursday. Rather showery" but finer than yesterday Harry and I were packing from the mill.

July 29th   Friday. Showery Harry and I brought potatoes from the Flour mill. Mother very poorly

July 30th   Saturday. Fine day Killed a pig in the morning. In the afternoon we felled dry trees of the flat and saw the first lamb of the season. Mother better. Eggs for the week 48 . . .

Aug 3rd   Wednesday. Fine day Father left for Wellington. Being unable to get to the bush we have been falling on the flat.

Aug 4th   Thursday. Fine day W. Wackrow called in. We have been digging in the garden. It seems very lonely without father . . .

Aug 6th   Saturday. Fine day Mother went to Wackrows in the morning. Harry and I were working round the house all day. Father came home about ten o'clock at night Eggs for the week 35

Aug 7th   Sunday. Very wet day Mother's birthday had a very quiet day

---

*   The originals are in the Turnbull Library, Wellington, NZ. They cover 1892, 1893 and 1896/7. In 1992 when I was in New Zealand, Vivian's son Arthur gave me a photocopy of them obtained by his daughter, Jane Clendon, (who worked at the Turnbull), and asked me to bring them to England for Susan Miller. Susan has kindly lent them to me. They consist of about 200 pages of A4, each page covering several days' entries (see illustration).

Aug 8th   Monday. Showery Sad day Harry very poorly he and and [sic]
            Father gone to Wellington to see the doctor

Aug 9th   Tuesday. Fine day Mother has a bad headache. Henry Salmons
            came to ask Mother to go down and see their baby as it was not
            very well, but she was too ill to go.

Aug 10th   Wednesday. Fine day Mother better. Still lonely Went down to
            Wackrows to get the milk. Dug a little in the garden.

Aug 11th   Thursday. Fine day To our surprise Father returned late last night,
            but had to return to Petone this afternoon, we accompanied him as
            far as Salmon's and stayed to tea. In the morning we planted
            blackberries.

The surprise expressed by Vivian on August 11th was probably because Tom had returned without Harry. There was bad news. Harry had a serious mental illness.

Meanwhile on August 12th, Eliza, alone in the house on a frosty morning, remembered the 24th birthday of her son Arthur – my grandfather – far away in England. That night Tom came back late, again without Harry. Next day Vivian and Sidney were sent to look after the sheep, while the parents stayed at home to share their anxiety about Harry's future.

Aug 12th   *Friday Fine day and hard frost this morning the Thermometre [sic] being 31 in our bedroom We have been clearing and pruning bushes. One of our hens died this morning. Arthur's birthday.*

Aug 13th   *Saturday Fine day Father and Sydney [sic] came home late last night without Harry. Sydney and I went to look after the sheep which we found all right. Eggs for the week 37 . . .*

Aug 17th   *Wednesday Very showery Fritz and Will Wackrow called in this morning. Sydney went to Wellington to see Harry . . .*

Oct 6th   *Thursday Fine day Sydney went to see Harry in Wellington early this morning. Mother and I took a pig to Wackrows and she waited while I went on to Salmon's to get the butter.*

Oct 7th   *Friday Showery this morning. I went to meet Syd at the Hutt and brought good news from Harry. Wackrows bought another half a pig . . .*

Despite the "good news" on October 7th, Harry was not mentioned again in the diaries. He never returned. He was to remain in hospital for the rest of his life.

Sidney was the next to leave, later in the 1890's. He went to Auckland, boarded with a Mrs McCarroll, a music teacher, and married her daughter on 12th July 1900.

Vivian remained for a few years longer. He left in the early 1900's when in his twenties to join Sidney in business in the Lower Hutt. And by the time he was married in 1906 he was established as a merchant there.

Tom and Eliza remained alone at Akatarawa, an ageing couple, enduring a life of increasing difficulty, and ill health. On 17th February 1907 when Arthur wrote from Birmingham to his brother Vivian he said: " . . . We were very sorry that Mother has been so ill and shall be relieved when they can sell the farm and come and live near you . . . "

By 1910 they had sold the land to a man called Clouston. They came down to live in Upper Hutt, at No 15 Eberton Road. I saw the house, a conventional "Hutt" single story building, on our way up to Akatarawa in 1992.

Also at about this time Tom & Eliza inherited some money. In 1906 Eliza's older brother George died in Ramsgate. He left her £1,000. Arthur represented her at the funeral and wrote a letter describing it to her. He ended with the words:

> *Uncle seems to have had a very peaceful & happy end. He was quite content. It upset me when I went into the old room & saw everything as it used to be. They say he mentioned my name two or three times the day before he died but could not say any thing more.*
>
> *Goodbye my dear Mother & Father – it was all very sad & I shall miss his kind face always very much*
>
> *ever your loving son Arthur.*

Reading his letter and the description of the funeral it is clear that Tom & Eliza were kept well informed of the goings-on in the Vye family at Ramsgate by their son Arthur, and others – and that the death of Eliza's especially favourite brother was another sad occasion for her.

The second inheritance was in 1910 – £500 from the estate of Tom's older brother John who had returned to Ramsgate after farming in Glens Falls. Arthur had been to see him at the time of Uncle George's funeral four years earlier, and had reported as follows:

> *I went on Sunday to see Uncle John Clendon & I make no doubt I shall come off pretty well there some day. He was most friendly & thought I should have had more . . .*

As it happened John Clendon left £8,338-4-10 altogether, and I do not know how much his nephew Arthur inherited. But the £500 which went to John's brother Tom in New Zealand is said to have paid for Tom and Eliza's house in Upper Hutt.

Tom and Eliza did not stay long in Upper Hutt. Their sons Sidney and Vivian were settled in Lower Hutt by then, so they came down to Lower Hutt. Within a few years Eliza had developed cancer, and fear of the disease was such that her grandson Jack, born February 21st 1913, was not allowed near her. He was held up as a baby outside the window of her house for her to see him. She died on March 16th 1915, aged 75.

Tom stayed on in the same house close to his two sons. By this time he was completely blind, used a white stick, and was looked after by a housekeeper. He would visit his sons on alternate evenings. Nancy Walker (Tom's granddaughter then age 9) remembered these visits, and in 1992 described them to me in the following words:

> *Father would read the paper to him in front of the fire – make a cup of tea – and then Grandpa would go home at 9 pm. I shall never forget the tap, tap, tap, of his white stick as he walked back home – it wasn't far to go.*

Tom died on June 17th 1921. He was 85.

He was buried, with Eliza, at the Taita Cemetery, Lower Hutt.

Their gravestone is inscribed:

> *Heaven's Morning breaks*
> *and earth's vain shadows flee*

Tom and Eliza ended their days a long way from their birthplace in Kent, in Ramsgate, as did Tom's parents and two of his brothers who died in USA. But they were near two of their married sons who, with their children after them, created a closely knit family enclave that still existed in and around Lower Hutt when we were there in 1992.

One son, however, was on the other side of the world. He was Arthur, then age 52, who had not seen his father, mother, or brothers since he was 18.

The next chapter reveals the significance of this separation. It describes the lives of Harry, Arthur, Sidney and Vivian. It highlights the effect – on them and on their families – of their parents' decision to emigrate to New Zealand in 1887, and of Arthur's to stay behind in England.

To set the scene, here is the formal genealogical record.

THOMAS (1836-1921) and ELIZA KELSEY (1839-1915) CLENDON had issue five children:

(i)	**EDITH CLENDON**	b	186?	Glens Falls, New York State, USA
	died in infancy	d	186?	Glens Falls
(ii)	**HENRY CLENDON**	b	1863 or 1864	Glens Falls
	(known as Harry)	d	1935 Sep 18	Wellington, New Zealand
	died without issue			
(iii)	**ARTHUR CLENDON**	b	1868 Aug 12	Glens Falls
	MA (Cantab) & MA (London)	d	1939 Sep 14	Colchester, Essex, England
	m. ELLEN ELIZABETH HICKINBOTHAM			
	(known as Elsie)	m	1896 Jan 14	Birmingham, England
		b	1870 May 19	Birmingham
		d 1936	July 24	interred in Colchester

(iv) **SIDNEY CLENDON**   b 1870 May 24   Ramsgate, Kent, England
                                  d 1957 Jun 7   Auckland, New Zealand

    m. (1st)   m 1900 Jul 12   Auckland
    ESTHER FLORENCE McCARROLL
    (mother of Kelsey & Nell)   b 1871 Oct 26   Auckland
                                  d 1906 Feb 27   Lower Hutt, New Zealand

    m. (2nd)   m 1907 Oct 9   Wellington
    ANNA LOUISA ORR   b 1872 Mar 7   Wellington
    (mother of Nancy & Jack)   i 1933 Jun 15   Lower Hutt

    m. (3rd)   m 1938 July 12   Wellington
    MARY TWEEDIE   b 1878 Aug 12   ?England, migrated to NZ in 1906
                                  d 1972 Oct 22   Auckland
    twice widowed, (1st) WORTHINGTON née CARTER, (known as Luki)

(v)   **VIVIAN CLENDON**   b 1878 Dec 1   Harborne, Birmingham
    (known as Vye or Vi)   d 1963 Sep 28   Lower Hutt

    m. ROSE CAROLINE COOPER
                                  m 1906 Aug 7   Havelock North, NZ
                                  b 1883 Dec 21   Havelock North
                                  d 1977 May 16   Lower Hutt

CHAPTER 7

A FAMILY DIVIDED

1860's to 1970's

THOMAS & ELIZA CLENDON's FAMILY

HARRY

Some of the early life of Tom and Eliza's children can be gleaned from the previous chapter. Apart from Edith who was born in Glens Falls and died in infancy, Harry was the oldest child. He was born in Glens Falls in either 1863 or 1864, and lived for the first five or six years of his life there, with his parents in his grandparent's house. The remainder of his childhood was spent in the beautiful farmhouse in Wales. By the age of fifteen he was in Birmingham, where he lived until he left with his parents for New Zealand. He would then have been a young man of 22.

Not much more is known about his early life. It is said that he had "a good time in London" before he left England. It is possible that he and his brother Sidney, then 17, were sent on ahead to New Zealand, in order to seek out a suitable farm. This was proposed as an idea in a letter written beforehand, and was mentioned to me in New Zealand. A search of ships' registers could prove the point one way or the other, but I do not think he did. I think it is more likely that he and Sidney went off in search of suitable land after the family had arrived in New Zealand and were living at Wadestown. If true, he must have been considered mentally fit and responsible at the time, although by January 1889 evidence of some ill health was emerging. His mother said of him in a letter then " . . . Harry is home now he has improved in health although not in finances since being here . . . "

The next references to him are found in Vivian's diaries. It is clear that he stayed at home on the farm, where he was given relatively straightforward tasks. Unlike Sidney who was travelling alone and taking responsibility for contracts in his teens, Harry, in his mid twenties, was doing the same kind of work as Vivian age 13.

On August 8th 1892, when about 26, Harry became so ill that he had to be taken to Wellington to see a doctor. He was certified as insane and admitted to hospital in Wellington. The circumstances of his departure from Akatarawa are described by Vivian in the previous chapter.

There are no stories of him passed down through the family. He was just not talked about. I knew about him vaguely from my father. His brothers Sidney and Vivian said nothing about him to their children. One of Vivian's sons, Arthur (b. 1908), told me in 1992 that he was stunned when his father told him one day that he had an Uncle Harry in the Porirua mental hospital who had just died. Arthur went to the funeral. He remembered Sidney and Vivian being there but no-one else. However, the family have recently recalled that Sidney and Vivian were in the habit of dressing up and going off together occasionally on Saturdays, and nobody had said where they were going. They could have been going to visit Harry in Porirua hospital. Harry died there on September 15th 1935, aged 71, and was buried in the Taita Cemetery.

He had spent 43 years, isolated from the family. Hospital records, discovered by Graham Clendon in 1997, reveal that throughout these years Harry was mentally very confused. However, he worked on the hospital farm and remained in good physical health until shortly before he died.

ARTHUR, SIDNEY & VIVIAN

The rest of this chapter is devoted to the other three sons – Arthur, Sidney and Vivian. Arthur and Sidney were only eighteen months apart in age – but Vivian was much younger – ten years younger than Arthur – and his early life, and education was very different.

Arthur and Sidney spent eight years of their childhood living on the farm in the beautiful valley of Cwm Rhaiadr in North Wales, described in the previous chapter. It must have been a delightful place for them to spend their childhood, while their parents were happily spending the fortune acquired in America. There would have been servants to do all the household chores, with a Nanny and later a Governess to see to the children's needs. This experience had a lasting effect on Arthur who retained a love of North Wales for the rest of his life. His fondness for that part of Wales influenced, I am sure, his choice to work there in later life. It was, in turn, passed on to his son Douglas, (my father), who was born there, and who took us there for holidays.

When the family moved to Birmingham, Arthur and Sidney went to King Edwards School. Both boys were intelligent, tall, well built, and physically strong. Arthur held the record for the half-mile, which stood for thirty years. I have the cup awarded to him in 1887.

As mentioned earlier Arthur and Sidney became very friendly with the

From left to right: Harry, Arthur and Sidney.

children of Dr James Hickinbotham. There were six. The oldest, the only
girl, was called Elsie. The rest were boys. The oldest boy was called Ryland,
who was, according to Nancy Walker, (Sidney's daughter), Sidney's best
friend at the time. The boys from the two families formed the
"Hickinbotham-Clendon" gang. Other boys may have been in it, but these
two families formed the nucleus. The gang had a special whistle by which
they identified themselves – they whistled the notes G-E-GG-E. This is now
known as "The Family Whistle". It has been used in subsequent generations
of both families. It is still used in several branches for calling children,

attracting the attention of husband or wife, or finding members of the family in a crowd.

Then, in 1887, the Clendon family parted. As described in the last chapter their father, Tom had decided to emigrate to New Zealand. However, Arthur who had done well at the school, and was clearly a scholar of some potential, wanted to go on to Cambridge University where he had obtained a place to read Classics at Emmanuel College.

Arthur did not have an easy choice because his father was by then unable to support him. My father told me that Arthur managed to borrow enough money from an uncle to enable him to take up his place at Emmanuel – and that Arthur then accounted for his expenses to this uncle regularly, and repaid the full amount in later life.

I strongly suspect it was Uncle George Vye, his mother Eliza's favourite brother, who came to the rescue. My evidence for this is in Arthur's letter to his mother in 1906, about Uncle George's funeral and the reading of the Will. He reported that two other members of the family owed Uncle George quite large sums of money, and then went on to say " . . . Of course I do not owe anything to the estate as I have told you before . . . ". My assumption is that this sentence refers to the money which Arthur had borrowed to go to Cambridge, and which he had by then paid back.

When these decisions were being made Arthur must have had mixed feelings. He had to say good-bye to his brothers and parents, not knowing when he would see them again. On the other hand the chance to go to Cambridge was an opportunity of a lifetime, that he could hardly refuse.

Vivian was only nine years old, too young to understand the significance of what was happening – but for Sidney it was different. He was close to Arthur in age, they had grown up together, and had mutual friendships in Birmingham. Sidney had a strong personality, was well educated and probably had equally good prospects. He was just a bit too young to be left behind. He had little choice. He set sail with his parents – to experience a way of living quite different from Arthur's – and on the other side of the world.

In autumn 1887 Arthur said good-bye to his parents and brothers. He went up to Cambridge and joined in the life of the College. He lived in superb architectural surroundings; the Wren chapel and cloisters, the dining hall, courtyards and the beautiful gardens at Emmanuel. A College servant would make his bed and clean his rooms. His life was civilised and gentlemanly, and he was getting good exam results. He was made an Exhibitioner, which signifies the award of a minor scholarship to help pay the fees. He ran for the College athletic team and rowed for the College as well. He won an oar in the 2nd VIII, which I have, and rowed for the 1st VIII in the May Races of 1889. He supplemented his income by coaching wealthier undergraduates who had difficulty with Latin.

The award of Arthur's exhibition was published in a list of honours gained by old boys of King Edwards School which Susan Miller has in her archives. I discovered that, by coincidence, the name of his friend Ryland Hickinbotham was also listed. Ryland was studying medicine at Birmingham University, and had been awarded the prize medal for Anatomy.

The Hickinbotham's house at 199 Monument Road, Birmingham, was Arthur's home address during the vacations, according to the College records. Arthur wrote to his parents regularly from England, and sent them a copy of Punch magazine each week. His mother, Eliza, also wrote regularly to him from New Zealand. But the only letter of hers that has survived was to Elsie Hickinbotham. The following extracts reveal the closeness of the two families, some news about Sidney and Vivian, and the deep attachment which had developed between Arthur and Elsie, then aged 18.

Wadestown
Wellington
January 25th '89

My dear Elsie
We were very pleased to hear from you & learn of all the doings of your family . . .

My love to your Mother & I thank her for her kind note I will write to her next time I thank her very much for her kindness to our dear Arthur, I hope he does not trouble her much, We could fancy you young folks are happy enough together. It is a great relief to us that Arthur will now be quite sure to finish his course of study at Cambridge. I am afraid you will get almost tired of waiting for him but he is such a dear old fellow that I feel there are not many Arthur's like him. I expect dear we both look at him through our great love for him & so we are not quite impartial judges of his talents but I think he will be sure to all. I really think Vie [Vivian then age 11] is quite as happy as in England as his great friend is living quite close to us, we have a charming home dear I wonder if you will ever see it as it is furnished prettily you would think we were as well off as ever. The plaque you painted hangs on the wall of the dining room . . .

I am sure you are busy if you are still teaching in the morning I hope it does not trouble you much, I was glad to hear you were feeling stronger & that your Mother too was better. I was so vexed dear Elsie that stupid Sidney should have written anything to annoy you he has been from home without any fixed address but I know he will write & apologise when he hears of it as he was always fond of you but had such a silly way of giving advice . . .

I could not resist reading dear Ryland's letter to Sidney before sending it off, it was just like having five minutes with him. I should indeed love to see him out

here for a trip before he settled down but he would do far better in England. No
one will have a Doctor without they are quite obliged . . .

I am glad Ryland does not even mind the unpleasant part of his study as
the professional part of his duties will be nothing after he has passed all examn.

With kind love to you dear & love to all the others in which Mr C joins
Believe me
Yours very affc.ly
E K Clendon

It turned out that Elsie Hickinbotham had to wait seven years before she
could marry "our dear Arthur" – a long time.

The Hickinbotham household had their problems as well. Elsie's father,
Dr James Hickinbotham had died five years earlier. He was an obstetrician
of growing distinction, and his career was cut short at the early age of 44
after a brief illness.

In addition to having to cope with six children as a widow, Elsie's
mother suffered from a painful chronic illness, I think osteomyelitis, for
which she was prescribed morphine to relieve the pain. She became
addicted to the drug, and her son Ryland took time off, perhaps as much as
a year, from his medical studies. He nursed her and helped her to overcome
the addiction.

At this point it is appropriate to digress for a moment to discuss the origin
of the christian name "Ryland". I discovered recently that a Miss Louisa Ann
Ryland made a great many gifts of land and buildings to the City of
Birmingham at around the time that Ryland Hickinbotham was born. One
of these was the Women's Hospital in Showell Green Lane where Ryland's
father, Dr Hickinbotham held a post as Physician. It seems that he named
his son "Ryland" after Miss Ryland. My father and I were named after him.
Also, like him, I am known as "Ryland" even though it is our second
christian name.

Meanwhile, in Wadestown the Clendons met a family from Ireland called
Orr. There were three sisters and two brothers, and they became very
friendly with the Clendon boys. One of the boys was Jack Orr, perhaps the
friend of Vivian's mentioned in the letter above.

When the family moved to Akatarawa the Clendons and the Orrs kept
in touch, and visited each other on several occasions. The first to be
mentioned in Vivian's diary was a visit by Jack Orr for Christmas. Jack
stayed from 23rd December 1893 to January 9th 1894, then Vivian returned
with him to stay at the Orr's house for ten days. Vivian describes these
events as follows:

1893

Dec 23rd   Saturday. Fine day Met Jack Orr at the station. Father has been working at the verandah all day and Syd falling. Weeks eggs 60 hens 29 ducks

Dec 24th   Sunday. Heavy showers Jack and I rode Bully and Rubie down to Salmons for some potatoes and had a swim in the river. Will W. and Hobbs called in this morning.

Dec 25th   Monday. Slight shower Christmas day. We had a goose and plum pudding for dinner. We saw no one all day.

Dec 26th   Tuesday. Fine day Syd started for Wellington this morning to spend a few days with a friend. Jack and I helped Father for a few hours and then went down and milked Wackrows cows for them as they are away.

Dec 27   Wednesday. Fine day We went down to Wackrows to milk but found that Will had returned and had milked them. We churned the butter and helped Father.

Dec 28th   Thursday. Very showery Mother had the toothache nearly all last night and she has felt very poorly all day. Jack and I helped Father, and we finished the dairy . . .

Jan 1st   Monday. Raining hard New Years day.
[1894]   Quiet day. I put in a window pane.

Jan 2nd   Tuesday. Showery The bees swarmed today and we have them all safely in the hive. This afternoon Jack and I took Bully and the sledge to the mill and fetched back a bag of pollard. Syd returned from Wellington this evening . . .

Jan 5th   Friday. Fine day Syd Jack and I mustered up all the sheep and Syd killed one . . .

Jan 7th   Sunday. Fine day Jack and I rode to the mill and fetched back some flour and wire . . .

Jan 9th   Tuesday. Fine day . . . I am going to return with Jack to Wellington in the morning to stay with him for a week.

Jan 20th   *Saturday. Fine day I returned home on Salmons cart with Mrs*
                Gunning and her two children after a very pleasant holiday. I
                bought a new suit of clothes in town . . .

Later that year, Eliza went to stay with Mrs Orr in Wellington, she was there
from April 3rd when Vivian wrote:

We borrowed a horse from the Wackrows and I took Mother down to the
Hutt station – she has gone to Wellington to spend a week there with some
friends . . .

Eliza returned home with Mrs Orr on April 14th – but beforehand there was
a good clear up!

This afternoon we all set to and cleaned the house up as we expected Mother back.
Mother arrived with Mrs Orr . . .

Mrs Orr stayed at Akatarawa until 21st April.

Two years later, there is a more significant entry about the Orrs in
Vivian's diary; two of the "Miss Orr's" came to stay for a fortnight. One of
them was called Anna, and Sidney wanted to marry her. The following
extracts are relevant.

1896

It is now the 12th Jan. I received this diary yesterday it is a present from Cyril
Morris I will write down all I can remember. Syd is now in Wellington we expect
him back tomorrow with two of the Miss Orr's who are going to stay a
fortnight . . . I borrowed two horses & met Syd with the girls at the Hutt & we
all got home about 6pm all feeling pretty tired . . .

We finished stacking the hay Mother & the girls went for a walk up to
Morgans this morning . . .

Very quiet day, we picked some fruit in the garden this afternoon . . .

Father played the guitar & sang we all had a pleasant evening . . .

Vivian did not often record that his father was enjoying life. Tom was
obviously very happy in the company of the Orr girls. He wrote a long
poem about one of them entitled "The Venus of Maoriland – by The
Akatarawa Settler".

In the poem he refers to her as 23 years old, which Anna was in
January 1896, so I have assumed that the poem was written then and
addressed to Anna.

THE VENUS OF MAORILAND

In far New Zealand's distant land,
The poet has taken a task in hand
To describe the Venus of Maoriland.
A settler poet among the hills
Who is troubled at times with a farmer's ills
Would say, if a cat may look at a King
It would not be presumptive for him to sing
And fearless, to strike the sounding *string . . .

If thou wer't the Goddess of Love, in short,
The love must have been of a very pure sort.
A fine tall girl of five feet nine
Radiant with health and beauty fine
Is the settlers Venus of Maoriland,
Whose charms the poet will seek to expand . . .

In the early morning taking a pail
She went out to milk in the old cow bail;
Her skirt to her waist she would gravely pin
Till the edge fell past the knee within.
These proceedings gave an infinite joy
To a rusty old shepherd and a hobadehoy.
At the strong firm touch, though soft as silk
The yielding udder gave down its milk . . .

When washing day at length came round
The girl at the tub was always found.
Now all the Poet knows about washing
Is a sort of indistinct rubbing and squashing
So we will picture the girl going out through the door
With a large heavy basket of clothes before.
With careless swing and easy grip
The basket would lodge on the rounded hip.
The beautiful figure admired by the boys
With head thrown up in graceful poise . . .

---

* The "sounding string" refers, presumably, to the strings on his guitar.

Her dress streamed out from her ankles fair
And a vagrant tress of her rich dark hair
Had escaped from the coils which had held it there . . .

Time wore on so she said she must go
And we all of us felt uncommonly low,
The hills looked down in mute dismay
When their beautiful mistress rode away.
Next morn the hills were in misty grief
But the sun rose up to their relief
He kissed their brows and drying their tears
Said "Try and be cheerful now my dears
For this girl if beautiful at all
Is only mortal after all" . . .

Akatarawa's hills still mourn with me
Their beautiful mistress of twenty-three . . .

The Akatarawa Settler

When Sidney proposed to Anna she refused him. Although born in New Zealand, she was of Irish descent and she wanted to return to Ireland before settling down. Sidney mourned with his father as in the poem, "Akatarawa's hills still mourn with me their beautiful mistress of twenty-three", when Anna departed for Ireland.

Sidney was based in Akatarawa for some years further, sometimes leaving for work opportunities for several months – and then returning. It was when he was in his late twenties that he finally left for a job in Auckland, and found another girl. She was his landlady's daughter – Esther McCarroll.

They married on July 12th 1900. He was 30 and she was 28.

Meanwhile back in England his older brother Arthur had graduated from Cambridge. Arthur later wrote of his success there as follows:

I proceeded to Emmanuel College, Cambridge where I obtained an open Exhibition. In 1890 I was placed in the 1st division of the 2nd class of the Classical Tripos.

He left with a reference from Mr J Adam, who was a Fellow of Emmanuel College, and Examiner for the Classical Tripos 1889-1890. It included the following:

I consider him to be one of the most satisfactory pupils whom it has been my good fortune to teach. He has steadily improved in scholarship and learning, in intelligence and breadth of view; and all his work shows him to be manly and robust.

He has a real interest not only in classical antiquity but in modern thought and life, and a keen feeling for the points at which ancient civilization touches our own . . .

In September 1890 he became a Master at Craigmore College, Bristol, and stayed for four terms. I have a leather bound copy of the school magazine, called the "Craigmore Echo", with the initials A.C. embossed on the front cover. It reveals some of his exploits there, including playing football for the school 1st XI of 1890-1 as the only Master in the team; after a poor start he improved as the year went on!

The following are extracts from the Craigmore Echo:

THE DAY ON THE RIVER

Excursions up the river have become quite an institution at Craigmore, and form a pleasant break in the monotony of school life . . . Mr Bruton, who has lost none of his old capacity for work, made his debut in a new role, that of photographer in chief. He pranced about the bank with all the paraphernalia of black shrouds and three legged stands. Mr Clendon made a superhuman effort to look pleasant for once in his life . . . but although Mr Clendon's smile was wasted on the desert air, the style of the late "3" of the Emmanuel "First Boat" was seen and admired by all. He was the cynosure of all eyes – at least, when he managed, by crafty strategy to get in front of the other boats . . .

FOOTBALL

Mr Clendon as a novus homo did pretty well, but failed to keep the ball close enough, and thus lost many chances . . .

Mr Clendon nearly scored for us, the leather shooting a foot outside the post . . .

Mention must be made of a rattling good shot by Mr Clendon which hit our opponents cross-bar, rebounding into play, but which, after a struggle in front of their goal, we failed to put through . . .

Mr Clendon played better at centre than we have ever seen him, before . . .

JOTTINGS BY THE UBIQUITUS

Mr Clendon has been indefatigable in helping at the Sports Practice . . .

As a result of Mr Clendon's elementary lessons in Roman History, the

College porter has won the cognomen of the "Vestal virgin", because he keeps the stove fire going . . .

Mr Roberts' Lecture on Spectrum Analysis, which some will remember had already been announced, came off on March 9th. Two limelight lanterns were used to project the spectra and pictures on the screen . . . The various kinds of spectra were explained and illustrated . . . On this and other occasions, to the great delight of the ladies, Mr Clendon's manly form has appeared on the screen . . .

At Christmas 1891 he left Craigmore College to take up an appointment as a Master at Allhallows' School at Honiton in Devon. Within three years, at age 26, he was applying for headships. He furnished an impressive array of printed testimonials.

He was unsuccessful in his application for the post of Headmaster at Welshpool County School on January 15th 1895, but in December of that year he was chosen from sixty applicants to be the Headmaster of Dolgelley* County School in Merionethshire, North Wales. He was then 27.

At last he could get married! His salary as Headmaster was £150 a year with a capitation fee of £1 per pupil – and he had a house. He didn't waste any time. The wedding was on January 14th 1896 at St John's Church, Ladywood, Birmingham. The church is not far down Monument Road from the Hickinbotham's house at No. 199 where his bride, Elsie, was still living. When I went there recently the church was rather run down. An inner city Victorian building, it stands now on the edge of an inner ring road roundabout. Much of Monument Road has been obliterated by this inner ring road. I suppose that when Arthur and Elsie were married there it was a fairly new and busy church in a pleasant prosperous district of Birmingham.

While Elsie was waiting to get married she had been teaching. She was also involved in the formation of the Birmingham Girls Old Edwardian Club for Working Girls. She was President at the time of the First Annual Report for the year ending 1892 – and was listed also as one of the workers.

According to the records Arthur took up his duties at the school in January, so there was hardly any time for a honeymoon. They moved into Bryn Marian, the school owned house where they lived for the next nine and a half years. They had up to six boarding pupils at a time there.

When Sue and I visited Dolgellau in May 1996 the house, a detached

---

*   "Dolgelley" is the English way of spelling of the town's name, in use at the time when Arthur was there, and when I visited it as a child. Dogelley was then the County Town of Merionethshire – a county which no longer exists – hence the name "County School". Nowadays the Welsh way of spelling the town, "Dolgellau", is used, and I have used this spelling in the genealogical tables.

Victorian stone faced building, had been divided into two. We saw the house from the outside only, but when we went to the school we were shown around by the caretaker. Enlarged out of all recognition, but with the building which had been opened in Arthur's day still there and in use, the school is now the comprehensive secondary school for the area. In the main corridor were portraits of previous head teachers – but Arthur's was not there. The earliest was of his successor.

For Arthur the headmastership of Dolgelley County School was no sinecure. He was faced, on appointment, with serious and difficult problems. His tenure from 1896 to 1905, turned out to be extremely critical in the development of the school.

This period is referred to as the "difficult years" in a dissertation entitled "The Development of Secondary Education in Dollgellau 1889-1946", by Gwyn Jones BA. A copy of this dissertation can be found in the Archives Department at Dolgellau.

The principal cause of his problem was the stiff competition from the Grammar School for most of this period, made more acute by the difficulty of obtaining qualified staff when other larger schools could offer higher salaries. There were only 36 boys in the school when he arrived, which had risen to 44 by 1905 when he left. Despite these small numbers he achieved high academic standards. After 1901 an increasing number of pupils remained at the school after taking the matriculation exam, a broad based qualification required for entry to University. They attempted more advanced work and to qualify for various university entrance scholarships. Five of these scholarships were awarded to pupils from the school between 1899 and 1903 – and a further two by 1905.

By the time Arthur left in 1905, the school was securely established in a new building, free from debt, and a major reorganisation of the curriculum had been completed. He had won the battle with the rival Grammar School. It was closed in 1903. Arthur had secured a united secondary education, under one roof, for boys in Dolgelley and the surrounding area. He had steered the school through the most difficult period of its development.

An interesting detailed history of the school over this period has been produced by Sue Miller in the form of an excellent illustrated booklet. It is called "The Difficult Years", and is based on the dissertation by Mr Jones. I would be glad to provide copies on request.

During these nine and a half years Arthur and Elsie established themselves in the town. Their two children were born there – Douglas (my father) in 1898, and Myfanwy in 1899.

Arthur clearly saw the Headship of this small school as a stepping stone in his career. He was conscious that although he had a good degree from Cambridge, his MA (Cantab) was not a true postgraduate qualification. So he matriculated with London University as an external student and pursued a course of studies that led to the award of a London MA.

Armed with this further qualification, and his record at Dolgelley, he applied for the post of Headmaster at Handsworth Grammar School in Birmingham. He was selected for the job from 125 applicants, and was to stay there for 28 years until he retired in July 1933.

Elsie with her son Douglas Clendon, 1898.

*Sidney's first wife
Esther, with
Kelsey.*

On leaving Dolgelley he was presented with a gold pocket watch from the staff and pupils of the school, past and present, with an inscription to that effect inside the case dated 24th July 1905. This watch was given to me on my 21st birthday by my father.

In New Zealand Arthur's parents and brothers would have known all about the progress of his career and family from Arthur's regular letters. Vivian recorded in his diary the joy of receiving the English mail. On some days his mother spent the morning opening it and reading it aloud.

Tom and Eliza were never to see their first two grandchildren, Douglas and Myfanwy – but the year after Myfanwy was born Sidney married Esther, his landlady's daughter in Auckland, and brought her down to Lower Hutt to live. So they were not too far away from Akatarawa to show Tom and Eliza their next grandchild when three years later, on November 12th 1903, Sidney and Esther had a daughter. She was Esther Kelsey, named after her mother and grandmother, but she was always known as "Kelsey".

Sidney bought a Coal and Produce business in Lower Hutt and Vivian came in with him. They called the firm "CLENDON BROTHERS". They were merchants. They bought coal, grain and other produce, which was stored in the yard and delivered throughout the area by horse and cart. They had a particularly fine set of horses, which were well known for their high quality. Sidney's main role was in the office – and Vivian's was in the yard, supervising the men. Sidney had a strong character, with drive and determination, and a good business brain, but he could be a little temperamental and difficult to deal with on occasions. Vivian was good natured and more easy going, at home with people, and skilled at creating good relationships. He was no fool either. Between them they were a good team.

Sidney and Vivian built up Clendon Brothers into a sound business that kept both of their families in comfort and security, for many years.

Then in February 1906, less than a year after Arthur had moved to Handsworth Grammar School, a tragedy struck Sidney in New Zealand. His wife, Esther, died as a result of childbirth. She died on February 27th, the day after their second daughter, Nell was born.

Mrs McCarroll, Esther's mother, came down from Auckland and kept house for Sidney, and looked after the children. She stayed for eighteen months.

Later that year, on August 7th 1906, Vivian was married. His bride was Rose Caroline Cooper from Havelock North. She was a school teacher. They met when Vivian was on holiday in Havelock North, and were married there. Vivian and Rose set up house in Lower Hutt.

Arthur learnt, through the letters from New Zealand, about Vivian's happiness and Sidney's misfortune. He wrote a letter to Vivian about them. Vivian kept this letter between two pages of his diaries, where I found it in the photocopied version. It is very difficult to read. Words which I cannot decipher are indicated thus: [?]

Here is the letter.

9 Handsworth Wood Rd
Birmingham
Feb 17 07

My dear Vivian
    I was delighted to get your very interesting and cheerful letter. It is comforting to know that we have one in the family who can write a letter full of real life; I seemed to understand things so well when I had your letter & it made me long to come & see you all & have long talks & pick up the links with the past.
    Nothing would give me more pleasure than to take a year off but it is too early at Handsworth to consider it.
    After good years of service I might get the Autumn free – leave England mid of July and get back in January. Wouldn't it be delightful. We ought to bring the children too to make it [?] [?] .
    I can quite imagine how happy you are now you have settled comfortably down in your own home. It is wonderful how much more pleasant it is here without boarders to upset things, or serious money difficulties to face us. We all

of us seem on [?the] our way to get on in the world although it has been rather a long time coming.

The school is flourishing – quite full very popular and doing good work. This is my chief satisfaction . . .

We are all very well, which is a blessing. Douglas is about the age when I last saw you – he is a bright jolly little chap . . .

We were very sorry that Mother has been so ill and shall be relieved when they sell the farm and come and live near you. Poor old Sid. he has had a hard time! It must have been a terrible blow to him. I hope he is not taking it too hard.

I am glad that you appreciate the blessings of a good wife as I knew you would. You manage well on your money. Living seems to get more expensive in England all the time – not so much actual cost of food & clothes as the outside expenses one has to incur: subscriptions are a serious item.

Love to yourself, Rose & all the family

Yr affectionate brother

Arthur

Later that year Sidney's unhappy situation was brought to an end, when he married his first love, Anna Louisa Orr, on October 9th 1907 in Wellington.

When, about three years later, the boys' Mother & Father eventually sold their farm, Thomas, Eliza & their family began to enjoy its most happy and settled phase since 1887 when they had left England for New Zealand.

Sidney and Anna Louisa Orr, 1907.

Vivian with his father Tom and son Tom, Lower Hutt, 1907.

Vivian and Rose had four children – Tom, Arthur, Hazel and Lorna. They were the first to produce a grandchild in New Zealand for Tom and Eliza. He was Thomas Vivian Clendon, named after his father and grandfather, and was born on 28th September 1907. Always known as Tom, he is still going strong at the time of writing, at the ripe age of 89! I have two photos of him as a baby – one in his grandmother Eliza's arms, and the other with his father and grandfather Tom. A year and a day later Arthur, named after his Uncle in England, was born on September 29th 1908. He was still alive when we went to New Zealand in 1992, and he gave us a farewell party in his garden in Penrose Street, Lower Hutt, on the day before we left. He died in August 1995. Hazel was born on October 31st 1913 and is still alive. She lives in Lower Hutt. Lorna was born in Lower Hutt in 1923. She qualified as a teacher at Victoria College, and after a few years teaching in New Zealand went to England in 1950. At first she lived in London, working at the Festival of Britain and then in a library. Later she lived in Colchester and became very friendly with the Boyton family who introduced her to Esmonde Nixon. Esmonde and Lorna married and lived near Chelmsford, where Esmonde worked at the Marconi Company. In 1962 Esmonde obtained a post at the Victoia University, Wellington and he emigrated with the family to New Zealand, living at Days Bay, Eastbourne. Lorna died of cancer in 1982.

Sidney and Anna had two children – Nancy and Jack – both still alive and living in Lower Hutt when we visited New Zealand. Nancy was born on December 1st 1911, four years after Sidney's marriage to Anna. Jack was born just over a year later, on 21st February 1913. Jack died on July 6th 1996. An appreciation of his life as delivered by his four children at his funeral is included in Part Five.

Sidney and Vivian lived within close walking distance of each other in Lower Hutt – and with their parents, while they were still alive. After their mother died, their father had a housekeeper to look after him – but he came round to his sons' houses regularly in the evening.

Later on Sidney and Vivian bought two adjacent *batches at Point Howard – a delightful spot around the bay from Wellington where you can swim and sail. During the summer the families would go out there to live, and Sidney and Vivian went to work each day in a horse and trap. Nancy has many happy childhood memories of family holidays there by the sea.

Another feature of their family life were the "Akatarawa picnics". They took place up at the old farm, usually on Boxing Day. All the family went. The outings were fun – great family occasions. They still take place occasionally. But when we visited New Zealand in 1992, I realised that to the older generation the picnics had evoked mixed feelings.

Nancy summarised them when talking about her father's life on the farm at Akatarawa one day:

> *The whole thing was a muck-up really – there was a sadness about it – Father and Uncle Vye didn't like going back there when we started the "Akatarawa picnics" – the whole thing was soured I think . . .*
>
> *We started picnics in our 'teens – when we had the first car, an old V8 Ford – then after we were married, we used to have them on Boxing Day – we took our kids – all grandma Clendon's grandchildren and great grandchildren*

So the Boxing Day picnics were a kind of pilgrimage – a mixture of sadness and pleasure – the children enjoying the countryside and swimming in the river. One of their favourite games was to search for "Grandma Clendon's ring" which she had lost there all those years ago. Sidney & Vivian, now grandparents themselves, looked on with mixed feelings – remembering the hardships of their youth – and reflecting that despite all that they and their parents had suffered, the farm had got nowhere in the end. It had been up to them to build from scratch their business, their homes, their families, and their now successful way of life down in the Lower Hutt.

There were four children in each family. Sidney's two oldest daughters, Kelsey and Nell, were the children of his first wife. Their stepmother, Anna

---

* "batch" – a word used in New Zealand to describe a holiday house

Vivian's wife Rose with Thomas and Arthur.

got on very well with Nell, but her relationship with Kelsey was more difficult. Kelsey was independent minded – always trying to be first in her father's eyes. Finally when she was sixteen, Kelsey left home and went to live with Auntie Rose.

In addition to coping with the family, and running the business – Sidney took part in local affairs. He was a member of the Lower Hutt Borough Council from 1911 to 1919 – and was a Justice of the Peace.

Likewise, in England, Arthur was prospering, and becoming deeply involved in public affairs. His school was steadily growing – it had expanded from around 100 or 200 pupils when he started, to 600 by the 1930's. He moved house from Handsworth to Edgbaston, then the most fashionable residential part of Birmingham. He undertook numerous public duties including membership of Staffordshire County Council, the Education Committee of Birmingham City Council, and the Governing Body of Birmingham University. As Treasurer of the Birmingham Library he served on all its committees. For many years he was a churchwarden, and an energetic member of various Diocesan committees. He became Master of the Bridge Trust Lodge of Freemasons, and President of the Birmingham Graduates' Club.

Despite these achievements, (or perhaps because of them!) Arthur was never able "to get the Autumn free – leave England mid of July and get back in January". He had to continue frustrated in his longing to go to New Zealand – "to come & see you all & have long talks" – for over twenty five years after he wrote that in 1907.

In fact it was Sidney who was the first to take the journey half way round the world. He came to England in 1928 with Anna. He was 58, and after 41 years he renewed his friendship with his brother Arthur, with Elsie, and her brother, Ryland Hickinbotham, his schoolboy friend. They went on the Norfolk Broads on a boat with Arthur wearing his Emmanuel College blazer.

Sidney also went back to his birthplace, Ramsgate, and visited his mother's family. There he saw a portrait of his mother as a young woman. He brought it back to New Zealand with him. It is now belongs to his daughter Nancy. We saw it when we stayed with her in Lower Hutt. The portrait is beautiful. It is a small oval photograph and surrounding it are mounted autumn leaves, gathered from the countryside. On the back is inscribed:

About 1860.

> *These leaves were gathered and arranged in Glens Falls USA by Eliza Kelsey Clendon (née Vye) soon after her marriage to Thomas Clendon. Mrs Clendon's portrait is in the centre. The picture was sent by her to her first cousin, Eliza Kelsey, of Ramsgate, England, who had it framed.*
>
> *Given to S. Clendon 1928*

While in England Sidney bought an engagement ring to take back for his nephew Tom, Vivian's oldest son, then 21, to present to his future bride Sheila Milne.

He met his English niece, Myfanwy Clendon, by this time married to her Vye second cousin Jack Boyton. He also met and made an impression on his English nephew, Douglas, my father. My father told me that he remembered Sidney a big man, strong and of great stature. He said Sidney developed a large goitre which had to be surgically removed. It was so large that it was preserved in a medical museum in New Zealand.

This visit was the first reunion of the two brothers since their youth, but they made plans for the second – in New Zealand. Arthur was then only five years from retirement, and he and Elsie promised to sail to New Zealand as soon as they retired and spend about a year there.

Not long after Sidney had returned the business began to decline. The severe economic depression of the thirties, and the emergence of electricity and gas as modern means of heating and lighting, combined to put the family firm of Clendon Brothers into serious difficulties. Then in June 1933 Anna died and Sidney was very downhearted. He decided to give up struggling with the ailing business, and retire.

He was 63.

Kelsey, age 29, was the only one of his family who was working. She was a shorthand writer in New Zealand Parliament Buildings, was quite independent and lived in a flat of her own in Wellington. Nell, 27, married in 1933, and was off his hands. But Nancy, 21, was a student at University in Wellington, as was Jack aged 20.

Sidney let his house in Lower Hutt, and moved to a small flat in Wellington in a house which had belonged to his wife, Anna. It was barely adequate for him with Nancy and Jack. Kelsey, mindful of her freedom, was not interested in joining forces with her father and the students. She lived independently, also in Wellington.

Vivian continued to run the business for a while without Sidney – but within a year or two it was closed down. Vivian, then in his mid fifties, took on a Land Agency.

As Sidney was on such hard times, he wrote to his brother Arthur, to tell him what had happened and to say that he could no longer offer him and Elsie the hospitality that he had planned. He suggested that the whole trip would have to be cancelled. Arthur replied immediately by cable to say that he was coming anyway, and would find his own accommodation if necessary.

Arthur retired from the school after 28 years as head. He was given a tremendous send off, many very generous gifts, and a special plaque was commissioned of him, side face, still hanging in the school hall to commemorate his years of service.

A description of his stewardship can be found in a book produced to celebrate the centenary of the school called "Handsworth Grammar School 1862-1962". This book is now out of print, but extracts from it, and various other documents which demonstrate the progress of the school under his leadership, are in my archives. I include here an extract from the centenary book. It gives an insight of the man as seen by one of his former pupils, Geoffrey Templeman MA PhD FSA, who later became the Vice-Chancellor of the University of Kent at Canterbury:

I was at School from September 1925 until July 1931. When I came Arthur Clendon was already within sight of sixty, and when I left he was within a year of retirement . . . . I only came to know him well in my last two years in the sixth form when he taught me Latin. Even now, after 30 years, I have a very clear picture of him, for he was by any standard a very remarkable man. His figure was large and bulky, and he was rarely, if ever, seen in the school without his gown. But the surprising thing about this large and rather shambling man was his eyes which glittered behind his thick spectacles, and which made those who

Arthur Clendon

met him immediately aware that they were in the presence of someone out of the
ordinary . . .

   Looking back it seems to me that Arthur Clendon must have had a
particularly difficult time in the last years of his tenure. Not only was his School
constantly getting bigger, but it was beginning to include a high proportion of
boys from social classes other than those from which it had hitherto drawn. My
guess is, too, that as a school community it was less easy to manage in my day
than it had been when Arthur Clendon was first appointed before the First War.

   Yet it is as a teacher above all else that I remember him, and I think it
would also be said by all those who had the good fortune to be taught by him in
the sixth form . . . two or three of us who were the Headmaster's pupils had him
to ourselves. He was a fine classical scholar . . . One year I read with him Book
V of Lucretius "De Rerum Natura" and Juvenal's "Satires". It was an

unforgettable experience, something quite different from anything I had known before. For me, at any rate, it was the first glimpse I ever had of what real scholarship means.

My other abiding memory of Arthur Clendon has nothing to do with teaching. I recall him standing each Armistice Day on the platform in what then used to be called Big School, reading the long list of the names of those, many of them his own pupils, who had been killed in the First War. He made no effort to conceal his emotion thus revealing how much he cared to those of us who only knew him as a formidable headmaster . . .

Without much delay Arthur and Elsie packed up and sailed for New Zealand. They arrived in Auckland on the night of Tuesday 7th November 1933. Elsie wrote: *"We could only see the lights around the harbour which looked very nice & the war memorial all flood lighted."*

After a day in Auckland, disembarking and being shown around by a friend of the family, they took the train to Wellington. Their meeting with the other half of the family, at last, is described by Elsie in the following letter to her daughter Myfanwy in England:

c/o V Clendon Esqre
58 Penrose St
Lower Hutt
Wellington NZ

Friday
Nov. 10th 1933

My dear Myfanwy,

We got here yesterday having travelled in the train for 15 hours from Auckland where we landed . . .

The train for Wellington left at 7 and we did not get in until ¼ to 10 the next morning but we had booked a sleeper so it wasn't so bad, but it shook us much more than the ship did. When we got there Uncle Sidney and Kelsie & Jack & Nancy – Uncle Vivian & Auntie Rose & Tom & Lorna were there. Hazel & Arthur could not get off from work. They had two cars & a [?lorry] there & Nancy drove us here to Lower Hutt (12 miles).

We are staying with Uncle Vi as Uncle Sidney has let his house . . . Uncle Sidney looks older and rather shaky I thought. The three children looked very nice, Jack & Nancy rather dark like their Mother but Kelsie is fair with red hair. Uncle Sidney came back here with us & stayed most of the day. We spent a quiet day as we had not had much sleep for 2 nights & a very tiring day in Auckland. We went to bed early and had a very good night.

This is a very nice house & a nice quiet residential neighbourhood. I did not go out at all yesterday. Father just went to Lower Hutt Post Office to send the cable which I hope you got, but this morning Uncle Vi got off from business & took us a lovely drive to the different bays round about. The scenery is beautiful.

The hills are covered with masses of bright yellow broom which looks wonderful. There is gorse too, but the broom is much finer, & the sea & sky are bright blue.

We have just come home and I am writing this while Aunt Rose is getting the lunch. She is very nice. They all are. Tom lives at the back. His wife Sheila seems quite a nice girl. They have 3 children, all girls, but I haven't seen the baby yet. He [Tom] reminds me of Douglas rather thin & quiet with spectacles, with the same shaped face. Arthur is like Father the same figure & complexion & eyebrows. He is engaged but not formally. Hazel is a nice girl – rather delicate looking girl with black hair & dark eyes she is a typist in an office & Lorna is 10. I don't know whether this will get in time for your birthday [38 days later]

. . .

I don't think we shall be here very long. When we can find a nice boarding house or rooms either here or in Wellington. There is a nice garden & tennis court here & they say they are going to make Father play tennis.

Many happy returns darling – with very best love from Mother – to all – I do hope you are all going on all right.

With best love

Mother

Within a few days they had found a suitable place – and were to live there for the rest of the time that they spent in New Zealand. It was in Oriental Bay, on the other side of Wellington from Lower Hutt. From there you can get magnificent views across the harbour. On the opposite shore lies Point Howard where the holiday batches were, and Eastbourne where Tom & Sheila live today. They brought home a watercolour painting of the bay. It is now in the possession of my brother David. On the back is written:

This picture of Oriental Bay was painted to order from the back of St. Ives hotel, Wellington where we stayed Nov 1933 – Aug 1934. A. Clendon

The artist was Nugent Welch. How Arthur came to choose him I do not know, but Welch subsequently became recognised as one of New Zealand's foremost landscape artists. A cutting from the Wellington Evening News of 20th July 1936, attached to the back of the picture, shows that within three years he was achieving some prominence, as he was one of three artists whose paintings of Wellington Harbour were presented to the Art Gallery, and were referred to as "NZ's three most prominent landscape artists".

Shortly after they moved Elsie wrote again:

St. Ives
Oriental Bay
Wellington NZ
Nov 21 [1933]

My dear Myfan,

As you see we have moved into a boarding house in Wellington to be near Uncle Sidney. I think we shall be comfortable . . .

For the Christmas holidays we are going on a tour with Uncle Sidney in his car, to see some of the show places of New Zealand, geysers and boiling mud etc.!!

We are quite sorry to leave Uncle Vi's. They were very kind & I think they liked having us. We may go back there later if we can find a place to stay. It is too much for Auntie Rose. She is on all day without a bit of help, but she is a very sweet woman. I like her very much. They have cut off a piece of their house & made it into a separate flat. All the rest is quite big enough for them & very nice, but I think the business has almost expired, that is why Uncle Sidney has retired to get out of it, and has let the nice house he bought at Lower Hutt after he came to see us. He is living now in a small flat in a house which belonged to Auntie Anna. There is only just room for him & Jack & Nancy . . .

The journey to see the sights took place as planned. Nancy drove her father's big Austin 20. He sat in the front seat, with Arthur and Elsie in the back. After lunch all three passengers would fall asleep. Nancy remembers driving for miles with the three old folk snoozing in the car. When they stopped overnight Arthur and Elsie had "Bed and Breakfast" accommodation, but Sidney and Nancy slept in the car.

Elsie also wrote about a visit to see Nell, Sidney's 2nd daughter, who had recently married Tom Massey; they were living in Masterton:

Dec 8th [1933]

. . . On Saturday afternoon we had an early lunch & got a 'bus to the Lower Hutt, Uncle Vi's, & he took us in his car to Nell's. She lives at Masterton 56 miles away. Kelsey went too. We went over some very steep hills, with a precipice on one side & a great many curves to go round I don't think you would have liked it. There was one place where there was notice "Beware of the Wind". A car had blown down there so we hear. Masterton is a very nice little place & Nell was charming. Their house is quite small, and all on one floor of course & very pretty – not quite complete yet of course. We slept in the one spare room in a bed lent them by "Auntie Ruth" while she is away. Uncle Vi slept in his car & Kelsie on the sitting room sofa. It was very good of her to have the 4 of us as she has no

help. She was very bright & jolly, not so much like you in looks as I had expected paler & shorter, they say she does not look quite her old self yet . . .

[Nell was dogged with kidney disease for much of her life, and died eight years later]

She was delighted with the entree dish. She had not got one. She took us to church on Sunday morning leaving Kelsie & Uncle Vi to look after the dinner. We went a little drive round in the afternoon and left there in the evening ¼ to 7, arriving at Lower Hutt at 9 & caught the bus from the village here – or rather into Wellington & then a tram to Oriental Bay . . .

On Wednesday evening we went to the Lower Hutt with Uncle Sidney & Nancy to see the Amateur play in which "Gwen", Arthur's fiancee, was acting. She took the part of a housekeeper, in black satin & a cap & was very good. I lent her the cameo brooch. We went there & back in Uncle Sidney's car. Jack drove & brought us back. It was a great help as the distances are rather great at night especially . . .

I have bought a navy blue plain straw hat for everyday. Do you like your winter coat. I should like to see Elizabeth in her coat & leggings. Have you found rooms yet.

Love from Mother

There are more letters from Elsie to Myfanwy in the possession of Sue Miller (Myfanwy's daughter). These first few letters are the best records of family history. They give Elsie's first impressions of New Zealand, and more importantly, her first hand description of the various members of the family whom she knew about from letters – but had not met. Her later letters take them, and their way of life, much more for granted.

The stay in New Zealand was seriously upset when Arthur had a heart attack. Elsie was understandably concerned, even though Arthur wrote encouraging letters as if to prove there was nothing to worry about. But from then on he suffered from angina – and he was never able to walk upstairs again.

Arthur and Elsie sailed home to England in late 1934 – to Colchester – to build a bungalow there for their retirement – and to be near their two children, Douglas and Myfanwy. By that time both were married, with two children, and well established in Colchester. Both had settled there because of the influence of their Uncle Ryland Hickinbotham, one of the Hickinbotham and Clendon gang from the 1880's in Birmingham, Sidney's best friend, Elsie's brother, who was in practice there as a doctor.

Because Colchester was to be the home town of the English branch of the Clendon family from 1927 for 50 years – and still is to some of us –

Ryland Hickinbotham

it is worth recording the story of Ryland Hickinbotham, and how it all began.

Ryland, on completing his training at Birmingham Medical School, worked for a while in the hospital there. He was becoming recognised as a skilful and promising young surgeon in the 1890's, when he decided to emigrate to Australia. He married Beatrice Sharpe, who was the theatre Sister at the hospital where he worked, and in 1895 they went to Coolgardie, Western Australia, a gold rush town, and set up together as doctor and nurse in medical practice. They dispensed medicine from a tent in the gold-fields, where water cost 5/- a bucket. He then went to Caenarvon, Western Australia, where he was a magistrate and helped to set up a hospital. They had three children, all boys – Arthur b 1897(?8), *Tom b 1903, and John. Although Ryland had become a prominent member of the town, he returned to England before the first war, probably for the sake of his children's education.

---

*   Sir Tom Hickinbotham KCMG KCVO CIE OBE, Governor of Aden 1951-1956

While in Australia Ryland negotiated the purchase of a general medical practice, with house and surgery, in West Bergholt which is a village near Colchester. On arrival he found that it was not as good as he had been led to believe. Nevertheless he took it, (or perhaps he had to), but after a while, he moved house into a developing area of Colchester, then called "New Town" where he bought a large property, formerly a school, at 52/53 Wimpole Road. He set up a practice there from scratch. He continued to operate a surgery in West Bergholt, and to visit patients there, as well.

His Wimpole Road practice steadily grew. Then sometime around the end of the first war his wife died, and her sister came to look after the family. He then married again – to Mary Godfrey. She was the Queen's Nurse for that district – doing her rounds on a bicycle. Mary was deeply religious, and had been a missionary in Africa; she was contemplating entering a Convent at the time when Ryland proposed to her. Ryland and Mary had five children: three boys – Hugh, Peter and Dick, and two girls – Elsie and Nancy who both still live in Colchester. By the late 1920's Ryland had built up a very busy practice and in 1927 the 'flu epidemic completely overwhelmed him – he just could not cope with the number of visits he had to do. He telephoned his nephew, Douglas Clendon, who had recently qualified as a doctor, to ask him to come and help. Douglas came, they divided the work between them, and survived the crisis. When it was all over they both realised it would be a good thing for Douglas to stay on permanently – so he did. A partnership was formed between them called "HICKINBOTHAM & CLENDON". The property fell naturally into two houses, the Hickinbothams lived at No. 52, and Douglas Clendon installed himself next door at No. 53. In 1929 he married another doctor, Phyllis Winter who had been at medical school with him at University College Hospital in London. Their children, Ryland (me) b. 1930 and David b. 1933, were brought up alongside the younger Hickinbotham children, and played together in the backyard almost as one large family.

Also in 1927 Myfanwy Clendon, Douglas's sister, married Jack Boyton a dentist who had recently qualified at Birmingham. He was looking around for somewhere to open up a practice. Ryland Hickinbotham wrote to him saying that there was plenty of work to be done in Colchester, as "most of my patients have rotten teeth". Jack came alone to start with in 1927, living at 52 Wimpole Road with his Uncle Ryland and Aunt Mary. He then found suitable premises for a surgery and living accommodation just a few yards around the corner, in Military Road, and Myfanwy joined him. They had two daughters, Elizabeth b. 1931 and Susan b. 1934.

So when Arthur and Elsie came to retire it was natural to choose Colchester as the place to live. In 1934, their bungalow in Lexden Road had not yet been built, so on return from New Zealand they came to stay at our house, No. 53 Wimpole Road, where a double bed was installed in the dining room.

They called the bungalow 'Holm Oak' and moved there in 1935 – but next year Elsie was killed in a car accident. Arthur was driving his almost new Austin 12 back to Colchester from a holiday at Ryland's seaside chalet at Scratby, near Great Yarmouth. A sudden violent gust of wind blew the car sideways – it lurched and turned over. The sunshine roof was open and Elsie was in the front passenger seat. Her skull fractured as her head hit the road. Their domestic servant, Nellie, was in the back with Myfanwy. Neither they nor Arthur were injured. Elsie died on July 24th 1936, was cremated, and her ashes were interred at Colchester Cemetery.

Soon afterwards, Arthur was joined at Holm Oak by Harvey Hickinbotham, Elsie's brother – the next in line after Ryland. He had returned to England to retire after a lifetime of service as a missionary in India.

In 1936, Sidney's oldest daughter Kelsey Clendon sailed to England and stayed for some time. She worked at New Zealand House in London. She went on a tandem bicycle down the Rhine Valley with a New Zealand friend. She stayed in Colchester with Arthur, who was very fond of her. She took me to the town on a Saturday. I was six years old. It was market day. I remember us walking down St. John's Street, my hand in hers, when she told me that in New Zealand all the shops were closed on Saturday as well as Sunday – so that everyone could have a good long week-end off!

Kelsey was tall with fair hair. She had a strong personality – bubbling with self confidence and a kind of naive charm. She was irrepressible and all the Colchester family took to her at once. She could talk the hind leg off a donkey, she never stopped talking. When she got home she wrote letters, usually typewritten, and always full of news and opinion, to both the Colchester families. This prolific correspondence continued for the rest of her life. I have a sack full of her letters to sort through and evaluate. Among other things they illustrate the tremendous warmth of feeling, and the friendship that grew up between the next generation across the world. It was fortuitous, perhaps that Kelsey was such a prodigious communicator, and that the two sides of the family were each clustered together in relatively small communities – Lower Hutt and Colchester.

After Kelsey returned Harvey and Arthur had a few years together, looked after by Nellie. But a few days after War broke out, Arthur was killed.

At 12.50pm on Wednesday September 13th 1939 Arthur stepped out from behind a parked car, only about fifty yards from his house, and was knocked down by a motor cyclist. He was admitted to hospital and died at about 3.30am the following morning. He was buried in the Cemetery, in a grave next to Elsie's. He was 71.

Harvey left Holm Oak and it was let. To help alleviate the shortage of Clergy during the war he became the Rector of Aldham – a village about 5 miles from Colchester. Myfanwy and Jack and their family also moved out from Colchester and lived at Aldham Rectory, partly as a safety precaution to avoid any bombing, and partly to keep house for Uncle Harvey.

Meanwhile, back in New Zealand, Sidney had re-married. This time it was to a widow who, like him, had been married twice before. Known as "Luki" her name was Mary Tweedie. When they became engaged Nancy was working as a teacher in Samoa, and Jack wrote to her from Wellington to tell her about the happy event. When Sue and I were in New Zealand Jack read it out to us. His description of the loving couple is very amusing. But as well as being witty Jack's letter displays his gratitude that his father was looking forward to a happy married life again.

Sidney married Luki in Wellington on July 12th 1938. A few years later they moved to Auckland. I was told when in New Zealand that Sidney really enjoyed the last phase of his life in Auckland with Luki.

Vivian was 60, and still working, when the war broke out. His land agency business fell apart because of the war. So Vivian took a job in a hardware shop, and worked there until he retired.

Kelsey refers to the effect of the war on the housing market, to her Uncle Vi, her father Sidney, and to many other things, in a typical letter of hers of which the following is only a brief extract!

C/o Hon. D. Wilson's Office,
Parliament Buildings,
Wellington, N.Z.
30th August 1943

Dear Douglas,

Your letter dated 10th June received about 3 weeks ago – quite quick travelling for these days. I also received one from Uncle Harvey which was very welcome . . .

I do appreciate your writing to me, Douglas. If we don't keep in touch with each other occasionally – our families I mean – we will just completely lose touch with each other, and I think that would be a shame . . .

*We used to write to relatives in Cleveland, Ohio – my sister *Nell used to write to a namesake over there – but we have long since lost touch with them.*

---

*   Nell, referred to in the above letter as a namesake in USA, was George II's granddaughter whom he described when she was aged 10 in a letter dated 11th March 1884, see Chapter 5.

They would be our second cousins I suppose.

Some people over here are very keen on America, and wouldn't mind if we were attached to the USA after the war, but personally I would a thousand times rather come under Britain as we are at present. Of course we are much nearer the States. We have Mrs Roosevelt in Wellington at present – she broadcast a speech last night so I suppose I'm allowed to mention it. She made a very good speech – it was directed to the women of NZ . . . We have quite a few well known people in Wellington from time to time, although I never know, as a rule, until they have left – everything is very "hush hush" these days even in this little outpost.

I took your letter out to Lower Hutt the last time I visited Uncle Vi and Auntie Rose, and they were most interested and said to give you their love and they hoped that you would come out and see us after the war. As you say, air travel will probably go ahead by leaps and bounds after the war, and you'll be able to pop over here for a fortnight's holiday – maybe! I believe a big Lancaster bomber which was here recently, flew from England in 6 1/2 days! and yet it took me 6 weeks to get back here – wonderful isn't it?

I felt very homesick for England when I read your letter . . . I still find it hard to realise that Uncle Arthur isn't in Colchester – in my memories he seems to be part of it, and I can still hear him telling me things about England – in his enthusiastic way. He certainly was a dear, and it is only now that I realise fully how good he was to me. I think in some ways he understood me better than my own father!

Talking about father [Sidney] I had a letter from Nancy the other day and she says father has been doing a lot of concreting of the back part of the house. He is 73 so is wonderful for his age. I am hoping to go up at Xmas time . . . Father likes Auckland . . .

It is terribly hard to get accommodation here now – with the war industries thousands more people have had to come to Wellington and building for civilian requirements has stopped in the meantime. Consequently houses are almost impossible to get – and flats and rooms as well. Even most of the hotels have been taken over for war purposes . . . The Govt here has just passed legislation . . . to control the prices of houses when they are offered for sale . . .

I often think of my cycle trip down the Rhine and wonder if it is true! Sometimes we cycled 75 miles a day. I remember my seat was sore at first, but soon it became acclimatised . . .

You would be interested in talking to our Jack, if ever he gets to England before the war is over. He has been with the 6th Field Ambulance for two and a half years now, and through some of the tough fighting . . .

I was very interested to read about David and Ryland – dear little David with his deep voice and blue eyes. I can picture him getting some extra "sweeties" from the little shop next door . . .

I seem to be going on for ever here, Douglas, so must close. I'm glad you

are managing to dodge the bombs so far and no injuries to the clan. I
hope Ryland enjoys Epsom College – that is where Uncle Harvey went to, is it
not? . . .

> *Do write soon, although I understand how busy you are.*
> *My fondest love to Phyllis & you*
> *Kelsey*

Jack was able to get to Colchester at the end of the war, before being repatriated. He remembers long chats with my father Douglas, and studying lots of bits of paper spread over the sitting room floor trying to make sense of the family tree. My memory of him then is seeing him off on the train in his army uniform at Colchester North station.

Vivian moved from Lower Hutt round the bay to Point Howard. He converted the two holiday batches there into a house where he and Auntie Rose lived after he stopped work.

After the war Sidney and Vivian were still going strong in retirement. On 20th September 1948 Kelsey reported as follows:

> *I was out at Uncle Vi's yesterday. He is 69 now and is beginning to look a bit*
> *older I think. He was always very young in his ways . . .*
>
> *Father and Luki are both well, I'm glad to report. They had their 10th*
> *wedding anniversary recently. Luki writes to me fairly regularly. Father has just*
> *chopped down a big tree in their garden! He has great strength even now*

Sydney was 78 then, and was 80 when Kelsey surprised everyone by getting married to a man she met on the boat coming to England in 1950. He was Charles Lindsay. They were married by Uncle Harvey [Hickinbotham] at Aldham Church where he was still going strong in his 70's – one of the original members of the Hickinbotham Clendon gang.

They were married by Archbishop's Licence on 11th November 1950, the day before Kelsey's 47th birthday. Douglas cabled the good news to her father Sidney, who replied by airletter – in a bold hand:

> *1 Sanders Avenue*
> *Takapuna*
> *Auckland NZ*
> *19 Nov '50*
>
> *Dear Douglas*
> *I thank you very much for your cable as you may imagine we were all*
> *thinking of you all and it was a relief to us to know it had passed off so well and*
> *our girl was so happy with Charles. I thank you all for your great kindness and*

generosity to my dear girl.

It is nice to feel that I and mine still belong to the family, although living so far away.

Give my love to your Uncle Ryland, and Mary. I can hardly realise that all their children have grown up since I saw you last, and your boys also, who were not seen then, must be pretty big now, and Myfanwy's daughters.

How very much I should like to see them but I shall hear all about them from Charles before long.

I expect you and your Wife are looking a bit older too. I am very well for my age and still find much to amuse me and much to be thankful for.

Love to you all from us both
Sidney and Wife.

That letter, and the following one, are the only writings by Sidney that I have seen, yet through my researches I feel I have come to know the man from his schooldays, through his tough hard life as a young adult, his troubles and his achievements, and his final period of peace with himself and the world. Characteristically the second letter, like most of those from New Zealand at that time, ends with a plea for my parents to come over and see them!

1 Sanders Avenue
Takapuna
Auckland NZ
16 Dec 1950

Dear Douglas and Phyllis

I am sending this with our Christmas greetings and with thanks to you both, and to Jack and Myfanwy, and Uncle Harvey, for the glorious wedding you gave to my Kelsey. It is a strange freak of fortune that she should be with you for the Celebration. If we had tried to arrange it something would have gone wrong.

I am feeling well but I have now and then a feeling like Rip Van Winkle had, when I realise I am over eighty and see the second generation in middle age and the third generation now grown up.

What about you two coming over for a Holiday, there are plenty of Clendons now over here and they would all be delighted to welcome you.

A very Happy Christmas to you all and love from us both
Sidney & May"

---

*   Luki was also known as May – and signed letters to my parents as May

Sidney lived for another seven years. He died in Auckland on June 7th 1957. He was 87.

Vivian carried on living with Rose at Point Howard until he died on September 28th 1963. He was 85.

Their widows lived on much longer. Both were alive when my parents went out to New Zealand in 1967/8 – and they met. Luki then wrote to my parents while they were still in New Zealand:

> *1 Sanderson Ave*
> *Takapuna*
> *March 12/ 68*
>
> *My dear Phyllis and Douglas*
> *The time is getting short now & you will be leaving us all in about a week & am sure you will need a rest on the ship after all the gadding about & visiting all the members of the Clendon family . . . However I feel I know you both quite well & Sidney talked so much to me about Arthur . . .*
> *The weather has been glorious today & I have been trying to clear up my old untidy garden burning rubbish. I have a nice boy to do the lawns & his father & mother come too & I make tea under the trees. The great gr. children also come round as the grapes & apples are getting ripe, but I'm feeling tired but I can always come inside & put my feet up . . .*
> *Mary [[her daughter by a previous marriage who lived with her] is enclosing a wee note so wishing the fondest love to you both and all good wishes for a happy trip home*
> *Yours affec.ly*
> *May*

When they got home they had another letter at Christmas time from Luki describing her 90th birthday party. She talked of the many people who came, including one from a family that had come out with her on the same ship in 1906. But she was not well – "I've had bro pneu [broncho pneumonia] & it has taken it out of me".

She survived for a few more years, and died in 1972. She was 94.

Auntie Rose continued to live at Point Howard after Vivian died. My parents visited her there. She also exchanged Christmas greetings with them after they had come home to England.

The following letter is full of news about various members of the family, and her handwriting and expression is so fluent that the letter could have been written by someone half her age – which was 85.

9. Howard Rd
Pt. Howard
Eastbourne
N.Z.
Dec. 16. 68.

  Dear Douglas & Phyllis,
    Thanks for your Xmas wishes, your card arrived last week. Hazel & I are
in the midst of a Xmas rush although we did try to be a bit beforehand this year.
    We are having Xmas at Arthur's, Joyce is intending to cook a huge turkey.
I hear there will be 7 adults present plus 4 children, quite a family party . . . It
would be much more sensible to have everything cold but tradition dies hard &
we still keep up the old customs handed down by our ancestors . . .
    Hazel & I both send our love & very best wishes to you & yours
    from Aunty Rose

Towards the end of her life she moved to Lower Hutt, and lived there with
Hazel, in the house where Hazel now lives. Rose died in Lower Hutt on May
16th 1977. She was 93.

EPILOGUE

The death of Rose signifies the end of an era. She was the last of the
generation who knew what it was to live in the Victorian age – and to be
settlers in a distant colony.

It is now 110 years since the parting in 1887 between Arthur and the
rest of the family, when they set sail for New Zealand. That event – and the
affinity which Arthur felt for his family in New Zealand influenced all who
were close to him. His two children were profoundly affected, and they, in
turn, influenced my generation.

Myfanwy was never able to make the journey to New Zealand, but she
and Jack were passionate about their relations over there. They welcomed
and looked after Vivian's youngest daughter, Lorna, when she came to live
in England. They made a second home for her, and introduced her to her
husband Esmonde Nixon who lived in Colchester. They formed a deep and
lasting friendship with Kelsey. They exchanged messages by audiotapes and
sent across colour slide shows. Both their daughters, Elizabeth and Susan
have been to New Zealand and stayed with Nancy in Lower Hutt – Susan
has been several times.

Douglas followed in his father's footsteps. On retirement he and Phyllis
made the long journey by sea in the SS Maasdam – out one way and back

the other. A round the world trip. They left Southampton on Friday 6th October 1967 – stayed in New Zealand – and arrived back on Tuesday 2nd April 1968.

Their tour is well documented in colour slides, letters, maps and notes. They were met by innumerable first cousins with their wives and husbands at Wellington harbour – and their arrival was recorded on tape by Johnny Walker, Nancy's husband. While there Douglas sought out as many relations as possible. He and Phyllis put together all the original data on the descendants of James Reddy Clendon that appears in the 1974 edition. But for Douglas the trip was far more than a genealogical expedition. It was also a romantic journey on a cruise ship around the world – with all his relations in New Zealand at the end of it. A once in a lifetime opportunity to meet them, to get to know them, to enjoy their company, and make new friendships among them. Phyllis was a little more apprehensive – we could see it in her eyes when we said good-bye on the boat train at Waterloo station. But enjoy it they both did!

When they returned we met them at Waterloo, and took them to our home in St Albans where they stayed for two nights before returning to Colchester. They told us that the best friends they had made were Nancy, Sidney's daughter, and her husband, Johnny Walker.

In 1970, Johnny and Nancy came to England for a long visit. Their itinerary had been planned jointly with my father, but by the time they came he was too ill to accompany them on any of the trips. He died while they were here. Nancy & Johnny came over again for a long stay some years later, as did Jack after Loris died, and Nancy and Kelsey as widows. Then the next generation (Tom and Eliza's great grandchildren) began to travel as young back-packers, some staying and working for a year or two. When in England they looked us up. They came to family weddings, to Christmases, and stayed in our homes.

In November 1979, Sally Clendon, my daughter, was the first of her generation (Tom and Eliza's great great grandchildren) to make the journey. At age 24 she went over to New Zealand and stayed with Nancy and Johnny for six months, returning in May 1980. Johnny died in 1981 but Nancy and two other New Zealand cousins, Alison Clendon (Sidney's granddaughter) and Elinor Clendon (Vivian's granddaughter) were in England a year later, and all three came to Sally's wedding in Derbyshire in July 1982.

After I had retired, Sue and I followed in my father and grandfather's footsteps, and made a visit to New Zealand. We were there for six weeks in January, February and March 1992. We flew in to Auckland and went by train to Wellington. We were met there at the railway station by Nancy and Jack with two cars – as were Arthur and Elsie, my grandparents, nearly 60 years before.

At 80, Nancy was still driving, as was Jack, and they drove us in separate cars to Lower Hutt. They had vivid memories of the visits of my grandparents, my parents, and my daughter. We stayed with Nancy while in Lower Hutt. She told us about the early days. She took us to Akatarawa. Much of what is written in this and the previous chapter about the family in New Zealand was recounted to me by Nancy. I am deeply grateful to her for this contribution to the family history – and for her friendship and hospitality to Sue and me, to my parents and grandparents, and to my daughter Sally, on our visits to New Zealand spanning almost 60 years.

While in New Zealand I met many of my cousins, the descendants of Sidney and Vivian. Some were old friends, some were new acquaintances. All of them extended to us a warm friendship and hospitality, and many have helped in bringing up to date the New Zealand branches in the genealogical tables which comprise the next chapter. Although I have further information about many members of the family these tables are, of necessity, largely restricted to the basic recording of births, marriages and deaths.

However, in Part Five a fuller account is given of the lives of two of them – Arthur's son Douglas, Sidney's son Jack, and there is a short tribute to Vivian's son Tom, who died shortly before the book went to press.

CHAPTER EIGHT

THE DESCENDANTS OF THOMAS CLENDON

(1836-1921)

This chapter consists of the genealogical tables of all
the known descendants of Thomas Clendon and Eliza
Kelsey Vye. For ease of reference the numbering is
identical to the 1974 edition, and the same method of
presentation is used. The information has been
updated to December 1996, where possible. The
occupations of Thomas's grandchildren and their
spouses have been included, but are omitted in
subsequent generations. Post-nominal qualifications
have been universally included from many countries,
and awarding bodies in England are signified.

I apologise for any errors or omissions that I may
have made.

(4) **THOMAS CLENDON**   b 1836 Jan 8   Ramsgate, England
                                 d 1921 Jun 17   Lower Hutt, New Zealand

     m. ELIZA KELSEY VYE   m 1861 Apr 9   Ramsgate
                                 b 1839 Aug 7   Ramsgate
                                 d 1915 Mar 6   Lower Hutt

Thomas and Eliza had five children.

(I)   **EDITH CLENDON**   b 186?   Glens Falls, New York State, USA
       died in infancy   d 186?   Glens Falls

(ii)   **HENRY CLENDON**   b 1863 or 1864   Glens Falls
       (known as Harry)   d 1935 Sep 18   Wellington, New Zealand
       died without issue

(iii) **ARTHUR CLENDON**   b 1868 Aug 12   Glens Falls
       MA (Cantab) & MA (London) d 1939 Sep 14   Colchester, Essex, England

       m. ELLEN ELIZABETH HICKINBOTHAM
       (known as Elsie)   m 1896 Jan 14   Birmingham, England
                                b 1870 May 19   Birmingham
                                d 1936 July 24   interred in Colchester

(iv)   **SIDNEY CLENDON**   b 1870 May 24   Ramsgate, Kent, England
                                d 1958 Jun 7   Auckland, New Zealand

       m. (1st)   m 1900 Jul 12   Auckland
       ESTHER FLORENCE McCARROLL
       (mother of Kelsey & Nell) b 1871 Oct 26   Auckland
                                d 1906 Feb 27   Lower Hutt, New Zealand

       m. (2nd)   m 1907 Oct 9   Wellington
       ANNA LOUISA ORR   b 1872 Mar 7   Wellington
       (mother of Nancy & Jack) i 1933 Jun 15   Lower Hutt

       m. (3rd)   m 1938 July 12   Wellington
       MARY TWEEDIE   b 1878 Aug 12   ?England, migrated to NZ in 1906
       (known as Luki)   d 1972 Oct 22   Auckland
       twice widowed, (1st) WORTHINGTON née CARTER

(v)   **VIVIAN CLENDON**   b 1878 Dec 1   Birmingham
       (known as Vye or Vi)   d 1963 Sep 28   Lower Hutt

       m. ROSE CAROLINE COOPER
                                m 1906 Aug 7   Havelock North, NZ
                                b 1883 Dec 21   Havelock North
                                d 1977 May 16   Lower Hutt

(iii) ARTHUR CLENDON

Arthur and Elsie had two children, Douglas and Myfanwy. They and their issue are tabulated below. All place names are in England unless otherwise stated.

I Douglas Clendon

I **DOUGLAS RYLAND THOMAS CLENDON**
MA (Cantab) MRCS LRCP of Colchester,
general medical practitioner & anaesthetist

b	1898 May 10	Dolgellau, Wales (then spelt Dolgelley)
d	1970 Jul 10	Colchester

m. PHYLLIS ADA RELPH WINTER JP
MB BS (London) MRCS LRCP
consultant anaesthetist

m	1929 Jun 25	Llanaber, Barmouth, Wales
b	1901 Aug 31	Bridlington, Yorkshire
d	1991 Dec 31	Colchester

The wedding of Douglas Clendon and Phyllis Winter.

1 **THOMAS RYLAND CLENDON**
(Ryland) MA (Cantab) MB BChir FIPD, of Hathersage, Derbyshire

b	1930 Jun 1	Colchester

m. SUSAN MARY CUNINGHAM SRN

m	1954 Jan 9	Bath, Somerset
b	1931 Mar 17	Bath

i **SARAH JANE CLENDON** SRN RSCN of Worcester
(known as Sally)

b	1955 Mar 17	Bath

m. IAN FRANCIS ROWE MA (Cantab) MB BChir MD FRCP

m	1982 Jul 17	Bradwell, Derbyshire
b	1952 Mar 29	Solihull, West Midlands

a JAMES EDWARD ROWE

b	1984 May 18	Harrow, Middlesex

b HANNAH JANE ROWE

b	1986 Feb 14	Roehampton, Middlesex

c FIONA MARY ROWE

b	1989 Jul 3	Roehampton

d RACHEL ALICE ROWE

b	1991 Nov 25	Worcester

1   **THOMAS RYLAND CLENDON** *(cont.)*
    m. *SUSAN MARY CUNINGHAM*

(cont.)

ii   **CAROLINE MARY CLENDON** BSc (Bath), of Oxford
                    b   1956 July 25   Bath

     m. CHARLES FULTON BAGGS BSc (Bath)
                    m   1978 July 22   St Albans
                    b   1956 July 10   Beverley

         a   MATTHEW FULTON BAGGS
                    b   1983 Aug 14   Reading

         b   ANDREW RYLAND BAGGS
                    b   1987 Apr 10   Ipswich

         c   SARAH MARY BAGGS
                    b   1989 July 24   Ipswich

iii **JUDITH SUSAN CLENDON** NNEB of Wing, Buckinghamshire
                    b   1958 Apr 13   St Albans

     m. NIGEL JOHN WESTALL
                    m   1983 Apr 4   Bradwell, Derbyshire
                    b   1957 Oct 17   St Albans

         a   CLAIRE LOUISE WESTALL
                    b   1984 Dec 4   Watford

         b   MARK JOHN WESTALL
                    b   1986 May 25   Watford

         c   SOPHIE VIVIEN WESTALL
                    b   1990 May 2   Aylesbury

iv   **PETER JAMES RYLAND CLENDON** of Crouch End, London
                    b   1960 Feb 17   St Albans

     m. BRIDGET THERESA CARROLL (known as Bridie)
                    m   1990 Aug 25   Kiltimagh, County Mayo, Ireland
                    b   1963 May 11   Castlebar, County Mayo

         a   CATHERINE ALICE CLENDON
                    b   1995 Mar 4   Highgate, London

(cont.)

Ryland (the author)
and
Susan Cuningham

David Clendon
and
Valerie Ford.

The children of Ryland and Susan from left to right:
Elizabeth, Tom, Peter, Judith, Caroline, Sally, 1996.

The grandchildren of Ryland and Susan, 1996.

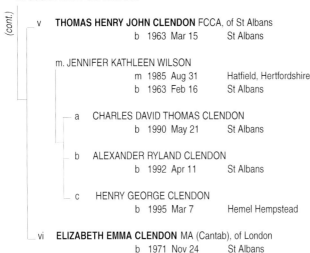

1   **THOMAS RYLAND CLENDON** *(cont.)*
    m. SUSAN MARY CUNINGHAM

(cont.)

v   **THOMAS HENRY JOHN CLENDON** FCCA, of St Albans
                              b   1963 Mar 15   St Albans

    m. JENNIFER KATHLEEN WILSON
                              m   1985 Aug 31   Hatfield, Hertfordshire
                              b   1963 Feb 16   St Albans

        a   CHARLES DAVID THOMAS CLENDON
                              b   1990 May 21   St Albans

        b   ALEXANDER RYLAND CLENDON
                              b   1992 Apr 11   St Albans

        c   HENRY GEORGE CLENDON
                              b   1995 Mar 7   Hemel Hempstead

vi **ELIZABETH EMMA CLENDON** MA (Cantab), of London
                              b   1971 Nov 24   St Albans

2   The Rev **DAVID ARTHUR CLENDON** MA (Cantab), of Pirton, Hertfordshire
                              b   1933 Feb 10   Colchester

    m. VALERIE MARGARET FORD SRN
                              m   1965 Jun 26   Digswell, Hertfordshire
                              b   1943 Mar 4   Southampton

        i   **CRISPIN JOHN ST ALBAN CLENDON**
                              b   1966 Jun 18   Caddington, Bedfordshire
                              d   1966 Jun 19   Luton

        ii **JANE KATHARINE CLENDON** RGN of London
                              b   1967 May 14   Luton

        iii **CHRISTOPHER RYLAND CLENDON** of Southampton
                              b   1968 Oct 3   Luton

II *Mary Myfanwy Boyton*

II **MARY MYFANWY CLENDON**
    (Myfanwy), of Colchester   b   1899 Dec 18   Dolgellau, Wales
    domestic science teacher   (then spelt Dolgelley)
                              d   1981 Apr 7   Colchester

    m. JACK LYONS BOYTON LDS MC
    (her VYE second cousin)   m   1927 Jan 12   Birmingham
    dental surgeon   b   1894 Apr 28   Dover
                              d   1977 May 31   Colchester

Jack, Myfanwy and family, with two New Zealand cousins.

(adults L. to r. Robin, Elizabeth, Jack; two New Zealand cousins, Susan, Myfanwy.)

1   **ELIZABETH ANN BOYTON** of Colchester
                          b   1931 Nov 23   Colchester

m. ROBERT MITCHELL   m 1955 Oct 15   Colchester
(known as Robin)   b   1931 Oct 30   Edinburgh

     i   **JANE SARAH BOYTON MITCHELL** BA (Open University), of Leavenheath, Suffolk
                          b   1957 July 4   Colchester

          m. RICHARD ADDIS ACII
                          m 1981 Apr 11   Colchester
                          b   1957 Oct 26   Park Royal, London

              a   IAIN ALEXANDER BOYTON ADDIS
                          b   1983 Nov 7   Colchester

              b   JACK CHRISTOPHER NORMAN ADDIS
                          b   1986 Sep 19   Sheffield

     ii   **ANN BELINDA MITCHELL** (Belinda), of Woodbridge, Suffolk
                          b   1960 Sep 28   Colchester

          m. ROGER ENO   m 1987 May 16   Woodbridge
                          b   1959 Apr 29   Woodbridge

              a   CECILY LORIS ENO
                          b   1993 Feb 17   Ipswich

              b   CHARLOTTE LIANA ENO (known as Lottie)
                          b   1994 Nov 11   Ipswich

2   **SUSAN JESSICA BOYTON** of Colchester
                          b   1934 Nov 30   Colchester

m. WILLIAM HENRY CHARLES MILLER (Henry),
died without issue   m 1964 Oct 10   Colchester
                          b   1925 Sep 15   Stamford
                          d   1966 Jan 16   Chelmsford

(iv) SIDNEY CLENDON

Sidney was married three times, and was twice widowed. His older two children, Kelsey and Nell, were from his first wife, Esther; the younger two, Nancy and Jack, were from his second wife, Anna.

There was no issue from his marriage to Luki, although she had a daughter, Mary Heslop, from a previous marriage.

Sidney's children and their issue comprise the next set of tables.

All the place names in the tables are in New Zealand unless otherwise stated.

(iv) SIDNEY CLENDON
(1st marriage to: ESTHER FLORENCE McCARROLL)

I Esther Kelsey Lindsay

I	**ESTHER KELSEY CLENDON**	b	1903 Nov 12		Lower Hutt
	(Kelsey), of Wellington	d	1985 Jan 30		Lower Hutt
	secretary to leader of NZ parliament				
	died without issue				

m. CHARLES JOHN LINDSAY				
taxidermist	m	1950 Nov 11		Aldham, near Colchester, Essex, England
	b	1902		Frome, Somerset, England
	d	1966 Feb 16		Wellington

II Ellen Mary Massey

II	**ELLEN MARY CLENDON**	b	1906 Feb 26	Lower Hutt
	(Nell), of Masterton	d	1941 Sep	Masterton

m. NOEL GISBORNE MASSEY			
(known as Tom)	m	1933 Apr 8	Lower Hutt
	b	1908 Dec 23	Gisborne
	d	1975 Oct 21	Wellington

1	**NOELA MARGARET MASSEY** of Havelock North		
		b	1935 Jun 29	Masterton

m. BRYAN AUSTEN-SMITH			
	m	1960 Apr 5	Wellington
	b	1932 Mar 25	Perth, Western Australia

i	**SIMON AUSTEN-SMITH**		
		b	1961 Jan 13	Lower Hutt

m. CHERIE JONES			
	m	1984 Apr 26	Havelock North
	b	19 Sep 11	?Napier

a	SARAH JANE AUSTEN-SMITH		
		b	1987 Jun 16	Auckland

(cont.)

*Kelsey Clendon
and Charles Lindsay*

Nell Clendon and Tom Massey

Noela Massey, Bryan Austen-Smith and Simon.

1   **NOELA MARGARET MASSEY** *(cont.)*
     m. *BRYAN AUSTEN-SMITH*

(cont.)
     ii   **BRIAR HELEN AUSTEN-SMITH**
                              b   1964 Aug 24   Lower Hutt

          m. JOHN TERENCE ANDREWS
                              m   1989 Oct 21   Havelock North
                              b   1953 Nov 5   Auckland

          a   LAUREN CLAUDIA AUSTEN ANDREWS
                              b   1995 Jan 19   Wellington

          b   HANNAH ANDREWS
                              b   1996 Oct 16   Wellington

2   **JOHN CLENDON MASSEY DOWNER**   of Otaki South
                              b   1938 May 19   Masterton
     John took the surname DOWNER, the married name of his father's sister who brought him up with her
     husband from the age of three when his mother died.

     m. ALISON WOOD   m   1960 Sep 10   Wellington
                             b   1938 Sep 26   Auckland
                             divorced

          i   **RICHARD DOWNER**
                              b   1962 Feb 10   Pahiatua, Nr. Masterton

(cont.)

2   **JOHN CLENDON MASSEY DOWNER** (cont.)
     m. ALISON WOOD

(cont.)

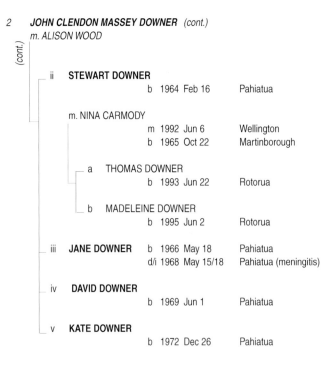

ii	**STEWART DOWNER**			
		b	1964 Feb 16	Pahiatua
	m. NINA CARMODY			
		m	1992 Jun 6	Wellington
		b	1965 Oct 22	Martinborough
	a	THOMAS DOWNER		
		b	1993 Jun 22	Rotorua
	b	MADELEINE DOWNER		
		b	1995 Jun 2	Rotorua
iii	**JANE DOWNER**	b	1966 May 18	Pahiatua
		d/i	1968 May 15/18	Pahiatua (meningitis)
iv	**DAVID DOWNER**			
		b	1969 Jun 1	Pahiatua
v	**KATE DOWNER**			
		b	1972 Dec 26	Pahiatua

(iv) SIDNEY CLENDON
(2nd marriage to: ANNA LOUISA ORR)

III Nancy Claire Clendon

Nancy Clendon, John Walker and family.
(L. to r. Brian, Nancy, Neil, Helen, Johnny)

III   **NANCY CLAIRE CLENDON** BA of Haverlock North (formerly Lower Hutt)
       school teacher   b 1911 Dec   Lower Hutt

       m. JOHN WALKER (Johnny)   m 1938 Dec 12   Samoa
       Chief Finance Officer   b 1912 Mar 9   Woodville
       Ministry of Education,   d 1981 Nov 19   Lower Hutt
       New Zealand

1   **NEIL JOHN WALKER** MSc PhD of Pennsylvania, USA
                                   b 1940 Nov 25   Auckland

       m. HELEN JOSEPH   m 1964 May 30   Timaru
                                   b 1939 Oct 25

           i   **ANDREW CLENDON WALKER**
                                   b 1968 Dec 22   Palmerston North

                m. MICHELLE LEANNE LE CLAIR
                                   m 1996 Sep 14   Napa, California, USA
                                   b 1972 Jan 18   Long Beach, California, USA

           ii   **JAMES JOSEPH WALKER**
                                   b 1971 Apr 6   Palmerston North

2   **BRIAN CLENDON WALKER** of Christchurch, NZ
                                   b 1943 Dec 9   Auckland

       m. WAIMARIE WOODS   m 1969   Tauranga
       (known as Lucky)   b 19
                                   divorced

           i   **NANCY WALKER**   b 1969 Aug   Tauranga

           ii   **JOHN WALKER**   b 1971   Tauranga

IV John Sidney Clendon

IV   **JOHN SIDNEY CLENDON** LLB (known as Jack), of Lower Hutt
      Chief Solicitor to the   b 1913 Feb 12   Lower Hutt
      Treasury, New Zealand   d 1996 July 6   Lower Hutt

      m. LORIS KATHLEEN SULLIVAN
                                   m 1947 May 10   Lower Hutt
                                   b 1917 May 16   Dunedin
                                   d 1977 Sep 9   Lower Hutt

Jack Clendon and Loris Sullivan

1   **JOHN HARVEY CLENDON** Dip Ag Dip VFM, of Johor, Malaysia,and Eastbourne, New Zealand
                          b   1948 May 15   Lower Hutt

     m. LOUISE STEVENS BSc MPhil
                          m   1984 Dec 12   Honiara, Solomon Isles
                          b   1955 Sep 25   Sawbridgeworth, Hertfordshire, England

        i   **ANNA-CLAIRE CLENDON**
                          b   1986 Apr 18   Bedford, England

        ii **JULIET LOUISE CLENDON**
                          b   1987 Sep 23   Bedford, England

2   **WILLIAM ROSS CLENDON** MA LLB (Ross), of Manila, Philippines, and Wellington, New Zealand
                          b   1951 Jun 25   Lower Hutt

     m. CAROL MARY DICKIE   m   1977 Apr 2   Ithaca, New York, USA
                          b   1951 Dec 30   Gore

        i   **SAMUEL JOHN CLENDON**
                          b   1985 Jan 12   Wellington

        ii **THOMAS ROBERT CLENDON**
                          b   1985 Jan 12   Wellington

3   **GRAHAM SIDNEY CLENDON** BSc of Wellington
                        b   1953 Jun 25   Lower Hutt

4   **ALISON JOAN CLENDON** NZRN of Auckland
                        b   1958 Sep 9   Lower Hutt

m. VAUGHAN ARUNDEL LAMBERT
                        m   1990 Feb 25   Upper Hutt
                        b   1957 Dec 9   Auckland

   i   **ISAAC JAMES ARUNDEL LAMBERT**
                        b   1991 Feb 16   Wellington

   ii **THOMAS KAHU ARUNDEL LAMBERT**
                        b   1993 Jun 10   Auckland

Left to right
Back: Graham and Ross
Middle: Nancy, Jack, Alison, Vaughan, Louise and John
Front: Juliet and Anna-Claire

(v) VIVIAN CLENDON

Vivian and Rose had four children, Tom, Arthur, Hazel, and Lorna.

Tom and Sheila have such a large and extended family that they are divided into separate sections, to make the tables easier to follow.

The term "de facto relationship", which occurs in some of the following tables, is in common use in New Zealand. It describes the relationship which exists when a couple live together as man and wife, without being married.

All place names in these tables are in New Zealand, unless otherwise stated.

The first table is of Tom and Sheila and their ten children. The subsequent ten tables contain the issue from each of their children.

I *Thomas Vivian Clendon*

I	**THOMAS VIVIAN CLENDON FICE** of Eastbourne		
	civil engineer	b 1907 Sep 28	Lower Hutt
		d 1997 May 23	Lower Hutt
	m. SHEILA McINTOSH MILNE	m 1930 Jan 11	Lower Hutt
		b 1910 Dec 28	Wellington
1	**VIVIENNE JEAN CLENDON** of Wellington		
		b 1930 Sep 10	Lower Hutt
	m. DENIS WALTER GOODWIN-COLLINGS		
		m 1951 Sep 22	Point Howard
		b 1926 Jan 24	Karori
2	**LESLEY ROSE CLENDON** of Lower Hutt		
		b 1932 Jan 17	Lower Hutt
	m. NEAL PATRICK O'NEILL	m 1955 Feb 12	Lower Hutt
		b 19	
		d 1987 Dec 5	Wellington
3	**JANETTE MARGARET CLENDON** of Eastbourne		
		b 1933 May 15	Lower Hutt
		d 1997 Feb 17	
	m. DENIS O'NEILL	m 1953 Oct 29	Petone
		b 19	
4	**THOMAS MILNE CLENDON** of Auckland		
		b 1935 Apr 28	Lower Hutt
	m. HEATHER VALE SWADLING NZRN		
		m 1960 Jan 30	Wellington
		b 1937 Oct 2	

Thomas Vivian Clendon and Sheila with their ten children.

I   **THOMAS VIVIAN CLENDON FICE** *(cont.)*
    m. SHEILA McINTOSH MILNE

5   **EWAN KEITH CLENDON** BEof Eastbourne
                              b 1936   Nov 3   Lower Hutt

    m. (1st)   m 1961   Dec 2   Tawa, Wellington
    JUDY ELIZABETH GRESHAM
                              b 1941 Mar 27   Gore
                              d 1970   Nov 21   Eastbourne

    m. (2nd)   m 1971   Dec 15   Lower Hutt
    SHEILA MARGARET COMBS NZRN
                              b 1940 May 19   Dunedin

6   **DOUGLAS ROBERT CLENDON** BE of Indonesia
                              b 1942 Sep 25   Lower Hutt

    m. KATHRYN RUTH STIRLING BA (known as Kate)
                              m 1967 Jan 7
                              b 1943 Apr 8

7   **RODERICK JAMES CLENDON** BA of Dannevirke
                              b 1948 Apr 24   Lower Hutt

    m. ANNETTE MARY GRAHAM-SMITH
                              m 1971 May 14
                              b 1947 Apr 6

I   ***THOMAS VIVIAN CLENDON FICE*** *(cont.)*
     m. SHEILA McINTOSH MILNE

8   **SHEILA VAUGHAN CLENDON** (known as Shelley)
                          b 1950   Aug 23   Lower Hutt

     m. ROBERT CHARLES FITNESS
                          m 1970 Mar 28   Eastbourne
                          b 1949 Oct 26   Lower Hutt

9   **DEBORAH VYE CLENDON** BA of Eastbourne
                          b 1952 Oct 20   Lower Hutt

     m. (1st)   m 1972 Jun 17   Eastbourne
     PETER JOHNSTON   b 19
                          divorced 1973

     m. (2nd)   m 1980 Jun 20   Welshpool, Wales
     ROBIN HUGH STUART McCOLL PhD
                          b 1942 Oct 3   Liverpool, England

10   **ELINOR MARY CLENDON** NZCS of Eastbourne
                          b 1955 Aug 30   Lower Hutt

     m. THOMAS SEVILLE   m 1987 Sep 3   London, England
                          b 1949   Apr 12   Manchester, England

1 Vivienne Jean Clendon

Denis and Vivienne have six children. They and their issue are tabulated below. The name of GOODWIN has been dropped from the hyphenated family surname, which is now COLLINGS.

1   **VIVIENNE JEAN CLENDON**
     m. DENIS WALTER GOODWIN-COLLINGS

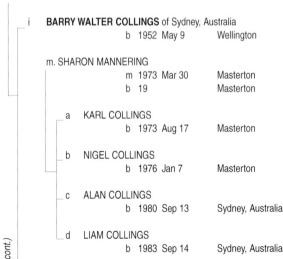

     i   **BARRY WALTER COLLINGS** of Sydney, Australia
                          b 1952 May 9   Wellington

         m. SHARON MANNERING
                          m 1973 Mar 30   Masterton
                          b 19   Masterton

     a   KARL COLLINGS
                          b 1973 Aug 17   Masterton

     b   NIGEL COLLINGS
                          b 1976 Jan 7   Masterton

     c   ALAN COLLINGS
                          b 1980 Sep 13   Sydney, Australia

     d   LIAM COLLINGS
                          b 1983 Sep 14   Sydney, Australia

(cont.)

1 **VIVIENNE JEAN CLENDON** *(cont.)*
   m. *DENIS WALTER GOODWIN-COLLINGS*

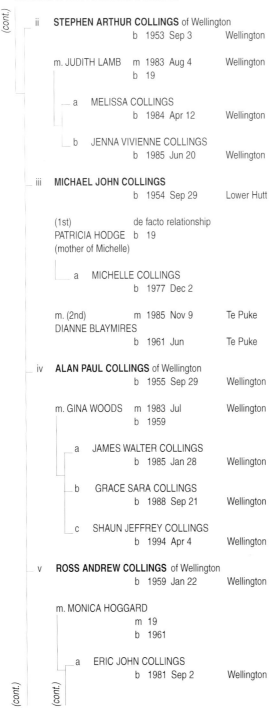

(cont.)

ii **STEPHEN ARTHUR COLLINGS** of Wellington
                          b   1953 Sep 3   Wellington

m. JUDITH LAMB   m 1983 Aug 4   Wellington
                   b   19

        a   MELISSA COLLINGS
                          b   1984 Apr 12   Wellington

        b   JENNA VIVIENNE COLLINGS
                          b   1985 Jun 20   Wellington

iii **MICHAEL JOHN COLLINGS**
                          b   1954 Sep 29   Lower Hutt

(1st)   de facto relationship
PATRICIA HODGE   b   19
(mother of Michelle)

        a   MICHELLE COLLINGS
                          b   1977 Dec 2

m. (2nd)   m 1985 Nov 9   Te Puke
DIANNE BLAYMIRES
                          b   1961 Jun   Te Puke

iv **ALAN PAUL COLLINGS** of Wellington
                          b   1955 Sep 29   Wellington

m. GINA WOODS   m 1983 Jul   Wellington
                   b   1959

        a   JAMES WALTER COLLINGS
                          b   1985 Jan 28   Wellington

        b   GRACE SARA COLLINGS
                          b   1988 Sep 21   Wellington

        c   SHAUN JEFFREY COLLINGS
                          b   1994 Apr 4   Wellington

v **ROSS ANDREW COLLINGS** of Wellington
                          b   1959 Jan 22   Wellington

m. MONICA HOGGARD
                          m 19
                          b   1961

        a   ERIC JOHN COLLINGS
                          b   1981 Sep 2   Wellington

(cont.)   *(cont.)*

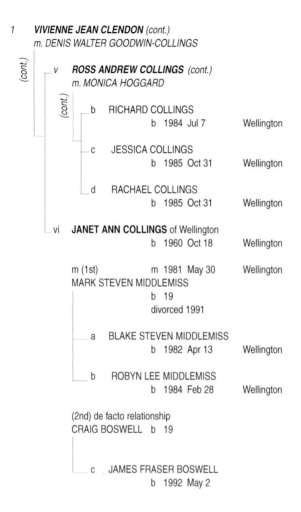

1 **VIVIENNE JEAN CLENDON** *(cont.)*
   m. DENIS WALTER GOODWIN-COLLINGS

(cont.)

v **ROSS ANDREW COLLINGS** *(cont.)*
   m. MONICA HOGGARD

(cont.)

   b RICHARD COLLINGS
        b 1984 Jul 7   Wellington

   c JESSICA COLLINGS
        b 1985 Oct 31   Wellington

   d RACHAEL COLLINGS
        b 1985 Oct 31   Wellington

vi **JANET ANN COLLINGS** of Wellington
        b 1960 Oct 18   Wellington

m (1st)   m 1981 May 30   Wellington
MARK STEVEN MIDDLEMISS
        b 19
        divorced 1991

   a BLAKE STEVEN MIDDLEMISS
        b 1982 Apr 13   Wellington

   b ROBYN LEE MIDDLEMISS
        b 1984 Feb 28   Wellington

(2nd) de facto relationship
CRAIG BOSWELL b 19

   c JAMES FRASER BOSWELL
        b 1992 May 2

2 Lesley Rose Clendon

Neal and Lesley O'Neill have six children. They and their issue are tabulated below.

2 **LESLEY ROSE CLENDON**
   m. NEAL PATRICK O'NEILL

(cont.)

i **KATHERINE THERESE MARY O'NEILL** of Eastbourne
        b 1955 Dec 27   Lower Hutt

m. ADRIAN MACNEE
        m 1981 Nov 7   Eastbourne
        b 19

   a JASON MACNEE
        b 1986 Apr 1   Lower Hutt

   b DANIELLE MACNEE
        b 1987 Aug 22   Eastbourne

2 **LESLEY ROSE CLENDON**
   m. NEAL PATRICK O'NEILL (cont.)

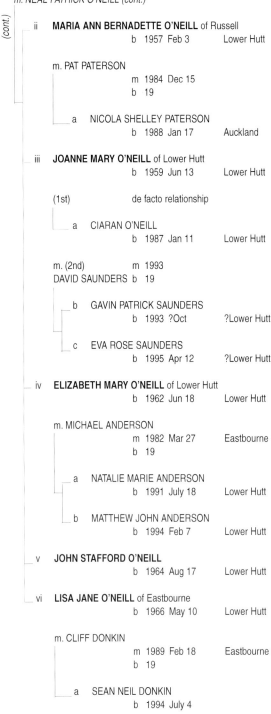

(cont.)

ii **MARIA ANN BERNADETTE O'NEILL** of Russell
                              b 1957 Feb 3   Lower Hutt

    m. PAT PATERSON
                        m 1984 Dec 15
                        b 19

         a   NICOLA SHELLEY PATERSON
                              b 1988 Jan 17   Auckland

iii **JOANNE MARY O'NEILL** of Lower Hutt
                              b 1959 Jun 13   Lower Hutt

    (1st)   de facto relationship

         a   CIARAN O'NEILL
                              b 1987 Jan 11   Lower Hutt

    m. (2nd)   m 1993
    DAVID SAUNDERS b 19

         b   GAVIN PATRICK SAUNDERS
                              b 1993 ?Oct   ?Lower Hutt

         c   EVA ROSE SAUNDERS
                              b 1995 Apr 12   ?Lower Hutt

iv **ELIZABETH MARY O'NEILL** of Lower Hutt
                              b 1962 Jun 18   Lower Hutt

    m. MICHAEL ANDERSON
                        m 1982 Mar 27   Eastbourne
                        b 19

         a   NATALIE MARIE ANDERSON
                              b 1991 July 18   Lower Hutt

         b   MATTHEW JOHN ANDERSON
                              b 1994 Feb 7   Lower Hutt

v   **JOHN STAFFORD O'NEILL**
                              b 1964 Aug 17   Lower Hutt

vi **LISA JANE O'NEILL** of Eastbourne
                              b 1966 May 10   Lower Hutt

    m. CLIFF DONKIN
                        m 1989 Feb 18   Eastbourne
                        b 19

         a   SEAN NEIL DONKIN
                              b 1994 July 4

3 Janette Margaret Clendon

Denis and Janette O'Neill had two children. They and their issue are tabulated below.

3   **JANETTE MARGARET CLENDON**
     m. DENIS O'NEILL

    i   **SHERI O'NEILL** of ?Tinopai
                           b   1955 May 24

        m. (1st)   m   1973
        DWIGHT DWAGG   b   19   Canada
        marriage dissolved

        a   DAEL DAGG
                           b   1973 July 14

        b   MELODY DAGG
                           b   1975 Mar 20

        c   HOLLY DAGG
                           b   1978 Mar 14

        (2nd)   de facto relationship
        MIKE COLONNA   b   19
        (father of Vittoria and Briget)

        d   VITTORIA O'NEILL
                           b   1982 Apr 30   Tinopai

        e   BRIGET O'NEILL
                           b   1983 Aug 17   Tinopai

        m. (3rd)   m. 1996 Apr 6   ?Tinopai
        WILLIAM SEDDON (Bill)
        (father of Jennifer) b   1957 Jan 16

        f   JENNIFER SEDDON
                           b   1995 Mar 3

   ii   **STACEY LEE O'NEILL** of Lower Hutt
                           b   1956 Nov 21

        m. (1st)   m 1981 Jan 15   England
        TERRY WATERHOUSE
                           b   19
                           divorced 1991

        a   HAMISH EWAN WATERHOUSE
                           b   1982 Oct 29   Wellington

        b   DYLAN WATERHOUSE
                           b   1985 Sep 29

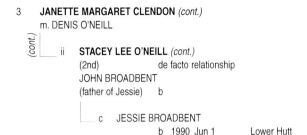

3   **JANETTE MARGARET CLENDON** *(cont.)*
m. DENIS O'NEILL

(cont.)

ii   **STACEY LEE O'NEILL** *(cont.)*
(2nd)   de facto relationship
JOHN BROADBENT
(father of Jessie)   b

c   JESSIE BROADBENT
b   1990 Jun 1   Lower Hutt

4 *Thomas Milne Clendon*

Thomas and Heather Clendon had four children.

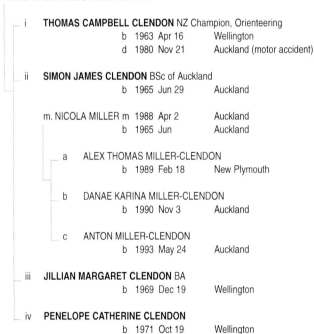

4   **THOMAS MILNE CLENDON**
m. HEATHER VALE SWADLING NZRN

i   **THOMAS CAMPBELL CLENDON** NZ Champion, Orienteering
b   1963 Apr 16   Wellington
d   1980 Nov 21   Auckland (motor accident)

ii   **SIMON JAMES CLENDON** BSc of Auckland
b   1965 Jun 29   Auckland

m. NICOLA MILLER m 1988 Apr 2   Auckland
b   1965 Jun   Auckland

a   ALEX THOMAS MILLER-CLENDON
b   1989 Feb 18   New Plymouth

b   DANAE KARINA MILLER-CLENDON
b   1990 Nov 3   Auckland

c   ANTON MILLER-CLENDON
b   1993 May 24   Auckland

iii   **JILLIAN MARGARET CLENDON** BA
b   1969 Dec 19   Wellington

iv   **PENELOPE CATHERINE CLENDON**
b   1971 Oct 19   Wellington

5 Ewan Keith Clendon

Ewan has nine children. His first wife, Judy, who died in 1970, was the mother the first three. In 1971, he married Sheila, by whom he had a further six. They and their issue are tabulated below.

5   **EWAN KEITH CLENDON**
      m. (1st) JUDY ELIZABETH GRESHAM

    i   **JEFFREY EWAN CLENDON** BE of Christchurch
                      b 1962 Jun 30   Lower Hutt

        m. BARBARA WILLIAMSON
                      m 1984 Feb 11   Wellington

          a   ALHANA CLENDON
                      b 1987 Nov 5   Christchurch

          b   JULIA CLENDON
                      b 1991 Mar 28   Christchurch

          c   GRACE CLENDON
                      b 1993 Nov 11   Christchurch

    ii   **FIONA MARGARET CLENDON** MB ChB, of Dunedin
                      b 1963 Sep 17   Lower Hutt

        m. ROBERT SMILLIE
                      m 1987   Eastbourne
                      b 19

          a   MATTHEW WILLIAM SMILLIE
                      b 1987 Aug 23   Dunedin

    iii **DIANA ROSE CLENDON**
                      b 1965 Nov 1   Lower Hutt

    iv **KATE ELIZABETH CLENDON**
                      b 1972 Jul 14   Lower Hutt

    v   **JAMES DOUGLAS CLENDON**
                      b 1974 Jul 10   Lower Hutt

    vi **DANIEL GEORGE CLENDON**
                      b 1976 Jun 21   Lower Hutt

    vii **NICHOLAS KEITH CLENDON**
                      b 1977 Dec 22   Lower Hutt

    viii **BEN ALFRED CLENDON**
                      b 1980 Jul 11   Lower Hutt

    ix **EDWARD JOHN CLENDON**
                      b 1983 Mar 9   Lower Hutt

6 Douglas Robert Clendon

Douglas and Kate have two children.

6   **DOUGLAS ROBERT CLENDON** BE of Indonesia
     m. KATHRYN RUTH STIRLING BA (known as Kate)

    i   **INDRA SARI** (by adoption)
                  b   1975 Jan 31   Jogjokarta, Java

    ii   **ARIFAH SARI** (by adoption)
                  b   1977 Nov 2   Jogjokarta, Java

7 Roderick James Clendon

Roderick and Annette have two children.

7   **RODERICK JAMES CLENDON** BA of Dannevirke
     m. ANNETTE MARY GRAHAM-SMITH

    i   **GENE MICHAEL CLENDON**
                  b   1971 Oct 28   Dannevirke
          m. JOANNE HALL   m   1995 Nov 18
                  b   19

    ii   **ELLANA TRACEY CLENDON**
                  b   1976 Feb 10   Dannevirke

8 Sheila Vaughan Clendon

Robert and Shelley have four children

8   **SHEILA VAUGHAN CLENDON** (known as Shelley)
     m. ROBERT CHARLES FITNESS

    i   **JODENE ELIZABETH FITNESS** BSc
                  b   1972 Oct 3   Petone

    ii   **KELLY MARIE FITNESS**
                  b   1974 Dec 5   Lower Hutt

    iii **JEREMY ALLAN FITNESS**
                  b   1978 Jun 12   Lower Hutt

    iv **ELEANOR SHANNON FITNESS**
                  b   1985 Aug 9   Lower Hutt

9 Deborah Vye Clendon

Robin and Deborah have three children.

9   **DEBORAH VYE CLENDON**
     m. (2nd) ROBIN HUGH STUART McCOLL PhD

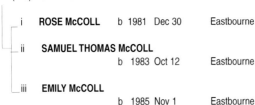

	i	**ROSE McCOLL**	b 1981 Dec 30	Eastbourne
	ii	**SAMUEL THOMAS McCOLL**	b 1983 Oct 12	Eastbourne
	iii	**EMILY McCOLL**	b 1985 Nov 1	Eastbourne

10 Elinor Mary Clendon

Thomas and Elinor have two children.

10   **ELINOR MARY CLENDON** NZCS of Eastbourne
     m. THOMAS SEVILLE

	i	**HARRY JAMES SEVILLE**	b 1988 Nov 5	Lower Hutt
	ii	**SARAH JEAN SEVILLE**	b 1990 Nov 9	Lower Hutt

II Arthur Cooper Clendon

This table covers Arthur and Joyce, their three children, and subsequent issue.

II   **ARTHUR COOPER CLENDON** of Lower Hutt, civil servant

	b	1908 Sep 29	Lower Hutt
	d	1995 Aug 4	Lower Hutt

m. DORIS JOYCE HAMILTON-OLNEY (Joyce)

	m	1937 Mar	Wellington
	b	1914 Jun 4	Wellington
	d	1983 Sep 14	Lower Hutt

Arthur and Joyce Clendon with their daughter Jane
and the Nixon children.

1   **ANNE MARY CLENDON** of Eastbourne
                          b   1940 July 2   Lower Hutt

m. BRUCE WILLIAM JOHNSTON TREEBY BSc Nat Dip AE Dip AE Dip A
                          m   1961 Feb 25   Taita, Lower Hutt
                          b   1936 Dec 11   Invercargill

    i   **AMANDA JEAN TREEBY**
                          b   1968 May 25   Lower Hutt

       m. WITEMARA TANIORA RAKETE (father of Tiana & Wikitoria)
                          m   1996 Feb 17   Lower Hutt
                          b   1965 May 7   Whangarei

      a   TIANA KIMIORA RAKETE
                          b   1987 Aug 4   Lower Hutt

      b   WIKITORIA HURIANA RAKETE
                          b   1994 Feb 7   Whangarei

   ii   **VICTORIA ANN JOHNSTON TREEBY** BA
                          b   1970 July 28   Lower Hutt

  iii   **CAMERON BRUCE WILLIAM TREEBY** Dip ID
                          b   1972 Oct 28   Lower Hutt

2   **KELSEY JOYCE CLENDON** of Paekakariki
     (surname now reverted to Clendon)
                              b   1942 Nov 24   Lower Hutt

     m. (1st)   m   1964
     JOHN SIDNEY ADAM   b   19

        i   **DAVID JOHN CLENDON-ADAM** of Sydney, Australia
                              b   1965 Mar 17

       ii   **ROBERT ARTHUR CLENDON** (dropped surname 'Adam')
                              b   1967 Dec 26

      iii   **JANE AMANDA CLENDON** of London, England (also dropped the 'Adam')
                              b   1967 Dec 26

             m. LEE DAVIS   m   1992 Oct 24   Marylebone, London, England
                                b   19   London, England

     (2nd)   de facto relationship
     PETER NORTH   b   19

3   **JANE CHRISTINE CLENDON** Dip Libr BA MA PhD, of Eastbourne
                              b   1951 Sep 26   Lower Hutt

     JULIAN LEICESTER LAKE BA (known as Bill)
                              de facto relationship
                              b   1947 Aug 30   Canberra, Australia

III Hazel Clendon

III   **HAZEL CLENDON** of Lower Hutt, shorthand typist
                              b   1913 Oct 30   Lower Hutt

Hazel Clendon

IV Lorna Christine Clendon

IV   **LORNA CHRISTINE CLENDON** BA of Lower Hutt (adopted a first name, HELEN)
school teacher   b 1923 Jun 16   Lower Hutt
                     d 1982 Nov 4   Lower Hutt

m. JOHN ESMONDE ARTHUR NIXON BSc(Eng) MIEE ACGI, of Lower Hutt
University lecturer   m 1953 Mar 28   Colchester, England
                     b 1915 Mar 14   Bristol, England
(changed his christian name by deed poll to ROBERT in 1983)

Lorna Clendon
and
Esmonde Nixon

1   **PAUL JOHN NIXON** of Eastbourne
                     b 1955 Mch 7   Braintree, England

    m. JULIE ROBERTSON   m 1991 Apr 27   Eastbourne
                     b 1958 Nov 21

       i   **JOSHUA NIXON** b 1993 Oct 29   ?Eastbourne

      ii **CHRISTOPHER NIXON**
                     b 1995 Sep 25   ?Eastbourne

2   **BRIDGET ROSE NIXON** of Cirencester, England (adopted a first name, EMMA)
                     b 1960 Dec 25   Lower Hutt

3   **KATHERINE HAZEL NIXON** (adopted a first name, LOUISE)
                     b 1964 Sep 22   Eastbourne

ON THE TRAIL OF JAMES REDDY CLENDON

BY ROSS CLENDON

In March 1994 I wrote a letter, reporting my discoveries about James Reddy Clendon, to Bette Edwards in Lenox, Massachusetts, USA, and also sent a copy to Tom Clendon in St Albans, England. When this book came to be written, Ryland asked me if he could include it. I readily agreed. Apart from a few minor editorial changes it is that letter which now follows.

Part 4 concludes with genealogical tables, showing all James Reddy Clendon's known descendents. These tables have been compiled by Philippa Holmes, a great great granddaughter of James Reddy, who has kindly made them available for publication.

BACKGROUND

As was mentioned in our 1993 Christmas newsletter, our visit home in December started with a short holiday in the Bay of Islands – that cradle of Clendon history and civilization in New Zealand. This isn't an attempt to inflict a blow-by-blow account of how four Clendons – aged 42, 41, 8 and 8 – enjoyed six days of sun, sea and sand, and other touristy activities besides, although this we certainly did. It was for me, however, and for Carol and Sammy and Thomas as well, our first visit to anywhere in New Zealand north of Auckland. It was probably therefore inevitable from the start that this short foray to the far north would end up becoming a search for the ghost of James Reddy Clendon. For me, it has also somewhat unexpectedly provided an incentive to reflect on ancestral roots generally. These are a few jottings about discoveries made during those six days last December and some reflections based on what I learnt then and what I have found out since.

Much – perhaps most – of what follows will not be new to you. In passing it on to you, therefore, I feel distinctly like the little drummer boy of Christmas carol fame – very much in awe of the Three Wise Men and only too well aware that I have "no gift to bring". Carrying that analogy a bit further, the nativity in this case could be considered the forthcoming birth of the third edition of the Clendon family tree which I know Ryland is working on with assistance from you both. I regard the three of you – Bette Edwards, Tom Clendon and Tom's father, Ryland – as the worldwide guardians of the Clendon family tree and of Clendon family lore generally – something for which Clendons present and future in New Zealand should be grateful, if not a little shamefaced.

This little drummer boy does in fact have one small nugget to offer – a letter, or rather a copy of a letter, which I came across in the Russell Museum. It is a letter written to Tom's great-great-great-great-grandmother (my great-great-great-grandmother) and was delivered to her via her nephew and son-in-law, Bette's great-great-grandfather. I came across the letter on the second day of our trip – a providential find that turned what would probably have been just a straightforward vacation into one with much more enduring memories. The letter, written from the Bay of Islands by James Reddy Clendon in 1848, is, with its dejected and defeatist tone, so much at variance with the image of James Reddy Clendon – prominent ship owner, merchant, consul and magistrate – that I and New Zealand's history-reading public have grown up with that it provided a spur to learn more. In doing so, I have not just learnt more than I knew before about James Reddy himself, but I think I have also developed a better understanding of what James Reddy's connection with New Zealand must have meant for those immediate family members he left behind in England. One hundred and sixty-five years after that connection with New Zealand began, it is natural for all us Clendons who have come after, either via direct or lateral lines, to bask in his reflected glory. But at the time those links were being forged, I can now see that New Zealand must have been a continual source of shocks, surprises, losses and disappointments as far as the rest of the family was concerned. But more of all this anon.

There still has not been a book devoted solely to James Reddy Clendon, or even a monograph as far as I am aware. This surprises me, more so now that I have finally made it to New Zealand's far north. Until 1990 the best place to find details of James Reddy's life was in an article on Clendon first published in the 1930s in the Dictionary of New Zealand biography. This same article was reprinted without alteration thirty years later in An encyclopedia of New Zealand. The author was James Rutherford, Professor of History at Auckland University. I know we used to have a copy of the Encyclopedia lying around the house in Lower Hutt when I was growing up although it has been many years since I read the Clendon article; certainly I have not read it since moving to Manila in 1986.

In the 1980s, as part of the build-up to New Zealand's sesquicentennial celebrations – the 150th anniversary of the proclamation of British sovereignty over New Zealand – the New Zealand Government funded a 10-year project to produce a new Dictionary of New Zealand biography (hereinafter "the DNZB"). The first volume covering the period 1769-1869 came out on time in 1990 and includes an entry on Clendon. As it happens, I have that volume in Manila. I have just finished reading the autobiography of Sir Keith Sinclair, New Zealand's foremost historian of recent years, in which the DNZB is described as New Zealand's greatest scholarly achievement. After my recent holiday in New Zealand, I now realize that the entry on Clendon has a number of mistakes, at least insofar as the more personal details of Clendon's family life and finances are concerned. These mistakes are all the more distressing given that the opening words of the DNZB entry are "According to family information . . . ". I know little about the author and can only guess that those family sources are the same ones that Rutherford is known to have spoken to in Northland sixty years ago when researching his article.

II. JAMES REDDY CLENDON – AN INTRODUCTION

Growing up a Clendon in New Zealand, I was aware from a very young age of our illustrious ancestor, James Reddy Clendon. So too were most other

New Zealanders, or at least so in my youthful pride and ignorance I used to think. Certainly, I came to expect that any history book about the days of early settlement in New Zealand would have a reference to James Reddy in the index. I always used to check and was generally not disappointed. Looking back, I am sure that this was one of the principal reasons why I became so interested in history at school.

The salient facts about James Reddy's life were handed down to us children initially not from history books or even family trees but in the traditional way – oral history from our forefathers, which in this case usually meant Dad and Aunty Nancy. We kids absorbed over time that James Reddy was born into a moderately well off Kentish family in 1800. His father, based first in Dover and later in Deal, was a Pilot of the Cinque Ports. James Reddy had far too many brothers and sisters to bother trying to remember them all by name (and, in any event, the only one who seemed to count as far as we were concerned was James' oldest brother, George), and they all sat down for dinner together only once in their lives. He also had many Chitty cousins, the result of intermarrying between the Clendon and Chitty families over two or three generations in ways which as a child I found too complicated to remember. There was a suggestion that James Reddy had been in the Royal Navy at some point, presumably in the late 1810s/early 1820s and perhaps through the influence of a naval relation on his mother's side who was supposed to have been the inspiration for James' unusual middle name. If James did enlist in the Royal Navy, he did not stay for long because by the mid-1820s, if not before, he had become a captain of merchant ships. The family tree (1974 edition) suggests that by the time he first acquired land in New Zealand in December 1830 he "had visited New Zealand several times as a trading master".

The family tree also indicates that his first marriage was to Sarah Hill (date not stated) and that their first child, a son, was born on 18 January 1827 in London. The baby was christened James Stephenson Clendon, and although it has still not been proven, the middle name presumably had some connection with James Reddy's future business partner in New Zealand, Samuel Stephenson. There was subsequently to be a falling out between Clendon and Stephenson for reasons that have never been explained but which I think can now be guessed at (more on this later).

As children we also learnt that the second child of James and Sarah, a daughter named Eliza Chitty Clendon, was born at sea at the entrance to the Hokianga harbour in New Zealand's far northwest. The birth took place on the City of Edinburgh with her father in command. The assumption always was that Mrs. Clendon, after enduring the hardships of a four months' voyage out from England, didn't quite make terra firma in time. The family tree shows the date of birth as 1828? Jan 16.

From 1832 when he moved permanently to New Zealand and settled at Okiato in the Bay of Islands, James Reddy steadily prospered. He owned ships. He acquired land. He fathered more children; by 1839 he and Sarah had had six*. Depending on how one looked at it, he gradually evolved into either a pillar of the community, or a sanctimonious prig. Both the DNZB and the family tree, for instance, mention that in the 1830s he was active in a movement for the prohibition of spirits and publicly drained his own rum casks in the hope that this would encourage sober habits among the riotous lower orders at the Bay.

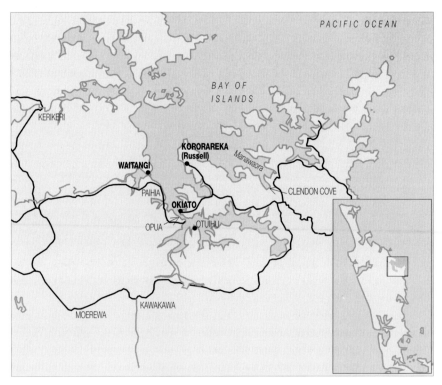

A map of the Bay of Islands

By the end of 1838 Clendon was becoming famous, although perhaps he didn't realize it yet. By 1840 he was really famous, although again he probably didn't know and, indeed, perhaps never lived long enough to appreciate that he was destined to rank forever alongside New Zealand's

---

*   After James and Eliza they had Fanny (b. 9 October 1831), Mary Parson Clendon (b. 11 September 1834), Sarah Ann Clendon (b. 5 May 1837) and Kate Erridge Clendon (b. 13 November 1839). I can find no further mention anywhere of Sarah Ann who presumably died at birth or soon after. Presumably, also, Sarah Ann was named after James Reddy's unmarried sister - the one later mentioned in The Letter.

great and good. Three factors were involved here. First, in October 1838 he became the United States consul in New Zealand. Secondly, in February 1840 he witnessed the signing of the Treaty of Waitangi. And thirdly, in May 1840 he sold his Okiato landholdings (300 acres in all) so that his house could become home for New Zealand's first British Governor and the surrounding land the site of New Zealand's first capital.

Growing up, I had always assumed that James Reddy's elevation to the position of United States consul was somehow related to the fact that his brother George together with other siblings or cousins had ended up emigrating to America. This I now realise was incorrect. He was chosen because he was presumably the best qualified for the job out of a very small field of eligible candidates. Good character would have been only one of several factors relevant to the appointment. In the late 1830s there were only a handful of men in the Bay of Islands who had trading establishments of any size where ships could be docked, caulked, repaired and so on, and also restocked. Clendon not only had such an establishment but it was also ideally situated. When it came time to pick a site for New Zealand's first capital in 1840, Clendon's property won out because it was adjacent to the best anchorage in the whole Bay of Islands.

Clendon was consul for only two years but it must have been a profitable appointment. Between 1839 and 1841 he recorded the arrival of 151 American vessels, mostly whaling ships. Presumably the Clendon establishment at Okiato received the lion's share of the business which accrued from these visiting Americans, particularly when one realises that, among other things, his trading station would have functioned as a post office where visiting Americans could come upon arrival to collect mail and news from home.

Profitable as the appointment must have been, its historical significance lies not in any economic windfall it provided but rather in the fact that New Zealand belonged to no colonial power at the time it was made. This is what brings Clendon's name to the fore in any account of a period in the nation's history when it was by no means clear which country, if any, would end up colonising New Zealand.

Nowadays the ordinary man in the street neither knows nor cares who the first American consul was. Still, Clendon's name surfaces in this connection from time to time, often in unexpected ways. I remember, for instance, that New Zealand had an American ambassador during the Nixon era who donated in a highly publicized fashion a portrait of James Reddy Clendon which when last seen by me held pride of place in the foyer of the American embassy in Wellington alongside a photograph of the reigning President of the day. A President's reign of course is a finite one and so those photographs get changed periodically but I suppose in theory James

James Reddy Clendon
A portrait that hangs in the US Embassy,
Wellington, New Zealand

Reddy's portrait should hang on unmolested.

But I digress. Let's move on to the Treaty of Waitangi which, as I mentioned, is the second reason for Clendon's lasting fame. The Treaty was signed just across the Bay from Clendon's Okiato home on a beautiful summer's day in 1840 on the front lawn of James Busby's house. Busby was Clendon's friend and counterpart, being British Resident at the time. Sir Keith Sinclair in his autobiography describes the Treaty of Waitangi as "the foundation document of our society and our state. It is not a constitution, but it is a sort of constitution". In simple layman's terms, it's a cross between the Magna Carta and the Declaration of Independence. Under the Treaty several hundred Maori chiefs ceded sovereignty to the British crown while at the same time reserving for themselves ownership over the land. New

Zealand thereby formally became a British colony. February 6, the anniversary of the signing, is New Zealand's national day and every year, on Busby's magnificent lawn with its glorious views across the Bay, there is usually some sort of shindig organized. Whenever possible we try to get the Queen to come. We can usually count on her to bring the Royal Yacht which, floodlit and anchored midstream, provides a fitting backdrop for the fireworks which usually end these affairs. I think the last time Her Majesty graced the event with her presence was in 1990 for the 150th birthday celebrations. This year we had to make do with Prince Charles who came accompanied by neither the Britannia nor his wife.

James Reddy Clendon was a witness to the Treaty of Waitangi. Whether he sailed across from Okiato on 6 February 1840 to join the assembled multitude (which included Busby; Queen Victoria's newly arrived envoy and soon-to-be Governor, William Hobson; and approximately fifty chiefs and several hundred assorted hangers-on from the northern Maori tribes) is not known with certainty. The odds I think are that he did. What is sure, however, is that he witnessed the important signature of the great chief Pomare II which was added later in the month. Whether he affixed his attesting signature to the Treaty on 6 February or eleven days later doesn't really matter. The important thing – at least if you're a Clendon – is that it's there.

In March 1840, Clendon agreed to the sale of his Okiato property to provide a home for the new Governor and his entourage, including a contingent of British troops. This is where the family mythology comes back into play. As children, we heard that this estate had been a magnificent place – after all, it must have been if the British Government agreed to pay over £15,000 for it. We heard stories of Mrs. Clendon's rose garden and a house big enough for servants, a governess and a piano and for the gracious entertaining required of a United States consul with a regular stream of ships' captains coming to call. For a year that house must effectively have been the seat of government in New Zealand while all around it the initial steps were being taken to survey the country's first capital which had been named Russell. It is possible today to see plans of the layout of this unbuilt city right down to the naming of the streets. All this was to come to an abrupt halt after only a year. The decision was made to move the capital to Auckland and the Governor departed, temporarily leaving behind some troops who remained living in the barracks down on the beach. On 1 May 1842 the house was totally destroyed by fire and never rebuilt. The name Russell was later transferred to Kororareka, that growing village with the unpronounceable name four miles or so downstream.

Okiata, re-named Old Russell, would in time become simply Okiato again. No traces of its brief fling with glory remained.

About twenty years ago we in Wellington learnt that this sacred land – the site of Mrs. Clendon's rose garden and New Zealand's first capital – had been taken over by a drug baron.

He was variously known as Terry Clark or Terry Sinclair and perhaps other aliases as well, but he achieved international renown as Mr. Asia – a Mr. Escobar of the '70s. He made a profitable business out of using young New Zealand women as couriers who stopped off in Asia on their way to get their O.E. (New Zealandese for "overseas experience") in Europe. He eventually came to a sticky end and died in prison in England. After his arrest and the publicity surrounding his lengthy trial, all sorts of stories came out in the New Zealand press about his Okiato property. He had not quite finished building it but it had already been the scene of wild parties at which Mr. Sinclair/Clark/Asia amused his guests by, among other things, cooking paper money in the microwave to show his audience the hidden metallic strip (microwaves must have been new in those days). There were also articles on such unusual architectural features as a roll-down steel grill at the foot of the hall staircase; this was apparently installed to make it more difficult for the police to spring a surprise night raid on those sleeping upstairs.

The early story of Okiata and its role as New Zealand's first capital is well documented. In the 1940s a well known historian, Ruth Ross, wrote a short book entitled New Zealand's First Capital. Much of what we heard as children from Dad and Nancy must have been based on that work.

As children, although we knew James Reddy had sold Okiato for £15,000, we also knew he didn't get it. Her Britannic Majesty's Government welshed on its contractual obligations to the representative of the United

Plaque on the approach to Mr Asia's House

States. Having vacated the property, Clendon was given only £2250 in cash and even this was in two widely spaced installments, one of £1,000 at the time of sale and the other of £1,250 in early 1842. In lieu of the balance still owing, he was granted in 1842 a 10,000 acre block at Papakura, just south of Auckland. This block, shown as "the Clendon block" on old maps of the area, was virtually worthless then and virtually worthless it must have remained until it passed from Clendon family ownership. Today it is part of Greater Auckland and must be worth many hundreds of millions of dollars. Growing up, there always seemed to me to be an unspoken assumption that we Clendons would now all be rich if only "the family" had hung onto this land. True this may have been in the case of James Reddy's direct descendants. But for those of us who are descended from George, not James, such surmising amounted to no more than wishful thinking.

This brings us to the last and what I always regarded as the best part of the family story. In 1855 James Reddy's first wife died (at the age of 49 and "of apoplexy" I have recently found out). This left James a 55-year old widower with four surviving children (not six as stated in the DNZB) aged between 28 and 16. Within five months of Sarah's death, Clendon had married a half-caste Maori girl by the name of Jane Cochrane, allegedly the daughter of a Maori "princess". The bride was not quite seventeen and a half at the time of this marriage, almost 40 years younger than the groom. There was always an assumption (supported, I now realise, by strong circumstantial evidence) that the turnout of Clendon's grown up children at this second wedding was not high.

After marrying Jane Cochrane, James Reddy proceeded to have eight more children. The first of these, a son, was born eleven months after the marriage and christened George Thomas, George being the name of James' father (and not Gordon as in the DNZB) and Thomas the name of James' grandfather and brother. Thereafter the children came at two yearly intervals for the rest of Clendon's life, the last being born after he had turned 70.

George Thomas, 14 December 1856
Jane, 21 July 1858
Edith Julia, 20 July 1860
William Frederick Ngaropo, 18 October 1862
Marian Takatowi, 16 June 1864
Clara Emily, 14 April 1866
Frances Louisa, 26 July 1869
John Chitty, 26 May 1871

Three years after their marriage, Jane and James moved north, first to Kerikeri, a short distance inland from the Bay of Islands, and two years later to Rawene on the Hokianga which, now that the kauri logs were running out and colonizing efforts were focused far to the south, was turning into an even sleepier backwater than the Bay of Islands itself by that stage had become.

Thus, when Clendon died on 24 October 1872 at the age of 72, he left a widow, then aged 34, with eight young children ranging in age from George, not quite 16, to a baby, not yet 18 months. Jane Clendon was to live on in Rawene until her death 47 years later. She never remarried.

This, then, is the James Reddy Clendon I grew up with. Before our recent holiday, I felt that I knew him fairly well, certainly much better than I knew his parents, siblings, wives or children. On the weekend before we left for New Zealand, I attended the annual Christmas bash hosted for the New Zealanders working at the Asian Development Bank by the New Zealand Government's representative on the ADB's Board. Last December the occasion doubled as a farewell for the Tongan Government's represent-ative, Edwin Nicholas, whose wife, Tepaeru (Pah for short), proved to be a New Zealander of Maori descent. Pah and I got to talking about our respec-tive Christmas plans, and the name of James Reddy came up. To my amaze-ment, my knowledge of James seemed to be more than matched by Pah's knowledge of James' second wife who in family circles had been called not Jane Cochrane or Jane Clendon but Mihi Kererene. Pah informed me that her grandmother, still alive at 96, was a "cousin" of Jane's and remembered her well (Jane died in 1919 at the age of 81). Pah knew nothing of Jane's husband, James Clendon, apart from the fact that he was an "American". This chance meeting was a salutary reminder that no man is an island, and that our family's tendency to concentrate the spotlight on James Reddy perhaps constitutes an injustice to the rest of the extended Clendon clan. My meeting with Pah did, however, seem an auspicious way to start our vacation. Driving home that night, I marvelled that there is a woman alive today in New Zealand whose cousin's husband grew to manhood during the reign of George III and learnt the art of sailing in the English Channel when Napoleon and his armies still held sway over most of Europe.

CLENDON'S HOUSES

During the 40 years he spent in New Zealand, James Reddy built four (possibly five) houses, three of which are still standing. The first was the one at Okiato. Next were the houses at Manawaora (Clendon Cove) and Kororareka (renamed Russell around 1846) which still survive, though much altered from their original appearance. There must have been another house at Kerikeri where Clendon lived in around 1858-1861 although it has not survived. Finally there is the house at Rawene on the Hokianga where Clendon spent the last years of his life. This is the house that was acquired from Clendon descendants in 1972 by the Historic Places Trust and is now open to the public. During our six days in the Bay of Islands we based ourselves throughout at Paihia, now the tourist hub of the area. Our search for Clendon involved a pilgrimage around these various sites, with one or two deviations on the side. If you are still with me up to this point but are now afraid of getting lost, I refer you to the map on page 158.

House No. 1 – Okiato

We visited Okiato on our first morning in the Bay of Islands. It is a sleepy little promontory of a hundred or so houses, no shops, no school. Full of holiday homes and retired people I suspect. It must be six or seven miles from the outer entrance to the Bay. The Bay of Islands, as the map should help make clear, is really a harbour with a total coastline (including the various islands) of approximately 500 miles. Captain James Cook on his epic voyage of discovery in 1769 "discovered" the Bay, which was heavily populated with Maori villages or 'pas' at the time, and it was he who named it the Bay of Islands. There is evidence that Cook sailed up as far as Okiato in a ship's boat lowered from the Endeavour.

We quickly found Mr. Asia's house. It lies at the end of the promontory on several acres of unkempt land with beautiful views in all directions. Across the water several hundred yards to the south and connected by a car ferry is Opua, almost as small and sleepy as Okiato but today probably the most popular yacht anchorage in the region. Many of the yachts are large oceangoing vessels, which, so I was informed by our motel keeper, are coming down each year in ever increasing numbers from various South Pacific islands in order to find a safe haven during the hurricane season.

Mr. Asia's house was large and ugly. It has never been lived in, nor has it been properly maintained. The microwave has long since been ripped out as has almost everything else of value. The grilled gate over the stairs, however, remains. There is a caretaker's cottage in the grounds inhabited by tenants who had never heard of Mrs. Clendon or her rose garden. We took a photo or two and drove on into Russell for lunch.

House No. 3 (chronologically speaking) –
the Clendon Bungalow at Russell (formerly Kororareka)

Russell has the air of a town resistant to change. Unlike booming Paihia across the Bay with its numerous hotels, motels and trendy tourist shops,

Russell slumbers on in a nineteenth century daze. This is the essence of its appeal. Tourists are today its lifeblood but one senses that the local definition of a well-behaved tourist is one who visits and spends but does not stay. One morning we awoke to find a glistening cruise liner anchored in the Bay with lighters buzzing to and fro ferrying passengers (predominantly American women of indeterminate age) to shore for the day. By evening they were all safely back where they belonged and during the night the liner sailed away. This, one suspects, is how Russellites would prefer us all to behave.

This modern air of peace and tranquility belies a very different past. Around the time Clendon brought his young family to settle in the Bay of Islands, Russell, or Kororareka as it was then called, was already well known for degradation and vice. By 1840 it had a world-wide reputation as the "hellhole of the Pacific" – a title which features in many contemporary journals. For sailors ashore "on liberty" after months at sea, tastes tended to be fairly basic: grog, women and perhaps a bit of brawling on the side. With no effective system of law and order, there was usually little captains could do about misbehaviour on shore except put to sea again as soon as possible. By 1840 it is estimated that Kororareka was supporting five hotels, fifty grogshops and many brothels. All this for a full-time population of around only 500-600.

There was no brawling on the beach the day we visited. In fact the town was awash with nuns and black-garbed Catholic clerics who had converged on Russell for the official reopening of Pompallier House. This building, after several years of restoration work, is now the showcase property of the Historic Places Trust in Northland. Built in 1839 by the Marist order, it belonged for several decades to the Catholic Church and then became a home in which some of Samuel Stephenson's descendants lived for many years.

Next door to Pompallier House right on the beachfront is the Clendon Bungalow. It too is now owned by the National Trust but not yet open to the public (and with no immediate plans in that direction). Those involved in the restoration and now the running of Pompallier House are living in it. Built in the 1850s, this house was the one which we had been brought up to understand was gifted by James to his daughter Fanny upon her marriage to Frank Gould. The marriage took place in 1853. Gould used the house to run a boys' school and boarding establishment. I suspect that the whole story is more complicated than this and am not sure when, if ever, Clendon himself lived in this house. Apparently most of the property's original features, outside as well as in, have long since disappeared which presumably explains why no one seems in any hurry to open the house to the general public.

Pompallier House proved to be of much more interest than the Clendon place next door. The Marist brothers had operated a printing press, a tannery and a bindery out of the premises, and these activities have all been revived. The attic floor, however, has been left bare, except for a couple of tables on which copies of Louisa Worsfold's unpublished Social History of Russell have been placed. Worsfold moved into Pompallier House as a young girl in the 1870s or 1880s. From her attic bedroom she would occasionally be awoken by flapping sails in the night as another visiting sailing ship dropped anchor in the bay. All this is graphically recounted, as are numerous tales, many of them hearsay, about Russell's former citizens. These, then, are the reminiscences of an old Russell identity written relatively late in her life. Although Worsfold was only born in the year Clendon died, she has much to say about him and about Samuel Stephenson too. The portraits that emerge are not particularly flattering to either man. Consideration is being given to publishing this scurrilous yet entertaining work.

Diversion 1 – Christ Church, Russell

On the following day, being the Sunday before Christmas, we decided to return to Russell for the morning service at Christ Church. In the days when Clendon was resident in the Bay, spiritual nourishment came from three different quarters – the Church Missionary Society (CMS) at Paihia where the mission and its church were run by the Williams brothers, Henry and William; the French Marist brothers at Korarareka (from 1839); or Christ Church, an Anglican church erected under the auspices of the CMS and dating from 1835.

Christ Church, built of white-painted kauri weatherboards with a high pitched roof, is small but charming without, light and peaceful within. During the first twenty years of the church's existence, Clendon family involvement must have been strong. Among the papers at Rawene, I discovered evidence that before the end of November 1834 Clendon had donated £10.00 to the church building fund, the largest individual contribution given in the seven years the subscription list was open. Three of Clendon's children – Eliza, Fanny and James – were presumably married there; at Rawene I recall reading details concerning one of those marriages, at which James Busby was among the guests.

Clendon's son-in-law, Frank Gould, in addition to running the boys' school at the Clendon Bungalow, was ordained as a Deacon in the Kororareka district in 1852. For his combined preaching and teaching services he was paid 4.00 per month which helps put that 10.00 contribution twenty years earlier into perspective.

One Clendon wedding which did not take place in Christ Church was that of James and Jane Cochrane in January 1856. Jane was an out-of-town girl being from the Hokianga, so Christ Church ought to have been the preferred venue for the marriage service. Instead, James and his bride sailed across to Paihia where they married in the mission church. Had they insisted on using Christ Church, the cooperation of the Reverend Frank Gould would have been required. Gould's reaction to the wedding (and to acquiring a new step-mother-in-law seven years younger than his wife) can be gauged from the following letter which he wrote to Archdeacon Abraham on 28 March 1856:

> My dear Archdeacon,
>
> I am very desirous to leave Kororareka, if it be possible, circumstances have lately occurred, of a family nature certainly, but still bearing so much on my position here as a Minister, that will I think make it advisable for the interest of the church – I have communicated with Archdeacon Henry Williams to whom the case is known, & he has given it as his opinion that it would be the best plan for me to be removed. Mr. St. Hill is acquainted with most of the particulars of the circumstances alluded to. You will most probably have heard of the connexion lately formed by Mr. Clendon, the father of Mrs. Gould, & I think that, should you feel disposed to learn the particulars from Mr. St. Hill, you will yourself approve my present course.

Frank Gould had to wait four years before his wish to be removed from Russell was granted. By the time the Goulds moved south, James and Sarah had already moved to Kerikeri so presumably the 'family reasons' for the shift were less compelling then than they were felt to be immediately after the marriage.

In addition to bearing witness to family festivities and feuds, Christ Church also saw the funerals of at least two Clendons. Buried side by side in the churchyard are James' first wife, Sarah, and his first child and namesake, James Stephenson Clendon*. A few feet away is the Stephenson family plot where Samuel Stephenson is buried†. These two families, in life once so close but then estranged, have been reunited in death. In years to come the monuments marking these graves will share the shade of a nearby sapling, planted by New Zealand's current Prime Minister, James Bolger, to commemorate the fact that this is New Zealand's oldest surviving church.

---

*   James Stephenson Clendon became a Magistrate and died in 1899 at the age of 72.
†   Samuel Stephenson out-lived James Reddy Clendon by 13 years, dying in 1885.

Diversion 2 – Russell Museum

Those who believe that God rewards good deeds will be gratified to learn that taking myself and my family to church that Sunday produced immediate results. Over tea and mince pies in the church hall after the service I enquired whether there was any acknowledged expert on local history among the congregation. I was thereupon introduced to the Deaconess, Heather Lindauer, who proved to have a second job as curator of the Russell Museum (formerly the Captain Cook Memorial Museum). Hearing of my interest in James Reddy, she kindly offered to open up her office there and then notwithstanding the hour and the day. So, having despatched the rest of the family to the waterfront verandah of the Duke of Marlborough (est. 1827) for what proved to be a very long pre-luncheon drink, I proceeded to spend a most enjoyable couple of hours ensconced with Mrs. Lindauer at the Museum.

I had visited the Museum a few minutes before closing the previous afternoon and made a lightning raid on the bookshop. Among my purchases were the following:

- A Most Noble Anchorage, subtitled 'A story of Russell and the Bay of Islands', written by Marie King and first published in 1992 by the Northland Historical Publications Society. Miss King had Mrs. Lindauer's job at the Russell Museum for many years, and the book has rightly been described in the foreword written by Jack Lee (of DNZB fame) as not a formal history but rather a folk-history of the author's homeplace. Its 210 pages, complete with the obligatory picture of Clendon – the same one as is in the family tree and at the American Embassy – made for engaging background reading while we were in the area, and since getting back to Manila as well. The book goes well on a coffee table. Its treatment of Clendon's early life, however, cannot be relied upon, in particular the author's claim that when he bought land at Okiato in 1830, "he had been back and forth to New Zealand for about 25 years and had spent his early married years in Port Jackson".

- Samuel Stephenson – Pioneer Merchant of Russell 1804 – 1885 by N.G. Stephenson and A.B. Stephenson, printed 1993 (second edition) – this is an excellent example of a family monograph and is written by two of Stephenson's descendants. There are many references to Clendon although the links between the Clendon and Stephenson families in England in the period before 1832 remain unclear. As a lesson to your goodselves, the work provides evidence that the best history writing may require distance as well as detachment: Dr. N.G. Stephenson's address is 17 Hamilton Close, Epsom, Surrey, KT19 8RG.

- Russell School; 150 Years of Education in Russell 1839 – 1989, edited by Alister Taylor & Heather Lindauer, published 1989. This was written for the Russell school's 150th Jubilee and, as one would expect, it is a chatty, entertaining work aimed at several generations assembling for a school reunion. There is an article on Fanny Clendon's husband, the Reverend Frank Gould, recounting how he came to New Zealand in 1845 as a member of Governor Grey's staff and then moved to Russell in early 1852.

He was ordained there on 6 June 1852 at the age of 25. He married Fanny Clendon in March the following year.

One book that was not for sale was T.B. Byrne's Wing of the Manakau; Captain Thomas Wing, his life and his harbour, published in Auckland by the author in 1991. Heather Lindauer introduced me to this work during the course of our meeting. Wing, born in 1810, was Samuel Stephenson's cousin and came out to New Zealand in 1832 serving under Clendon as first mate on the Fortitude. For two years after that he served in the same capacity on the Fortitude, then after 1834 became master of the schooner Fanny which Stephenson and Clendon had built in New Zealand. He seemed to be in Clendon's employ off and on throughout the 1830s. Just as I had never heard of Wing before, so too I have never come across Byrne, but his work as a naval historian, based on my quick perusal of this weighty and heavily footnoted volume on Wing, seems impressive and his research very thorough. I brought back with me to Manila half a dozen photocopied pages from Byrne's book. A close study of the complete work and its sources would appear to be essential for anyone contemplating a serious study of Clendon's life.

Heather Lindauer helped out in other ways as well. She quickly set me right on the Okiato site, pointing out that the Mr. Asia house is not the site of the original homestead. There is only one extant picture of Okiato showing how things must have looked in Clendon's day. This is a pencil sketch by Felton Mathew, New Zealand's first surveyor general. It was done in April 1840 and was later included in a volume presented as a farewell gift to Mrs. Hobson when her husband's term as Governor expired. On the highest point of the headland is a tall flagpole flying the Union Jack. In Clendon's day it would have been the Stars and Stripes. Otherwise the estate looks just as it must have done on the day James and Sarah left it.

I know that Ruth Ross' book contains all the details right down to the location of the rose garden. However, based just on the picture and on a brief description I came across in the Rawene house, it is clear that this was a substantial establishment. The house, built on an elevated site on the more sheltered northern side of the Okiato promontory, had ten rooms not including outhouses. Verandahs on what appear to be three sides looked out over surrounding lawn and garden and then out across the bay. Below the house spread along the beachfront were a large store of three floors and a smaller store of two floors, two timber cottages, and a blacksmith's shop. Adjacent to these was a wharf and a jetty 180 feet long in a bay with deep water and complete shelter. A desirable residence, in other words, and in its time probably the biggest and most lavishly appointed in the country.

The cost to Clendon of creating this estate lay not so much in the land itself but rather in the improvements. The land was purchased for not much more than the proverbial beads and trinkets used by settlers in America to acquire land from the Indians. In 1830s New Zealand the hard currency of the day was muskets. Ruth Ross' book will have all the details although I did bring away from the Russell Museum a copy of the 1837 Agreement between Clendon and Pomare whereby Pomare sold 80 more acres to augment the original 220. The concluding portion reads "The whole of which Land I, Pomare and others acknowledge to have sold to the said James Reddy Clendon, his heirs, executors, and administrators and assigns for ever for the consideration of a Double Barrelled Gun, two Casks of Powder, Box of Pipes, Two Great Coats, Ten Spades. In Witness whereof . . . etc." Later in Rawene I saw reference to the original purchase in 1830-32 where the total price for the land was expressed as being under £170 equivalent.

House No. 2 – Clendon Cottage, Manawaora

It was through Heather Lindauer that I found out about Clendon's house at Manawaora. The name meant nothing to me although I did have vague memories of childhood stories about one bay in the Bay of Islands being named after Clendon. Clendon Cove and Manawaora proved to be one and the same. The back cover of Marie King's A Most Noble Anchorage shows an official Government map of 1849 in which present day Manawara (sic) Bay is marked as including some smaller bays and coves including Clendon Cove, with Clendon Point at one end of it. I suspect that Manawaora, like Okiato, may have had new official English names imposed upon it, only to see time and common usage lead eventually to a reassertion of the old. Or maybe the name Clendon Cove is still used. To answer that, one would need to ask a few of the locals. The trouble is, there appear to be very few locals around to ask. New Zealand with its tiny population is full of lonely places but Manawaora struck me as being lonelier than most. It is on the Bay of Islands' seaward coast and there is no settlement between it and

Russell, about 15 miles away on a little-travelled road. We drove out on Sunday afternoon with directions from Heather on how to get there and after she had made a call to the owner, Bob McConnell, to check that it was alright for us to come. Twenty minutes out of Russell we found the letter box and turned down a long drive at the end of which was a sudden glimpse of sea. Mr. McConnell was out on his tractor mowing the lawn (several acres of it) when we arrived. He was in his 70s and had retired there with his wife more than a decade ago. He is now a widower and lives on the property alone. There are two houses side by side. One is Clendon's house, unoccupied but furnished and kept in reserve for when family and guests turn up on holiday. Less than 100 feet away is a new bungalow where McConnell lives.

Both houses look out across what for these purposes I shall call Clendon Cove, a narrow finger of water that turns a corner in the far-off distance so that the open sea is not visible. The cove is framed by gently sloping hills on either side. Like much of the Bay of Islands' shoreline, this particular cove is markedly tidal. When we were there the tide was out so it was necessary to walk several hundred yards across the mudflats to reach the sea.

Mr. McConnell retreated into his house after we arrived but the Clendon house was open and he told us to make ourselves at home. Clendon's cottage proved to be deceptively large. From the front it looks like the small cottage it presumably once was; this is the original part. But at the back, extensions over the years have added on several bedrooms and a big farmhouse kitchen. One of New Zealand's better known artists (Fassett Burnett) was living there in the 1970s and prints of some of his pictures hang on the walls. I suspect that there are many paintings of Clendon Cove in existence, not just because this particular artist lived here but also because this is a truly beautiful spot. The cottage is solid kauri and from the two front rooms the view though the original windows is straight across the unfenced lawn to the mudflats, then the sea framed by green hills with a wide, open sky above. With changes in light and tide and cloud, the colours must change throughout the day, but in essence it is a timeless, unchanging scene. Perfect for a holiday, although, as an estate agent in Pahia later told me, the isolation tends to get to you after a while if you're thinking of settling there for good (sentiments, I might add, which today are still applied by many to New Zealand as a whole).

The peacefulness now associated with Clendon Cove was not always so. When Clendon moved there with his family from Okiato in 1840 there may still have been several Maori settlements in this general area. This had certainly been the case seventy years earlier, a fact to which Heather Lindauer alerted me. There are some dark episodes in the story of early

European contact with New Zealand and Clendon Cove, so Heather told me, is closely connected with one of the worst. When Clendon first came to isolated Manawaora, and perhaps unbeknownst to him, he was far from being the first pakeha (white man) to set foot there.

Three years after Captain Cook's famous first voyage to New Zealand in 1769, a Frenchman, Marion du Fresne, made a landing in the Bay of Islands. His two ships were badly in need of repair and several members of his crew were suffering from scurvy. Du Fresne anchored off Moturua Island on 3 May 1772 and established a hospital and smithy onshore. His second-in-command then rigged up a carpenter's camp in Clendon Cove where kauri spars were to be dressed after being brought down from the ranges above the camp. All went well for over a month and relations with the local Maoris were good. But when a party of seventeen led by du Fresne failed to return to the ships after an outing ashore, a dozen men were sent to look for them. This second group was immediately attacked. One lone survivor managed to make it back to the ships to raise the alarm. More men were promptly despatched to Clendon Cove where all was found to be well. But camp was immediately struck. Before the departing Frenchmen had time to leave, however, some hostile Maoris appeared and imparted the news that du Fresne and their other missing shipmates had been eaten at a cannibal feast. This indeed proved to be true. Immediate reprisals for the twenty-eight dead Frenchmen were carried out at Clendon Cove by the fleeing sailors. Further vengeance was exacted on Moturua Island where the three largest villages were wiped out. The expedition then limped out of the Bay, its vessels unrepaired. Before leaving, the survivors buried a bottle in the sand in classic pirate style with a message claiming New Zealand for France.

According to the DNZB, Clendon owned 3,342 acres at Manawaora. I have no way of checking the veracity of this figure from Manila. According to Heather Lindauer, the local expert on this subject is Murphy Shortland, who manages the farm down the road from McConnell's place. Time ran out, and we never met him. The DNZB also claims that Clendon did not purchase this land – "the Clendon farm" – until 1838. Evidence found by Ruth Ross in the Rawene House seems to indicate that it was purchased at the same time and in the same manner as the Okiato land, i.e. in two installments in 1830 and 1832. Development of the land, however, probably did not begin until the late 1830s. How much land was actually cleared and farmed during Clendon's lifetime is also unclear to me. I saw a reference somewhere to Clendon wanting to raise horses there for the Sydney market. It is not particularly fertile land – nowhere near as good as the land he spurned in South Auckland, for example – but Clendon Cove was home for the entire Clendon family during certain periods after 1840, and in the case of James Stephenson Clendon it became his home on a long-term basis.

When a land titling exercise was carried out in 1860, the title which issued showed J.S. Clendon and one of his sisters as the legal owners. I am not sure when the land eventually passed out of family ownership.*

House No. 1 (Okiato) revisited

Armed with Heather Lindauer's directions and Felton Mathew's sketch, we revisited Okiato late on Sunday afternoon. The actual site of Clendon's house has been made a public reserve and Heather informed me that plans are afoot to have a proper archeological dig carried out in a year or so. Presently there is nothing to suggest that a house was ever there except for a collapsed hole nearby where the well once stood.

There is no longer a rose garden, of course, but there is a norfolk pine at the bottom of the path leading down to the beach. Norfolk pines from Norfolk Island (the most feared of all the Australian convict settlements) must have been fashionable in the 1830s because all the 'best' families seem to have planted one – the Busbys at Waitangi, the Williams at Paihia, the Mairs at Te Wahapu, the Stephensons at Tapeka (to where Samuel withdrew after his break with James in 1836). The Clendons planted one at Okiato and another at Clendon Cove. Now 160 years later they tower like sentinels above their pygmy neighbours, mute reminders of a vanished age.

Impressive as they are to the modern eye, these exotic (i.e. not native) trees also serve as a silent rebuke, a reminder of how much man has altered the landscape of northern New Zealand in the last two centuries, almost always for the worse. The forests which once covered all of Northland were dominated by kauri trees, with many being well over 1,000 years old. Less than 1% (20,000 ha) of this original forest cover is left. The birdlife too has been decimated, and in the past 150 years many species have become extinct. Clendon will forever be associated with the political birth of New Zealand, and rightly so. Easily overlooked in this context, however, is the fact that the arrival of so-called western civilization with Clendon in the vanguard was to spell ecological death in certain specific cases and environmental disaster generally. Certainly the Eden that was the Hokianga in 1829 when Clendon first laid eyes upon it is now no more.

I suspect that the physical changes to the landscape in the Bay of

---

* The family tree makes no mention of Manawaora/Clendon Cove but states that Clendon owned land at Orongo Bay. Orongo, the "round bay", lies between Okiato and Russell and there is a restored building there known locally as the American Consulate. But this was never James Reddy's home and the building post-dates Clendon's period as consul. I have come across no indication that Clendon ever owned land at Orongo Bay.

Islands are much less marked. The high concentration of Maori settlements in the area would have doomed much of the surrounding forest before Europeans arrived. Nevertheless, it is clear that Clendon did his bit to tame and anglicize this wilderness. The author of that sole surviving sketch remarked after his first visit to Okiato in 1840 that "the Clendons have a very pretty comfortable, English looking place. The house is handsomely furnished and is very prettily situated with a nice lawn and paddock green with clover and commands a fine view of the harbour". His wife in her diary noted that Sarah had all the comforts and most of the luxuries of civilized life around her. The house is very neatly finished and seems well furnished. There is a splendid piano by Broadwood in the drawing room, but so woefully out of tune that it is impossible to touch it. We drank tea from splendid china served on a silver salver . . . ".

Unlike Manawaora, Okiato could never have been an isolated and lonely place while the Clendons resided there. We know that Clendon employed on a regular basis a schoolmaster, a carpenter and a boatbuilder, two of these having been brought from England on the Fortitude. Throughout the 1830s, in the course of running their marine store Clendon and Stephenson must have been providing work at different periods for sizeable numbers of carpenters, coopers, blacksmiths and labourers. Samuel Stephenson himself lived at Okiato until 1836 although without any family.* And whenever the Fortitude was in port, its captain (never Clendon himself after 1832) and crew would have been based at Okiato.

In the decade 1831-1840, the number of vessels visiting the Bay of Islands doubled and doubled again to average 118 visits each year. Thus, although Kororareka, New Zealand's first and at this stage still its biggest town, was hardly big by modern standards, it had a relatively large transient population. With about 20 to 30 crew and passengers on each vessel, the Bay was receiving about 3,000 visitors a year at the end of the decade. Many of these visitors presumably found time to call on the Clendons.

Until 1834 British whalers were the major visitors; thereafter the Americans took this honour. American visits increased sharply over the decade from 11 in 1833 to average close to 60 each year from 1836 to 1840. After the American and British whalers came the French – on average 15 of their vessels visited each year by the end of the decade. Whaleships of other nations were never numerous: during the decade before 1840 there were nine visits by Canadian ships, three from Bremen, two from Lisbon, one from Chile and just one, the Tokirau, recorded as whaling from New

---

*   Stephenson anticipated Clendon's second marriage to Jane Cochrane by marrying in 1844 an 18 year old local girl of mixed Maori-pakeha lineage.

Zealand. I have discovered that Clendon and his closest European neighbour, Gilbert Mair who ran the marine store at Te Wahapu, as a joint venture in 1838 purchased the American vessel Independence which had been stranded in the Bay of Islands. She was recommissioned and named Tokirau, a Maori term for the northern reaches of New Zealand. So we can claim that our illustrious ancestor, in addition to being a prominent merchant, American consul etc. etc., was a whaler too.

The fact that there were always plenty of English-speaking neighbours, both permanent and temporary, three or four miles away at Kororareka does not of course mean that Sarah and her growing brood of children frequently availed themselves of such company. On the contrary, they almost certainly did not. It was very noticeable to visitors to the Bay in the 1830s how the respectable segment of the population – the merchants and missionaries – deliberately lived a respectable distance from the unseemly sights and sounds that were daily fare along the Kororareka beach.

If Clendon's neighbours to the north at Kororareka left something to be desired, the situation just to the south was not exactly ideal either. Clendon had bought Okiato from Pomare II, the great Ngapuhi leader and war chief. Pomare lived a few minutes away by boat just beyond Opua at Otuihu and he and Clendon knew each other well and seem to have been good friends. The two men were not dissimilar in age with Pomare probably just a decade or so older. This was the chief who, so the story goes, signed the Treaty of Waitangi on 17 January 1840 on the strength of Clendon's assurances, and then went on to induce several other important chiefs to sign as well.

Pomare was described by the missionaries as "graceful, well proportioned, strong and attractive to women". He had several wives and many children. He put most of his energy during the 1830s into making Otuihu both impregnable and a rival to Kororareka as a centre of attraction for Europeans. He became a major dealer in spirits, several grog shops were established in the pa (the Maori word for fort or village), and he may have possessed his own still. He traded in pork, potatoes and timber, derived profit from the prostitution of the slave women of the pa, and encouraged gambling.

The 1830s were years of frequent inter-tribal warfare in the Bay. On one occasion in 1837 a force of 40 war canoes with 800 men sailed past the beach below Clendon's Okiato house in an unsuccessful attempt to take Otuihu. Pomare had as many as 3,000 warriors under arms, and in that particular year, 1837, he was aided by 131 Europeans living in his pa. Most of these had probably drifted across the Tasman from Australia. Many New Zealanders have a tendency to regard Australia as a nation of former convicts although I concede that this generalization is not always supported by the facts. However, in the case of the 131 Europeans who were among the Clendons' closest neighbours in the 1830s, I think there is a strong probability that many, if not most, were fugitives from the law who had been unavoidably detained in Australia before reaching New Zealand. Whether these neighbours were the sort of people Sarah felt called upon to impress with her best china and silver salver must for the present remain in doubt. Similarly, we can only guess at how much socializing took place between the Clendon and Pomare children. Quite apart from the armed warriors, escaped convicts, slave girls, inebriated ruffians and so on, the Otuihu pa was also famous for its collection of dried human heads (Pomare's uncle having been an acknowledged expert in this area) so Sarah may not have fancied the idea of her impressionable youngsters being let loose in such an environment.

If it was indeed the case that the Clendon children were infrequent visitors at the Otuihu pa, one can only hope for their sake that Mr. Pomare was accustomed to bringing his own children with him when he visited his friend, James Reddy. One of Pomare's sons, Hare, who would have been a contemporary of Clendon's children must have had an engaging personality. As a young man he was taken to England in 1863 as part of a travelling road show along with his pregnant wife. The whole party was introduced to Queen Victoria at Osborne who was so taken with Hare that she offered on the spot to become Godmother to his future child. The child, the first Maori to be born in England, was christened Albert Victor after the Queen's late husband and 'oohed' and 'aahed' over at Windsor by the Queen and her daughters. The value of the Queen's christening gifts exceeded the annual salary of Fanny Clendon's husband. To top it all off, Queen Victoria ensured that Hare and his family returned to New Zealand first class (they had come steerage). All these facts and more can be gleaned from the DNZB.

Okiato has certainly changed since the time of James Reddy and Pomare. Contemporary observers in the 1830s noted that it was common to see ships at anchor along the whole five mile stretch from Kororareka to Otuihu. One of the best vantage points to observe all this would have been Okiato. The views from Okiato are less busy now but still impressive. Until recently the closest habitation to the site of Clendon's house was a holiday house on the flat ground near the beach where the barracks once stood. In the mid-1980s, the area around the Clendon house was sub-divided into eleven sections and since then two new houses have appeared. The bigger of the two occupies the best site on the crest of the rise and has a discrete sign on its letter box reading "Okiato Lodge". I was surprised to learn afterwards from my Paihia estate agent that this is no ordinary home but an exclusive and expensive hotel catering to foreign VIPs seeking privacy and rest. A former Prime Minister of Australia had been a recent guest. I was told that an overnight stay costs NZ$750 (US$400)- approximately ten times what we were paying in Paihia for our two-bedroomed serviced motel. One of the suites is apparently named after James Reddy Clendon.

I have received since my return to Manila a letter from my sales consultant in Paihia informing me that the property originally known as the barracks – water front position, land area of approximately one hectare – may be for sale at around NZ$500,000. As this amount would buy a substantial family home in the best part of Auckland, I have decided not to pursue this further.

House No. 4 – Kerikeri

Kerikeri, citrus capital of New Zealand, is today the biggest town in the Bay of Islands (population circa 1,500). Situated fourteen miles north of Paihia, Kerikeri has become a thriving centre for handicrafts and cottage industries, its equable climate and relaxed lifestyle attracting many creative and artistic residents. It was Clendon's home for a two year period between 1859 and 1861 when he was based there as a circuit magistrate. We spent a day in the vicinity as tourists not aware at that stage of Clendon's earlier involvement with the town. I have since learnt that my brother, John, during a visit to the area in 1982, was informed that Clendon's residence at Kerikeru was in close proximity to the Stone Store but that no trace remains. The Stone Store was built from 1832-36 as a mission storehouse. It is New Zealand's oldest stone building and popular with tourists.

House No. 5 – Clendon House, Rawene

Rawene is approximately eighty miles from Paihia and we made a day trip of it. Eighty miles can make a big difference in New Zealand. Outwardly the Hokianga is not too different from the Bay of Islands – both share the same pleasant weather and easy access to a profusion of outdoor pursuits. But scratch beneath the surface, especially by investigating some of the economic indicators, and it quickly becomes apparent that the Hokianga has suffered as much as anywhere from the savage economic recession in New Zealand over the past several years. The Hokianga is today considered one of the poorest areas in the country. Rawene (with a population of 461 in 1992) is at the end of a long, narrow peninsula on the Hokianga's southern shore. A car ferry departs hourly for North Hokianga but, even so, Rawene has a definite feel of being at the end of the line. Certainly, there is no disputing that it is off the beaten track. But it is the biggest place around and it seemed a pleasant, friendly town – a good place to be poor. I came away from our day there not only more knowledgeable about my Clendon roots, but more sure too about my New Zealand ones.

Clendon House is the biggest tourist attraction in town. However, given Rawene's relative isolation, it draws only a handful of visitors each week. Although Clendon House is the most important of James Reddy Clendon's surviving properties, it is also the one I will mention least. Built in the late 1860s, it was lived in for only a few years by James Reddy before his death in 1872. There is a good guidebook to the house written by Ruth Ross in 1978 and you may both have read it at some stage, especially you, Tom, in view of your parents' visit to Rawene in March 1992. As the guidebook remarks, the dominant personality in the history of Clendon House is not Captain Clendon, the Kentishman who became United States consul and colonial magistrate, but two New Zealanders: Jane Clendon, his second wife, and George Thomas Clendon, their eldest son. Although many of the family treasures which the New Zealand Historic Places Trust purchased with the house were James Reddy's belongings, it was, as Ruth Ross points out, his widow and the eldest son who treasured them. To them is due the credit of keeping home and possessions together for the ultimate enjoyment of all New Zealanders.

Clendon House is indeed a home, not just a house. When the Historic Places Trust purchased the property in 1972 it seems to have been literally stuffed with Clendon family papers, photos and memorabilia. After Ruth

Clendon House, Rawene

Ross had sorted through everything (following in the steps of Professor Rutherford who completed a similar exercise after staying there for a week in 1936), all of the most important items were removed to the Auckland Public Library where they have remained. I have not laid eyes on any of this material although copies of a few items are available for viewing at Clendon House or referred to in notes left at the house by Ruth Ross.

I bought a Visitors' Guide to Hokianga while I was in Rawene. In it James Reddy Clendon is described at least twice as being "a prosperous Bay of Islands merchant" immediately before coming to Rawene. In Rawene Clendon was to become the customs inspector, the registrar of births, deaths and marriages and the resident magistrate, although not necessarily all at the same time or in that order. The same Visitors' Guide also credits Clendon with building "a large elegant house, the first in town with glass windows". I am not sure that large and elegant are words that I would have used (particularly bearing in mind that this was home for a family of ten, plus a governess) but Clendon House certainly has a warm, lived-in feeling about it.

One of the nicest touches about the house is that there are now two visitors books – one for the hoi polloi and another for members of the family (which I was pleased to see has been liberally interpreted as including the extended clan). We now feature four lines from the bottom of page 2. Sue and Ryland's names occupy the same position on page 1 – that's an average of about ten Clendons visiting each year. With one exception, all Clendon visitors to date claim descent from either James Reddy or his brother George. The sole exception was John Clendon Gilbert who visited the house six weeks before we did from Victoria, Australia and indicated that he is a great-great-grandson of James Reddy's sister, Rebecca. This led me to investigate further and I was somewhat amazed to find from the family tree that Rebecca, who became a Mrs. Howard in 1829, ended up in New Zealand too as a result of her husband becoming a postmaster in Canterbury. This is one branch of the family that I cannot ever recall hearing discussed. Nancy and Dad may contest this, but I personally know nothing whatever about any of Rebecca's descendants.

CLENDON'S AUSTRALASIAN VOYAGES

When did Clendon first visit New Zealand? How many round trips between England and New Zealand did he make before finally settling in the Bay of Islands? On the weight on the evidence I have available before me in Manila, the answer to the first question is 2 April 1829, and to the second, one.

In 1826 as master of the Medora Clendon made his first visit from

England to Australia. I am relying on Byrne's book for this. If Byrne's book does not provide the answers to when this vessel arrived and left, the published Shipping Arrivals and Departures for Sydney almost certainly would. My guess is that Clendon was in Port Jackson (Sydney) by March/April 1826 at the latest and was there again in September/October of that year. In between times, the Medora may have been getting refitted somewhere in Sydney harbour but more likely was ranging along the Australian coast assembling a cargo for the return voyage. I consider it unlikely that the Medora got as far as New Zealand. Although this fact is often not appreciated, New Zealand is as far from Australia as England is from Italy and the Tasman Sea which separates New Zealand from Australia can be as rough and dangerous as any in the world. In other words, a trans-Tasman crossing was not one to be taken lightly or quickly. In support of my contention that the Merode probably did not visit New Zealand, the two obvious first ports of call for any ships coming from Australia at that time were the Hokianga harbour on New Zealand's north-western tip and the Bay of Islands on its north-eastern side. The Hokianga is New Zealand's fourth largest harbour but its entrance is narrow and has a treacherous bar. The narrowness of the entrance was the reason for the harbour not being "discovered" until 1819 when a missionary travelling overland from the Bay of Islands eighty or so miles away came upon it. A small missionary and settler presence was established in the Hokianga by the mid-1820s. If the Medora had visited the area in 1826, I believe that in one of the surviving diaries or journals recording the first European contact there this fact would have been recorded.

And what of the Bay of Islands? One of the books I found for sale in the Russell Museum was Bay of Islands Shipping Arrivals and Departures 1803-1840 by Rhys Richards and Jocelyn Chisholm, the Paremata Press, 1992. It begins thus:

The pioneer "Shipping Arrivals and Departures" list was compiled for Sydney from 1788 to 1825 by the late Dr. John Cumpston. At first glance it seemed dry and intimidating, with a cast of thousands and no plot, as indigestible as a telephone book. However on closer acquaintance, by working carefully and using his invaluable indexes, its true worth became apparent. His first "S.A.D." made it possible to extract innumerable sub-plots or sub-themes, such as the course over several decades of a single ship, the career of a captain, the interests of an owner or partnership, or the scope of a trade. Given the paucity of other early material and the capacity of the lists to help cross-check what other fragments remain, it soon became impossible to conceive of writing Australasian maritime history, and indeed, Australasian history before 1840, without frequent recourse to Cumpston's S.A.D. lists.

This S.A.D. list prepared by Richards and Chisholm for the Bay of Islands is the first attempt to bring together from all sources a cumulative and comprehensive list of shipping arrivals and departures at a New Zealand port.

On the strength of the book's opening paragraph, I promptly purchased this Bay of Islands S.A.D. list and secreted it away until after we had left the area. Carol got it for her birthday at the end of December. If something that outwardly is as indigestible as a telephone book does not strike either of you as the most romantic of birthday presents for one's wife, let me explain. Carol and I first met in 1974. Carol was working at New Zealand's premier research library, the Alexander Turnbull Library in Wellington, and I was near the end of the final year of my law degree. Shortly afterwards, I found out that I had an opportunity to do some postgraduate work in the United States. Eager to see and experience the bright lights and big cities of America's northeast, I chose Cornell in Ithaca, New York, not realising until it was too late that Ithaca is small, bucolic and at the most centrally isolated point on the entire eastern seaboard. Still, I ended up thoroughly enjoying the three years I spent there.

Carol's hold on me by the time I left New Zealand in August 1975 had not yet reached the stage of matrimony. Being a resourceful woman, however, she got in touch with Dr. John Cumpston, the self-same gentleman referred to above. Dr. Cumpston, already by then an elderly man, was about to embark on a final expedition to New England on behalf of the Pacific Manuscripts Bureau, an Australian-based organization partly funded by the Turnbull Library. Carol got herself a job as his Girl Friday (and an American work permit to boot). For much of 1976 she travelled throughout the northeast looking for whaling logs to microfilm.

What I came to realise after following Carol's progress along the United States' northeastern coast was how closely New England had been linked to the New Zealand of the 1830s when Kororareka was headquarters of the South Pacific whaling fleet. Whalers based in such places as Edgartown, Nantucket, Salem, New Bedford, Sag Harbor, Plymouth and Newport were likely in that period to be as familiar with Kororareka as with Boston or New York.

One of the fruits of that 1976 expedition and the stream of microfilm reels to the Turnbull Library which resulted from it is the S.A.D. list referred to above. Now one can say with almost complete certainty whether a particular vessel did or did not visit the Bay of Islands between 1803 and 1840. A total of 1575 visits are listed. A visit by the Medora is not among them.

The Medora appears to have departed Sydney in October 1826 and we find Clendon back in England by the end of January 1827. The usual length of a voyage between England and Australia or New Zealand was around four months.

The next we hear of Clendon is as master of the City of Edinburgh. Byrne refers to Clendon as being a part owner of this vessel although I have not seen such a claim made anywhere else. The Byrne claim is footnoted, but again I do not have the page with the footnote on it. I do, however, find this claim somewhat surprising in view of what, through Byrne's book, I came to know of James Reddy's next vessel.

The 366 ton City of Edinburgh sailed from Cork on 23 June 1828 and travelled directly to Sydney with a cargo of 80 female convicts. Clendon's wife and 18 month old son were also on board. The voyage took 142 days, the arrival date in Sydney being 12 November 1828.

Now Clendon could turn his sights to New Zealand for what I believe was the first time. In March 1829 the City of Edinburgh left Sydney with the whole Clendon family still aboard. Its arrival date in Hokianga is recorded as being 2 April 1829. This was not the arrival which coincided with the birth of Clendon's second child, although that child must have been conceived in the Hokianga shortly after the vessel arrived.

For the next five months the City of Edinburgh remained in New Zealand waters. Leaving the Hokianga at the beginning of June it got stuck on the bar at the harbour entrance. For a time it appeared all might be lost. Sarah and the child were lowered over the side and at considerable risk a small boat succeeded in getting them back to dry land. When the ship eventually floated free, it was rudderless so the vessel drifted helplessly over the horizon leaving Sarah uncertain as to its fate. The ship was rescued several days later and taken in tow around the top of New Zealand to the Bay of Islands. Clendon's introduction to his future home appears to have been on a bitterly cold winter's night when, leaving his incapacitated ship far out at the heads, he came in by small boat as far as Paihia where he asked the missionary Henry Williams to organise as many boats as possible to help guide his ship in. Williams' wife, Marianne, has left us a vivid account of that first evening with Clendon. Her journal entry covering that day finishes with the words, ". . . having refreshed the poor captain and his boat's crew, we retired to rest admitting how wonderfully God works in His providence". The City of Edinburgh must have been guided in safely the next day and word was sent overland to Sarah informing her that James was safe.

The City of Edinburgh returned to Sydney around August 1829 but was back in the Bay of Islands at the end of November. For the next twelve months Clendon was engaged in procuring a cargo of kauri spars and timber to take back to England. It was probably during this period, as his ship travelled from harbour to harbour throughout the north in search of kauri, that the Maoris gave him the nickname "Tuatara" after the reptile that links New Zealand to the Mesozoic era (and is now almost extinct), the idea apparently being that Clendon was like a lizard seeking food in holes and crannies.

During these meanderings James Reddy returned to the Hokianga and it was on the occasion of this return visit that Eliza Chitty was born at sea off Hokianga heads on 16 January 1830. The evidence suggests that the vessel was in no hurry to go in, as a Hokianga resident recorded in his diary going on board for dinner a couple of days before Eliza's birth. Clendon had sent an overland messenger to the Hokianga before setting sail from the Bay of Islands so perhaps, with the harrowing experience of their last crossing of the bar still fresh in their minds, they considered it prudent to wait offshore until a pilot boat appeared from the inner harbour settlement at Rawene, then named Herd's Point. Rawene is situated several miles from the harbour entrance.

Eliza Chitty was not the first white child born in New Zealand (1815 seems to be the earliest date in that respect) but to her younger sister, Ellen Frances or Fanny as she was known within the family – James' and Sarah's third child – may well go the honour of being the first pakeha child conceived in New Zealand but born in England. The City of Edinburgh left the Bay of Islands on 10 December 1830. It could well have dawdled on the New Zealand coast for a few more weeks as it did not arrive in Deal until 6 June 1931. Four months later on 9 October 1831 James' and Sarah's third child was born.

On 7 December 1830, three days before leaving the Bay of Islands, James Reddy entered into agreements with Pomare and two other chiefs relating to the purchase of land at both Okiato and Manawaora. Clearly he intended to come back. The first trading establishment in the Bay had been opened in 1830 (by Gilbert Mair at Te Wahapu, half way between Okiato and Kororareka) and Clendon correctly saw scope for more. So once back in England he proceeded to spend the next ten months preparing for his return. A more suitable ship was acquired, the 125 ton schooner Fortitude, and into it was loaded all that was deemed necessary to establish a ship's chandlery and general trading store and construct and furnish a home on the other side of the world. The Fortitude set sail at the end of April 1832. This second trip to New Zealand was expected to be one-way only. And so it proved.

SHOCKS AND SURPRISES

The 1827 return to Deal

I indicated earlier that as far as the Clendons in England were concerned, they were far from unaffected by James Reddy's connection with the antipodes. That connection caused shocks and surprises, losses and disappointments. Let us start with the former.

Chief among the shocks and surprises I would include both daughters-in-law. We have already seen how James Reddy's second marriage upset his own children and there is no reason to believe that his 82 year old widowed mother and his middle-aged siblings reacted any differently when they heard the news.

But what of James' first marriage to Sarah? The circumstances surrounding this marriage were still being recounted in the Bay of Islands many years later, if the account left to us by Louisa Worsfold is anything to go by. Mrs. Worsfold's reminiscences are clearly unreliable. Some of her comments on the Clendons are demonstrably wrong and others I would hope are so. However, this little tale relating to James' and Sarah's marriage has a general ring of truth about it, at least in its salient details. Based on those reminiscences of Louisa Worsfold, my guess is that the beginnings of James' first marriage went somewhat as follows. James arrived in Sydney as captain of the Merode in the first part of 1826 (see Sydney S.A.D. list for exact date). Shortly thereafter he met Sarah. In late April Sarah became pregnant. By the time Sarah became aware of her condition, Clendon and the Merode had departed Sydney, although not yet on the return voyage to England. Before that final departure, the Merode re-visited Sydney where young James was greeted by the avenging fury of his future mother-in-law. I quote from Mrs. Worsfold's reminiscences:

Sarah Isabella Hill and James Reddy Clendon

Mr. Clendon (James Reddy) was called Capt. Clendon . . . He left the sea after he married a Sydney girl, a Miss Hill. Her Father had a butcher's shop in Sydney & this daughter had been to England as lady's maid to the wife of the Governor of New South Wales of that time, & returned in the same capacity, & Mr. Clendon, as Capt. of the ship did a bit of courting. There were some great tales of the reception he got on his arrival in Sydney, by Mrs. Hill, who chased him with a butcher's knife & all the Englishmen gathered at the water-front to welcome the ship & the latest news from England, made an alley way to aid his escape. However she must have tracked him down as he married Miss Hill & in time came to New Zealand & stayed here.

Marry Miss Hill he did. On 2 October 1826 at St. Phillips Church in Sydney. Details of the time and place and of the minister and witnesses are to be found among the papers in Clendon house, Rawene and the DNZB confirms the date. My guess is that the wedding took place within hours of the Merode's departure because the next we hear of the former Miss Hill is less than four months later when she gave birth in England on 27 January 1827 to James Stephenson Clendon.

*James Stephenson
Clendon*

In all probability, news of James' marriage and of his bride's condition would not have preceded him to England. The news, therefore, would have coincided with James' own arrival when nine-months pregnant Sarah, the former lady's maid from the convict settlement of Port Jackson, accompanied him down the gangplank.

The 1831 return to Deal

If Clendon's first return from down under in 1827 caused some shock and surprise among the family, I think it likely that his second and last return, and the only return ever from New Zealand, must have been memorable as well. Clendon had been gone three years and now had with him his growing family: wife Sarah (5 months pregnant), son James (now four and a half years old), and daughter Eliza (18 months). From Byrne's book we also know that:

> Among the passengers Clendon took to England were two Maori chiefs, Taraia and 'Ahouiffe', who were 'curious to have an interview' with King William IV. He also took "three others (Maori) of inferior note". When the City of Edinburgh arrived at Clendon's home town of Deal, Kent on 6 June 1831, the Maori chiefs caused considerable interest, as the following extract from a contemporary English newspaper records.
>
> On Monday (June 6), two New Zealand chiefs with three others of inferior note, landed at Deal from the ship City of Edinburgh, Captain Clendon. The faces of the chiefs, fantastically tattooed, presented a formidable and grotesque appearance, while those of their less privileged brethren exhibited no indication of artificial embellishment. In the course of the day they visited several gentlemen in Deal, and gratified curiosity by a routine of national exhibitions; the war-whoop was given in good style; and in a sham fight they flourished their clubs with such imposing celerity, as to produce a feeling of astonishment, not unmixed with apprehension, lest a luckless blow should spoil the sport of the pseudo combatants. A tobacco-pipe was given by a boatman to one of the chiefs, but instead of conveying it to his mouth, he very deliberately suspended it by a convenient cavity of the ear. This preposterous appendage seemed to elevate his self-importance, and was regarded, no doubt, as a very valuable ornament.

If nothing else, Clendon seemed to have a knack for bringing home unexpected guests for dinner.

LOSSES AND DISAPPOINTMENTS

The final departure, 1832

The most obvious loss that I have in mind here was the personal loss of family and loved ones that was associated with emigration generally in nineteenth century England. With the sailing of the Fortitude in 1832, James Reddy bade farewell to his parents, to the rest of his family and to his country of birth for the final time. James was 31 and had more than 40 years to live. Nevertheless, as far as I am aware neither he nor Sarah nor any of James' children, including the eleven yet to be born, would ever return to England or see again the Clendon family members who remained behind. Maybe some family correspondence exists that will prove me wrong on this.

The final parting from Deal must have less difficult for Sarah. She, after all, was heading homeward and the Bay of Islands S.A.D. list does indicate that the Clendons during the 1830s themselves used the Fortitude to visit Sydney at least once; the whole family went across together in June 1834. Maybe Sarah was even relieved to be getting away from class conscious England to the more egalitarian air that she knew awaited her in Australasia. I have no evidence that relations between James' mother, Elizabeth Chitty, and Sarah were anything but cordial. But James' and Sarah's respective mothers seem cut from quite different cloth if Louisa Worsfold's wharfside account is to be believed. Looking at Elizabeth Chitty's portrait in the family tree, I find it hard to imagine this rather superior looking lady chasing prospective sons-in-law down Deal High Street with a butcher's knife.

We have Byrne to thank for the following details of James' and Sarah's final departure*:

> . . . it was late April before the Fortitude was finally ready and brave farewells had been uttered. Leaving the safety of its berth the Fortitude, under the guidance of a Thames river pilot, slipped quietly down London's historic waterway, passing Wing's home county of Essex on the port side and the greening Kent countryside on the starboard. Turning into the Channel the Fortitude eventually came to anchor in the Downs, the famous roadstead lying between Deal and the treacherous Goodwin Sands, where it remained overnight on 22 April 1832.
>
> There is reason to believe that the Fortitude anchored off Deal in order that Clendon could collect his wife and three children who lived there and say farewell to his own family. It is also possible that Miss Maria Coldham [the sister of Marianne Williams of Paihia] may have joined the Fortitude at Deal and

---

*   In Byrne's book on Wing, this passage comes complete with four footnotes, none of which I have seen.

William Gardner, a boatbuilder, whom Clendon had engaged to work at Okiato. Although the reference to Clendon's wife and children is partly supposition, there is no doubt that a meeting took place on 23 April between George Clendon and Samuel Stephenson, probably at Clendon's father's home in view of one of the witnesses at that meeting being James Clendon's sister, Sarah Ann. One of the outcomes of the meeting was a signed agreement . . . [on which, see more below].

With the formalities completed and everybody on board, including possibly the two Maori chiefs and 'three others' Clendon had brought to England in the City of Edinburgh, the order was given to weigh anchor. Soon the Fortitude [was] heading for Tenerife in the Canary Islands, and thence for New Zealand. Of the voyage itself nothing is known except that over four months passed before [the] first glimpse of New Zealand.

At first light, on a fine early spring morning, [31 August 1832], the Fortitude entered the Bay of Islands and came to anchor off the CMS station at Paihia, where its arrival had been watched with keen interest by the Rev. Henry Williams.

In Rawene, I came across this extract from Henry William's journal dated 31 August 1832:

A Schr. obs'd at day light standing into the Bay and in a short time a boat pulling on shore. All was anxiety to know who it might be, when the name of Cap. Clendon was passed in an instant along the settlement.

So began Clendon's permanent association with New Zealand. England's loss had become New Zealand's gain.

The 1848 letter

We shall return to that signed agreement shortly, the one signed on 23 April 1832 at Deal. First though, let's take a closer look at the letter written by James Reddy to his mother sixteen years later. That letter, a ship letter sent to Mrs. Clendon care of Charles Chitty Esq. at the Stock Exchange, London was written on 21 March 1848 from the Bay of Islands. It reads as follows:

My dear Mother,

Many months have elapsed since I wrote to any part of the family – my last was to George. The truth is I have no good tidings to communicate and I do not like to trouble you with my difficulties – all our losses [and] removings(?) etc(?) I have at different times written about. We are now living at Kororarika – upon a piece of land belonging to one of the young Williams at a nominal rent,

and doing business in a petty retail way – and so little of it we could not make
a living but for the assistance of Sarah's mother who frequently sends a case
containing cloathing for us all . . . tea sugar etc. Mary is with her – to be
educated and will be provided for. Eliza, Fanny & Kate are at home. James has
still the contract in connection with one of the Williams' for the supply of Beef
for the troops, but the competition is so great that the price is hardly a paying
one.

I see no other prospect than to work hard to the end of my days. I cannot
say the government have done much for me beyond ruining me. I have written
to both George & John to ask them to take my land near Auckland in liquidation
of my debt to you, it is daily becoming of more value. Yet all depends upon the
British Government – if they attempt to carry out Earl Grey's instruction i.e. to
take all the land not cultivated by the Natives – there will be a rebellion
throughout the Island – and certainly an extermination but not of the Natives –
the Whites will suffer. It will require half the British Army to conquer New
Zealand – judging from what has already taken place – in every case the Natives
have been victorious.

I receive occasionally a newspaper I suppose from Sarah Ann as her name
and address is upon it. I shall be happy to hear that you are still enjoying good
health – I wish I could add to your comfort. Sarah and the children are well and
join me in love to you, Sarah Ann and all the family.

Believe me my dear Mother

Your affectionate son
James R. Clendon

First, how did I come by this letter? The original is owned by a woman who
lives in Arundel, Sussex. She was in the Bay of Islands last year as a tourist
and gave a copy of it to the Russell Museum. I do not think she has any
connection with the family because she had typed out the handwritten letter
and in doing so misread "James R" for "Samuel". According to the Museum
curator, the letter had been acquired quite recently. Through a friend who
lives just down the road from Arundel in Rye, I managed to track down the
donor earlier this month. My friend informs me that she has recently
acquired another letter, written also he believes by James Reddy, this one
dated 1820. I am investigating further and will keep you informed.

Now for the letter itself. How was it possible for James Reddy Clendon
– the shipowner, trader, consul and man of "commercial pre-eminence" (to
use a DNZB phrase) of eight years earlier – to have sunk so low so quickly?
His spirits were presumably to sink even further by the end of the year for,
unbeknownst to Clendon at the time of writing this letter, he was never to
see one of his children again. Mary, the daughter staying with her

grandmother in Sydney, would be dead six months later barely a week after her fourteenth birthday. She is buried with other members of the Hill family in Vaucluse, now among the ritziest of Sydney's eastern suburbs.

Much had happened in the Bay of Islands in the eight years since that optimistic day in 1840 when the Treaty of Waitangi was signed. Many local Maoris, led by Chief Hone Heke, had become increasingly disgruntled, regarding the Treaty as being more honoured in the breach than the observance. The year 1844 marked the beginning of the Native Wars, later to be re-named the Maori Wars and now, in this more politically correct age, the New Zealand Wars. In 1845 most Europeans living in the Bay of Islands fled in fear of their lives. In March 1845, the farm at Clendon Cove was abandoned and the whole Clendon family moved temporarily to Auckland following the fall of Kororareka. The town was sacked and only Christ Church and Pompallier House were spared. Several of the town's defenders were killed in the grounds of the church and are buried close to where they fell.

The British soon regained control of the area. Clendon's friend Pomare was arrested and taken to Auckland. His people were forced to abandon the great pa at Otuihu and British gunboats were despatched to raze it to the ground. By 1846 the war in the north would be over, and the rebuilding of Kororareka could begin. Rebuild it did, but never again would Kororareka (now officially re-named Russell, a fact Clendon chose to disregard in his 1848 letter) be the commercial hub of earlier years. Even before the war, whaling's role in the economy of the Bay of Islands had been suddenly and dramatically waning. Americans, then as now foes of government interference, had started going elsewhere after 1840 when British sovereignty resulted in the introduction of tonnage duties, port charges and revenue taxes. The whales too stopped coming to this part of the South Pacific or perhaps it was just that their numbers had been depleted. Almost overnight, the whaling industry – that lifeblood of the Bay of Islands in the 1830s – died.

Administration of the colony was now being carried out from Auckland. It was said that the new Governor* did not think highly of his countrymen in the Bay, and the feeling seems to have been reciprocated. The area stagnated as the colony's focus shifted steadily to the south. Clendon and his family eventually returned to the Bay but it would seem that they did not all go back to the isolated Clendon farm. Instead, as indicated in the letter, we find them in 1848 living upon a piece of land

---

*   The Governor by this time was Sir George Grey. The Earl Grey referred to in James Reddy's letter was Secretary of State for the Colonies in London.

belonging to a young Williams*. This date also coincides with the single two year period between 1840 and 1867 when Clendon was not in the employ of the Government in some form or another. So this letter, then, although written by someone who saw "no other prospect than to work hard to the end of my days", is essentially the work of a 47 year old who is unemployed.

Loss of the Fortitude

But what of Clendon's ships? In particular, what had happened to the Fortitude? The answers here are interesting for they touch on Clendon's continuing connections with his family back in England. It has hitherto been assumed and accepted (as, for example, in the DNZB entry) that James Reddy Clendon and Samuel Stephenson between them purchased the Fortitude. But the manuscript material studied by Byrne in his words "provides conclusive evidence that, contrary to the hitherto accepted assumption, James Clendon never held any title to the Fortitude".

On what was probably James Reddy's last night in England, James' father and James' business partner, Samuel Stephenson, met at the Clendon home in Deal. The outcome of that meeting was that signed agreement of 23 April 1832 referred to earlier. This agreement, expressly stating who owned the Fortitude and its cargo, is quoted in full below. The combined value of the vessel and the stores and cargo was £2,304. As Byrne says, the agreement is a document of some importance as, by its discovery, together with the ship's accounts, the question of the Fortitude's ownership is put beyond doubt.

Agreement between George Clendon and Samuel Stephenson. It is hereby understood and agreed by the undersigned that the Schooner Fortitude, James Clendon Master, with the whole of her cargo bound for New Zealand belongs two thirds to Mr. George Clendon of Deal and the remaining one third to Mr. Samuel Stephenson, late of London now passenger on board the said Schooner.

Witness our hands this 23rd April 1832 at Deal.
    George Clendon, Samuel Stephenson
Witness to the Signature of Mr. George Clendon and Mr. Samuel Stephenson
    Jones, Sarah Ann Clendon

---

* James Stephenson Clendon married Elizabeth Frances Williams. Mrs. Lindauer informed me that this was not one of 'the' Williams i.e. of Paihia missionary fame, but a local Kororareka Williams whose family had convict origins in Australia.

The Fortitude, a vessel owned by James' father and James' business partner, became the foundation of the Clendon/ Stephenson joint venture in New Zealand. In the Bay of Islands S.A.D. list we can trace its sailings to and from Sydney, beginning at the end of 1832. In 1833 there were four arrivals of the vessel in the Bay of Islands, in 1834 there were five and in 1835 three. The pattern in other words was well established. Then, in a dramatic break with this pattern, the vessel was chartered to a Mr. Harvey for a voyage to Tahiti. Mr. Byrne takes up the story:

> *Under the terms of the charter-party, the Fortitude's ports of call were clearly defined: sail to Tahiti in the Society Islands from there to the Sandwich Islands, and return to the Society of Islands, prior to proceeding to Port Jackson. The object of the voyage being to sell its cargo of kauri spars and to procure a cargo for the return run. On 1 November 1835 the Fortitude, which "had only a fortnight's provisions as they intended getting a supply at Tahiti", left Okiato under Capt. Robert MacKay, with Harvey and Mitchiner as passengers, and a Mr. Cunningham travelling as supercargo. If Clendon and Stephenson watched its departure, little did they realise the Fortitude was about to vanish from their sight forever.*

Normally the run to Tahiti would have taken approximately two weeks. The Fortitude should have arrived around mid-November 1835. The first inkling that Clendon and Stephenson probably had that something was amiss would have been when the next visiting vessel arrived in the Bay of Islands from Tahiti. From the S.A.D. list we can see that the first vessel from Tahiti after the Fortitude's departure arrived seven weeks later on 21 December 1835. It was HMS Beagle calling at the Bay towards the end of her long voyage of 1831-36. The naturalist on board was Charles Darwin. It can reasonably be assumed that Clendon made enquiries of Darwin and the Beagle's captain, Robert FitzRoy (later to be a Governor of New Zealand), together with other members of the crew, to see if they had any news of the Fortitude. There would have been none.*

Returning now to Byrne's narrative of the Fortitude's final voyage:

> *According to Cunningham's letter and Thompson's declarations, the vessel's course was shortly altered whither the seamen knew not, as Thompson expressly said their destination was kept secret". By late November provisions and water had*

---

* The Beagle's captain wrote in his narrative of this epic voyage "...we anchored between Kororareka and Paihia (the missionary settlement): farther up the harbour [i.e. near Okiato] were several whale-ships which had anchored there, I was told, in order to avoid the spirit shops of Kororareka".

virtually run out and the crew "subsisted on peas". "It was only when we were two or three days from Valparaiso that we knew where we were going. We arrived at Valparaiso on Christmas Day". It appears the Fortitude was in need of some repair work to its masts and that the proceeds of the sale of the spars were applied "to pay for the repairs". Apparently the sale proceeds were "not enough and Harvey ordered her (the Fortitude) to be sold, despite Capt. MacKay's protests that Clendon should be notified and asked to send "money to repair her". Furthermore, it is evident from Thompson's statement: there was not a seaman on board who would have refused to have sailed round the world in her", and that the overall soundness of the Fortitude was not in question. Clearly Harvey had other thoughts on the matter and the awkward matter of ownership was overcome by some devious stratagem. "The vessel was sold for $6,000 to Harvey [who] afterwards sold it for $7,000 to a Mr. Lyons, a merchant of Valparaiso. She is now under Chilean colours in the employ of Mr. Lyons and manned by Frenchmen.

Capt. MacKay left Valparaiso in January or February 1836 for England and John Thompson arrived there on 3 August 1836.

How long Clendon and Stephenson expected the charter voyage to take is not known, but as the months slipped by and no word of the Fortitude was heard or received, "neither by her owners, nor the agent in Sydney", quite understandably their anxiety deepened. After a silence of over a year, when they had probably given up hope, they "heard indirectly that the [Fortitude] had been taken into Valparaiso and sold [and] sailed under Chilean colours on the South American coast." Judging by Mary Clendon's letter of 23 March 1837 acknowledging her brother's letter advising of "the loss of the Fortitude", Clendon had learnt from Mr. Cunningham about the vessel's sale. Mary Clendon immediately sent her brother's letter to their father, who had already been "informed of the loss and was only awaiting to hear from [James] that it was quite true before he took any decisive measures".

How George Clendon, the registered part owner of the Fortitude, came to hear the grim news is not known but in a letter dated 16 January 1837 from his son, John Chitty, it is clear he knew about the position at the beginning of January 1837. He had written to John, in London, urgently requesting him to try and locate John Thompson in order to obtain his statement regarding the illegal sale of the Fortitude. By good fortune John's difficult task was accomplished, as he reported on 16 January: "I have succeeded in finding the cook/steward of the Fortitude at the time she was sold." Thompson was found on board a brig in the West India Docks, which was loading for Trinidad.

It is unknown what action, if any, followed John Chitty Clendon's visit to the Foreign Office, where he went to seek assistance. He was:

"unhesitatingly advised to lay a statement of the case before Lord Palmerston and that the government would render prompt assistance." Similarly, it is not known whether George Clendon, who renewed the Fortitude's marine policy, recovered his loss. It appears he did not, judging by the surviving papers of his estate.

The loss of the Fortitude almost certainly resulted in a substantial financial loss, both to James Clendon and his father. It was a loss "borne . . . with great composure", by George Clendon. The effect on part owner Samuel Stephenson is not known but it too was probably hard. Taken in isolation, the loss, although a heavy body blow, could have been painfully absorbed by Clendon and Stephenson. However, when combined with the earlier loss of their second vessel* . . . the partnership was placed under very considerable strain."

Extent of financial losses

George Clendon invested heavily in New Zealand and lost. Those losses were also borne by James Reddy's mother, and his brothers and sisters, for on George's death the deceased's estate was diminished as a result of those financial reverses in New Zealand. The reference in James Reddy's 1848 letter to the money he owed to his mother was presumably money owed to her under the terms of his father's will. James would have been communicating with his brothers, George and John, in their capacity as executors of their father's estate.

The extent of the Clendon family losses is difficult to gauge but I have a feeling it went well beyond the loss of the Fortitude. What is obvious, however, is that James Reddy came to New Zealand at the age of 31 with very little of his own capital behind him. He did what many a young man has done before and since: he went to his father for help. George appears to have been extremely generous with the assistance he provided and I find it hard to believe that the Clendon family at that time could have been so wealthy as to enable George to provide financial help on the same scale to his other eight adult children.

In Clendon House, Rawene, I came across a short (11 page) research

---

*   This second vessel, and as far as I am aware the only vessel the Clendon/Stephenson partnership ever owned outright, was the Fanny, a 31/41 ton schooner built at Hokianga in 1834 and intended largely for coastal trading. There are six recorded arrivals of this ship in the Bay of Islands before she was lost off the East Coast of New Zealand in May 1836. The only other vessel I came across associated with Clendon's name was the Tokirau referred to earlier - the stranded American whaler re-commissioned by Clendon and Mair in 1839 just as whaling was dying out in this part of the Pacific.

paper written by an Auckland University history student in 1970 entitled
"New Zealand's First American Consulate". During the research for this
paper, the author, George Harron, had gone through many Clendon family
papers at the Auckland Public Library. Mr. Harron estimates that before
taking up residence at Okiato James Reddy borrowed about £5,000 from his
father. Whether this was inclusive or exclusive of the amount George spent
on the Fortitude is unclear. According to Harron "By the end of 1837
[Clendon's] mercantile establishment had prospered so well that his
indebtedness to his father was only £3,126.19.6, and by the end of 1838 he
had repaid another £1,270.17.10. Harron's researches would have stopped
in 1841, and I am assuming that he found no evidence up to that time of a
further reduction in the £1,850 still owing. After 1841, Clendon's financial
position must have quickly deteriorated, particularly after the Okiato sale
turned sour, and it must have become more and more difficult for him to
make any inroads unto the amount still owing. By the time James Reddy
Clendon died he was penniless and his widow only succeeded in saving the
Rawene house because it was mortgaged to her father (to whom James
owed three years' rent at the time of his death).

Where had all the money gone? Some must have been spent on the
"fleet" – operating and maintaining the Fortitude, building the Fanny and
buying and re-commissioning the Tokirau. Several thousand pounds must
have been spent on the improvements at Okiato. An equally impressive sum
must have been sunk into the Clendon farm at Manawaora. Ruth Ross found
among the papers in Rawene the following statement of evidence filed by
Clendon in March 1858 in the Land Claims Court at Kororareka.

> I spent on this property [Manawaora] Three Thousand pounds in clearing,
> building, cultivating, and fencing, but at the time of the war we thought it
> inexpedient to remain there. Afterwards a good deal of the fencing was destroyed
> by fires that had been made, most likely by natives. As soon as peace was
> destroyed my son returned to the property: he is now 30 years old and has been
> at Manawaora (excepting during the war) since he was 11 years old.

Manawaora did not merit this sort of investment. I now realise that James
Reddy Clendon shared with a number of his other city-bred relations (such
as those who tried farming in Glens Falls, New York, in Louisa County,
Virginia and in Akatarawa, New Zealand) an unerring eye for selecting the
wrong land in which to invest large amounts of family toil and treasure. As
I said earlier, Manawaora is a great place for a holiday, but it was not the
right place for Clendon to realise any aspirations he may have had of
becoming a wealthy pastoralist and a foundation member of New Zealand's
landed gentry.

JAMES AND HIS WIVES: AN ASSESSMENT

Sarah Hill Clendon

Clendon's first wife remains for me a shadowy figure, in large part perhaps because I have not seen a picture of her at any age. Reports on Sarah that I came across were mixed. Her obituary, in all likelihood written by her husband, is flattering as one would of course expect:

> *Died*
> *On Saturday, the 11th instant [11 August 1855], at Russell, Bay of Islands of apoplexy, Sarah Isabella, aged 49 years, wife of James Reddy Clendon, Esq., Resident Magistrate. Her death is universally and sincerely regretted, for her well known charity and disinterested benevolence have rendered her, for years, the beloved benefactress of the poor, the sick and the afflicted. Requiescat in pace!*

Village gossip in Russell, as transmitted down to us via Mrs. Worsfold's acerbic pen and unreliable memory, paints a somewhat different picture. According to Mrs. Worsfold (who I should emphasize was not even born until 1872), "Mrs. Clendon was quite a militant lady and report went that [James Reddy's] life was not very peaceful". There appear to be quite a number of diaries and whaling logs where references to Mrs. Clendon's hospitality are included. To her visitors and contemporaries she appeared hospitable, kind to those in need, a good homemaker – in short, an excellent settler's wife in a raw, new country. But her origins were clearly humble as more than one visitor noted. One of Sarah's most literate visitors was Sarah Mathew, the wife of New Zealand's first surveyor general, Felton Mathew. The two Sarahs met in 1840 when they were both aged 34. Sarah Mathew is described in the DNZB as well educated, intelligent and an avid reader. Back in England the poet John Keats had been a family friend. After their first meeting, Sarah Mathew summed up her hostess thus: "Mrs. Clendon seems a very kind sort of creature, and has a numerous family but I can not say much for her refinement or education".

Jane Cochrane Clendon

Jane was clearly an impressive woman in her own right. She had mana (prestige) independent of any her husband may have attained during his lifetime. The respect in which she seems to have been held throughout the Hokianga increased rather than diminished through her long widowhood. Jane's education was almost certainly superior to Sarah's. Born in the Hokianga at a time when educational opportunities were very limited, Jane appears to have been at school in either Paihia or Russell (perhaps the same school the two youngest Clendon daughters were attending) at the time she met James Reddy.

Ruth Ross carried out an inventory of the books in Clendon House and found some that belonged to Jane before her marriage. How many sixteen year old girls today possess books with such titles as A Memoir of Felix Neff, Pastor of the High Alps, and of his Labours among the French Protestants of Dauphine, a remnant of the primitive Christians of Gaul?

Quoting from Ruth Ross' notes made in 1974 shortly after she finished the task of collating the Clendon papers, "A photograph of Jane as a young woman shows her to have been good-looking, even beautiful, if rather solemn. One might reasonably judge her to have been a person of character, poise and determination on the evidence of this photograph alone. Later events were to prove she had all these qualities."

Ruth Ross continues:

> [Jane] had a commanding presence and great strength of character. Her natural sense of dignity, her certainty of her rightful place as a leader of Herd's Point, these carried her through the lean times and the indignities of indebtedness. There never was much affluence in the Clendon House at Rawene -- though there may have been a certain amount of living beyond their means -- but one has the impression it was always a warm, hospitable and loving home. In that remarkable first and second generation Pakeha-Maori world of later nineteenth century Hokianga, there was an appreciation of cultural and spiritual values which would have been more expected -- and perhaps harder to find -- in a more sophisticated social milieu. Money may have been short and occupational pursuits humble, but in manners, in intellectual interests and in genuine neighbourliness (notwithstanding family jealousies), Jane Clendon and her children were no colonial yokels.

I remain ignorant of how much interaction there was between James Reddy's first and second families. James Stephenson Clendon spent time in Rawene assisting his father as a translator so he at least must have got to know Jane and her older children quite well. Whatever the objections of Clendon's first family to their father's remarriage to a young girl within months of his first wife's death, Ruth Ross, for one, thought that Jane may have won them all over in the end, if not at the beginning. But as Ross herself admitted, the picture that emerges from the surviving family correspondence is ambiguous on this point. Ross has referred in her notes to a letter written by Jane almost three years after her husband's death. She had been in a dispute with her father (who wanted his £200 loan to James repaid together with the back rent) and in this letter to an old friend of James, she wrote:

Mr. Manning can you picture to yourself my sorrow & dismay when I reflect on the uncertainty of life & the probability of my poor & very little children being left homeless or at the mercy of their not over fond relatives, from whom they will receive but little or no cheer in fact who regard their existence in the world at the same time as themselves a most unpardonable offence as obstacles or objects of their bounty, as I have most bitterly experienced.

Who was it that Jane had in mind here – her own relatives or her stepchildren? As Ruth Ross says, "an interesting speculation".

Just as I remain ignorant of last century's inter-family relationships, so, too, I remain largely ignorant of Jane's background apart from knowing that she was the product of an Irish father and a Maori mother. I find it now very easy to believe that her Maori lineage was a distinguished one and that her mother was indeed a "princess" in her own tribe. Many, perhaps most, of the offspring of James' and Jane's marriage would have quickly opted for the pakeha world and their present-day descendants have presumably long since left their Maori heritage behind. But in other cases, particularly in the far north, I suspect that James' and Jane's joint influence over those of their descendants who chose to retain and nourish their Maori roots lives on in ways that for the present, and without much more research, can only be guessed at. But to give one possible example, in 1989 I read an obituary here in Manila of Sir James Henare, scion of one of Maoridom's most distinguished families and widely tipped in the 1980s to become Governor General of New Zealand; his full name apparently was James Clendon Henare. My suspicion is that the marriage of James Clendon and Mihi Kererene could remain a genealogist's dream for a long time to come.

James Reddy Clendon

In this century of exponential world population growth, it gives one pause for thought to realise that if James Reddy Clendon had had "only" thirteen children, the Clendon name in the direct male line from James would have died out within two generations. The name has survived, however, thanks to his fourteenth and last child, John Chitty, born in his father's seventy first year*. James Reddy had three other sons. The first, and the only son of his first marriage, himself produced one son, Bowen Clendon, but Bowen had

---

* John Chitty's birth followed seven months after the death in London of James Reddy's youngest brother who bore the same name. According to the DNZB, James Reddy Clendon "began his career as a ship owner in London, in partnership with his brother John Chitty Clendon". According to the family tree, John Chitty was born on 16 December 1809 and ended up a successful dental surgeon (with Dowager Queen Adelaide as one of his patients) so this seems to be another DNZB mistake.

only daughters. The next son was George, first child of his second marriage. George's own marriage was childless. To quote Ruth Ross, George "was a Justice of the Peace, a loyal son, a staunch husband, everyone's friend and father of none". Next came Fred (christened William Frederick Ngaropo Clendon) whose tenth birthday was probably overshadowed by his father's death which followed four days later, after a lingering illness. There was a touching letter concerning Fred found among the papers at Clendon House, written by Jane soon after James Reddy's death when she was forced to make the arduous trip to Auckland to confront her husband's creditors. Sixteen year old George, now the man of the house, was instructed in the letter to keep an eye on Fred's infected toe and "tell him don't, don't forget the well". Perhaps Fred was responsible for making sure the four littler ones did not fall in. Sadly Fred himself was to suffer an unexpected immersion twelve years later, the result of which was that he caught a chill and died at the age of twenty- two. The Methodist minister at Rawene contributed this obituary: "Fallen Asleep – F.W. Ngaropo Clendon. Having grown to manhood on the river, he was an expert oarsman, and had twice proved champion in Hokianga waters. He was accordingly invited by Kaipara experts to join them in contesting the great Auckland race". But on the way to Auckland by sailing boat the crew capsized in rough weather; one was drowned and Fred's drenching led to the illness from which, two months later, he died. The obituary went on to note that "the deceased spoke perfectly the Maori language". To quote from Ruth Ross' notes again, "The minister's account is of a young man of simple, almost childlike goodness and faith. Photographs suggest a thoughtful, almost a beautiful youth, whose apparent slightness of build was presumably deceptive. Telegrams of condolence to the bereaved mother are still preserved".

The descendants of John Chitty Clendon and of James Reddy Clendon's various daughters from both marriages now number in the many hundreds and are scattered throughout New Zealand and beyond. In Rawene I obtained a copy of the genealogical table of the family of James Reddy Clendon compiled originally in 1954 by Tom's grandfather, Douglas, with the help of you, Bette, and Erik Chitty. The table was updated in 1990 by Philippa Ann Holmes of Tauranga, which, with more recent additions, has been included in this book. Although I have since discovered that Ryland knows her and stayed with her when he was in New Zealand, I had never heard of Philippa Holmes – nor are any of the currently living descendants on her list personally known to me. As must by now be clear, from my perspective the Wellington branch of the Clendon family (i.e. my branch) has always been quite distinct from the Auckland and North Auckland branches that are descended from James Reddy, and even more distinct, if that is possible, from any South Island branch that has descended from James' sister, Rebecca.

This joint letter began as an effort to kill two birds with one stone and has long since got out of hand. Since I returned from Wellington in the New Year, I have taken it with me – largely in my head – on Bank missions to Xiamen in January and then to Qingdao last month. My research began in airport lounges and hotel rooms and led down many unexpected avenues. I first put pen to paper on a wintery Sunday in Beijing earlier this month in the Palace Hotel looking out over the Forbidden City. It seemed somewhat incongruous at the time, and even more so now when I reflect upon it, but after making the attempt to get under James Reddy's skin I have welcomed this chance to try and set the record straight in certain areas and to set down one or two of my own thoughts in the process. The thoughts that occupied me most, however, I have elected not to answer here: how typical a Clendon was James Reddy? Is there such a thing as a typical Clendon? If so, how does it come through – in the choice of marriage partner, choice of career, choice of life style? Do we Clendons value the spiritual over the temporal, or vice versa? Are we by birth destined to be risk takers or risk averse, adventurers or stay-at-homes, successes or failures? How do we judge success? Are we doers or thinkers, farmers or sailors, merchants or professionals, drop-outs or ambitious strivers? Are we loners or joiners, leaders or followers, optimists or pessimists? Why do we have this inordinate pride in our family name which is still so evident on three continents? Is it normal, is it justified? In other words, what have we inherited from our forebears and what are we passing on, either deliberately or subconsciously, to our own descendants? This for me is what has made this first serious delving into genealogy so fascinating and so distinct from the ordinary type of historical research.

As I said, I am going to duck all these questions for now – ask me again in forty years and I may be willing to proffer some answers. Suffice to say for the moment that I do consider James Reddy to have been a true Clendon. His place in New Zealand history is assured and nothing that I or anyone else now says will change that. The Clendon that the history books will always remember, however, is the dashing young captain in his twenties and the successful pioneer settler in his thirties. Easily overlooked will be the fact that Clendon's final thirty years presented a marked contrast to his earlier life. In terms of what he did longest and probably did best, James Reddy Clendon could be considered above all a public servant. Of some of his missionary contemporaries it was later cynically said that they had come to New Zealand to do good but ended up doing well instead. In Clendon's case I think that rather the opposite proved true.

Descendants of James Reddy Clendon

CLENDON James Reddy		b	1800 Oct 1	Deal, Kent, UK
		d	1872 Oct 24	Rawene
m. Sarah Isabella Hill (1)		m	1826 Oct 2	Sydney
		b	1804/5	
		d	1855 Aug 11	Russell
m. Jane Takotowi COCHRANE (2)		m	1856 Jan 9	Paihia
		b	1838 Jul 18	Mangamuka
		d	1919 May 21	Rawene

He had fourteen children who are listed below and their issue follow generation by generation on the subsequent pages.

1(1)	CLENDON James Stephenson (1)	b	1827 Jan 18	London
	(Resident magistrate at Whangarei)	d	1899 Nov 9	Russell
	m. WILLIAMS Elizabeth Frances	m	1861 Dec 7	Bay of Islands (m. by Henry Williams)
		b	1843	
		d	1910 May 20	m.i. Russell
1(2)	CLENDON Eliza Chitty (1)	b	1830 Jan 16	on Board Ship off Hokianga
		d	1908 Jul 28	Auckland
	m. William Bertram WHITE	m	1851 Oct 4	Russell – Rev Robert BURROWS
		b	1821 Jun 23	France
		d	1910 Jan 10	Auckland
1(3)	CLENDON Ellen Frances (Fanny) (1)	b	1831 Oct 9	London
		d	1888 Jun 18	
	m. Frank Arthur GOULD (Rev.)	m	1853 Mar	
		b	1827 Mar 3	Exeter
		d	1923 Apr 30	
1(4)	CLENDON Mary Parson (1)	b	1834 Sep 11	Sydney or Okiato
		d	1848 Sep 22	Memorial South-head cemetery, Sydney
1(5)	CLENDON Sarah Ann (1)	b	1837 May 5	Okiato
	(No further information)	d		
1(6)	CLENDON Kate Erridge (1)	b	1839 Nov 13	Okiato
		d	1910 Jul 4	Auckland
	m. William Frederick HOWARD	m	1860 Oct 20	Kororareka
	(Farmer)	b	1830 Dec 22	
		d	1912 Dec 10	Kamo
1(7)	CLENDON George Thomas (2)	b	1856 Dec 14	
		d	1933 Jan 27	
	m. Juliet Catherine QUIGLEY	b		
	(No issue)	d	1946 Jul 6	
1(8)	CLENDON Jane (2)	b	1858 Jan 23	
	(Not married)	d	1912 Oct 6	
1(9)	CLENDON Edith Julia (2)	b	1869 Sep 20	
		d	1877 Jul 25	
1(10)	CLENDON William Frederick Ngarapo (2)	b	1862 Oct 18	
	(Not married)	d	1895 Mar 17	
1(11)	CLENDON Marion Takotowi (2)	b	1864 Jun 16	
		d	1961 Sep 9	
	m. Thomas Lumsden MILLAR	m	1882 Feb 22	Rawene
		b	18	
1(12)	CLENDON Clara Emily (2)	b	1866 Apr 14	
		d	1889 Jul 21	
	m. William Andrew WEBSTER	m	1884	
		b	1858	
		d	1921	

1(13)	CLENDON Frances Louisa (2)	b	1869 Jul 3	Rawene
		d	1964 Nov 10	Tauranga
	m. Robert Patrick FLOOD	m	1892 Jun 9	Hokianga
		b	1861 Aug 11	Ireland
		d	1934 May 20	Okaihau
1(14)	CLENDON John Chitty (2)	b	1871 May 26	
		d	1944 Nov 26	
	m. Annie BEAZLEY	m	1898 Aug 30	
		b	1881 Jan 18	
		d	1952 May 13	

2(1)(i)	CLENDON Fanny Kate	b	1862 Oct 20	
	(Spinster)	d	1936 Aug 10	M.I. Russell
2(1)(ii)	CLENDON Edwin John	b	1864 Oct 2	Bay of Islands
	(Admitted Bar 1887)	d	1936 Oct 4	Prominent Thames
	m. Eleanor Calvert CARR	m	1893 Dec 28	
		b	1869 Jun 21	
		d	1939 May 16	

2(2)(i)   WHITE Eliza Louisa   b   1852 Aug 25
(Not married – baptised at Kororareka 1852 Sep 52 by Frank GOULD)
(Lived at Mangonui – father described as Police Magistrate)
          d   1926 Jan 27   Auckland

2(2)(ii)   WHITE Caroline Ellen   b   1854 Jun 19   Kerikeri
(Born at Kemp House, baptised at Kororareka 1854 Jul 9 by Frank GOULD)
(Lived at Mangonui – father Police Magistrate)

		d	1945 Nov 5	Auckland
	m. John Martin Hawkins LUSH	m	1883 Apr 5	Auckland
	(Solicitor)	b	1854 Sep 9	Auckland
		d	1893 Jun 4	Auckland

2(2)(iii)	WHITE Kate Sarah Ann	b	1856 Mar 9	
	(Not married)	d	1939 Apr 4	Auckland
2(2)(iv)	WHITE Fanny Edith	b	1858 Jan 6	
	(Not married)	d	1945 Nov 19	Auckland
2(2)(v)	WHITE Emily Howard	b	1859 Dec 10	
	(Philatelist)	d	1943 Jul7	Auckland
	m. John KENDERDINE	m	1890 Sep 18	Auckland
		b	1860 Jul 15	
		d	1931 Jan 26	Auckland
2(2)(vi)	WHITE William Bertram	b	1862 Sep 24	Oruru, Northland
		d	1943 Jun 30	Takapau
	m. Grace Rosalie RESTALL	m	1906 Jan 10	
		b	1877 Jul 29	Christchurch
		d	1976 Apr 2	Waipukurau
2(2)(vii)	WHITE Frederick Foster Clendon	b	1864 Sep 24	Mangonui
		d	1946 Jun 29	
	m. Eva Muriel Rutherfurd WARD	m	1905 Jan 11	St Marks, Carterton
		b	1881 Sep 6	Carterton
		d	1919 Mar 9	Havelock North

When Frederick F. C. White was married he lived at Maurpataniwha, Hawkes Bay.
His wife E. M. R. Ward was the only daughter of Mrs W. N. Ward.
She is listed in Bertha Mabel Holmes's (née WARD) birthday book. She must have been a WARD relation.

2(2)(viii)	WHITE Rosa Mabel (May): Twin	b	1867 Oct 7	
	(Not married)	d	1962 Oct 21	
2(2)(ix)	WHITE Henry James: Twin	b	1867 Oct 7	
	(Died young)	d	1872 Feb 16	
2(2)(x)	WHITE Mary Ashburnham (Aunt Molly): Twin	b	1870 Jul 20	
		d	1936 Nov 4	Auckland
	m. James Preston STEVENSON	m	1894 Sep 12	
		b	1871 Mar 26	At sea
		d	1948 Jul 28	Auckland

2(2)(xi)	WHITE Alice Florence (Flossie): Twin	b	1870 Jul 20	
		d	1944 Jun 14	Auckland
	m. John William NICHOL	m	1895 Feb 26	Auckland
		b	1865 Oct 20	
		d	1944 Dec 6	Auckland
2(2)(xii)	WHITE Minnie Gould	b	1873 Jun 21	
	(Died in infancy)	d	1873 Jul 18	
2(2)(xiii)	WHITE Brenda Mary	b	1872	
	(Died in infancy)			
2(3)(i)	GOULD Mary Parson	b	1854 Jan 5	Russell
	(Baptised 1854 Jan 29 at Kororareka by Frank GOULD)			
		d	1940 Jun 15	
	m. Charles Lamb LONG	m	1874 Apr 8	Otahuhu
		b	1851 Jan 22	Sheffield
		d	1903 Feb 20	
2(3)(ii)	GOULD Francis Arthur	b	1855 Jun 17	
	(Baptised at Kororareka 1855 Jul 15 by Francis Gould)			
	(Assumed name of Simpson)	d		Honolulu
	m. Ellen Fanny EMPSON	m	18	
		b	1856 Oct	
2(3)(iii)	GOULD Kate Fanny	b	1856 Sep 6	Auckland
	(bapt 1856 Sep 28 at Kororareka by Frank GOULD; lived at Kororareka)			
		d	1947	Auckland
	m. Henry Percy GILFILLAN	m	1880 Oct	Holy Trinity Otahuhu
	(Public Accountant)	bc	1855	
		d	? 1950	Auckland
2(3)(iv)	GOULD George Alfred	b	1857 Dec 5	
	(Baptised 1858 Jan 3 by Fr GOULD;			
	lived in Kororareka)	d	1944 Dec 23	
	m. Mary Jane WEBBER	m	18	
		b	1865 Aug 8	
		d	1926 May	
2(3)(v)	GOULD Ellen Julia	b	1859 Feb 8	
	(Baptised 1859 Mar 8 at Kororareka by Fr GOULD: lived Kororareka)			
		d	1934	
	m. James Wrey NOLAN	m	1881 Jul 23	
	(Solicitor of Gisborne)	b	1854 May 24	Bathurst
		d	1938	
2(3)(vi)	GOULD Rose Eliza	b	1860 May 10	
	(Baptised 1860 Jun 14 at Kororareku			
	by Fr GOULD – lived Kororareku)	d		
	m. William Endell WANKLYN	m	1889 Oct 1	
		b		of Christchurch
2(3)(vii)	GOULD Henry Howard	b	1861 Oct 10	
		d	1925?	
	m. Mary MacFARLANE	b	18	
2(3)(viii)	GOULD Charles Herbert	b	1863 Jul 21	
	m.			
2(3)(ix)	GOULD Mabel Edith	b	1865 May 29	
		d	1952	
	m. Francis Travers MORGAN	b		
	(Bank Manager)	d	1931	
2(3)(x)	GOULD Percy Clendon	b	1866 Sep 3	
	(Accountant)	d	1928 Apr 6	
	m. Elizabeth Margaret McCOWAN	m	1902	
		b		
		d	1953 Apr 19	
2(3)(xi)	GOULD Amy Beatrice	b	1868 Jan 31	
		d	1945	
	m. William Alexander D'ARCY	m	1893	
		b	1863	Lived Wanganui
		d	1940	
2(3)(xii)	GOULD Ernest Trevor	b	1869 Apr 6	of Sydney
		d		Sydney

2(3)(xiii)	GOULD Maude Heywood	b	1870 Jun 16	
		d	1922	Gisborne
	m. Walter Richard BARKER	m	1896	
	(Sheep-farmer of Gisborne)	b	1866	
		d	19	
2(3)(xiv)	GOULD Ethel Nellie	b	1872 Jul 13	
		d	1951 Nov 10	
	m. Harold Edwin FORDE	m	1901 Apr 15	
		b	1876 Jan 14	Otahuhu
		d	1937 Jan 7	Auckland
2(3)(xv)	GOULD Sydney Harold	b	1873 Nov 3	
	(Baptised Otahuhu)	d	1891 Sep 13	
2(3)(xvi)	GOULD Lille Gertrude	b	1874 Dec 16	
	(Baptised Otahuhu)	d		
	m. Walter Richard BARKER	b	1866	
	(Widower of Maude Heywood GOULD – 2(3)(xiii))			
2(6)(i)	HOWARD Harry Frederick	b	1861	Auckland
		d	1941 Jul 4	Whangarei
	m. Mabel Florence HILL	m	1893	Auckland
		b	1870	Dunedin
		d	1943 Feb 20	Whangarei
2(6)(ii)	HOWARD Mabel Kate	b	1862 Dec 3	Auckland
	(Baptised St Johns 1863 Jan 18; lived Tamaki; father farmed.			
	Sponsors: E. C. White; F. Gould; W. B. White)	d		Auckland
2(6)(iii)	HOWARD Arthur Harry Spowers	b	1866 May 23	
	(Baptised St Johns 1866 Jun 24; lived Tamaki East; settler)			
	m. Florence GUNN			
2(6)(iv)	HOWARD Claude Gladwyn Wynyard	b	1871 Apr 9	
	(Aunt Fanny's birthday book shows Claude Howard on Apr 9)			
	(Not married)	d	1946	Hamilton
2(6)(v)	HOWARD Ida Kate Clendon	b	1873	Auckland
	(D.I.)	d	1873	Auckland
2(6)(vi)	HOWARD Ella	b	1876	Auckland
	m. Horace CRAMOND			
2(6)(vii)	HOWARD Frank Clendon	b	? 1878 Aug 25	Otahuhu
	(? died in infancy)	d		
2(6)(viii)	HOWARD Florence Louise	b	1881	
	(Not married)	d	1967 Jul 18	Wellington
2(6)(ix)	HOWARD Trevor Clendon	b	1883 Aug 2	Onehunga
		d	1945 Oct 20	Otahuhu
	m. Florimel Lilian STEWART	m	1912 Sep 7	
		b	1889 Jul 10	Onehunga
		d	1978 Oct 13	Howick
2(11)(i)	MILLAR George Frederick Graham	b	1885 Dec	
	(No issue)	d	195?	
2(11)(ii)	MILLAR Edward Lumsden	b	1887	
		d	1893	
2(11)(iii)	MILLAR Francis Edith	b	1889 Sep 11	Rawene
		d	1986 Dec 11	Whangarei
	m. David Christopher INGRAM (1)	m	1916 March	
		b	1873	
		d	1942 Oct	
	m. Paul SPENDER (2)	m	1928	
2(11)(iv)	MILLAR Ruth	b	1891 Oct 14	
		d	1948 Feb 7	Auckland
	m. Charles Henry GUTHREY	m	1913 Nov 11	Rawene
		b	1888 Jul 16	
2(11)(v)	MILLAR Trevor Clendon	b	1893 Nov 12	Rawene
		d	1966 Dec 11	Rawene
	m. Marjorie Alice SPEIGHT	m	1935 Jan 22	Auckland
		b	1903 Jul 11	Te Puke
		d	1977 Dec 10	Auckland

2(11)(vi)	MILLAR Marion Elizabeth (Peggy)	b	1895 Dec 17	
		d	1991 May 26	
	m. Leonard William KEENE	m	1922 Feb 22	
		b	1891 Nov 20	
		d	1968 Oct	
2(11)(vii)	MILLAR Thomas Lumsden	b	1905 Jul 1	Rawene
		d	1981 Apr 19	
	m. Connie COSSON	b	1907 Feb 6	Awanui
2(12)(i)	WEBSTER Frederick	b	1885	
	(Died young)			
2(12)(ii)	WEBSTER Edith May	b	1887	
		d	1957	
	m. WEBSTER	b		
2(12)(iii)	WEBSTER James Reddy	b	1889	
		d	1949	
	m. Hazel Annie Emily CHAFFEY	b	1903	
		d	1960	
2(13)(i)	FLOOD Thomas Frederick	b	1893 Mar 6	Rawene
	(Killed in WWI)	d	1917 Oct 2	
2(13)(ii)	FLOOD George Robert	b	1895 May	Rawene
		d	1895 Nov 6	Rawene
2(13)(iii)	FLOOD Katherine Mary	b	1896 Oct 3	Rawene
		d	1989 Jun 11	Auckland
	m. Nicholas BROWNE	m	1926 Jan 11	Okaihau
		b	1891 Dec 10	Te Aroha
		d	1960 Jul 27	Auckland
2(13)(iv)	FLOOD Jane Margaret	b	1898 Nov 14	Hokianga
		d	1989 Aug 18	Auckland
	m. Florence Daniel DONOVAN	m	1928 Apr 10	Okaihau
		b	1902 Nov 14	
	(No issue)	d	1982 Dec 4	Tauranga
2(13)(v)	FLOOD George Patrick	b	1903 Feb 21	Rotorua
		d	1976 Oct 6	Hamilton
	m. Mary Josephine Ann McHUGH	m	1927 Jun 20	
		b	1905 May 13	Auckland
		d	1982 Apr 28	Auckland
2(13)(vi)	FLOOD Mary Frances	b	1906 Aug 15	TePuke
2(14)(i)	CLENDON George Thomas (Tom)	b	1899 Jan 27	
		d	1978 Apr 18	
	m. Edith HOPKINS (Edie) (1)	m	1925 Nov 25	
		b	1892 Dec 9	
		d	1958 Dec 23	
	m. Katherine Mary COPPINS (2)	b	1923?	
		d	1977 Feb 23	
2(14)(ii)	CLENDON John Frederick (Jack)	b	1900 Oct 17	
		d	1966 Jul 3	
	m. Elsie JOHNSON	m	1925 Jul13	
		b	1907 Aug 9	
2(14)(iii)	CLENDON Hugh Chitty	b	1902	Lives in Takapura
	m. Ellen Elizabeth BEAZLEY (Len)	b	1908	
2(14)(iv)	CLENDON James Edwin (Jim)	b	1903 Jun 2	
		d	1971 Feb 12	
	m. Margaret Caroline HAIGH (Topsy)	m	1924 Nov 12	
		b	1905 Apr 18	
		d	1982 Jul 21	
2(14)(v)	CLENDON Sidney Hamilton (Dick)	b	1907 Aug 15	Lives in Paeroa
	m. Barbara Ellen ELLIOT (Ella) (1)			
	m. Ivy Thelma WAH (Biddy) (2)			
2(14)(vi)	CLENDON William Henry: Twin	b	1912 Jul 12	
	m. Eleanor PAIN (Goldie)	m	1939	

2(14)(vii)	CLENDON Gordon Eric: Twin	b	1912 Jul 12	
		d	1963	
	m. Ilene Myrtle ALLPORT			
2(14)(viii)	CLENDON Alma Joyce Takatowi	b	1917 Mar 16	
	m. Colin Hartley VINCENT	m	1940 Nov 16	
3(1)(ii)I	CLENDON Marie de Beauvoir	b	1894 Nov 12	
	m. Horace Augustus JOYCE	b	1886	
		d	1935 Sep 22	
3(1)(ii)II	CLENDON Erridge Brown	b	1898 Oct 20	Thames
	(Akd. Solicitor)	d	1976 Aug 28	
	m. Kathleen Constance SMITH	b	1899 Nov 4	
		d	1993 Mch 4	Remuera
3(2)(ii)I	LUSH Charles Martin	b	1884 Apr 27	Auckland
	(Not married – baptised St Mary's)	d	1955 Apr 30	Auckland
3(2)(ii)II	LUSH Bertram	b	1885 Dec 30	Auckland
	(Baptised St Mary's)	d	1921 Aug 5	Wellsford
	m. Jessie Beatrice GRAHAM	m	1913 Aug 14	Whangaripo
		b	1886 Nov 11	Sydney
		d	1955 Apr 30	Whangaripo
3(2)(ii)III	LUSH Arthur	b	1888 Nov 11	Auckland
		d	1978 Aug 9	Wellington
	m. Phyllis Mary TRIFFITT	m	1921 Nov 9	Auckland St Mary's
		b	1896 Aug 12	England
		d	1971 Nov 28	Christchurch
3(2)(ii)IV	LUSH Caroline Ellen (Nell)	b	1893 Aug 3	Akd. Ewelme
	Not married	d	1981 Feb 24	Auckland
3(2)(v)I	KENDERDINE Brenda Mary	b	1892 Jan 13	
		d	1977 Nov 12	Auckland
	m. William Edward QUIGLEY	m	1916 Jul 5	
		b	1882 Oct 20	
		d	1958	Wellington
3(2)(v)II	KENDERDINE Edna	b	1894 Nov 18	
	(Not married)	d	1976 May 26	
3(2)(vi)I	WHITE William Bertram	b	1907 Apr 3	? Auckland
	(Not married)	d	1924 Nov 29	Takapau
3(2)(vi)II	WHITE Geoffrey Bertram	b	1908 Sep 12	Waipukurau
	(Not married)	d	1970 Jul 19	Waipukurau
3(2)(vi)III	WHITE Kathleen Clendon Bertram	b	1910 Jan 20	Auckland
	m. John Anderton DAKINS	m	1940	Takapau
		b	1909 Dec 21	Hastings
3(2)(vi)IV	WHITE Lesley Alison Bertram	b	1919 Apr 7	Auckland
		d	19	
	m. Edgar Delmage SAUL	m	1939 Apr 5	
		b	1912 May 28	
		d	1979 Sep 4	
3(2)(vii)I	WHITE Gordon Rutherfurd	b	1905 Nov 11	
	m. Bettina Lois RANSOM	m	1941 Mar 1	
		b	1916 Jan 24	
3(2)(vii)II	WHITE Marjorie Clendon	b	1906 Dec 2	
	(Not married)	d	1979 Nov 1	
3(2)(vii)III	WHITE Muriel Mary	b	1908 Dec 3	
	(Not married)	d	1929 Jan 11	
3(2)(vii)IV	WHITE Evelyn Freda	b	1909 Nov 10	
	(Not married)			

3(2)(x)I	STEVENSON Joyce Preston	b	1898 Aug 4	Auckland
		d	1990 Nov 21	Auckland
	m. Lester Henwood ROBERTS	m	1927 Nov 24	Auckland St Mary's
		b	1897 May 2	Christchurch
		d		
3(2)(x)II	STEVENSON Brian Preston	b	1900 Jul 22	Auckland
		d		
	m. Joanna Maud MAKGILL	m	1927 Oct 5	Auckland St Mary's
		b	1898 May 29	
		d	1975 Dec	
3(2)(xi)I	NICHOL Hilda Florence	b	1897 Sep 14	
		d	1989 Nov 4	Levin
	m. James TODD	m	1922 Dec 20	Diocesan School Chapel, Auckland
		b	1899 Dec 19	Gisborne
		d	1982 Jan 11	Levin
3(2)(xi)II	NICHOL Jack Crompton	b	1900 Jan 17	
	(Not married)	d	1974 Aug 11	Auckland
3(3)(i)I	LONG Eleanor Woodford	b	1875 Feb 7	
		d	1965 Jun 14	
	m. Basil BRENNAND	m	1914 Jan 14	
		b	1884	West Lydford
	(Flu epidemic)	d	1918 Nov	
3(3)(i)II	LONG Frank Clendon	b	1876 Apr 29	
		d	1954 Jan 29	
	m. Doris LIDDELL	m	1912 Dec 26	India
		b	1890 Sep 23	
		d	1965 Feb 8	
3(3)(i)III	LONG Alfred Charles	b	1878 Mar 16	
	m. Maude ELLIS	m	1908 Jul 15	
		b		
		d	1967 Aug 9	
3(3)(i)IV	LONG Ivy	b	1881	
	(Died in infancy)	d	1882 Feb 23	
3(3)(i)V	LONG Cyril Gervaise	b	1885 Aug 30	
		d	1966 Dec 7	
	m. Dorothy CARDNO			
	(No children)			
3(3)(i)VI	LONG Trevor	b	1891 Oct 13	
		d	1915	at Gallipoli
3(3)(ii)I	GOULD Charles Arthur Selwyn	b	1879 Jun 17	Bapt Otahuhu
	(When born abode Blenheim: father telegraph operator)			
3(3)(ii)II	GOULD Herbert Stanley	b	1880 Oct 22	Bapt Otahuhu
	(When born abode Dargaville: father telegraph officer)			
3(3)(ii)III	GOULD Alfred Mervyn	b	1882 May 12	Bapt Otahuhu
	(When born abode Dargaville: father telegraph officer)			
	(Sponsors: Ellen Julia NOLAN, J. N. Nolan, F. Gould. Baptised 1882 Jun 4 by Frank Gould)			
3(3)(iii)I	GILFILLAN Elsie Muriel Gould	b	1885	Auckland, bapt Otahuhu Dec 2
		d	1947	
	m. Henry Percy LEWIS	m	1906	divorced
3(3)(iii)II	GILFILLAN Dagmar Gertrude Gould	b	1885	Auckland
	m. George Richard MEDHURST	m	1909	Melbourne, Australia
		b	1874	
		d	1926	
3(3)(iii)III	GILFILLAN Trevor Vincent			
	m. Gertrude			
3(3)(iv)I	GOULD Frank Ernest	b	1887 Feb 25	of Dargaville
		d	1973 Aug 11	
	m. Frances Mickle NUIR	b	1889 Jun 3	
	(No issue)			
3(3)(iv)II	GOULD Vera Ida	b	1891 Feb 1	Bapt Otahuhu
	(Not married)	dc	1971	Lived Dargaville

3(3)(iv)III	GOULD Bernard Dudley	b d	1892 Nov 16 1985	Bapt Otahuhu Lived Kaipara
	m. Mary Hilda FAITHFULL	m b	1921 1894 Oct 19	
3(3)(iv)IV	GOULD Elsa Mabel m. William Ferrier HADWIN	b m b d	1894 Jan 10 1916 1893 Feb 8 1951 Aug 18	
3(3)(iv)V	GOULD Una Amy Maude m. Edward Crawford ROBINSON	b m b d	1899 May 13 1927 1909 Jan 27 1974	Lives Dargaville
3(3)(v)I	NOLAN Frank Wrey	b d	1882 1965 Jul 23	
	m. Lucy PRICE née KITSON (Daughter: Pam PRICE)	m b	1921 1889	Christchurch
3(3)(v)II	NOLAN Mary	b d	1883 Jul 9 1935 Apr 24	
	m. Richard Eyre BARTON	b d	1883 1952	
3(3)(v)III	NOLAN Gordon m. Cathie BRANDON	b b	1885 1890	Wairoa
3(3)(v)IV	NOLAN Mabel Etta	b d	1888 1960	
	m. Ian Roderick Coleridge MURCHISON	b d	1888 1964	
3(3)(v)V	NOLAN Hazel	b d	1891 1973 Sep 17	
	m. Charles OLIVER (No further information)			
3(3)(v)VI	NOLAN Henry Clyde (Toby)	b d	1893 1959	
	m. Sylvia Muriel WESTENRA	b	1898	
3(3)(v)VII	NOLAN James Gould (Pat)	b d	1899 1971	
	m. Hope Eversley BELFIELD	m b	1933 1905	Wellington Belinda
3(3)(vi)I	WANKLYN Douglas Endell m. Katherine LANE	b m	1893 1921	
3(3)(vi)II	WANKLYN John (Not married. Lieutenant in WWI.)	b d	189 1917	
3(3)(vii)I	GOULD Douglas	b		of Sydney
3(3)(vii)II	GOULD Elsie m. PATTERSON			
3(3)(vii)III	GOULD Mavis	b		
3(3)(vii)IV	GOULD Madge	b		of Brisbane
3(3)(vii)V	GOULD William m.	b		
3(3)(vii)VI	GOULD Howard	b		of Auckland
3(3)(vii)VII	GOULD Mollie	b		
3(3)(vii)VIII	GOULD Daphne	b		
3(3)(vii)IX	GOULD Tracey	b		
3(3)(vii)X	GOULD Joseph	b		
3(3)(viii)I	GOULD Leslie (Doctor in Waikato)	b		

3(3)(viii)II	GOULD Kenneth	b		
3(3)(ix)I	MORGAN Travers Grenfell (Clips)	b d	1894 1980 May	Gisborne Wellington
	m. Alison Mary Balcombe BROWN	m b d	1920 Dec 23 1898 1992 Feb	Wellington St Pauls Wellington
3(3)(x)I	GOULD Frank Clendon	b d	1904 Oct 29 1959	of Dargaville
	m. Anna WYNYARD	m b d	1929 1905 1990 Jul	
3(3)(x)II	GOULD Sir Trevor Jack	b d	1906 Jun 24	of Auckland
	m. May MILNE	m	1934	
3(3)(x)III	GOULD Peter Lyndsay	b d	1911 May 10 1988	of Auckland
	m. Olive Joy BISHOP	m	1936 Oct 31	
3(3)(xi)I	D'ARCY William Selwyn	b d	1894 1968	
	m. Constance NIXON (1)	m d	1930 1957	
	m. Doreen SWARBRICK	m	1959	
3(3)(xi)II	D'ARCY Noel Heathcote m. Jean Margaret CAMERON	b m	1898 1927	
3(3)(xi)III	D'ARCY Frank Hedworth	b d	1906 1945	
	m. Joan Aldridge CARVER	m	1937	
3(3)(xi)IV	D'ARCY Douglas Clendon m. Marcia Millicent McKENZIE	b m	1908 1932	
3(3)(xii)I	GOULD Jack Trevor	b	1903	
3(3)(xii)II	GOULD Innes m. Richard CHAPMAN			
3(3)(xiii)I	BARKER Maude Fanny Victoria	b d	1897 1955	
	m. Maurice Joseph BROWNLIE	m b d	1932 1897 1957	
3(3)(xiii)II	BARKER Percival Frank (Sheep-farmer)	b	1898	
	m. Mildred SHERRATT	m b	1921 1900	
3(3)(xiii)III	BARKER Lesley Millicent m. Frederick Ensor HUMPHREYS (Sheep-farmer)	b m b	1900 1922	of Gisborne
3(3)(xiii)IV	BARKER Walter Denzil m. Annette THORNE GEORGE	b m	1904 1935	
3(3)(xiv)I	FORDE Harold Glenis	b d	1903 Jan 22 1960 Oct 24	Auckland Auckland
	m. Dorothy Florence WHITESIDE	m b	1927 Nov 12 1900 Dec 8	St Andrews Auckland India
3(6)(i)I	HOWARD Kathleen Violet Clendon	b d	1893 Nov 21 1983 Dec 1	Auckland Wellington
	m. Harold Alexander PEEBLES	m b d	1917 Feb 24 1895 May 5 1970 Aug 27	Whangarei Kuaotunu Wellington
3(6)(i)II	HOWARD Gladys Muriel Clendon (Sissie) (Not married)	b d	1895 Jul 16 1984 Aug 16	Auckland Whangarei
3(6)(iii)I	HOWARD Ian m. Mary MILSOM	b		

3(6)(vi)I	CRAMOND Hazel m. Henry DAY	b		
3(6)(vi)II	CRAMOND Manu m. John JAMIESON (No issue)	b		
3(6)(vi)III	CRAMOND Zika M. Harry BAKER	b		
3(6)(vi)IV	CRAMOND Vida m. Raymond STOKES	b		
3(6)(ix)I	HOWARD Julie Clendon m. Ronald Herbert LEWIS	b d m b d	1916 Feb 6 1942 Nov 21 1918 Aug 18 1977 Apr 14	Otahuhu Otahuhu Te Aroha Auckland
3(6)(ix)II	HOWARD Ross Clendon m. Dulcie Joan GOW	b d m b	1923 Jul 4 1947 Jan 25 1921 Apr 28	Otahuhu Auckland Mt. Eden Auckland
3(6)(ix)III	HOWARD Joan Clendon m. George Palmer CADE	b m b d	1925 Jun 18 1969 Apr 23 1909 May 10 1987 Sep 26	Otahuhu Auckland
3(11)(iii)I	INGRAM Trevor David (1) (in the R.N.Z. Navy) m. Thelma VEART	b d m b d	1916 Dec 11 1980 Nov 20 1939 Oct 6 1919 Apr 16 1994 May	 Auckland Auckland
3(11)(iii)II	INGRAM Francis Lumsden (1) m. Elizabeth LEAF	b m b	1918 Jun 1949 1928 Mar 5	 Kaikohe
3(11)(iv)I	GUTHREY Albert Ronald m. Mary Aldyth NORRIS	b m b	1916 Jan 15 1944 Feb 10 1915 Oct 28	Rawene
3(11)(iv)II	GUTHREY Shirley Marion m. Ivan Alfonso JOHNSON	b m b	1919 Oct 3 1942 Oct 24 1917 May 4	Rawene
3(11)(iv)III	GUTHREY Nona (lives in Devon UK) m. Arthur HUNT (No issue)	b	1922 Apr 22	Rawene
3(11)(iv)IV	GUTHREY Ngaere Clendon m. Neville LANGFORD	b m b d	1925 Apr 3 1950 May 15 1914 Jun 26 1982 Jun 13	Rawene Auckland Huntly Tauranga
3(11)(iv)V	GUTHREY Barbara Ruth Takotowi m. Frans BLOM	b m b	1931 Dec 9 1955 Oct 15 1932 Jun 15	Hokitika
3(11)(v)I	MILLAR Mary Marion	b d	1936 Mar 22 1936 Mar 24	Rawene
3(11)(v)II	MILLAR Thomas Richard Clendon (Chemist) m. Audrey Maisie MONK	b m b	1937 Sep 7 1961 Feb 4 1938 Jul 5	Rawene Auckland Cambridge
3(11)(v)III	MILLAR Marjorie Ruth	b d	1939 Jan 10 1939	Rawene
3(11)(v)IV	MILLAR Geoffrey George	b d	1942 Jan 19 1942 Jan 20	Rawene
3(11)(vi)I	KEENE Richard Lumsden (Not married)	b	1925 Sep 3	

3(11)(vi)II	KEENE Lesley Dorothy	b	1932 Nov 14	
	m. Leslie MILLS	m	1967 Nov	
		b	1926 Apr 17	
3(11)(vii)I	MILLAR Joan	b	1934 Mar 19	Rawene
	m. Ronald DOBBS	b	1933 Jan 8	Whangarei
3(11)(vii)II	MILLAR Robin	b	1939 Nov 29	Rawene
	m. Jane B.	b	1940 Mar 3	Auckland
3(12)(ii)I	WEBSTER Trevor	b	1910	
		d	1973	
	m. Maisie KILGOUR	b	1915	
3(12)(iii)I	WEBSTER Philip Stephen	b	1920 Dec 23	Rawene
	m. Gladys TAPP			
3(12)(iii)II	WEBSTER Harold	b	1935	
		d	1938	
3(12)(iii)III	WEBSTER Geoffrey	b	1938	
	m. Betty WILLIAMS			
3(13)(iii)I	BROWNE Louise Margaret Clendon	b	1927 Sep 23	Auckland
	m. Breton Clyde PENMAN	m	1956 Jan 21	Hong Kong
		b	1927 Feb 13	Auckland
3(13)(iii)II	BROWNE Thomas Nicholas	b	1930 May 13	Rawene
	m. Margerat Pratricia SIMPSON	m	1953 May 23	Aukland
		b	1930 Jul 16	Aukland
3(13)(iii)III	BROWNE Adrienne Mary	b	1941 Dec 22	Te Puke
	m. Derrick Edwin DAVID	m	1961 Dec 6	Auckland
		b	1939 Feb 19	Penang
3(13)(v)I	FLOOD Mary Louise	b	1928 Jul 14	Auckland
	m. James Brennan SMITH	m	1948 Jan 10	Auckland
		b	1925 Mar 26	Auckland
3(13)(v)II	FLOOD Thomas Clendon	b	1930 Jan 2	Rawene
3(13)(v)III	FLOOD Ann Patricia	b	1931 Sep 3	Rawene
3(14)(i)I	CLENDON Trevor George (1)	b	1926 Nov 21	
	m. Valerie June SHEAT	m	1953 May	
	(No issue)	b	1933 Jun 13	
3(14)(i)II	CLENDON Frederick Thomas (1)	b	1928 Mar 3	
	m. Heather Mary BAKER	m	1952 Feb 23	
		b	1930 Feb 28	
3(14)(i)III	CLENDON Ailene Elsie (1)	b	1930 Apr 20	
	m. Peter Raoul CRIBB (1) (Divorced)	m	1951 May 19	
		b	1926 Jan 28	
	m. Cedric Stanley SMALLER (2)	m	1981 Mar 14	
		b	1926 Feb 28	
3(14)(ii)I	CLENDON John Frederick	b	1926 Jan 10	
	m. Oliver Elias JONES	m	1947 Nov 15	
		b	1926 Jul 1	
3(14)(ii)II	CLENDON Lynette Ann Maureen	b	1929 Oct 25	Lives in Queenstown
	m. Reginald PARKER	m	1947	
3(14)(ii)III	CLENDON Robin Keith Chitty	b	1937 May 17	
	m. Adele Margaret TAFT (1) (Divorced)	b	1939	
	m. Evon HARRIS (2) (Divorced)			
3(14)(ii)IV	CLENDON Helen (Adopted)	b	1939	
	m. Ralph HONEY			
3(14)(iii)I	CLENDON Leslie Hugh	b	1926 Jan 14	
		d	1942	
3(14)(iii)II	CLENDON George Melton (called Melton)	b	1927	
	m. Anne TAPP	b	1925	

3(14)(iii)III	CLENDON Joyce Ramona m. Duncan Albert McGREGOR	b m b	1928 Dec 4 1949 Dec 10 1921 Feb 24	
3(14)(iii)IV	CLENDON Daphne Mary m. McGREGOR	b m	1930 Apr 10 1950 Jun 5	
3(14)(iv)I	CLENDON Sidney James m. Doris SWANN	b d	1925 Sep 10 1947 Jan 12	
3(14)(iv)II	CLENDON Douglas Haigh m. Jillian CURRIER	b m b	1926 Dec 6 1955 Nov 26 1936 Sep 16	Live in Santa Cruz Singapore
3(14)(iv)III	CLENDON Joyce Ramona m. Duncan Albert McGREGOR	b m b	1928 Dec 4 1949 Dec 10 1921 Feb 24	
3(14)(iv)IV	CLENDON Daphne Mary m. McGREGOR	b m	1930 Apr 10 1950 June 5	
3(14)(iv)V	CLENDON Dorothy Margaret (Peggy) m. Walter Raymond BOURNE	b m b	1931 Aug 20 1952 Jan 26 1924 Oct 5	
3(14)(iv)VI	CLENDON Hilda Shirley m. Raymond Leslie LOCKWOOD	b b	1932 Feb 1 1928 Jan 25	
3(14)(iv)VII	CLENDON Beverley Anne m. Basil Raymond BOWMER	b m	1934 Jan 20 1955 Apr 11	
3(14)(iv)VIII	CLENDON Marion Dawn m. Donald Keith HALE (1) (Divorced) m. John Harvey BRADBURY	b m	1937 Jul 7 1955 Oct 8	
3(14)(iv)IX	CLENDON Murray Ronald m. Coral REID	b m	1938 Jul 16 1960 May 28	
3(14)(iv)X	CLENDON Graham Lawrence m. Merle WYATT	b m b	1942 Feb 18 1965 Jan 9 1941 May 29	
3(14)(v)I	CLENDON Norma Barbara (1) m Douglas Sydney LESLIE	b b	1931 Feb 24 1932 Mar 25	Auckland? Wellsford?
3(14)(v)II	CLENDON David Sidney m. Patricia June UNDERWOOD	b m b	1932 Oct 26 1957 1934 Sep 28	Auckland Maungaturoto
3(14)(vi)I	CLENDON William	b	1940 Feb 6	
3(14)(vi)II	CLENDON Terence m. Carol IVICH (Divorced)	b	1942 Jan 20	
3(14)(vii)I	CLENDON Maurene m. Arthur Joseph HAWKES	b	1935	
3(14)(vii)II	CLENDON Judi Anne m. Fred MORTENSEN (Divorced)	b	1939	
3(14)(vii)III	CLENDON Barry Gordon m. Karen JOHNSON	b m b	1941 1964 1945	
3(14)(vii)IV	CLENDON Dennis Keith: Twin	b d	1947 Oct 24 1947 Oct 24	
3(14)(vii)V	CLENDON Robert Eric: Twin m. Faye Esther MERCER	b m	1947 Oct 24 1970 Dec 18	
3(14)(viii)I	VINCENT Hartley Clendon m. Maureen FLEET	b m	1942 Jun 18 1960 Nov 12	
3(14)(viii)II	VINCENT Lindsay John	b	1944 Jan 24	Lives in London

3(14)(viii)III	VINCENT Julie Kathryn Adele m. Nigel Eric FRITH	b m	1948 Mar 27 1968 Apr 29	Lives in London
3(14)(viii)IV	VINCENT Gregory Hugh m. Juliana GRANICH (1) (Divorced) m. Amanda (2)	b m	1954 Feb 7 1989 Dec 13	
3(14)(viii)V	VINCENT Colin Grant (Unmarried in 1990)	b	1956 May 24	
4(1)(ii)I1	JOYCE Peter Edwin Clendon m. Beverley Mayfield WEST	b m b	1926 Jul 9 1952 Sep 6 1925 Apr 19	
4 (1)(ii)I2	JOYCE Barbara Clendon m. Stephen John Hindmarsh COX	b m b d	1929 Sep 22 1952 Jan 26 1926 May 31 1979	
4(1)(ii)II1	CLENDON Rosemary Agatha m. Donald Collins FAULL	b m b d	1926 Aug 6 1953 Jun 11 1926 Feb 14 1983 Jul 17	
4(1)(ii)II2	CLENDON Mercia Eleanor m. John Walton SIDDORN	b d m b d	1929 Feb 13 1975 Apr 21 1951 Sep 3 1924 Jun 4 1969 Jan 28	
4(2)(ii)II1	LUSH Bertram Graham m. Alethia STEVENSON	b d m b	1914 Dec 19 1978 194? 	Whangaripo Auckland England
4(2)(ii)II2	LUSH Nancy Ellen m. Reginald Edwin HUGHES (Had engineering business: Hughes & Son)	b m b d	1917 Feb 8 1942 Apr 4 1907 Jan 28 1992 Sep	Whangaripo Auckland, St Mary's Wellington Whangarei
4(2)(ii)III1	LUSH Martin Triffitt m. Elisabeth Cameron GIBSON	b m	1923 Aug 9 1951 Mar 31	Wellington Nuneaton, U.K.
4(2)(ii)III2	LUSH Phyllis Alison m. Ian Arthur WILLIAMSON	b m	1925 Apr 17 1952 Feb 2	Arapuni Christchurch St Mary's
4(2)(ii)III3	LUSH Cynthia Marjorie D.Y. Diphtheria	b d	1928 Feb 9 1930 Mar 26	Arapuni Auckland
4(2)(ii)III4	LUSH Janet Marion D.I.	b d	1931 Dec 10 1931 Dec 26	Wellington
4(2)(v)I1	QUIGLEY Margaret m. Robert Mitchell MILNE	b m b	1917 May 21 1936 Aug 12 1908 Aug 27	Auckland Auckland
4(2)(v)I2	QUIGLEY John Kenderdine m. Pamela Mary ROBINSON	b m b	1921 May 16 1945 Mar 21 1924 Apr 4	Oamaru
4(2)(vi)III1	DAKINS Pamela Rosalie m. Donald BYNG (now divorced)	b m b	1941 Mar 20 1963 Jan 28 1934 Jan1	Takapau London Bromsgrove, UK
4(2)(vi)III2	DAKINS Dianne Mary m. William George LISHMAN	b m b	1942 Sep 5 1967 May 13 1942 Nov 11	Takapau Takapau Auckland
4(2)(vi)III3	DAKINS Paul Anderton m. Denise Helen McKIRDY	b m b	1944 Jul 30 1972 Mar 31 1947 Nov 28	Stokes Valley, Wellington Lower Hutt
4(2)(vi)IV1	SAUL Judith Alison m. Ross St James DAHM	b m	1941 Sep 5 1962 Oct 6	

4(2)(vi)IV2	SAUL Antoinette Elizabeth	b	1943 May 27	Takapau
	m. Robert James COOPER (now divorced)	m	1965 Feb 20	
4(2)(vi)IV3	SAUL Gay Merle Bertram	b	1945 Sep 24	
	m. Peter George SEARLE	m	1967 Sep 30	
4(2)(vii)I1	WHITE Janet Eva Rutherfurd	b	1944 Mar 16	
	m. John Charles ROBERTS	m	1973 Nov 29	
4(2)(vii)I2	WHITE Anne Clendon	b	1945 Feb 19	
4(2)(x)I1	ROBERTS Anthony Lester	b	1928 Nov 4	Auckland
	m. Alison Gay BEDDEK	m	1953 Sep 19	Auckland
		b	1933 Jul 24	Auckland
4(2)(x)I2	ROBERTS Pauline Clendon	b	1939 Jul 28	Auckland
	m. William Frederick GORTON (Fred)	m	1961 Nov 30	Auckland St Mary's
		b	1928 May 29	Dunedin
4(2)(x)II1	STEVENSON Cynthia Mary	b	1928 Jul1	Auckland
	m. John Hampden HYATT	m	1962 May 19	Flamstead, UK
	(1992 lived in Edinburgh)	b	1928 Jun 12	Surrey
4(2)(x)II2	STEVENSON Miriam Rosemary	b	1930 Dec 18	Auckland
	m. David LESLIE	m	1986 Jul 27	
		d	1991 Apr 25	Sydney
4(2)(x)II3	STEVENSON Joanna Muriel	b	1932 Apr 18	Auckland
	m. Charles Henry FAIRWEATHER (Jock)	m	1961 Oct 21	Chelsea, London
		b	1927 Jun 27	North London
		d	1975 May 3	Tauranga
4(2)(x)II4	STEVENSON Rodney Brian Preston	b	1935 Feb 1	Auckland
	m. Suzanne GILES (1) (Divorced)			
	m. Virginia HIBERDINE (2)	m	1982 Aug 28	Auckland
		b	1944 Feb 17	Invercargill
4(2)(xi)I1	TODD Philippa Ann	b	1924 Jan 13	Auckland
	m. Peter Douglas Ledger HOLMES	m	1947 Dec 20	Levin
		b	1923 Aug 13	Auckland
		d	1991 Jul 20	Tauranga
4(2)(xi)I2	TODD David John	b	1927 Jul 23	Tokomaru Bay
	m. Sybil Alice LANCASTER	m	1951 Apr 21	
		b	1928 Feb 16	Petone
4(2)(xi)I3	TODD Alison	b	1931 Aug 14	Tokomaru Bay
	m. Keith Robert LINES	m	1951 Aug 4	Levin
		b	1920 Aug 7	Wellington
4(3)(i)I1	BRENNAND Gwendolyn Mary	b	1914 Dec 30	
	m. Stanley Malcolm SHARP	m	1942 Mar 23	
		b	1905 Jan 15	
		d	1972 Nov 23	
4(3)(i)II1	LONG Arthur Clendon	b	1913 Sep 21	
	(Airforce Instructor)	d	1943	
4(3)(i)II2	LONG Mary Ethel	b	1915 Sep 4	
	m. Claude Leslie GARNER	m	1947 Jul 12	
		b	1912 May 9	
		d	1985 May 31	
4(3)(i)II3	LONG Eileen Eleanor Lillian	b	1916 Aug 31	
	m. Alexander Henry WAKELIN	m	1940 Jan 13	
		b	1914	
		d	1982 Apr 4	
4(3)(i)II4	LONG Beryl Lydia	b	1919 Aug 19	
	m. Ronald George WAKELIN	m	1942 Jan 22	
		b	1917 May 1	
4(3)(i)II5	LONG Pamela Ruth	b	1926 Dec 14	
4(3)(i)III1	LONG Meta Erena	b	1909 May 6	
	m. Neil SMALL	m	1933 Jun 21	
		b	1905 May 5	
		d	1973 Nov 18	

4(3)(i)III2	LONG Audrey Millicent	b	1908 Jan 21		
		d	1984 Oct 18		
	m. Robert FERGUSSON	m	1931 Apr 21		
		b	1900 Jun 16		
4(3)(i)III3	LONG Charles Alfred	b	1912 Aug 6		
		d	1974 Aug		
	m. Phyllis WRATT				
4(3)(iii)I1	LEWIS Murray	b	1909	Wanganui	
		d	1974		
	m. Jean de Graaf WATERMEYER	b	1921		
4(3)(iii)I2	LEWIS John Derek	b	1913	Wanganui	
	m. Margaret SHAW (1)	m	1940		
		d	1949		
	m. Elizabeth DAY (2)	m	1951		
		b	1927		
	m. Laura (3)				
4(3)(iii)I3	LEWIS Diana Christine Neville	b	1919		
	m. John Stanhope Harrison LISTER	b	1923	England	
		d	1977		
4(3)(iii)II1	MEDHURST Shirley Travers	b	1911	Wanganui	
	m. Robert Verdon PERFECT	m	1944		
		b	1904	England	
		d	1957	Southampton	
4(3)(iii)II2	MEDHURST Vivien Barbara Gould (Baptised				
	when a child in New Zealand by Rev Frank Gauld)	b	1914	Wanganui, lives in Petersfield UK	
	m. Robert Keith CHRISTOPHERSON	m	1949 May 18	Beaulieu Abbey	
		b	1921 Jun 21	London	
4(3)(iii)II3	MEDHURST Peter Thurston	b	1917 Oct 25		
		d	1943 Aug 3	at sea on active service, Fleet Air Arm	
4(3)(iii)III1	GILFILLAN James	b			
	(RAF Pilot killed in tropical storm on active service)				
4(3)(iii)III2	GILFILLAN Janet PHD				
	m. Dr E. A. CARR (Divorced)				
4(3)(iii)III3	GILFILLAN Susan				
	m. Peter STANLEY (Divorced)				
4(3)(iv)III1	GOULD Dudley Lloyd	b	1921 Nov 8		
		d	1943	Italy	
4(3)(iv)III2	GOULD Marjorie Rae	b	1922 Oct 9		
		d	1971		
	m. Clifford VAUSE	m	1946		
		b	1917 Jun 12		
4(3)(iv)IV1	HADWIN Elsa Mary (Glory)	b	1917 May 18	Lives Waikanae	
	m. Brian Copeman WILLSON	m	1941 Jan 1		
		b	1911 Apr 26		
		d	1987		
4(3)(iv)V1	ROBINSON Jill	b	1929 Oct 18		
	m. Gordon Wright UPTON	m	1959		
		b	1921 Aug 23		
4(3)(iv)V2	ROBINSON Clendon Garth	b	1932 Sep 16		
	m. Barbara Joan MORSE	m	1960		
		b	1936 Feb 6		
4(3)(v)I1	NOLAN Penelope Ann	b	1922		
	m. Peter REYNOLDS	m	1942	Wellington	
		b	1920		
4(3)(v)II1	BARTON Richard Wynne	b	1909		
		d	1981		
	m. Pam PRICE	b	1915		
4(3)(v)II2	BARTON Patrick Arnold	b	1912		
	m. Jean SAINSBURY	b	1912		

4(3)(v)II3	BARTON John Wrey m. Patricia GIBBONS	b	1918	
4(3)(v)III1	NOLAN Nancy Brandon	b	1914	
4(3)(v)III2	NOLAN Mary Joyce m. Terence Leslie Carleton WILLIAMS	b m b	1916 1941 1916	Wairoa
4(3)(v)III3	NOLAN Gordon William m. Judith IRONS	b d	1919 1982	
4(3)(v)IV1	MURCHISON John Nolan m. Jean Catherine GILBERT	b b	1928 1932	
4(3)(v)IV2	MURCHISON Michael Roderick m. Patricia Barbara GERARD	b b	1929 1929	
4(3)(v)VI1	NOLAN Patricia Elizabeth m. Heathcote Beetham WILLIAMS	b m b	1924 1946 1922	Gisborne
4(3)(v)VI2	NOLAN Gerald James m. Basil Phyllis Howard UNWIN	b		
4(3)(v)VI3	NOLAN Juliet Mary m. Hugh Bradley RICKARD	b m	1938 1984	Gisborne
4(3)(v)VII1	NOLAN David Belfield m. Aline Janet STUDHOLME	b m	1934 1958	Hinds South, Canterbury
4(3)(v)VII2	NOLAN Jacquetta Bridget m. John Frederick CADELL	b m b	1937 1958 1929	Gisborne
4(3)(v)VII3	NOLAN Caroline Margaret m. Hugh Spearman JOHNSTONE	b m b	1939 1961 1934	Gisborne
4(3)(v)VII4	NOLAN Kerry Gould Louis m. Nicola Mary VAVASOUR	b m b	 1972 1947	Blenheim
4(3)(vi)I1	WANKLYN Patrick Endell m. Diana Maude HUMPHREYS	b d b	1922 1986 1925	See (3)(xiii)III2
4(3)(vi)I2	WANKLYN Prudence Rose Endell m. Owen Christopher JOHNSTONE	b m b	1924 1946 Nov 12 1920	
4(3)(vi)I3	WANKLYN John Endell m. Roma NORTHCOTE	b m	1928 1956	
4(3)(vii)V1	GOULD (son)	b		
4(3)(ix)I1	MORGAN Alan Grenfell (Surgeon) m. Ina June LAYBOURN (June)	b d m b	1925 Sep 7 1949 Dec 3 1925 Jun 30	Wellington Wellington St Pauls Thames
4(3)(x)I1	GOULD Patricia Ann m. Michael Dargaville MALLOY (Solicitor)	b m b	1929 1950 1926	
4(3)(x)I2	GOULD Margaret Lucy m. Keith Dargaville HARDING	b m b	1933 1953 1925	of N. Wairoa
4(3)(x)I3	GOULD Elizabeth Barbara Wynyard m. Charles Eric PARR (Gynaecologist in Auckland)	b m b	1936 Jul 30 1964 1925 Jun 12	
4(3)(x)II1	GOULD Josephine Margaret m. Arthur William YOUNG (Divorced)	b m b	1936 Mar 31 1961 1935 Mar 12	of Auckland

4(3)(x)II2	GOULD Frances Diana m. George Terence CREAGH	b m b	1936 Feb 11 1963 1933	
4(3)(x)II3	GOULD Trevor Clendon m. Mary Anne WATT (1) (Divorced) m. Janine (2)	b m b	1947 Nov 9 1971 1950 Jul 2	
4(3)(x)III1	GOULD Beverley Joy m. Ross Harry SEYMOUR	b m	1937 Sep 11 1959 Feb 12	
4(3)(x)III2	GOULD Philippa Mary m. Geoffrey Francis LINDBERG	b m	1940 Dec 4 1960 Nov 4	
4(3)(xi)III1	D'ARCY Jill Alison m. Neil Corbet BRYANT	b m	1939 1961	
4(3)(xi)III2	D'ARCY Kathryn Frances m. Michael Hugh O'Donnell ALEXANDER	b m	1945 1968	
4(3)(xi)IV1	D'ARCY Patricia	b d	1936 1940	
4(3)(xi)IV2	D'ARCY Ann Kathleen m. Nigel Bruce NATION	b m	1941 1963	
4(3)(xii)II1	CHAPMAN Colin m.	b		
4(3)(xii)II2	CHAPMAN Richard	b		
4(3)(xiii)I1	BROWNLIE Virginia Norah m. Richard Barton JOHNSON	b m b	1931 May 8 1955 Aug 24 1931 Nov 16	Gisborne of Canterbury
4(3)(xiii)I2	BROWNLIE Alexa Maude m. Thomas Christopher GRIGG	b m b	1932 Aug 21 1950 Feb 18 1926 Mar 3	Gisborne of Canterbury
4(3)(xiii)II1	BARKER Janet Maude m. Ian McNEIL (1) m. Derrick HANSEN (2)	b m	1922 1946	
4(3)(xiii)II2	BARKER Patrick Walter	b d	1923 1936	
4(3)(xiii)II3	BARKER Annette Alys m. Robert George EIVERS	b m b	1926 Dec 5 1949 May 21 1918 Mar 20	
4(3)(xiii)II4	BARKER Philip John m. Jennifer MOORE	b m	1928 1952	
4(3)(xiii)III1	HUMPHREYS Richard Ensor m. Erica Cecil ROBERTSON	b d m	1923 1972 1948	
4(3)(xiii)III2	Diana Maude HUMPHREYS m. WANKLYN Patrick Endell	b b d	1925 1922 1986	See (3)(xiii)III2
4(3)(xiii)IV1	BARKER Peter Richard Thorne m. Diana Templeman JAMES	b m b	1936 1959 1935	
4(3)(xiii)IV2	BARKER Jennifer Jane m. Michael HOLDEN	b m	1937 1959	
4(3)(xiii)IV3	BARKER Gail Maude m. Douglas DYMOCK	b m	1940 1987	
4(3)(xiv)I1	FORDE Jocelyn Barbara m. Robert JAMIESON	b m b d	1929 Apr 8 1950 Mar 28 1919 Mar 20 1974 Cot 24	Auckland Kilmarnock Auckland

4(3)(xiv)I2	FORDE Cynthia Joan	b	1932 Mar 8	Auckland
		d	1936 Aug 18	Auckland
4(3)(xiv)I3	FORDE Pamela Dorothy	b	1938 Aug 7	Auckland
4(6)(i)I1	PEEBLES Howard Jackson	b	1920 Apr 30	Whakatane
		d		
	m. Margaret Allison ROSS	m	1946 Oct 12	Wellington
		b	1925 Jan 16	Wellington
4(6)(i)I2	PEEBLES Donald Clendon	b	1922 Mar 5	Taneatua
	m. Prudence Alison CORKILL	m	1960 Aug 6	Wellington
		b	1931 Dec 28	Wellington
4(6)(i)I3	PEEBLES Graeme Ross	b	1929 Nov 28	Wellington
	m. Patricia Margaret NEWTON	m	1965 Feb 25	Wellington
		b	1937 Jan 26	Christchurch
4(6)(iii)I1	HOWARD Nicholas	b		
	m.			
4(6)(iii)I2	HOWARD Jane	b		
	m. Barry HUNTER			
4(6)(iii)I3	HOWARD Arthur Russell	b		
4(6)(vi)I1	DAY Manu	b		
	m. Raymond BAILEY			
	(No issue)			
4(6)(vi)III1	BAKER Dariel	b		
	m. Michael HOLIBAR			
4(6)(vi)IV1	STOKES Judith Gilian	b		
	(Now deceased)	d		
	m. John BARNEY			
4(6)(vi)IV2	STOKES Peter	b		
	m. Joan ROBERTSON			
4(6)(ix)I1	LEWIS Trevor Ronald	b	1945 Jul 1	Auckland
	m. Yvonne ANDREW	m	1975 Jul 8	
		b	1949 Feb 8	Auckland
4(6)(ix)I2	LEWIS Raymond Clendon	b	1950 Jun 12	Auckland
4(6)(ix)I3	LEWIS Anne Margaret	b	1956 Feb 16	Howick
4(6)(ix)II1	HOWARD Christine Clendon	b	1948 Feb 18	Remuera Auckland
	m. Giovanni Bruno TONETTO	m	1970 Feb 26	Auckland
		b	1934 Jul 27	Italy
4(6)(ix)II2	HOWARD Rosalind Anne	b	1950 Oct 24	Auckland Mt. Albert
4(6)(ix)II3	HOWARD Graeme Timothy	b	1958 Nov 12	Auckland
	m. Shirley HICKMORE	m	1984 Jan 21	Auckland
		b	1956 Oct 14	Auckland
4(11)(iii)I1	INGRAM Patricia Frances	b	1941 Sep 16	
	m. Morrie CHALLINOR	b	1932	
4(11)(iii)I2	INGRAM Marienne Gae	b	1946 Oct 14	
	m. Leon POINGDESTRE	m	1966 Jan	
4(11)(iii)I3	INGRAM David Roy	b	1944 May	
	m. Rae WHITAKER	m	1968 Nov	
4(11)(iii)II1	INGRAM Francis Keith	b	1949 Dec 30	Rawene
	m. Ann PERI	m	1969	Waima
		b	1949 Dec 2	Waima
4(11)(iii)II2	INGRAM Arthur Kenneth	b	1953 Apr 28	Rawene
	m. Audrey MITAI	m		Murupara
4(11)(iii)II3	INGRAM Marion Edith	b	1955 Jun 21	Rawene
	m. David TEWHUI	m	1974 Nov 30	Rawene

4(11)(iii)II4	INGRAM Jack m. Jenny SMALL	b m	1959 Sep 18	Rawene Wellington
4(11)(iv)I1	GUTHREY Peter Charles m. Robyn Lorraine SMITH	b m b	1944 Nov 14 1973 Feb 1 1948 Aug 13	
4(11)(iv)I2	GUTHREY Richard Norris m. Ruth Mary	b m b	1947 Jan 29 1970 1948 Nov 7	
4(11)(iv)I3	GUTHREY Philip	b	1948 Nov 25	
4(11)(iv)I4	GUTHREY John Norris m. Louise	b m b	1952 Feb 26 1980 1954	
4(11)(iv)I5	GUTHREY David m. Rosalind NEWMAN	b m b	1956 Jan 14 1987 Nov 7 1953 Sep 13	
4(11)(iv)I6	GUTHREY Mary Jane Ruth	b	1959 Apr 15	
4(11)(iv)II1	JOHNSON Paul Guthrey m. Merle WOODLEY	b m b	1944 Nov 24 1967 May 13 1945	
4(11)(iv)II2	JOHNSON Robert Guy m. Dianne IRVING (1) (Divorced) m. Jill (2)	b m m	1946 Feb 5 1967 Aug 26 1974	
4(11)(iv)II3	JOHNSON Geoffrey Ian m. Linda CAREY	b m	1950 Jan 6 1973 May 13	
4(11)(iv)II4	JOHNSON Dudley Charles m. Wendy GRIFFITHS	b m	1952 Jan 25 1973 Dec 15	
4(11)(iv)II5	JOHNSON Margot Anne m. Donald GOODMAN	b m	1955 Oct 1 1978	
4(11)(iv)II6	JOHNSON Glen Harold m. Jennifer HARE	b m	1959 Dec 7 1985 Jan 3	
4(11)(iv)IV1	LANGFORD Joanna Mary m. David GUTHRIE	b m b	1951 Oct 25 1974 May 24 1949 Oct 26	Auckland Christchurch Dunedin
4(11)(iv)IV2	LANGFORD Barbara Ruth m. Darryl WOODS	b m b	1955 Nov 1 1981 Oct 18 1946 Jul 29	Tauranga Tauranga Australia
4(11)(iv)IV3	LANGFORD Philippa Ann	b d	1957 Sep 20 1957 Nov 3	Katikati Katikati
4(11)(iv)IV4	LANGFORD Mark David m. Christine VIVIAN	b m b	1959 Oct 12 1983 May 14 1959 Mar 17	Katikati Wanaka
4(11)(iv)V1	BLOM Sabrina m. Bernd KAEHLIG (1) (Divorced) m. Raymond ALVEREZ (2) John PAXINOS (3)	b m m	1957 Apr 15 1980 1983	Melbourne
4(11)(iv)V2	BLOM Murray Anthony (Often based in the Persian Gulf – on an oil rig in Caspian Sea Christmas 1993)	b	1963 Jun 17	Takapuna
4(11)(v)II1	MILLAR Susan Ruth (Worked in her father's Mangakino pharmacy, 1994) m. Paul Terrence McMAHON	b m b	1961 Dec 5 1986 May 31 1955 Jul 22	Kaikohe Mangakino Hawera
4(11)(v)II2	MILLAR Kathryn Alice m. Owen Lewin LEWIS	b m b	1965 May 16 1984 Oct 6 1959 Sep	Auckland Rotorua Rotorua
4(11)(v)II3	MILLAR Joanne Robyn	b	1971 Apr 22	Mangakino

4(11)(vi)II1	MILLS Marion Elizabeth	b	1968 Sep 3	
	m. Dennis Reece GOWER	m	1985 Dec 8	
		b	1964 Dec 9	
4(11)(vii)I1	DOBBS Sandra	b		
	m. Brian LEE	m	1979	Kaikohe
4(11)(vii)I2	DOBBS Terry Ann			
4(11)(vii)I3	DOBBS Karen			
	m. Belnnerhassett BOYD	m	1984 Jul 30	Waimate N
4(11)(vii)I4	DOBBS Neil			
4(11)(vii)II1	MILLAR Dirk	b	1964 Apr 11	Kaikohe
	m. Helen	m	1989	Cambridge
4(11)(vii)II2	MILLAR Wade			
4(11)(vii)II3	MILLAR Susan			
4(12)(ii)I1	WEBSTER Anthony Douglas: Twin	b	1946	Marton
	m. Dorothy CALLOW			
4(12)(ii)I2	WEBSTER Dennis: Twin	b	1946	Marton
	m. Margaret SEABROOK			UK
4(12)(ii)I3	WEBSTER Susan	b	1949	Marton
	m. Louis LIND			
4(12)(ii)I4	WEBSTER Katherine	b	1952	Marton
	m. Francis LIND			
4(12)(iii)I1	WEBSTER Gregory James	b	1949	
	m. Joanne OWEN (1)			
	m. Judy SANDS (2)			
4(12)(iii)I2	WEBSTER Jennifer	b	1951	
	m. Franz SONNTAG			
4(12)(iii)I3	WEBSTER Stephen	b	1954	
	m. Annette HILL			
4(12)(iii)III1	WEBSTER Kevin	b	1953	
4(12)(iii)III2	WEBSTER Sharyn	b	1955	
	m. Peter GRIFFITHS			
4(13)(iii)I1	PENMAN Mark Adrian	b	1957 Mar 6	Hong Kong
	m. Donna EVERSON	m	1983 Jun 11	Auckland
		b	1960 Dec 15	Auckland
4(13)(iii)I2	PENMAN John Anthony	b	1958 May 4	Hong Kong
4(13)(iii)I3	PENMAN Sarah Louise	b	1959 Jun 10	Hong Kong
	m. Richard McARLEY	m	1986 Dec 21	Auckland
		b	1949 Dec 12	South Island
4(13)(iii)I4	PENMAN Helena Chan (Yee Man)	b	1961 Jun 5	Hong Kong
	m. Mark David Courtenay GREEN	m	1988 Oct 21	Auckland
		b	1956 Oct 29	South Africa
4(13)(iii)I5	PENMAN Nicholas Andrew	b	1962 Jan 16	Hong Kong
4(13)(iii)I6	PENMAN Paul Breton	b	1964 Aug 12	Hong Kong
4(13)(iii)II1	BROWNE Jennifer Mary	b	1954 Mar 12	Auckland
	m. Michael John Graham GOODGER	m	1973 Dec 23	Auckland
		b	1950 Jan 8	Fiji
4(13)(iii)II2	BROWNE Michael Thomas	b	1955 Jul 2	Auckland
	m. Rosemarie Malika UBEDA	m	1985 Jun 1	Auckland
		b	1956 Jan 31	France
4(13)(iii)II3	BROWNE Mark Nicholas	b	1956 Dec 5	Auckland
	m. Grace Debrila ZENZIC	m	1980 Sep 6	
		b	1957 May 28	Auckland

4(13)(iii)II4	BROWNE Philip Anthony	b	1959 Oct 11	Auckland
	m. Katja NOHRA	m	1984 Oct 20	Auckland
		b	1961 Mar 19	Lebanon
4(13)(iii)II5	BROWNE Katherine Mary	b	1962 Jan 24	Auckland
4(13)(iii)II6	BROWNE Nicola Mary	b	1963 Nov 20	Auckland
4(13)(iii)III1	DAVID Jerome Christian Nicholas	b	1962 Jul 19	Auckland
4(13)(iii)III2	DAVID Louise Mary	b	1963 Oct 22	Auckland
4(13)(iii)III3	DAVID Jane Katharine	b	1964 Nov 14	Auckland
4(13)(iii)III4	DAVID Catherine Theresa	b	1966 Mar 17	Penang
	m. Michel NEFF	m	1988 Nov 28	Germany
		b	1963 Apr 17	Germany
4(13)(iii)III5	DAVID Andrew John	b	1968 Feb 27	Penang
4(13)(v)I1	SMITH Vivienne Mary	b	1948 Sep 7	Auckland
	m. Maurice CHORLEY	m	1969 Dec 20	Auckland
		b	1940 Sep 7	Launceston, Tasmania
4(13)(v)I2	SMITH Jacqueline Theresa	b	1952 May 21	Auckland
	m. Charles Alexanda STEPHEN	m	1978 Oct 27	Sydney
		b	1937 Oct 2	London
4(14)(i)II1	CLENDON Raewyn Joy	b	1952 Nov 24	
	m. Grant LOWE			Opotiki
4(14)(i)II2	CLENDON Lorraine	b	1955 Sep 16	
	(Not married in 1990)			
4(14)(i)II3	CLENDON Jill Shirley	b	1957 Apr 6	
	m. Glenn ROGERS			Rotorua
4(14)(i)II4	CLENDON Bryce Frederick	b	1960 Feb 20?	
	m. Franca			
4(14)(i)III1	CRIBB Murray Peter (1)	b	1952 Aug 10	
	m. Judith Ann WARRINGTON	m	1973	
		b	1957 Feb 5	
4(14)(i)III2	CRIBB Diana Gay (1)	b	1954 Sep 3	
	m. Stephen George HAMILTON (1) (Divorced)	b	1975	
	m. John Edward HEATLEY (2)	m	1986 Jul 11	
		b	1956 Jun 16	
4(14)(i)III3	CRIBB Roger Lindsay Alan (1)	b	1955 Dec 14	
	m. Kim HIGHAM (1) (Divorced)	m	1976 May	
	dfr. Helen MOSES (2)	b	1957 Aug 15	
4(14)(ii)I1	CLENDON Peter John	b	1948 Nov 14	
	m. Barbara CATTERALL	m	1971 Mar 22	
		b	1951 Jan 4	
4(14)(ii)I2	CLENDON Janice Patricia	b	1950 Apr 3	
	m. Gilbert Lewis GODSMARK	m	1970 May 23	
		b	1948 Jun 2	
4(14)(ii)I3	CLENDON Raewyn Joy	b	1951 Jun 16	
	m. John BELL (Divorced)	m	1972 Jul 8	
4(14)(ii)I4	CLENDON Dianne Elizabeth	b	1954 Aug 16	
	m. Gary Bertram TROUP	m	1975 Apr 12	
		b	1952 Oct 3	
4(14)(ii)I5	CLENDON David James	b	1955 Sep 11	
	m. Ruth WILSON	b	1954 Aug 1	
4(14)(ii)I6	CLENDON Bruce Douglas	b	1959 Jun 8	
	m. Laura TYKODI	m	1987 Jul 25	
		b	1964 Jul 25	
4(14)(ii)I7	CLENDON Katherine Louise	b	1962 May 12	
	m. Ian KERR	m	1988 Jan 30	
		b	1951 Aug 1	

4(14)(ii)II1	PARKER Philip Geoffrey	b	1949 Sep 22	Lives in USA
4(14)(ii)III1	CLENDON Lance Robin	b	1959 Jul 17	
4(14)(ii)III2	CLENDON Grant Alan John	b	1960 Dec 4	
4(14)(iii)I1	CLENDON Heather Margaret m. Frank PEARS	b	1946 May 2	
4(14)(iii)II1	CLENDON Mark John m. Cherry DONALD (Divorced)	b	1951	
4(14)(iii)II2	CLENDON Geoffrey Hugh (Unmarried in 1990)	b	1953	
4(14)(iii)II3	CLENDON Jill	b	1961 Sep 17	
4(14)(iii)II4	CLENDON Mark	b	1964 Mar 15?	
4(14)(iii)II5	CLENDON Rory	b	1977 May 11	
4(14)(iii)III1	McGREGOR Stephen Robert m. Carolyne WYLDE	b m b	1951 Oct 28 1975 Feb 15 1946 Apr 22	
4(14)(iii)III2	McGREGOR Grant Irwin (Unmarried in 1990)	b	1953 Dec 7	
4(14)(iii)III3	McGREGOR Philip Wayne m. Patricia Jean SHARP	b m b	1957 Apr 20 1986 May 24 1961 Sep 9	
4(14)(iii)III4	McGREGOR Mark Lindsay m. CIndy Jo PEEL	b m	1960 Jan 4 1981 Dec 11	
4(14)(iii)IV1	McGREGOR Charmaine m.	b		
4(14)(iii)IV2	McGREGOR Dennis m.			
4(14)(iii)IV3	McGREGOR Susan			
4(14)(iii)IV4	McGREGOR Wendy m.			
4(14)(iv)II1	CLENDON Dale m. Sandie	b m	1957 May 10 1986	
4(14)(iv)II2	CLENDON Neil	b	1959 Mar 6	
4(14)(iv)V1	BOURNE Neville James	b	1953 Nov 30	
4(14)(iv)V2	BOURNE Peter Raymond George (Possum) m. Lynn STEPHENS (Divorced 1988)	b m	1956 Apr 13 1984 Oct 13	
4(14)(iv)V3	BOURNE Geoffrey Lawrence m. Lynda Jane THORNTON	b m	1958 Apr 28 1985 Mar 30	
4(14)(iv)V4	BOURNE Deborah Margaret	b	1959 Jul 31	
4(14)(iv)V5	BOURNE Kristine Grace m. Bryan David NICOL	b m	1961 Aug 21 1985 Apr 28	
4(14)(iv)VI1	LOCKWOOD Gregory Lance	b	1954 May 13	
4(14)(iv)VI2	LOCKWOOD Warren Leslie m. Caroline	b	1955 Jul 17	
4(14)(iv)VI3	LOCKWOOD Marilyn Fay	b	1958 Apr 16	
4(14)(iv)VI4	LOCKWOOD Craig Lee m. Suzanne BALL	b	1961 Jan 25?	
4(14)(iv)VII1	BOWMER Karen Joy	b	1956 May 2	

4(14)(iv)VII2	BOWMER Gavin Ross m. Helen BROWN (1) (Divorced) m. Shelley REES (2)	b	1958 Jan 18	
4(14)(iv)VII3	BOWMER Rodney	b	1960 Sep 27	
4(14)(iv)VIII1	HALE Robert Alan (1) m. Sharon BYRNE	b	1957 Feb 26	
4(14)(iv)VIII2	Vickie	b		
4(14)(iv)VIII3	Paul	b		
4(14)(iv)IX1	CLENDON James	b	1964 Apr 26?	
4(14)(iv)IX2	CLENDON Peter (Dougal)	b	1967 Dec	
4(14)(iv)X1	CLENDON Cary Edward m. Lorraine Joy OLIVER	b m b	1966 May 25 1987 Mar 28 1966 Feb 16	
4(14)(iv)X2	CLENDON Tony Ramon	b	1968 May 17	
4(14)(iv)X3	CLENDON Dene Nicholas	b	1970 Jun 15	
4(14)(iv)X4	CLENDON Cherie Ann Louise	b	1971 Sep 20	
4(14)(v)I1	LESLIE Barbara Mary m. Stan WATTON	b b	1955 Apr 28 1951 Oct 25	Warkworth Whangarei
4(14)(v)I2	LESLIE Sydney Wayne m. Linda Elizabeth SMALL	b b	1956 Jul 12 1959 Oct 28	Warkworth
4(14)(v)I3	LESLIE Sandra Delwyn m. Brian Geoffrey SHAW	b b	1959 Nov 24 1955 Apr 8	Warkworth
4(14)(v)I4	LESLIE Allan Douglas	b	1962 Oct 21	Warkworth
4(14)(v)II1	CLENDON Donna June m. Kerry Joseph ERCEG	b	1958 Apr 18	Paparoa Wellsford
4(14)(v)II2	CLENDON Carol Patricia	b	1960 Feb 24	Paparoa
4(14)(v)II3	CLENDON Yvonne Anne m. Anthony Francis ATKINS	b m	1961 Apr 12	Paparoa Wellsford
4(14)(v)II4	CLENDON Judy Diane	b	1963 Jun 20	Kaikohe
4(14)(vi)II1	CLENDON Yvette Lee	b	1975 Dec 12	
4(14)(vi)II2	CLENDON Phillip	b	1982 Jun 30	
4(14)(vii)I1	HAWKES Angela (now Anna) Josene m. FORRESTER	b	19	
4(14)(vii)I2	HAWKES Susan Glenda	b	19	
4(14)(vii)I3	HAWKES Michael Joseph	b	19	
4(14)(vii)I4	HAWKES Josie Lisette	b	19	
4(14)(vii)I5	HAWKES Kim Daryl	b	19	
4(14)(vii)I6	HAWKES Amanda	b	19	
4(14)(vii)III1	CLENDON Kerry Lee m. Hubert Clarence NICHOLSON	b m	1965 1985	
4(14)(vii)III2	CLENDON Stephen Roger m. Jennifer Gladys WEIR	b m	1966 1987	
4(14)(vii)III3	CLENDON Jarrad Dean	b	1972	
4(14)(vii)V1	CLENDON Jason Eric	b	1972 Dec 6	
4(14)(vii)V2	CLENDON Tracy Lee	b	1975 May 16	

4(14)(viii)I1	VINCENT Brett Hartley	b	1961 May 3
4(14)(viii)I2	VINCENT Kellie Maree	b	1968 Jan 6
4(14)(viii)I3	VINCENT Sarah Jane	b	1970 Feb 19
4(14)(viii)II1	VINCENT Tui Moana	b	1972 Mar 19
4(14)(viii)II2	VINCENT Polyanna Leonora Mary	b	1981 Oct 29
4(14)(viii)III1	FRITH Lucy Kathryn	b	1973 May 4
4(14)(viii)III2	FRITH Miles Eric	b	1978 Jun 20
4(14)(viii)III3	FRITH Alice Adele	b	1981 Sep 10
4(14)(viii)III4	FRITH Henry Clendon	b	1983 Jul 4

5(1)(ii)I1i	JOYCE Christopher Clendon m. Gael Campbell	b m b	1953 Jul 15 1981 Mch 6 1952 Sep 3	
5(1)(ii)I1ii	JOYCE John Simon m. Sharyn Rose BHANA	b m b	1956 Jun 14 1982 Jan 29 1958 Apr 23	
5(1)(ii)I1iii	JOYCE Philippa Anne m. Michael CHARLTON	b m b	1961 Jun 29 1987 Jan 15 1961 Jan 25	
5(1)(ii)I2i	COX Jeremy John Hindmarsh (Adop) m. Megan Jane ALEXANDER	b m b	1953 Jun 24 1988 Apr 15 1963 Sep 3	
5(1)(ii)I2ii	COX Rosemary de Beauvoir (Adop) m. Tony Marko PECOTIC	b m b	1955 Jun 5 1988 Nov 7 1947 Aug 12	
5(1)(ii)II1i	FAULL Angela Clendon m. Richard HURLEY	b m b	1955 Aug 25 1987 Jul 3 1955 Sep 3	
5(1)(ii)II1ii	FAULL Richard John Collins m. Sara ROBINSON	b m b	1957 May 21 1984 Nov 24 1957 Dec 8	
5(1)(ii)II2i	SIDDORN Anne Clendon m. Richard GREEN-WILKINSON	b m	1952 Jun 18 1972 Sep 3	
5(1)(ii)II2ii	SIDDORN Gillian Mary m. Philip FOSTER	b m	1954 Jul 4 1977	
5(2)(ii)II1i	STEVENSON Rodney Eric (Adopted)			
5(2)(ii)II2i	HUGHES Pamela Anne m. Anthony Clifton Frank LANGTON	b m b	1943 May 7 1966 May 7 1942 Dec 1	Whangarei Auckland Auckland
	(Called 'Tony' – was Farm Adviser with Dept of Agriculture; 1993 Independent Adviser.) (1992 – Pam did remedial teaching part time)			
5(2)(ii)II2ii	HUGHES Barbara m. Maxwell James HARRIS (Farmer)	b m b	1946 Aug 30 1966 Sep 3 1934 Sep 11	Whangarei Whangarei Auckland
5(2)(ii)III1i	LUSH Philippa Mary m. Neville Andrew IDOUR	b m b	1952 Apr 11 1941 Sep 14	Crowborough, U.K. Dunedin
5(2)(ii)III1ii	LUSH Katherine Elisabeth (Kate)	b	1954 Aug 19	Dunedin
5(2)(ii)III1iii	LUSH Andrew Martin m. Susan Elizabeth STOCKWELL	b m b	1957 Dec 4 1990 Jan 20 1954 Aug 22	Dunedin Wanganui

5(2)(ii)III2i	WILLIAMSON Margaret Lorna	b	1953 May 3	Wellington
	m. Anthony Edward STRATTON	m	1976 Aug 28	
		b	194? Dec 24	
5(2)(ii)III2ii	WILLIAMSON Arthur Ross (Ross)	b	1955 Jul 26	Wellington
	m. Wendy KING	m	1977 Nov 26	Auckland
		b	1955 Aug 14	
5(2)(ii)III2iii	WILLIAMSON Peter Hawkins	b	1958 Feb 17	Wellington
5(2)(ii)III2iv	WILLIAMSON Helen Janet	b	1960 Oct 14	Wellington
	m. Keith Ian CHALLANDS	m	1986 Mar 29	
		b	1955 Sep 25	England
5(2)(v)I1i	MILNE Roderick Ian	b	1942 Jan 14	Auckland
	m. Irene Faith BUTLER	m	1973 Mar 31	
		b	1947 Nov 14	
5(2)(v)I1ii	MILNE Alistair Robert	b	1945 Feb 16	
	(Died young)	d	1946 May 5	Auckland
5(2)(v)I1iii	MILNE Andrew Kenderdine	b	1948 Jul 30	Auckland
	m. Janice Ruth WATSON	m	1971 Feb 27	
		b	1950 Mar 12	
5(2)(v)I2i	QUIGLEY Nicholas John Kenderdine	b	1946 Aug 20	Auckland
	m. Helen Margaret BULL	m	1973 Sep 1	
		b	1950 Apr 16	
5(2)(v)I2ii	QUIGLEY Michael Meredith	b	1948 Aug 11	
5(2)(v)I2iii	QUIGLEY Elizabeth Mary	b	1950 Jun 6	
	m. Ian Robert STANLEY	m	1983 Nov 26	
		b	1950 Jul 11	
5(2)(v)I2iv	QUIGLEY Amanda Caroline	b	1956 Mar 27	
	m. Gregory John TWINAME	m	1989 Nov 4	
5(2)(vi)III1i	BYNG Michelle Susan	b	1965 Jun 20	Amsterdam
5(2)(vi)III1ii	BYNG Simon Andrew	b	1969 Dec 31	Melbourne
5(2)(vi)III2i	LISHMAN Nicola Marie	b	1968 Feb 17	Auckland
	m. Glen WHEELER	m	1990 Apr 25	Edinburgh
		b	1965 Aug 1	Hamilton
5(2)(vi)III2ii	LISHMAN Rachel Dianne	b	1970 Jan 18	Auckland
5(2)(vi)III2iii	LISHMAN Paul William	b	1972 May 28	Auckland
5(2)(vi)III3i	DAKINS Richard Anderton	b	1975 Mar 15	Waipukurau
5(2)(vi)III3ii	DAKINS Matthew Charles	b	1978 Mar 26	Waipukurau
5(2)(vi)III3iii	DAKINS Louise Clendon	b	1980 Feb 5	Waipukurau
5(2)(vi)IV1i	DAHM Ian Ross	b	1963 Nov 20	
	m. Michele EATON	m	1985 Apr 6	
5(2)(vi)IV1ii	DAHM Murray William	b	1965 Apr 7	
5(2)(vi)IV1iii	DAHM Kerryn Marie	b	1967 May 15	
5(2)(vi)IV2i	COOPER Vicki Elizabeth	b	1970 Mar 2	
5(2)(vi)IV2ii	COOPER Jarrod Stephen Robert	b	1971 Oct 21	
5(2)(vi)IV2iii	COOPER Clinton Andrew	b	1973 Oct 29	
5(2)(vi)IV3i	SEARLE Dianne Cherie	b	1969 Jan 29	
5(2)(vi)IV3ii	SEARLE Bradley Peter	b	1971 Jan 20	
5(2)(vi)IV3iii	SEARLE Trudi Lee	b	1973 Jan 27	
5(2)(vii)I1i	ROBERTS Anna Louise	b	1975 May 27	

5(2)(vii)I1ii	ROBERTS Peter John	b	1977 May 12	
5(2)(vii)I1iii	ROBERTS Catherine Mary	b	1978 Jan 12	
5(2)(x)I1i	ROBERTS Anne Elizabeth	b	1955 Mar 15	Auckland
	m. Peter A SAVORY (1) (divorced)	m	1975 Dec 15	
		b	1951 Dec 10	
	m. Quentin Keith HILLS (2)	m	1984 Jan 6	
		b	1957 Dec 17	Wellington
5(2)(x)I1ii	ROBERTS Prudence Gay	b	1958 Feb 19	Auckland
	m. David Blair Francis BROWN	b	1954 Jan 1	Auckland
5(2)(x)I2i	GORTON Peter Howard	b	1962 Oct 12	Auckland
	m. Louise Jean WARD	m	1991 Jun 8	Waipukurau St Mary's
		b		
5(2)(x)I2ii	GORTON Mark Clendon	b	1964 Nov 7	Rotorua
	m. Leanne DAY (1) (Divorced)	m	1986 Apr 19	
	m. Pauline McKECHNIE (2)	m	1989 Dec 27	Brisbane
		b	1962	Scotland
5(2)(x)II1i	HYATT Michael John Guthrie	b	1963 Jun 9	Edinburgh
	(1992 lived in Edinburgh)			
5(2)(x)II1ii	HYATT Juliet Mary	b	1964 Aug 21	Edinburgh
	m. Kevin John BROWN	m	1991 May 17	Edinburgh
	(1992 lived in Toulouse)	bc	1963 Jun 4	
5(2)(x)II1iii	HYATT Susan Joanna	b	1967 Oct 18	Auckland
	(1992 lived in Edinburgh)			
5(2)(x)II3i	FAIRWEATHER Alistair Andrew Chalmers	b	1962 Nov 30	Dunfermline,Scotland
5(2)(x)II3ii	FAIRWEATHER Sarah Joanna	b	1966 May 9	Tasmania
	m. Steven James COWIE	m	1992 Mar 7	Tauranga St Johns
		b	1964 Jun 18	Marton
5(2)(x)II4i	STEVENSON Mark Preston (1)	b	1958 Sep 11	Auckland
5(2)(x)II4ii	STEVENSON Victoria Anne (1)	b	1960 Feb 29	Auckland
5(2)(xi)I1i	HOLMES Elizabeth Ann	b	1951 Jun 10	Auckland
	m. David MichaeL AYRES	m	1982 Sep 4	Sydney
		b	1952 Sep 8	Sydney
5(2)(xi)I1ii	HOLMES Wendy Joy	b	1955 Oct 15	New Plymouth
	m. David Anthony PAUL	m	1974 Aug 31	New Plymouth
		b	1954 Jan 8	New Plymouth
5(2)(xi)I1iii	HOLMES Alison Pamela	b	1959 Mar 13	New Plymouth
	m. John Alexander LAURENSON	m	1980 Oct 3	Nettlebed
		b	1952 May 13	Glasgow
5(2)(xi)I2i	TODD Geoffrey Arthur	b	1952 Mar 26	Lower Hutt
	m. Linda Lola DYETT	m	1973 Jan 21	Wellington
		b	1952 Aug 28	Wellington
5(2)(xi)I2ii	TODD Patricia Ann	b	1955 Dec 11	Lower Hutt
	m. Patrick Mark CAMPION	m	1986 Jun 7	Sydney
		b	1952 Mar 20	Ireland
5(2)(xi)I2iii	TODD Gary James	b	1957 Nov 8	Lower Hutt
	m. Marilyn Lisevy ROSE (1) (Divorced)	m	1984 Mar 31	Sydney
	m. Debbie (2)	m	1993 Feb	Sydney
5(2)(xi)I3i	LINES Victoria Jane	b	1952 Jul 7	Levin
	m. David Graham PALMER	m	1974 Feb 8	Levin
		b	1951 Aug 19	
5(2)(xi)I3ii	LINES Anthony James	b	1954 May 17	Levin
	m. Mary LAWSON	m	1982 Feb 17	Napier
		b	1956 Dec 21	Napier
5(2)(xi)I3iii	LINES Robert Andrew	b	1955 Oct 9	Levin
	m. Dorothy Joy GARLICK	m	1979 Oct 20	Auckland
		b	1956 Jan 28	Karamea

5(2)(xi)I3iv	LINES Peter Keith	b	1959 Oct 16	Levin
	(Died in infancy)	d	1959	Levin
5(2)(xi)I3v	LINES David Keith	b	1962 Oct 15	Levin
	m. Rebecca Mary CHRISTOPHERS	m	1986 Feb 22	Matamata
		b	1962 Aug 27	
5(3)(i)I1i	SHARP Malcolm Russell	b	1943 Feb 10	
	m. Maxine Elizabeth DARROW	m	1964 Oct 10	
		b	1943 Jun 6	
5(3)(i)I1ii	SHARP Eleanor Gwendolyn	b	1944 May 25	
	m. Rex McMaster KEYS	m	1966 Jan 15	
		b	1944 Jul 23	
5(3)(i)I1iii	SHARP Geoffrey Clendon	b	1947 Mar 13	
	m. Lynn WILKINSON (1)	m	1967 May 20	
		b	1949 Mar 18	
	m. Aileen NORRISH (2)	m	1979 Jul 27	
		b	1945 Sep 7	
5(3)(i)I1iv	SHARP Margaret Marian	b	1949 Oct 24	
	m. Ron LICHTWARK	m	1971 Nov 6	
		b	1937 Jul 23	
5(3)(i)II2i	GARNER Pauline Elizabeth	b	1948 Aug 20	
	m. Gary BROWNE (Divorced 1982)	m	1978 Jul 22	
5(3)(i)II2ii	GARNER Peter Arthur	b	1950 Nov 12	
	m. Judy (1) (Divorced)			
	m. Anna Marie (2)	m	1987	
5(3)(i)II2iii	GARNER Claudia Kay	b	1952 Oct 20	
	m. John			
5(3)(i)II3i	WAKELIN Judith Marie	b	1941 Jan 10	
	m. Keith Ashton WHITE (Alan)	m	1960 Feb 6	
		b	1938 Jan 5	
5(3)(i)II3ii	WAKELIN Roger Dudley	b	1946 Apr 26	
	m. Vicki Cromwell			
		b	1948 Jul 4	
5(3)(i)II3iii	WAKELIN Deborah Anne	b	1957 Jun 13	
	m. Craig OLIVER	m	1988 Feb 24	
5(3)(i)II4i	WAKELIN Barbara Joan	b	1942 Nov 5	
	m. Joe BENTLEY (1) (Divorced 1979 Apr 7)	m	1964 Sep 7	
	m. John Antill GAWITH (2)	m	1979 Apr 7	
5(3)(i)II4ii	WAKELIN Linda Rosalind	b	1948 Dec 1	
	m. John Anthony DEAN	m	1969 Apr 11	
5(3)(i)III1i	SMALL Neil Bruce	b	1934 Oct 24	
	m. Rosemary LARKIN	m	1955 Dec 27	
		b	1932 Jun 8	
5(3)(i)III1ii	SMALL Trevor John	b	1937 Jan 6	
	m. Beverley BRIGHT	m	1960 Dec 17	
		b	1937 Oct 8	
5(3)(i)III1iii	SMALL Erena Maude	b	1940 May 27	
	m. John NEILSON	m	1960 May 10	
		b	1937 Oct 17	
5(3)(i)III1iv	SMALL Alan Keith	b	1943 May 8	
	m. Louise FISHER	m	1969 Dec 4	
		b	1943 Mar 17	
5(3)(i)III2i	FERGUSSON Murray	b	1933 Nov 24	
	m. Anne WESNEY	m	1958 Mar 15	
		b	1936 Mar 10	
5(3)(i)III2ii	FERGUSSON Roger	b	1936 Aug 6	
	m. Eileen TROY	m	1965 May 8	
		b	1935 Jun 3	

5(3)(i)III2iii	FERGUSSON Warren	b	1940 Aug 16
	m. Rosemarie ALABA	m	1983 Sep 25
5(3)(i)III2iv	FERGUSSON Basil	b	1942 May 22
	m. June WING	m	1964 Dec 12
		b	1946 Mar 29
5(3)(i)III3i	LONG Janice (Adopted)		
5(3)(i)III3ii	LONG Marian (Adopted)		
5(3)(iii)I1i	LEWIS Charles	b	1951	South Africa
5(3)(iii)I1ii	LEWIS Janet Christine Anne	b	1953	South Africa
	m. Clifford Andrew JORDAN	m	1977
		b	1949
5(3)(iii)I2i	LEWIS John Elliot (1)	b	1942
	(headmaster of Eton College)		
	m. Vibeka JOHANNSON	b	1947
5(3)(iii)I3i	LISTER Simon John (Adopted)	b	1960
5(3)(iii)I3ii	LISTER Mark Harris (Adopted)	b	1961
5(3)(iii)II1i	PERFECT Victoria	b	1945
	m. Michael Mawan MEGUID	m	1967	Boston, USA
		b	1944
5(3)(iii)II1ii	PERFECT Timothy Robert	b	1948
	m. Maureen HYAMS	b	1950	divorced 1995
5(3)(iii)II2i	CHRISTOPHERSON Peter Dormen	b	1952 Aug 14	Cornwall
	m. Christine O'NEILL	m	1984 Aug 12	Richmond
		b	1986 Oct 3	Belfast
5(3)(iii)III2i	CARR Anthony		
5(3)(iii)III2ii	CARR Nicholas		
5(3)(iii)III2iii	CARR Sarah Jane (Sally) PHD		
5(3)(iii)III3i	STANLEY Elizabeth	b	1951
5(3)(iii)III3ii	STANLEY Anne (triplets)	b	1954	Cuckfield, Sussex
5(3)(iii)III3iii	STANLEY Ruth (triplets)	b	1954	Cuckfield, Sussex
5(3)(iii)III3iv	STANLEY Mary (triplets)	b	1954	Cuckfield, Sussex
5(3)(iii)III3v	STANLEY Judith	b	1960	Haywards Heath, Sussex
5(3)(iv)III2i	VAUSE Gail Lorraine	b	1950 Jan 18
5(3)(iv)III2ii	VAUSE Janice Anne	b	1952 Sep 29
5(3)(iv)IV1i	WILLSON Patricia Mary (Adopted)	b	1947 May 22
	m. Errol LATTENSON (1)	m	1973
	m. Donald DELBRIDGE (2)	m	1978
5(3)(iv)IV1ii	WILLSON Alan Hadwin (Adopted)	b	1949 Feb 14
	m. Susan Margaret CRIMENS (1)	m	1971 Jun 26
	m. Lynnette Rona ROWLEY (2)	m	1981 Feb 14
5(3)(iv)V1i	UPTON Simon Guy	b	1961 Jun 7
	m. Joanne Pamela DAVIES	m	1983
		b	1965 Jun 22
5(3)(iv)V1ii	UPTON André Scott	b	1964 Oct 7
	m. Janet Christine KEMP	m	1983
		b	1962 Jun 23
5(3)(iv)V1iii	UPTON Fiona Anne (Adopted)	b	1967 Mar 24
	m. Michael Alan RADFORD	m	1984
		b	1957 Mar 21
5(3)(iv)V2i	ROBINSON Diane Lynne	b	1964 Jul 9

5(3)(iv)V2ii	ROBINSON Susan Jane	b	1967 Aug 16	
5(3)(v)I1i	REYNOLDS Eva Sally	b	1943	
	m. Simon Charles PARKER	m	1964	Gisborne
		b	1939	
5(3)(v)I1ii	REYNOLDS Guy Morris	b	1946	
		d	1988	
	m. Annabell SHERRATT	m	1972	Gisborne
5(3)(v)I1iii	REYNOLDS Martin Wrey Morris	b	1950	
	m. Caroline UPHAM	m	1975	Christchurch
5(3)(v)I1iv	REYNOLDS William Peter Morris	b	1964	
5(3)(v)II1i	BARTON Richard Hugh	b	1939	
	m. Jillian Mary BUNNY (1)	b	1940	
	m. Anne HAISMAN (2)			
5(3)(v)II1ii	BARTON Peter Howard	b	1941	
	m. Judith Sybella DYMOCK	m	1975	
		b	1951	
5(3)(v)II1iii	BARTON Tessa Mary	b	1945	
	m. Frederick Charles Richard LEVINGE	b	1939	
5(3)(v)II2i	BARTON Timothy Patrick	b	1954	
	m.	m	1989	
5(3)(v)II3i	BARTON Mary Ann	b	1947	
	m. John C. CHAMBERS			
5(3)(v)II3ii	BARTON Susan Gibbons	b	1950	
	Desmond John COWIE	m	1977	Ruatoria
		b	1950	
5(3)(v)II3iii	BARTON Jane Gibbons	b	1953	
	m. Robert Bertram TAIT	m	1978	Ruatoria
		b	1950	
5(3)(v)II3iv	BARTON Sally Gibbons	b	1955	
	m. Hamish Duncan SPENCER	m	1983	Ruatoria
		b	1952	
5(3)(v)III2i	WILLIAMS Andrew Carleton	b	1941	Gisborne
	m. Katherine VEITCH	m	1972	
5(3)(v)III2ii	WILLIAMS Timothy Nolan	b	1948	Christchurch
	m. Jennifer CHAPMAN	m	1970	
		b	1947	
5(3)(v)III2iii	WILLIAMS John Terence	b	1950	Waimate
	m. Helen Frances MEYER	m	1973	
5(3)(v)III2iv	WILLIAMS Christopher Henry	b	1955	Auckland
	m. Jillian KIDDLE	m	1985	
5(3)(v)III3i	NOLAN Lucy Gordon	b	1948	Wairoa
	m. John Anthony LARSEN			
5(3)(v)III3ii	NOLAN Sally Gordon	b	1951	Wellington
	m. Neil McLAUGHLIN			
5(3)(v)III3iii	NOLAN Annabel Gordon	b	1956	Wairoa
	m. Mark FRANKLIN			
5(3)(v)IV1i	MURCHISON John Gilbert	b	1958	
5(3)(v)IV1ii	MURCHISON Susan Mabel	b	1960	
	m. Peter John LAMBIE	b	1958	
5(3)(v)IV1iii	MURCHISON Lucy Jean	b	1961	
5(3)(v)IV1iv	MURCHISON Cushla Mary	b	1963	
	m. Brent George MURDOCH	b	1960	

5(3)(v)IV2i	MURCHISON Francis Meg	b 1953	
	m. John Bassett MORTEN	b 1951	
5(3)(v)IV2ii	MURCHISON Deborah Coleridge	b 1954	
	m. John David McKELVIE	b 1952	
5(3)(v)IV2iii	MURCHISON Christine Jane	b 1956	
	m. Richard CROUCH	b 1953	
5(3)(v)VI1i	WILLIAMS James N. Marcus	b 1948	
5(3)(v)VI1ii	WILLIAMS Susan Rosemary	b 1950	
	m. Gerald Bruce KEMP	m 1976	Gisborne
		b 1947	
5(3)(v)VI1iii	WILLIAMS Hamish Beetham Nolan	b 1952	Turihua, Gisborne
	m. Angela BEAMISH	m 1979	Otamuri, Hawkes Bay
		b 1956	
5(3)(v)VI1iv	WILLIAMS Philida Anne	b 1954	
	m. Michael Patrick EIVERS	m 1976	
		b 1952	
5(3)(v)VI1v	WILLIAMS David Heathcote Beetham	b 1958	Gisborne
	m. Kirsty Anne WILSON	m 1984	Wellington
		b 1961	Wellington
5(3)(v)VI1vi	WILLIAMS Arnold Henry Beetham	b 1960	Gisborne
		d 1962	
5(3)(v)VI1vii	WILLIAMS Amanda Mary	b 1963	Gisborne
	m. Ian Duncan CRISP	m 1989	Gisborne
		b 1962	Gisborne
5(3)(v)VI2i	NOLAN Vicki Jane	b 1960	
	m. John S. TIETJEN	m 1988	
5(3)(v)VI2ii	NOLAN Peter Gerald	b 1962	
5(3)(v)VI2iii	NOLAN Hamish William	b 1970	
5(3)(v)VII1i	NOLAN Julia Elizabeth	b 1959	
	m. Richard CODRINGTON	m 1987	London
5(3)(v)VII1ii	NOLAN Bridget Alexandra	b 1961	
5(3)(v)VII1iii	NOLAN Michael Studholme	b 1964	
5(3)(v)VII2i	CADELL Caroline Elizabeth Scarlett	b 1960	
5(3)(v)VII2ii	CADELL Alexandra Jane	b 1962	
5(3)(v)VII2iii	CADELL Charles Belfield Mallock	b 1965	
5(3)(v)VII3i	JOHNSTONE Charlotte Sarah Hope	b 1962	
5(3)(v)VII3ii	JOHNSTONE James Nolan Spearman	b 1966	
5(3)(v)VII3iii	JOHNSTONE Phoebe Jacquetta Mary	b 1970	
5(3)(v)VII4i	NOLAN Rosamund Mary Hope	b 1974	
5(3)(v)VII4ii	NOLAN David Patrick Hugh	b 1976	
5(3)(v)VII4iii	NOLAN Abigail Charlotte	b 1978	
5(3)(v)VII4iv	NOLAN Ineke Rachel Claire	b 1982	
5(3)(vi)I1i	WANKLYN Jennifer Lesley	b 1948	
	m. John PETERS	m 1977	
		b 1932	
5(3)(vi)I1ii	WANKLYN Robert Endell	b 1950	
	m. Pauline Loraine WILLS	m 1976	
		b 1953	
5(3)(vi)I1iii	WANKLYN William Roger	b 1953	
	m. Penelope FERGUSON	m 1981	
		b 1958	

5(3)(vi)I1iv	WANKLYN John Humphreys m. Georgina Ann CAMERON	b 1955 m 1985 b 1960	
5(3)(vi)I1v	WANKLYN Timothy Donald m. Suzanne WARREN	b 1963 m 1985 b 1964	
5(3)(vi)I2i	JOHNSTONE Philip Harry Bell m. Bronwyn GRAINGER	b 1948 Nov 18 b 1952 Jul	Timaru
5(3)(vi)I2ii	JOHNSTONE Richard Own m. Beverley BELL	b 1950 May 26 m 1974 Dec 14 b 1948 Oct 23	Timaru Ashburton
5(3)(vi)I2iii	JOHNSTONE Joanna Rosemary m. Wayne Terrence MORGAN	b 1951 Jul 7 m 1979 Dec 22 b 1951 Aug 13	Timaru Timaru
5(3)(vi)I2iv	JOHNSTONE Fiona Elizabeth	b 1955 Mar 10	Timaru
5(3)(vi)I2v	JOHNSTONE Christopher Endell m. Julia BARCLAY	b 1964 May 5 m 1988 Nov 12	Timaru Timaru
5(3)(vi)I3i	WANKLYN Catherine Francis m. David John THACKER	b 1957 Nov 28 m 1983 Mar 27 b 1955 Oct 14	Gov. Bay
5(3)(vi)I3ii	WANKLYN Jacquetta Jane m. Andrew Robert HAZELDINE	b 1958 Nov 11 m 1982 Nov 20 b 1956 Apr 16	Gov. Bay
5(3)(vi)I3iii	WANKLYN David Endell	b 1959	
5(3)(ix)I1i	MORGAN Wayne Grenfell m. Margaret TOMLINSON (Maggie)	b 1951 Jan 22 m 1979 Feb 10 b	Wellington Wellington St Pauls England
5(3)(ix)I1ii	MORGAN Wendy Jane m. Bernard Matthew HILL	b 1952 Jun 1 m 1974 b	Wellington Wellington St Marys
5(3)(ix)I1iii	MORGAN Philippa Mary m. Andrew Roderick MEEHAN	b 1958 Dec 10 m 1981 Mar 6	Wellington Wellington St Pauls
5(3)(ix)I1iv	MORGAN Suzanne Margaret m.	b 1963 Apr 14	Wellington
5(3)(x)I1i	MALLOY Kathleen Anne m. Timothy Peter GREVILLE (Solicitor)	b 1951 m 1973 b 1948	
5(3)(x)I1ii	MALLOY John Clendon m. Claude Anne-Marie J. LOLLINGER	b 1953 m 1983	
5(3)(x)I1iii	MALLOY Timothy Michael m. Wynanda Johanna Maria JANSEN	b 1956 m 1981	
5(3)(x)I1iv	MALLOY Barbara Mary m. Ronald Frederick GASTON	b 1958 m 1984	
5(3)(x)I1v	MALLOY Catherine Elizabeth	b 1972	
5(3)(x)I2i	HARDING Judith Margaret m. Ross Duncan MIDDLETON	b 1954 m 1973	
5(3)(x)I2ii	HARDING Josephine Anna m. Norman FOY	b 1956 m 1984	
5(3)(x)I2iii	HARDING Harold Keith m. Penelope Fiona SMART	b 1957 m 1985	
5(3)(x)I2iv	HARDING Patricia Lynn m. Athol Ross FRIEDRICH	b 1959 m 1982	
5(3)(x)I2v	HARDING Peter Clendon m. Lynette May GAUSEL	b 1960	

5(3)(x)I2vi	HARDING Robert Frank	b	1963	
5(3)(x)I2vii	HARDING Brian Charles	b	1967	
5(3)(x)I3i	PARR Anna Frances	b	1965 Feb 28	
5(3)(x)I3ii	PARR Jennifer Margaret	b	1966 Nov 18	
5(3)(x)I3iii	PARR Elizabeth Hilary	b	1969 May 30	
5(3)(x)II1i	YOUNG Diana Margaret	b	1962 May 5	
5(3)(x)II1ii	YOUNG Michael John	b	1966 Jan 2	
5(3)(x)II1iii	YOUNG David William	b	1970 Feb 12	
5(3)(x)II2i	CREAGH Helen Mary	b	1964 Jun 17	
5(3)(x)II2ii	CREAGH Adrienne Margaret	b	1966 Jul 23	
5(3)(x)II2iii	CREAGH Christine Anne	b	1971 Jul 20	
5(3)(x)II3i	GOULD Anna (1)	b		
5(3)(x)III1i	SEYMOUR Geoffrey Clendon	b	1960 Mar 17	
5(3)(x)III1ii	SEYMOUR William Ross	b	1961 Aug 4	
5(3)(x)III1iii	SEYMOUR John Lyndsay: Twin	b	1968 Jan 12	
5(3)(x)III1iv	SEYMOUR Justine Beverley: Twin	b	1968 Jan 12	
5(3)(x)III2i	LINDBERG Sally Ann	b	1963 Mar 5	
5(3)(x)III2ii	LINDBERG Craig Francis	b	1965 Jan 6	
5(3)(x)III2iii	LINDBERG Phillip Lyndsay	b	1966 Sep 28	
5(3)(xi)III1i	BRYANT Nicola Kathryn	b	1962	
5(3)(xi)III1ii	BRYANT Richard D'Arcy	b	1964	
5(3)(xi)III2i	ALEXANDER Philippa Joan	b	1969	
5(3)(xi)III2ii	ALEXANDER Christopher Hugh O'Donnell	b	1970	
5(3)(xi)IV2i	NATION Sarah Elizabeth	b	1966	
5(3)(xi)IV2ii	NATION Kathryn Margaret	b	1969	
5(3)(xi)IV2iii	NATION Paul Bennington	b	1972	
5(3)(xii)II1i	CHAPMAN Angus	b	1972	
5(3)(xii)II1ii	CHAPMAN Iain	b	1973	
5(3)(xiii)I1i	JOHNSON Anna Maude m. David Michael ABBOTT	b m b	1956 Oct 2 1984 Mar 23 1957 Jul 11	 Springfield
5(3)(xiii)I1ii	JOHNSON Lucinda Eleanor m. David John Lennox DOUGLAS	b m b	1957 Oct 20 1980 Nov 29 1955 Jun 25	 Springfield
5(3)(xiii)I1iii	JOHNSON Fiona Virginia m. William Turnbull STEVENS	b b	1960 Sep 29 1956 Jan 18	
5(3)(xiii)I1iv	JOHNSON Richard WIlliam Maurice	b	1970 Mar 23	
5(3)(xiii)I2i	GRIGG Tessa Maude	b	1959 Apr 17	
5(3)(xiii)I2ii	GRIGG John Maurice m. Audrey Hilary CULLEN	b m b	1962 Jul 28 1989 Jun 17 1963 Oct 12	 Devon, UK
5(3)(xiii)II1i	McNEIL Alys Kay (1) m. John LANDON-LANE	b m b	1947 1971 1945	

5(3)(xiii)II3i	EIVERS Linda Marion	b	1950 Feb 21
	m. Richard Harold GADDUM	m	1977 Feb 26
		b	1953 Oct 29
5(3)(xiii)II3ii	EIVERS Dinah Annette	b	1951 May 10
	m. Angus John GORDEN	m	1981 Feb 21
		b	1950 Apr 16
5(3)(xiii)II3iii	EIVERS Michael Patrick	b	1952 May 31
	m. Phillida Anne WILLIAMS	m	1976 Oct 22
		b	1955 Sep 28
5(3)(xiii)II3iv	EIVERS Midge Veronica	b	1954 Mar 18
	m. Robert Francis Thomas CURRAN	m	1980 Mar 1
		b	1952 Apr 11
5(3)(xiii)II3v	EIVERS Sandra Gay	b	1956 Sep 15
	m. John Halten BOJESEN-TREPKA	m	1979 Oct 27
		b	1956 Nov 12
5(3)(xiii)II3vi	EIVERS Carol Jan	b	1959 Jan 3
	m. David William GEORGE	m	1989 Mar 11
		b	1951 Aug 4
5(3)(xiii)II3vii	EIVERS William George	b	1962 Dec 26
	m. Bronwen Lisa HORDER	m	1987 Jul 24
		b	1967 Oct 19
5(3)(xiii)II4i	BARKER Jennifer Kim	b	1953
	m. David Ross GARDINER	m	1972
		b	1947
5(3)(xiii)II4ii	BARKER Derry	b	1956
	m. Philip Vincent STOVELL	m	1978
		b	1953
5(3)(xiii)II4iii	BARKER Jenny Lea	b	1960
	m. Michael Hugh STOVELL	m	1980
		b	1958
5(3)(xiii)II4iv	BARKER Robin Wynne	b	1962
	m. Hamish Bayly de LATOUR	m	1982
		b	1960
5(3)(xiii)III1i	HUMPHREYS Christine Lesley	b	1950
	m. Timothy Charles TAYLOR	m	1972
		b	1947
5(3)(xiii)III1ii	HUMPHREYS Peter Richard	b	1952
	m. Suzanne Mary BULL	m	1978
		b	1956
5(3)(xiii)III1iii	HUMPHREYS Guy Murray	b	1960
	m. Margaret Diana GUNSON	m	1985
		b	1961
5(3)(xiii)III2i	WANKLYN Jennifer Lesley	b	1948
	m. John PETERS	m	1977
		b	1932
5(3)(xiii)III2ii	WANKLYN Robert Endell	b	1950
	m. Pauline Loraine WILLS	m	1976
		b	1953
5(3)(xiii)III2iii	WANKLYN William Roger	b	1953
	m. Penelope FERGUSON	m	1981
		b	1958
5(3)(xiii)III2iv	WANKLYN John Humphreys	b	1955
	m. Georgina Ann CAMERON	m	1985
		b	1960
5(3)(xiii)III2v	WANKLYN Timothy Donald	b	1963
	m. Suzanne WARREN	m	1985
		b	1964

5(3)(xiii)IV1i	BARKER Penelope Jane	b	1960	
5(3)(xiii)IV1ii	BARKER Ian m. Lynne McLEAN	b m b	1962 1985 1961	
5(3)(xiii)IV1iii	BARKER William James	b	1967	
5(3)(xiii)IV2i	HOLDEN Jane Barker m. Jeremy Kenneth WILLIAMS	b m b	1960 1986 1954	
5(3)(xiii)IV2ii	HOLDEN Thomas Michael m. PARKER	b m	1961 1989	
5(3)(xiii)IV2iii	HOLDEN Paul	b	1964	
5(3)(xiv)I1i	JAMIESON Susan Kay	b	1954 Oct 2	Auckland
5(3)(xiv)I1ii	JAMIESON Janet Ann m. Raymond Sydney EVERITT	b m	1956 Sep 24 1985 Feb 9	Auckland Sydney
5(6)(i)I1i	PEEBLES Jan Lesley m. Wayne George MOYLE	b m b	1949 Apr 18 1969 1949 Feb 9	Wellington Wellington
5(6)(i)I1ii	PEEBLES Bruce Russell m. Jacky DANIEL	b m	1950 Apr 15 1983 Jan 8	Wellington Paraparaumu
5(6)(i)I1iii	PEEBLES Noel Scott	b	1954 Oct 1	Wellington
5(6)(i)I1iv	PEEBLES Dale Lynette m. Gerald HARPUR	b m b	1957 Jul 3 1981 Jan 17 1956 Jan 18	Wellington Raumati Sth Wellington
5(6)(i)I2i	PEEBLES Karen Clendon	b	1963 Nov 19	Wellington
5(6)(i)I2ii	PEEBLES John Eric m. Catherine HUNT	b m	1966 Jan 30 1991 Mar 9	Christchurch Christchurch
5(6)(i)I2iii	PEEBLES Colin Mark	b	1969 Jul 18	Christchurch
5(6)(i)I3i	PEEBLES Murray Clendon	b	1967 Dec 18	Wellington
5(6)(i)I3ii	PEEBLES Alastair Newton	b	1969 Feb 18	Wellington
5(6)(i)I3iii	PEEBLES Catherine Janet	b	1970 Jul 23	Wellington
5(6)(i)I3iv	PEEBLES Ross Alexander	b	1972 Aug 19	Wellington
5(6)(iii)I2i	HUNTER Amanda	b		
5(6)(vi)III1i	HOLIBAR Jane	b		
5(6)(vi)III1ii	HOLIBAR Marie	b		
5(6)(vi)III1iii	HOLIBAR Robyn	b		
5(6)(vi)III1iv	HOLIBAR Jennie	b		
5(6)(vi)IV1i	BARNEY Victoria Judith	b	1971	
5(6)(vi)IV1ii	BARNEY Michelle	b		
5(6)(vi)IV1iii	BARNEY Belinda	b		
5(6)(vi)IV2i	STOKES Richie Graham	b		
5(6)(vi)IV2ii	STOKES Robbie Clendon	b	1971	
5(6)(vi)IV2iii	STOKES Lesley	b		
5(6)(ix)I1i	LEWIS Carol Anne	b	1972 May 29	Auckland
5(6)(ix)I1ii	LEWIS Philip Trevor	b	1974 Nov 18	Auckland
5(6)(ix)II1i	TONETTO Michael Antony	b	1972 Nov 2	Wellington

5(6)(ix)II1ii	TONETTO Daniella Christine Rita	b	1974 Dec 7	Palmerston North
5(6)(ix)II3i	HOWARD Gemma Ruby	b	1984 Aug 6	Auckland
5(11)(iii)I1i	CHALLINOR Karen Marie	b	1964 Oct 20	
5(11)(iii)I1ii	CHALLINOR Christine Lynda	b	1966 Jan 13	
5(11)(iii)I1iii	CHALLINOR John Michael	b	196 Feb 25	
5(11)(iii)I1iv	CHALLINOR Warren David	b	1969 Aug 26	
5(11)(iii)I2i	POINGDESTRE Michele Gae	b	1967 Oct	
5(11)(iii)I2ii	POINGDESTRE Philip Marc	b	1969 Sep	
5(11)(iii)I2iii	POINGDESTRE Yvette Danielle	b	1972 Sep	
5(11)(iii)I3i	INGRAM David Terence	b	1970 Oct	
5(11)(iii)I3ii	INGRAM Lee Sebastian	b	1972 Jan	
5(11)(iii)II1i	INGRAM Rhonda	b	1969 Feb 11	Rawene
5(11)(iii)II1ii	INGRAM Ken George	b	1974 Jun 5	Rawene
5(11)(iii)II1iii	INGRAM Ihaka	b	1976 Sep 9	Auckland
5(11)(iii)II2i	INGRAM Shamus	b	1989 Mar 7	Hamilton
5(11)(iii)II3i	TEWHUI Elizabeth Dawn	b	1972 Mar 21	Rawene
5(11)(iii)II3ii	TEWHUI Leo Lumsden	b	1973 Aug 24	Rawene
5(11)(iii)II3iii	TEWHUI Marion	b	1974 Oct 6	Rawene
5(11)(iii)II3iv	TEWHUI Joshua	b	1976 Jun 8	Rawene
5(11)(iii)II4i	INGRAM Niklas	b	1982 Apr 27	Wellington
5(11)(iv)I1i	GUTHREY Nicholas	b	1975 Sep 8	
5(11)(iv)I1ii	GUTHREY Anna	b	1977 Jul 1	
5(11)(iv)I1iii	GUTHREY Timothy Peter Ronald	b	1979 Jun 25	
5(11)(iv)I1iv	GUTHREY Andrew Richard	b	1982 Aug 15	
5(11)(iv)I2i	GUTHREY Christopher	b	1970 May 5	
5(11)(iv)I2ii	GUTHREY Hamish	b	1974 Nov	
5(11)(iv)I4i	GUTHREY Francis Diana	b	1981 Feb 1	
5(11)(iv)I4ii	GUTHREY George	b	1982 May 7	
5(11)(iv)I4iii	GUTHREY Antonia Mary Louise	b	1983 Oct 28	
5(11)(iv)I5i	GUTHREY Julia Mary	b	1985 Jun 1	
5(11)(iv)I5ii	GUTHREY Elizabeth Clare	b	1989 Sep 18	
5(11)(iv)II1i	JOHNSON Darinee Ann	b	1969 Aug 29	
5(11)(iv)II1ii	JOHNSON Anthony	b	1971 Jun 1	
5(11)(iv)II1iii	JOHNSON Madeline Kate	b	1973 Aug 3	
5(11)(iv)II2i	JOHNSON Toni Nicola (1)	b	1970 Feb 17	
5(11)(iv)II2ii	JOHNSON Anna Rachel (1)	b	1971 Jun 3	
5(11)(iv)II2iii	JOHNSON Matthew Guy (1)	b	1972 Oct 28	
5(11)(iv)II2iv	JOHNSON Katie Jane (1)	b	1974 Feb 5	
5(11)(iv)II2v	JOHNSON Andrew (2)	b	1975 Jun 26	

5(11)(iv)II2vi	JOHNSON Sarah (2)	b	1980 Nov 4	
5(11)(iv)II2vii	JOHNSON Sophie (2)	b	1986 Sep 2	
5(11)(iv)II3i	JOHNSON Emma Kate	b	1980 Jul 17	
5(11)(iv)II3ii	JOHNSON Hamish Ian	b	1983 Sep 5	
5(11)(iv)II4i	JOHNSON Haydon	b	1981 Dec 13	
5(11)(iv)II4ii	JOHNSON Jeremy	b	1984 Sep 2	
5(11)(iv)II5i	GOODMAN Nigel	b	1979 Jan 3	
5(11)(iv)II5ii	GOODMAN Claire Ruth	b	1983 Jan 20	
5(11)(iv)IV1i	GUTHRIE Racquel Cara	b	1977 Sep 1	Auckland
5(11)(iv)IV1ii	GUTHRIE Simon David	b	1984 Apr 18	Auckland
5(11)(iv)IV2i	WOODS Robert Mark	b	1992 Sep 30	
5(11)(iv)V1i	PAXINOS Julia (3)	b	1992 May	
5(11)(v)II1i	McMAHON Bridget Jane	b	1981 Oct 15	Tokoroa
5(11)(v)II1ii	McMAHON Adam Richard	b	1984 Mar 13	Tokoroa
5(11)(v)II2i	LEWIS Emma Louise	b	1985 Mar 20	Auckland
5(11)(v)II2ii	LEWIS Annette Joyce	b	1987 Mar 14	Whangarei
5(11)(vi)II1i	GOWER Dana Lee	b	1986 Feb 3	
5(11)(vi)II1ii	GOWER Martin Lewis	b	1988 Feb 13	
5(11)(vi)II1iii	GOWER Daniel Walter	b	1989 Jul 3	
5(11)(vii)I1i	LEE Casey	b	1980 Apr 9	
5(11)(vii)I1ii	LEE Nathan	b	1981 Oct 19	
5(11)(vii)I1iii	LEE Samuel	b	1983 Oct 8	
5(12)(ii)I2i	WEBSTER Leyshon	b	1972	Palmerston North
5(12)(ii)I2ii	WEBSTER Lara	b	1974	Marton
5(12)(ii)I3i	LIND Louisa m. Roger DAYSH	b m	1967 1988 Dec 6	
5(12)(ii)I3ii	LIND Cory	b	1970	
5(12)(ii)I3iii	LIND Gavin	b	1973	
5(12)(iii)I1i	WEBSTER Michelle (1)	b	1973	
5(12)(iii)I1ii	WEBSTER Dionne (1)	b	1976	
5(12)(iii)I2i	SONNTAG Claire	b	1974	
5(12)(iii)I2ii	SONNTAG Marcus	b	1976	
5(12)(iii)I2iii	SONNTAG Jacob	b	1979	
5(12)(iii)I2iv	SONNTAG Gabrielle	b		
5(12)(iii)III2i	GRIFFITHS Michelle	b	1971	
5(12)(iii)III2ii	GRIFFITHS Tanyia	b	1973	
5(12)(iii)III2iii	GRIFFITHS Stacey	b	1976	
5(13)(iii)I3i	McARLEY Charlotte Louise	b	1979 Jan 26	Auckland
5(13)(iii)I3ii	McARLEY Leilani Yee Man	b	1982 Jul 13	Auckland

5(13)(iii)I3iii	McARLEY Tristan John	b	1985 Jul 9	Auckland
5(13)(iii)I3iv	McARLEY Peter Emrys	b	1986 Oct 12	Auckland
5(13)(iii)I4i	GREEN Sebastian Dennis Courtenay	b	1989 Sep 23	Auckland
5(13)(iii)II1i	GOODGER Talia	b	1977 Apr 24	Auckland
5(13)(iii)II1ii	GOODGER Nicholas	b	1978 Nov 8	Auckland
5(13)(iii)II1iii	GOODGER Sophie	b	1982 Oct 14	Auckland
5(13)(iii)II2i	BROWNE Melina Malika Rosa Maria Katherine Ubeda	b	1986 Jul 2	Auckland
5(13)(iii)II3i	BROWNE Nicholas Andrew Zenzic	b	1987 May 18	Hong Kong
5(13)(iii)II3ii	BROWNE André James Zenzic	b	1989 Dec 18	Hong Kong
5(13)(v)I1i	CHORLEY Clinton Matthew	b	1971 Mar 27	Auckland
5(13)(v)I1ii	CHORLEY Daniel John	b	1975 Sep19	Auckland
5(13)(v)I2i	STEPHEN Peter Alexander	b	1977 Nov 2	Sydney
5(13)(v)I2ii	STEPHEN Alexis Josephine	b	1981 Dec 14	Sydney
5(14)(i)II1i	LOWE Andrew	b		
5(14)(i)II1ii	LOWE Jamie	b		
5(14)(i)II1iii	LOWE Mathew	b	1987 Jul 14	
5(14)(i)II3i	ROGERS Megan	b	1987 Jul 14	
5(14)(i)II3ii	ROGERS Daniel Thomas	b	1989 Dec 18	
5(14)(i)III1i	CRIBB Ronald Thomas	b	1973 Dec 19	
5(14)(i)III1ii	CRIBB Caroline Diana	b	1976 May 25	
5(14)(i)III2i	HEATLEY Alexandra Rose (2)	b	1988 May 21	
5(14)(i)III2ii	HEATLEY Thomas Elliot Clendon (2)	b	1989 Dec 13	
5(14)(i)III3i	CRIBB Tammy Julia (1)	b	1976 Oct 15	
5(14)(i)III3ii	CRIBB Kelly Ann (1)	b	1978 Jan 29	
5(14)(i)III3iii	CRIBB Rebecca Mary (2)	b	1990 Mar 7	
5(14)(ii)I1i	CLENDON Petra Jane	b	1971 Feb 16	
5(14)(ii)I1ii	CLENDON Penny Jan	b d	1973 Sep 6 1974 Nov 15	
5(14)(ii)I1iii	CLENDON David Peter (Adopted)	b	1975 Feb 5	
5(14)(ii)I2i	GODSMARK Lewis John	b	1970 Nov 8	
5(14)(ii)I2ii	GODSMARK Robert James	b	1972 Jan 11	
5(14)(ii)I2iii	GODSMARK Emma Elizabeth	b	1979 Mar 10	
5(14)(ii)I3i	BELL Michael William	b	1976 Aug 21	
5(14)(ii)I3ii	BELL Stephen John	b	1978 Apr 19	
5(14)(ii)I4i	TROUP Russell William	b	1979 Sep 26	
5(14)(ii)I4ii	TROUP Clare Elizabeth	b	1981 Oct 24	
5(14)(ii)I4iii	TROUP Warwick James	b	1985 May 19	
5(14)(ii)I5i	CLENDON Kaya Ruth	b	1980 Mar 1	
5(14)(ii)I7i	KERR	b	1990 Jun	

5(14)(iii)I1i	PEARS Marnie			
5(14)(iii)I1ii	PEARS Mathew			
5(14)(iii)II1i	CLENDON Alexander Guyan	b	1971 Apr 20	
5(14)(iv)II1i	CLENDON Brian Patrick	b	1990 Apr 5	
5(14)(iii)III1i	McGREGOR Daniel James Clendon	b	1983 Apr 14	
5(14)(iii)III4i	PEEL-McGREGOR Zachary	b	1983 Jan 13	
5(14)(iii)III4ii	PEEL-McGREGOR Ry	b	1984 Jun 1	
5(14)(iii)III4iii	PEEL-McGREGOR Katala	b	1988 Aug 25	
5(14)(iii)IV1i				
5(14)(iii)IV1ii				
5(14)(iii)IV1iii				
5(14)(iii)IV1iv				
5(14)(iv)V3i	BOURNE Christopher James Oliver	b	1987 Jun 2	
5(14)(iv)V3ii	BOURNE Mathew David	b	1989 May 2	
5(14)(iv)VI2i	LOCKWOOD Paul			
5(14)(iv)VI2ii	LOCKWOOD Tony	b		
5(14)(iv)VIII1i	HALE Amanda	b	1985 Feb 24	
5(14)(iv)VIII1ii	HALE Mathew	b	1987 Feb 28	
5(14)(v)I1i	WATTON Craig Eric Brice	b	1976 Dec 27	Whangarei
5(14)(v)I1ii	WATTON Phillip Leslie	b	1978 Jan 5	Whangarei
5(14)(v)I1iii	WATTON Steven Allan	b	1981 Oct 10	Whangarei
5(14)(v)I2i	LESLIE Delwyn Manie	b	1980 Nov 22	Warkworth
5(14)(v)I2ii	LESLIE Wayne Bruce	b	1982 Nov 1	Warkworth
5(14)(v)I3i	SHAW Katie June	b	1990 Aug 21	Paparoa
5(14)(v)II1i	ERCEG Kirsten Koran	b		
5(14)(v)II1ii	ERCEG Shanell May	b		
5(14)(v)II1iii	ERCEG Melissa Clendon	b		
5(14)(v)II3i	ATKINS Monique Jelvon Clendon	b	1984 Sep 11	Warkworth
5(14)(v)II3ii	ATKINS Blake Anthony Clendon	b	1986 Dec 21	Warkworth
5(14)(vii)I1i	FORRESTER Tristan	b	19	
5(14)(vii)I1ii	FORRESTER Rosemary	b	19	
5(14)(vii)III1i	NICHOLSON Sam	b		
5(14)(vii)III1ii	NICHOLSON Zak	b		
5(14)(vii)III2i	CLENDON	b	1990	
6(1)(ii)I1iia	JOYCE Nicholas Clendon	b	1983 Jan 25	
6(1)(ii)I1iib	JOYCE Stuart William	b	1984 Oct 10	
6(1)(ii)I1iic	JOYCE Sophia Louise	b	1987 Sep 9	
6(1)(ii)I2iia	PECOTIC Stephen Peter Clendon	b	1987 Nov 12	

6(1)(ii)II1iia	FAULL Lucy Alexander	b	1987 Jun 4	
6(1)(ii)II1iib	FAULL Olivia	b	1989 Mch 21	
6(1)(ii)II2ia	GREEN-WILKINSON Claire	b	1978 Feb 21	
6(1)(ii)II2ib	GREEN-WILKINSON Edward	b	1980 Jun 18	
6(1)(ii)II2ic	GREEN-WILKINSON Laura	b	1984 Jun 19	
6(1)(ii)II2iia	FOSTER Jake	b	1988 Jul 3	
6(2)(ii)II2ia	LANGTON Kay Suzanne	b	1967 Dec 29	Masterton
	(1992 – Kay an air traffic controller at Tauranga)			
6(2)(ii)II2ib	LANGTON Jennifer Ann (Jenny)	b	1969 Feb 14	Masterton
	m. Neil FERRIS	m	1990 Jun 9	Whangarei
	(1992 lived at Whareora)	b		
6(2)(ii)II2iia	HUGHES Karen Judith	b	1968 Apr 10	Whangarei
	(BA, LLB Barrister June 1990, Family and Criminal Lawyer			
	1992 with Ross, Holmes & Low, Auckland)			
	m. Brian FERRIS	m	1995 Feb	
6(2)(ii)II2iib	HUGHES David Maxwell	b	1970 Aug 13	Whangarei
	(BEngElectrical, 1st Class Honours, Akd. Uni			
	1991 design engineer with Design Power in Hamilton)			
6(2)(ii)II2iic	HUGHES Roslyn Tracey	b	1973 Mar 29	Whangarei
	m. Mark Tony LINGS	m	1993 Feb 6	Kamo
	(Plumber, then trained as a nurse)	b	1967 Jun21	Hammersmith, UK
6(2)(ii)III1iiia	LUSH Emily Kate	b	1991 Sep 4	Nelson
6(2)(ii)III2ia	STRATTON Julia Mary	b	1979 May 14	Hamilton
6(2)(ii)III2ib	STRATTON Richard Edward	b	1982 Sep 28	Te Puke
6(2)(ii)III2ic	STRATTON Fiona Gillian	b	1985 June 20	Te Puke
6(2)(ii)III2iia	WILLIAMSON Hannah Alison	b	1981 Jan 20	Thames
6(2)(ii)III2iib	WILLIAMSON Sarah Dawn	b	1982 May 27	Thames
6(2)(ii)III2iic	WILLIAMSON Philip Ross	b	1983 Oct 29	Thames
6(2)(ii)III2iid	WILLIAMSON Luke Ian	b	1986 Apr 9	Thames
6(2)(ii)III2iva	CHALLANDS Michael John	b	1988 Dec 8	Wellington
6(2)(ii)III2ivb	CHALLANDS Caroline Alison	b	1991 Jul 3	
6(2)(ii)III2ivc	CHALLANDS Stephen	b	1994 Mar	
6(2)(v)I1ia	MILNE Virginia Louise	b	1977 Nov 21	
6(2)(v)I1ib	MILNE Paul Roderick	b	1984 Nov 2	
6(2)(v)I1iiia	MILNE Melanie Sarah	b	1973 Jan 14	
6(2)(v)I1iiib	MILNE Katherine Philippa	b	1977 Mar 14	
6(2)(v)I1iiic	MILNE Lucy Margaret Kenderdine	b	1978 Aug 31	
6(2)(v)I2ia	QUIGLEY Andrew John (Adopted)	b	1984 Jun 27	
6(2)(v)I2iiia	STANLEY Charlotte Caroline	b	1986 Jul 25	
6(2)(v)I2iiib	STANLEY Thomas George	b	1988 Jul 5	England
6(2)(vi)III2ia	WHEELER Jessica Leigh	b	1990 Sep 8	London
6(2)(vi)III2ib	WHEELER	b	1992	
6(2)(x)I1ia	HILLS Justin Barrett (2)	b	1988 Apr 15	Sydney
6(2)(x)I1ib	HILLS Alexandra Clare (2)	b	1992 Feb 21	Melbourne

6(2)(x)I1iia	BROWN Sarah Louise	b	1986 Jan 14	Auckland
6(2)(x)I1iib	BROWN Helen Frances	b	1988 Aug 13	Auckland
6(2)(x)I2iia	GORTON Sarah Kate (2)	b	1992 Feb 26	Brisbane
6(2)(xi)I1ia	AYRES Jeffrey David	b	1984 May 22	Sydney
6(2)(xi)I1ib	AYRES Nicholas Peter	b	1987 Apr 9	Sydney
6(2)(xi)I1iia	PAUL Amber Jean	b	1981 Jan 20	Rotorua
6(2)(xi)I1iib	PAUL Briar Alexandra	b	1983 Jun 16	Rotorua
6(2)(xi)I1iic	PAUL Hannan David	b	1985 Mar 14	Rotorua
6(2)(xi)I1iiia	LAURENSON Rosie Alice	b	1988 Apr 18	Tauranga
6(2)(xi)I1iiib	LAURENSON Sophie Emma	b	1990 Aug 9	Tauranga
6(2)(xi)I2ia	TODD Laurence David	b	1983 Oct 2	Wellington
6(2)(xi)I2ib	TODD Heather Robin	b	1986 Nov 2	Wellington
6(2)(xi)I2iiia	TODD Alexander James (1)	b	1986 Apr 23	Sydney
6(2)(xi)I3ia	PALMER Jessica Mary	b	1975 Jul 18	Carteron
6(2)(xi)I3ib	PALMER Nicholas James: Twin	b	1977 Mar 15	Carteron
6(2)(xi)I3ic	PALMER Lauren Melissa: Twin	b	1977 Mar 15	Carteron
6(2)(xi)I3iia	LINES Alexandra Louise	b	1987 Jan 22	Wellington
6(2)(xi)I3iib	LINES Emma Clare	b	1988 May 23	Wellington
6(2)(xi)I3iiia	LINES Alice Rose	b	1982 Sep 2	Auckland
6(2)(xi)I3iiib	LINES Sophie Camille	b	1984 Oct 21	Auckland
6(2)(xi)I3iiic	LINES Oliver Robert	b	1987 Sep 6	Waikare North Canterbury
6(2)(xi)I3va	LINES Christopher Jacob	b	1994 Mar 22	Auckland
6(3)(i)I1ia	SHARP Byron Maxwell (Lived in Adelaide 1989) m. Rosemary Anne STAPLES	b m b	1966 Oct 17 1987 Mar 7 1967 Apr 18	
6(3)(i)I1ib	SHARP Paul Clendon	b	1968 Oct 26	
6(3)(i)I1ic	SHARP Vincent Malcolm	b	1972 Mar 14	
6(3)(i)I1id	SHARP Catherine Audrey (Adopted)	b	1973 Mar 28	
6(3)(i)I1iia	KEYS Lynda Maree	b	1969 Feb 19	
6(3)(i)I1iib	KEYS Annette Ruth	b	1970 Aug 9	
6(3)(i)I1iiia	SHARP Kristene Helen (1)	b	1968 Apr 29	
6(3)(i)I1iiib	SHARP Michael John (1)	b	1971 Dec 21	
6(3)(i)I1iiic	SHARP Natalie Jane (2)	b	1981 Jan 24	
6(3)(i)I1iva	LICHTWARK Stephen Bryan	b	1974 Feb 4	
6(3)(i)I1ivb	LICHTWARK Geoffrey Craig	b	1975 Oct 15	
6(3)(i)II2ia	BROWNE Laura	b	1981 Jan 2	
6(3)(i)II3ia	WHITE Adam Ashton m. Anita D'SOUZA	b m	1964 May 31 1987 May 16	
6(3)(i)II3ib	WHITE David Alexander	b	1965 Jun 6	
6(3)(i)II3ic	WHITE Christian Alan	b	1967 Apr 14	

6(3)(i)II3id	WHITE Susan Elizabeth	b	1970 Feb 2
6(3)(i)II3iia	WAKELIN Sacha Roselle	b	1974 Jul 17
6(3)(i)II4ia	BENTLEY Jenifer Nadine (1)	b	1967 Nov 21
6(3)(i)II4ib	BENTLEY Lisa Rachel (1)	b	1971 Jan 1
6(3)(i)II4ic	BENTLEY Michael Joseph (1)	b	1972 Aug 8
6(3)(i)II4id	BENTLEY Stephen Robert (1)	b	1974 Dec 26
6(3)(i)II4ie	GAWITH Thomas Ione (2) (Adopted)	b	1984 Sep 9
6(3)(i)II4iia	DEAN Lori Joanna	b	1973 Jul 4
6(3)(i)II4iib	DEAN Jonathan	b	1974 Nov 1
6(3)(i)III1ia	SMALL Ingrid m. John CLARK	b	1958 Jun 8
6(3)(i)III1ib	SMALL Mary m. Ali ALI	b	1959 Jan 27
6(3)(i)III1ic	SMALL Duncan	b	1961 Mar 2
6(3)(i)III1id	SMALL Bruce	b	1962 Jul 23
6(3)(i)III1ie	SMALL Virginia m. Chris LUKE	b	1963 Sep 3
6(3)(i)III1if	SMALL Jacqueline	b	1964 Sep 14
6(3)(i)III1ig	SMALL Richard	b	1967 Nov 20
6(3)(i)III1iia	SMALL Graham	b	1962 Feb 14
6(3)(i)III1iib	SMALL Rachel	b	1964 Jun 16
6(3)(i)III1iiia	NEILSON Murray m. Sandra WILLIAMSON	b	1963 Feb 18
6(3)(i)III1iiib	NEILSON Fiona	b	1964 Feb 10
6(3)(i)III1iiic	NEILSON Diane m. Carey BURR	b	1965 May 12
6(3)(i)III1iiid	NEILSON Andrew	b d	1966 Sep 8 1985 Aug 24
6(3)(i)III1iiie	NEILSON Mathew	b	1971 Jul 24
6(3)(i)III2ia	FERGUSSON Deidre	b	1963 Jan 23
6(3)(i)III2ib	FERGUSSON Kathryn	b	1965 Oct 19
6(3)(i)III2ic	FERGUSSON Hamish	b	1971 Feb 1
6(3)(i)III2id	FERGUSSON Charlotte	b	1972 Dec 16
6(3)(i)III2iia	FERGUSSON Anthony	b	1967 Jan 29
6(3)(i)III2iib	FERGUSSON Mark	b	1969 Sep 18
6(3)(i)III2iiia	FERGUSSON Russell	b	1984 Jun 24
6(3)(i)III2iva	FERGUSSON Sally	b	1968 May 12
6(3)(i)III2ivb	FERGUSSON David	b	1970 Feb 15
6(3)(iii)I1iia	JORDAN Alistair	b	1979
6(3)(iii)I1iib	JORDAN Leanne	b	1982
6(3)(iii)II1ia	MEGUID Bonnie Matha	b	1973
6(3)(iii)II1ib	MEGUID Robert Alexander	b	1975

6(3)(iii)II1iia	PERFECT Matthew Robert	b	1979	
6(3)(iii)II1iib	PERFECT Daniel Stephen	b	1981	
6(3)(iii)II2ia	CHRISTOPHERSON Kathryn Annabel	b	1986 Oct 1	London
6(3)(iii)II2ib	CHRISTOPHERSON Eliza Rose	b	1990 March 27	Guildford
6(3)(iii)II2ic	CHRISTOPHERSON Saoirse	b	1992	Guildford
6(3)(iv)IV1ia	LATTENSON Adam Christian (1)	b	1974 Jul15	
6(3)(iv)IV1ib	LATTENSON Jarrod Scott (1)	b	1976 Jan 31	
6(3)(iv)IV1iia	WILLSON Hamish Hadwin (1)	b	1973 Jan 31	
6(3)(iv)IV1iib	WILLSON Dean Francis (1)	b	1974 Aug 26	
6(3)(iv)IV1iic	WILLSON Ashley Brian (1)	b	1978 Dec 23	
6(3)(iv)IV1iid	WILLSON Blair Alan (2)	b	1982 Jun 29	
6(3)(iv)IV1iie	WILLSON Matthew Brian (2)	b	19 Aug 29	
6(3)(iv)V1ia	UPTON Christopher Stephen	b	1984 Dec 12	
6(3)(iv)V1ib	UPTON Daniel James	b	1987 Mar 11	
6(3)(iv)V1ic	UPTON Matthew William	b	1989 Mar 18	
6(3)(iv)V1iia	KEMP-UPTON Benjamin James	b	1983 May 6	
6(3)(iv)V1iib	KEMP-UPTON Jeremy Alex	b	1984 Oct 9	
6(3)(iv)V1iic	KEMP-UPTON Martine Nicola	b	1986 Apr 3	
6(3)(iv)V1iid	KEMP-UPTON Erin Leigh	b	1989 Apr 12	
6(3)(iv)V1iiia	RADFORD Brook Adam	b	1984 Oct 20	
6(3)(ix)I1ia	MORGAN Thomas Grenfell	b	1983 Feb 27	Wellington
6(3)(ix)I1ib	MORGAN William James	b	1984 Dec 8	Wellington
6(3)(ix)I1ic	MORGAN Annabel Jane	b	1987 Jul 19	Wellington
6(3)(ix)I1iia	HILL Christopher	b	1978 Nov 25	Wellington
6(3)(ix)I1iib	HILL Richard	b	1982 Apr 30	Wellington
6(3)(ix)I1iic	HILL Jacqueline	b	1983 Sep 16	Wellington
6(3)(ix)I1iiia	MEEHAN Samantha Jane	b	1985 Oct 25	Wellington
6(3)(ix)I1iiib	MEEHAN James Victor Grenfell	b	1988 Apr 16	Wellington
6(3)(ix)I1iiic	MEEHAN Kate	b	1990 Oct 6	Wellington
6(3)(v)I1ia	PARKER Tanya Sally	b	1965	
6(3)(v)I1ib	PARKER Victoria Susan	b	1967	
6(3)(v)I1ic	PARKER Caroline Ann	b	1969	
6(3)(v)I1iia	REYNOLDS Sarah	b	1973	
6(3)(v)I1iib	REYNOLDS George Morris	b	1976	
6(3)(v)I1iic	REYNOLDS Joseph Morris	b	1979	
6(3)(v)I1iid	REYNOLDS Matthew Morris	b	1988	
6(3)(v)I1iiia	REYNOLDS Charles Upham Morris	b	1979	
6(3)(v)I1iiib	REYNOLDS Emma Pepita	b	1981	
6(3)(v)I1iiic	REYNOLDS Patrick Peter Upham	b	1985	

6(3)(v)II1ia	BARTON Richard Mark	b	1964
6(3)(v)II1ib	BARTON Amanda Lucy m. Dene Jonathan MINTY	b	1966
6(3)(v)II1ic	BARTON Andrew William	b	1969
6(3)(v)II1iia	BARTON Hamish Dymock	b	1976
6(3)(v)II1iib	BARTON Richard Price	b	1978
6(3)(v)II1iic	BARTON William Wynne	b	1981
6(3)(v)II1iiia	LEVINGE Georgina Rona	b	1971
6(3)(v)II1iiib	LEVINGE Charles Richard Wynne	b	1973
6(3)(v)II3ia	CHAMBERS Benita Barton	b	1982
6(3)(v)II3iia	COWIE Matthew Barton	b	1978
6(3)(v)II3iib	COWIE Andrew Barton	b	1980
6(3)(v)II3iic	COWIE Jessica Barton	b	1983
6(3)(v)II3iiia	TAIT David Edward	b	1981
6(3)(v)II3iiib	TAIT Julia Barton	b	1982
6(3)(v)II3iiic	TAIT Anita Barton	b	1985
6(3)(v)II3iva	SPENCER Olivia Barton	b	1986
6(3)(v)II3ivb	SPENCER Annabelle Barton	b	1988
6(3)(v)III2ia	WILLIAMS Margo Joyce	b	1976
6(3)(v)III2ib	WILLIAMS Hamish Richard	b	1979
6(3)(v)III2iia	WILLIAMS Samuel	b	1972
6(3)(v)III2iib	WILLIAMS Angus	b d	1974 1978
6(3)(v)III2iic	WILLIAMS James Chapman	b	1975
6(3)(v)III2iid	WILLIAMS Kate	b	1979
6(3)(v)III2iiia	WILLIAMS Nicholas Leslie	b	1976
6(3)(v)III2iiib	WILLIAMS Ben Meyer	b	1978
6(3)(v)III2iiic	WILLIAMS Rosa Mary	b	1981
6(3)(v)III3iia	McLAUGHLIN David	b	1975
6(3)(v)III3iib	McLAUGHLIN James Anthony	b	1977
6(3)(v)III3iiia	FRANKLIN Hamish William	b	1983
6(3)(v)III3iiib	FRANKLIN Simon Mark	b	1985
6(3)(v)III3iiic	FRANKLIN Rachael Kate	b	1989
6(3)(v)IV1iia	LAMBIE Catherine Laura	b	1985
6(3)(v)IV1iib	LAMBIE Fiona Evelyn	b	1987
6(3)(v)IV2ia	MORTEN Frances Kate	b	1977
6(3)(v)IV2ib	MORTEN Caroline Jane	b	1979
6(3)(v)IV2iiia	CROUCH Thomas Wilfred Michael	b	1983
6(3)(v)IV2iiib	CROUCH Anna Frances	b	1985
6(3)(v)VI1iia	KEMP Caroline Rose	b	1978

6(3)(v)VI1iib	KEMP Jeremy Arnold	b	1980	
6(3)(v)VI1iic	KEMP Hamish Gerald	b	1982	
6(3)(v)VI1iiia	WILLIAMS Toby Heathcote Beetham	b	1980	
6(3)(v)VI1iiib	WILLIAMS Belinda Patricia	b	1982	
6(3)(v)VI1iiic	WILLIAMS Paul Michael	b	1985	
6(3)(v)VI1iva	EIVERS George Wynn	b	1978	
6(3)(v)VI1ivb	EIVERS Rebecca Sylvia	b	1979	
6(3)(v)VI1ivc	EIVERS William Michael	b	1983	
6(3)(v)VI1ivd	EIVERS James Robert	b	1984	
6(3)(v)VI1ive	EIVERS Henry Beetham	b	1986	
6(3)(v)VI1va	WILLIAMS Anna Nicola	b	1987	Gisborne
6(3)(v)VI1vb	WILLIAMS Libby Anne	b	1989	Gisborne
6(3)(vi)I1iia	WANKLYN Mark Robert	b	1980	
6(3)(vi)I1iib	WANKLYN Andrew David	b	1983	
6(3)(vi)I1iiia	WANKLYN Demelsa Anne	b	1985	
6(3)(vi)I1iiib	WANKLYN Samuel Roger	b	1987	
6(3)(vi)I1iva	WANKLYN Craig (Adopted)	b	1980	
6(3)(vi)I1ivb	WANKLYN Anna (Adopted)	b	1983	
6(3)(vi)I2ia	JOHNSTONE Simon	b	1976 Mar 15	Waimate
6(3)(vi)I2ib	JOHNSTONE Vashti Frances	b	1978 Jan 17	
6(3)(vi)I2ic	JOHNSTONE Fenella	b	1981 Sep 8	
6(3)(vi)I2iia	JOHNSTONE Samuel Richard	b	1976 Dec 14	Timaru
6(3)(vi)I2iib	JOHNSTONE Nicholas	b	1978 Seb 14	Timaru
6(3)(vi)I2iic	JOHNSTONE Joseph	b	1980 Nov 19	Timaru
6(3)(vi)I2iiia	MORGAN Henry	b	1982 Nov 13	Timaru
6(3)(vi)I2iiib	MORGAN Abigail Katherine	b	1984 May 24	Timaru
6(3)(vi)I2va	JOHNSTONE Bridget Lucy Rose	b	1989 Sep 8	
6(3)(vi)I3ia	THACKER Rebecca Jane	b	1984 Sep 28	Gore
6(3)(vi)I3ib	THACKER Katie	b	1987 Apr 1	Gore
6(3)(vi)I3iia	HAZELDINE Jennifer Francis: Twin	b	1987 Jul 7	
6(3)(vi)I3iib	HAZELDINE Josie Amanda: Twin	b	1987 Jul 7	
6(3)(x)I1ia	GREVILLE Richard Warwick	b	1978	
6(3)(x)I1ib	GREVILLE Nicola Patricia	b	1980	
6(3)(x)I1ic	GREVILLE Christopher Francis	b	1983	
6(3)(x)I1iia	MALLOY Danielle René	b	1983	
6(3)(x)I1iib	MALLOY Michael John	b	1986	
6(3)(x)I1iiia	MALLOY Jesse Charles	b	1985	
6(3)(x)I1iiib	MALLOY Willem Johannus	b	1986	
6(3)(x)I1iiic	MALLOY Shaun Clendon	b	1988	

6(3)(x)I1iva	GASTON Steven Kant	b	1988	
6(3)(x)I2ia	MIDDLETON Melissa Joy	b	1973	
6(3)(x)I2ib	MIDDLETON Nigel Duncan	b	1976	
6(3)(x)I2iia	FOY Henry John	b	1985	
6(3)(x)I2iib	FOY Emma Margaret	b	1989	
6(3)(x)I2iva	FRIEDRICH Benjamin Ross	b	1984	
6(3)(x)I2ivb	FRIEDRICH Shane Kendall	b	1985	
6(3)(x)I2va	HARDING Kirsten May	b	1983	
6(3)(x)I2vb	HARDING Andrew Thomas	b	1985	
6(3)(xiii)I1iia	DOUGLAS Polly Anna	b	1983 Oct 24	
6(3)(xiii)I1iib	DOUGLAS Benjamin David John	b	1985 Jul 15	
6(3)(xiii)I1iic	DOUGLAS Lucinda Rose	b	1988 Sep 22	
6(3)(xiii)I1iiia	STEVENS William Turnbull	b	1989 May 17	
6(3)(xiii)II1ia	LANDON-LANE Richard James	b	1976 Sep 21	New Plymouth
6(3)(xiii)II1ib	LANDON-LANE Sarah Kate	b	1980 Oct 24	Auckland
6(3)(xiii)II3ia	GADDUM James Robert	b	1980 Feb 5	
6(3)(xiii)II3ib	GADDUM Nicholas Richard	b	1982 Sep 15	
6(3)(xiii)II3ic	GADDUM Georgina Midge	b	1983 Nov 9	
6(3)(xiii)II3iia	GORDEN Thomas Edward	b	1983 Nov 23	
6(3)(xiii)II3iib	GORDEN Abigail Alice Rose	b	1985 Sep 14	
6(3)(xiii)II3iiia	EIVERS George Wynne	b	1978 Jan 9	
6(3)(xiii)II3iiib	EIVERS Rebecca Sylvia	b	1979 Nov 23	
6(3)(xiii)II3iiic	EIVERS William Michael	b	1983 Mar 25	
6(3)(xiii)II3iiid	EIVERS James Robert	b	1984 Oct 5	
6(3)(xiii)II3iiie	EIVERS Henry Beetham	b	1986 Jan 12	
6(3)(xiii)II3iva	CURRAN Michael Thomas Samuel	b	1982 Mar 27	
6(3)(xiii)II3va	BOJESEN-TREPKA Christopher John	b	1982 Sep 28	
6(3)(xiii)II3vb	BOJESEN-TREPKA Sarah Jane	b	1984 Apr 25	
6(3)(xiii)II3vc	BOJESEN-TREPKA Michael James	b	1987 Sep 28	
6(3)(xiii)II3vd	BOJESEN-TREPKA Claire Anna	b	1989 Jan 6	
6(3)(xiii)II3viia	EIVERS Kimberly Jane	b	1989 Feb 3	
6(3)(xiii)II4ia	GARDINER Mark Douglas	b d	1975 1976	
6(3)(xiii)II4ib	GARDINER Paul Philip	b	1977	
6(3)(xiii)II4ic	GARDINER Robin Lea	b	1978	
6(3)(xiii)II4id	GARDINER Rick	b	1983	
6(3)(xiii)II4ie	GARDINER Christy Kim	b	1986	
6(3)(xiii)II4iia	STOVELL Benjamin Vincent	b	1980	
6(3)(xiii)II4iib	STOVELL Anna	b	1982	

6(3)(xiii)II4iic	STOVELL Kate	b	1984	
6(3)(xiii)II4iiia	STOVELL William Hugh	b	1982	
6(3)(xiii)II4iiib	STOVELL Margo	b	1984	
6(3)(xiii)II4iva	de LATOUR Caroline	b	1985	
6(3)(xiii)II4ivb	de LATOUR Harry	b	1988	
6(3)(xiii)III1ia	TAYLOR Daniel Charles	b	1976	
6(3)(xiii)III1ib	TAYLOR Luke Richard	b	1978	
6(3)(xiii)III1ic	TAYLOR Alexandra Mary	b	1980	
6(3)(xiii)III1iia	HUMPHREYS Richard Peter	b	1982	
6(3)(xiii)III1iib	HUMPHREYS Fleur Lesley	b	1984	
6(3)(xiii)III1iic	HUMPHREYS Ben Michael Frederick	b	1988	
6(3)(xiii)III1iiia	HUMPHREYS Hannah Elizabeth	b	1989	
6(3)(xiii)III2iia	WANKLYN Mark Roert	b	1980	
6(3)(xiii)III2iib	WANKLYN Andrew David	b	1983	
6(3)(xiii)III2iiia	WANKLYN Demelsa Anne	b	1985	
6(3)(xiii)III2iiib	WANKLYN Samuel Roger	b	1987	
6(3)(xiii)III2iva	WANKLYN Craig (Adopted)	b	1980	
6(3)(xiii)III2ivb	WANKLYN Anna (Adopted)	b	1983	
6(3)(xiii)IV1iia	BARKER Matthew Peter	b	1987	
6(3)(xiii)IV2ia	WILLIAMS Jennifer Rose	b	1988	
6(3)(xiii)IV2ib	WILLIAMS Julia	b	1989	
6(6)(i)I1ia	MOYLE Brian Wayne	b	1969 Oct 16	Wellington
6(6)(i)I1ib	MOYLE Glenn Steven	b	1976 Mar 1	Wellington
6(6)(i)I1iia	PEEBLES Brent John (Son of Jacky)	b	1975 Nov 3	
6(6)(i)I1iib	PEEBLES Rebecca Jane	b	1984 Oct 29	Brisbane
6(6)(i)I1iva	HARPUR Nadene Leigh	b	1984 Jul 28	
6(6)(i)I1ivb	HARPUR Stephanie Jennifer	b	1986 Nov 14	
6(6)(i)I1ivc	HARPUR Victoria	b		
7(2)(ii)II2ibA	FERRIS Megan Samantha	b	1992 Mar 1	
7(2)(ii)II2ibB	FERRIS Michael John	b	1993 Jul 7	
7(2)(ii)II2ibC	FERRIS	b	1995 Apr	
7(2)(ii)II2iicA	LINGS Anthony Francis	b	1992 Apr 14	
7(2)(ii)II2iicB	LINGS Brendon Mark	b	1993 Jul12	

PART 5
MISCELLANY

CHAPTER NINE

DOUGLAS CLENDON *(1898-1970)*
PHYLLIS CLENDON *(1901-1991)*

An Appreciation – by Ryland Clendon.

Douglas Clendon was born on 10th May 1898 at Dolgellau, then spelt Dolgelley. His birth certificate shows that he was born at home, a house called "Bryn Marian", and that his father was "Arthur Clendon, Schoolmaster and MA Cambridge". Arthur was the Headmaster of Dolgelley County School, Dolgelley being then the County Town of Merionethshire.

Bryn Marian still stands, on the north side of the town, a substantial Victorian stone-built house. Douglas's sister Myfanwy was born there on 18th December 1899. It was a school house. Part of their mother's job was to manage it as a boarding house for a handful of pupils who lived in outlying villages and farms, and were unable to get to and from school each day. Staff were employed to do the cooking and housework, and Douglas was often downstairs in the servants quarters. They talked in Welsh, and he grew up to speak both Welsh and English. He used to sneak into a store room where large stocks of flour and sugar in sacks, and jam in huge pots, were kept. He would help himself to jam, thinking that a small portion missing each day would not be noticed – but in the end it was – and he was severely scolded by his mother.

Jam was a luxury to him as a boy. He was given the choice of cake or jam for tea, never both, except on Sundays. He visited the girls school nearby, Dr William's School, with his parents, and was allowed to go and play there. He walked about barefoot for a lot of the time, and the soles of his feet became very tough.

In 1905 the family moved to Birmingham, where his father had been appointed Headmaster of Handsworth Grammar School. Douglas missed the life of a small town, the countryside and the mountains. He remained very fond of North Wales, and the area around Dolgelley. He returned for walking holidays as a young man, was married there, and came back again with his own family on holidays in 1932, 1938, 1939 and twice after the war in the late 1940's.

He was seven when he arrived in Birmingham, and his life changed considerably. He had to wear shoes and went to a "Dames School". He enjoyed life, but was not good at school, and did not take it very seriously. On February 17th 1907, when Douglas was coming up to nine years of age, his father Arthur wrote to Vivian in New Zealand referring to him as follows:

> . . . Douglas is just about the age that you were when I last saw you – he is a jolly little chap but rather careless in his school work. I doubt whether he will ever get a Scholarship at King Edwards but I intend him to go there in a year or two . . .

Within a year Arthur had entered Douglas at his own school, Handsworth Grammar School. When I visited the school in 1993 I was given a copy of Douglas's school record card. It was filled in (in Arthur's handwriting as head master) as follows:

_155_   SCHOOL REGISTER
_2026_

NAME Clendon, Douglas R.T.   BIRTHDAY May 10.98
                                     ENTRY Jan.08
PARENT'S NAME Arthur Clendon   PROFESSION Schoolmaster
ADDRESS 9 Handsworth Wood Rd. H.   PREVIOUS EDUCATION Private

RECORD	DATE	CLASS	POSITION	REMARKS
ENTRANCE V. Fair	Jan 08	ii	18	
EXAMS	Sep '08	iii	25	
GAMES				
SOCIETIES				
DATE OF LEAVING July 1909				

SUBT. CAREER   K.E.H.S '09 -'16
                   Sandhurst 1916

As can be seen from this record card Douglas did not excel himself at his father's school. But he did gain entrance to King Edwards High School in 1909 although not as a scholar. He did not shine in class there either.

He enjoyed going for cycle rides with his father in the country at week ends. Their bikes had fixed wheels. The pedals were "fixed" via the chain to the rear wheels, so there was no freewheeling or gear changing facility. The gearing was rather high, so to assist starting off there was a step protruding from the rear axle on which the rider placed his left foot, and then proceeded gather speed by scooting along with the right foot. When the bike had got up speed the rider put his right leg over the back of the bike – lowered himself onto the saddle – and found the revolving pedals. Once they had got up speed they tried not to slow down if possible. The brakes were not very efficient either, and he and his father came off into the hedge on corners at the bottom of a fast hill on a number of occasions.

He liked catching and getting off trams in between stops while they were slowing down for traffic, and watching Aston Villa play football on Saturday afternoons. His usual method of entry was over the fence at the back of the ground.

The aspect of school life that he preferred most at King Edwards was the Officers Training Corps (OTC), which was the name (and expectation!) given to the School Cadet Corps in those days. He was an avid reader of G A Henty's books which glamourised the adventures of British soldiers in the Boer War. He was aged 16 at the outbreak of the Great War and soon became caught up in the mood of patriotism and excitement that then pervaded the youth of the country.

 By 1915 he had decided to make the Army his career. To become an officer he had to get to Sandhurst. That meant passing an entry examination. And so at the age of 17 he started to take his school studies seriously for the first time in his life. He was put in a form called "The Remove" which existed to cram people like him for such examinations. He worked hard and in 1916 he sat the Sandhurst entrance exam. The pass list was published in order of merit – with a line drawn under the name of the lowest candidate to be admitted. He looked there first, and saw his name just above the line. He had scraped in by the skin of his teeth!

He was overjoyed, not only because he had got in, but also because it was the last course to be of only six months duration; succeeding courses were to be longer. So he was delighted that he would be able get to his regiment and to the front line as quickly as possible. His regiment was the infantry regiment for the area – the South Staffordshire regiment.

While at Sandhurst he had to learn to ride a horse. Infantry officers rode while the troops marched and it was essential that they could control a horse at all times, especially on parade. They spent hours on well trained horses trotting round a field with a sergeant-major in the centre shouting instructions and commands. The horses knew all the drill backwards! When the sergeant shouted "Trot" they trotted; when he said "Gallop", they galloped. So in a short time the cadets thought they could control a horse easily! But the real learning came when the sergeant gave instructions such as: "When I say "Gallop" you are to trot – when I say "Trot" you are to canter – and so on! That was when the men began to be sorted from the boys!

Douglas made good progress at Sandhurst. He passed out comfortably above the minimum mark – about one third the way up the class, but he did not join his regiment. He joined the Royal Flying Corps – the RFC. In the days before the RAF was formed, the RFC was part of the Army, operating over the enemy lines in France in support of the troops on the ground. An RFC officer had visited Sandhurst at the end of the course to recruit volunteers to train as pilots – and Douglas decided to have a go. The expectation of life of a pilot in France was then under six months. He was 18.

He was stationed at the RFC School of Instruction at Hendon airfield in north London. Nowadays there is an RAF museum on the site. The first entry in his flying log book was on 9th January 1917. His first flight was on the following day – dual control – for 25 minutes. He rose to 300 feet doing circuits around Hendon. Then he did very little flying – only three and a half hours in the first month, all dual control. He went solo for the first time, for 16 minutes on 19th February – and the comment "Flying well" was entered in the log. By the 24th February he had flown solo for a total of 2 hours and 18 minutes, mainly short flights circuiting round the airfield. There was a clear month before he flew again – this time a concentrated effort over four weeks which culminated in a cross country flight to Farnborough reaching an altitude of 5,000 feet on 16th April.

It was extremely cold flying those early machines. He felt as though the wind was blowing right through him. His only protection in an open cockpit was a thin (by present day standards) fur lined leather flying jacket, a fur lined cap, goggles, knee boots and gloves. The engine was very noisy, with strong vibrations. One plane had a rotary engine which sent oil everywhere as it spun round. The engines were unreliable and parachutes were not in use. If the pilot got into difficulty he had no alternative but to dive down to the nearest field and attempt a crash landing.

On return from Farnborough on 16th April he damaged the starboard aileron and wing skid on landing. Nevertheless he was told that he had qualified as a Pilot, and would be posted to France. He had flown solo for a total of 15 hours 33 minutes.

He was told that he was to be a night bomber, and would need to make two night landings before going to France. Later that day he flew an altitude test for 1 hour 25 minutes, and when it was dark took off for his first night flight. He circled three times and came in to land. There were some trees at the edge of the airfield, and as he approached he misjudged their height and his wheels caught the top of a tree. The plane overturned and Douglas fell into the trees. He came to rest hanging upside down. He put his hand down, felt the ground, and realised that he had only just missed breaking his neck. Rather shaken he reported to his Commanding Officer to be told that he had done one night landing, and that he should take a few days leave and come back to do the second!

Douglas Clendon in his RFC days.

Date and Hour	Wind Direction and Velocity	Machine Type and No.	Passenger	Time	Height	Course	Remarks
11/4/17	F.E.	4972	Solo	15	700	1 landing	
12/4/17	FE	5208	"	40	2000	4 landings	
12/4/17	FE	4972	"	75	2000	4 landings	
13/4/17	FF	4280	"	50	2000	2 landings	engine trouble.
15/4/17	FE	5208	"	70	4500	3 landings	
16/4/17	FE	6363	"	40	2500	2	
16.4.17	FE	5208	"	45	5000	Farnboro.	Cross country. Damaged starboard aileron and wing skid in landing

TIME IN AIR DURING W. E. 16·4·17 =   5 · 35
     "   SOLO   "   "   =   5 · 35
TOTAL TIME SOLO TO DATE   =   15 · 33

[signature] CAPTAIN,
ADJUTANT No. 19 RESERVE SQUADRON,
ROYAL FLYING CORPS.

16/4/17	FE	5208	Solo	1h.25—		Altitude test	
16/4/17	FE	5208	Solo	10 mins		right landing	Crashed.
23/4/17	FE	4972	"	45 mins.			
23/4/17	FE	4972	"	80 mins			
23/4/17	FE	4972	"	70 mins			
23/4/17	FE	6363	Self	45 mins		bombs with Capt Cole Hamilton (passed)	

[signature] CAPT

A page from Douglas Clendon's flying log book.

A week later he returned and began flying again. On April 23rd he flew aircraft no. FE 4972 on three solo flights of 45, 80 and 70 minutes duration. He then flew as a passenger for 45 minutes described in his log as "Bombs with Capt. Cole Hamilton (passed)". That night he took off for the fifth time that day for his second night flight. This time the engine caught fire. In an attempt to extinguish the fire, he dived. This was the recognised procedure, but it failed. His plane crashed as he landed on the airfield. He could remember nothing about the accident. The last moment he could recall was seeing the airfield lights along the wing as he circled around for the third and last time – and thinking that the flight would soon be over.

He woke up in a military hospital with a fractured skull, blind, and the bones of his left forearm shattered. His sight recovered, but he was left with impaired vision in one eye. A metal plate was inserted in his left forearm, and the bones screwed to it. It was permanently fixed and rotation of the wrist was no longer possible.

After convalescence in the north of England at Lytham St Annes, he was classified as unfit for active service. A document with his log book shows that he departed from the 19th Reserve Squadron, Royal Flying Corps, on 23rd November 1917, seven months after his crash. He was seconded to the Machine Gun Corps and remained with them, training gunners in England, until the end of the War in November 1918.

He was then a 1st Lieutenant. After the War, because flying was considered as dangerous as active service in France, he was categorised as "wounded on active service". This made him eligible for retirement and a War Pension of half his pay. He applied and in 1919 he was released from the Army.

He decided to train to be a doctor and was admitted to Emmanuel College Cambridge on October 1st 1919. College records show that he was granted exemption from the Previous Examination, (the University entrance exam), by virtue of his military service, and that he was matriculated on October 22nd.

He was put into digs, and his mother sent him a desk. The letter which he wrote to thank her is one of the documents that, together with some photographs, I gave to the College in January 1993. It was printed, and illustrated with a pen and ink drawing, under the title "Letter From a Freshman" in the 1992-93 edition of Emmanuel College Magazine, and is included in the section on links with Emmanuel College in Part Five of this book. It displays Douglas's sense of fun, his warmth, and his love of humanity – as well as saying something about Cambridge landladies.

He loved the way of life at Emmanuel and made some good friends there. When he moved into College he shared a set of rooms in Front Court with Charles Bigger, a fellow medical student. He and Charles were in the

Boat Club. Douglas, being rather short and slightly built was a cox. In 1922 they were both in the first boat and that summer they competed at the Henley Royal Regatta.

Douglas took the usual medical course as an undergraduate, and took an honours BA in 1922. Unlike most Cambridge men he never bothered to take his MA when he became eligible. However when his younger son, David, was due to take his MA in 1961 he invited Douglas to join him. Douglas did so and they were awarded it together.

In 1922 Douglas entered University College Hospital Medical School in London to undertake his clinical training. His friend Charles Bigger went to St Thomas's Hospital, but they took digs together at Mornington Crescent in London.

At last Douglas had found his vocation. Emmanuel had been an enjoyable way for him to complete his education and adjust to a civilian way of life after the excitement and tragedy of war. The dilettante in him, although never quite lost – for example in his penchant for driving fast in open cars – became replaced at UCH by a seriousness and devotion to medicine that was to develop and mature into a full professional life. He qualified with the Conjoint diploma (MRCS LRCP) in 1925.

Coming under the influence of Professor Choyce, to whom he was House Surgeon, and as House Physician to Dr Batty Shaw, he experienced as a young doctor the beginnings of the scientific approach to medicine that we take for granted today.

On the medical side intravenous drips were being used for the first time in the wards by Batty Shaw. Douglas was responsible for setting them up, monitoring their effect and keeping them going properly. Insulin had just been discovered by Banting and Best in Canada, and was also being tried out experimentally by Batty Shaw. Diabetes, hitherto incurable and rapidly fatal, had become a treatable disease, but no-one knew how to manage it. Douglas as the House Physician had to cope with the problems of hypo and hyper-glycaemic comas in the night with very little knowledge or experience to guide him.

On the surgical side he enjoyed the world of the operating theatre. He had no ambition to be a surgeon, but he quickly became deeply fascinated by anaesthetics. Then considered an unpopular and rather boring task, it consisted of rendering the patient deeply unconscious by the use of an open mask of gauze on which the anaesthetist sprinkled ether or chloroform. Douglas, however, was interested in the art of keeping the patient deep enough, but not too deep so as to minimise the after effects of the anaesthetic. He developed considerable skill at observing and assessing the unconscious patient's state, and adjusting the depth of anaesthesia. He offered to give anaesthetics in place of his colleagues, who were glad to be relieved of the job, and spent many long hours in the theatre doing so.

One of the women students in his year was Phyllis Winter. She was born on 31st August 1901 in Bridlington, Yorkshire. Her father was a painter and decorator who had died shortly before she was born, leaving her mother, Alice Winter, with no means of support for her six children. The youngest four, including Phyllis, were placed in the care of the National Children's Home. After an initial spell at their London Branch in Bonnar Road, Bethnal Green, Phyllis was moved to Harpenden. There she lived in the Home's Sanatorium and was brought up by Sister Helen Suart, in association with Sister Emma Goodin who was the Sister-in Charge.

She did not live the conventional life of a child in a Branch, but was one of two girls brought up as "their own" by these two Sisters, always known later in our family as the "Big Aunties".

Although most girls had an elementary education and went into domestic service on leaving school, Phyllis was sent to the Modern School in Luton and from there gained entrance to University College, London to read medicine. On completion of her pre-clinical studies at the College, she crossed Gower Street to enter UCH for clinical training. The Children's Home supported her throughout her training, both by paying her fees and living expenses, and by providing accommodation at the sanatorium in Harpenden until she had qualified as a doctor and was able to support herself. In later life she must have repaid the Home several times over. She supported it, and the work of her sister Ethel who dedicated her life to working as a Sister in the Home, throughout the rest of her life.

When she first met Douglas they were both students on the wards at UCH. She was travelling each day by train to London, and did not do much socialising, although her favourite student at that time, Timmy Flew who was later a Consultant Obstetrician at UCH, took her to dances and taught her the Charleston. However it was Douglas who took her out to a champagne dinner when she passed her finals – but being brought up in a strict Methodist establishment she had not tasted alcohol before, and did not like it at all. She also worked at UCH after she had qualified, and was House Physician to Sir Thomas Lewis FRS. Douglas proposed marriage to her at about this time, but she declined him.

In 1927 Douglas joined his Uncle Ryland, Dr J R Hickinbotham, in his general practice in Wimpole Road Colchester. Shortly afterwards he was appointed Honorary Anaesthetist to the Essex County Hospital, Colchester.

Uncle Ryland owned a large house in Wimpole Road which had once been a school, and had since been divided into two, with a surgery in each. Uncle Ryland lived in No. 52 which was the larger, with the original reception rooms, hall, and front stairs; Douglas rented No. 53 from his Uncle. It had smaller and fewer rooms and used the old back stairs. He installed himself there with a housekeeper called Ethel, and bought himself a car, a bull-nosed Morris Cowley.

Soon afterwards Phyllis, who had in the meantime been working in hospitals in London, was appointed resident physician at the Sanatorium at Nayland, about ten miles from Colchester. Founded by Dr Jane Walker, a Harley Street specialist in the treatment of Tuberculosis, the "San" had been built by her using wealth accumulated by her family who were textile manufacturers in the north of England. Phyllis had become a protégé of Jane Walker, who sacked the dispenser at the San. in order to be able to afford to employ Phyllis – who had to make up the medicines alongside her other duties. Within a year Phyllis had full responsibility for the day to day running of the sanatorium with Dr Jane Walker visiting from London about once a week. When it came to Christmas time, Jane Walker laid on a party and dance and asked Phyllis to find a partner. Somewhat at a loss she decided to approach Douglas, the only suitable person she knew in the vicinity, and he accepted. Their friendship was renewed and he began visiting her frequently at Nayland on his off duty, taking her for rides in the car – and teaching her to drive. He proposed again – and this time she accepted.

They were married on June 25th 1929 at Llanaber, near Barmouth in Merionethshire. Jane Walker had offered to give them a wedding at Nayland, but they chose a village in Wales not far from where Douglas was born, and which Phyllis knew because she had been for holidays to Barmouth with the children's home in her youth. He was 31, and she was 27 years of age.

They were married by Douglas's godfather, Uncle Harvey Hickinbotham. They had to return home to Colchester immediately where Douglas needed to help Uncle Ryland who was overloaded with work because of a flu epidemic, and they postponed their honeymoon in the Wye Valley until later.

On return Phyllis was at a loss as to what to do. Never having lived in a private house she was unsure where to start. Ethel the housekeeper was firmly ensconced and resented Phyllis's presence on the scene. To her delight Ethel quickly realised that the new mistress of the house had not the first idea how to manage, and put the knife in quickly: "What would you like me to order from the butcher today, Madam?" . . . "The doctor doesn't like that for tea, madam" . . . "He never eats tomatoes madam!". etc.

Phyllis tried to assume her new and completely unaccustomed role with good grace, although she could not see initially what was expected of her. Douglas was fully preoccupied with his general practice, spending most of the day visiting patients in their homes; for several sessions each week he attended the hospital to give anaesthetics, and his evening surgeries went on very late. He was on call each night for the practice, and often had to go the hospital in the night to give emergency anaesthetics.

However, life began to improve for her. She was roped in to judge baby competitions, joined the League of Health and Beauty, undertook charity work for the League of Pity, became active in the Medical Women's Federation – and soon became pregnant. Her first child (myself) was born at home on 1st June 1930. A second son, David, followed on 10th February 1933.

She then joined the British Red Cross Society as Commandant of the Colchester Women's Detachment – Essex 48. And within a few years she was also helping Douglas out with his practice by doing home visits for him when he was busy. I remember being out with her doing visits in about 1937. It was a cold winter's evening and raining. We were in the "grey car" – an Austin 12 tourer AEV 899 owned jointly by Douglas and Uncle Ryland as an extra car. She returned to the car from a patient's house in a back street, complaining that the old man in there had attempted to prevent her examining his chest, thinking she was merely the doctor's wife on a social visit. A social visit was the last thing on earth that the shy Phyllis would ever contemplate giving anyone if she could help it! And she let him know in no uncertain terms who she was and why she was there, and to take his pyjama top off without any further nonsense! As a doctor she was quite confident with men and women of all classes and types. In social situations she could be shy, gauche, and often wished that the floor would open and swallow her up.

In 1939 the outbreak of World War II changed the lives of Douglas, Phyllis and their children for good. Many of the doctors in the town were called up to serve in the Forces. They were taken in age order, the youngest first. Douglas was left behind and his workload was considerably increased. Phyllis was recruited into the Emergency Medical Service as an Anaesthetist, having been trained initially by Douglas. Colchester was a potential invasion zone and the children were evacuated with their school to the Malvern Hills, initially for six months from June to December 1940, and thereafter for the term time only.

With the children away at boarding school, and a severe shortage of doctors in the town, Douglas and Phyllis threw themselves into their work as their contribution to the War effort. In addition Phyllis became Assistant County Director of the Essex Red Cross (with a Rank equivalent to Colonel). Douglas took part in trials as part of the research into new anaesthetic drugs being carried out by the Medical Research Council. He was one of the first anaesthetists to use an intravenous muscle relaxant, curare, in England. He also analysed the pulmonary complications occurring after 579 consecutive operations (all cases operated on in one year at a small EMS hospital in

Colchester) and published the results jointly with the hospital medical superintendent.

After the War their life settled down to a more steady pace, but remained centred on their professional work. Phyllis was appointed to the staff of the hospital as Honorary Anaesthetist, alongside Douglas. With the advent of the National Health Service (NHS) in 1948 they became salaried as Senior Hospital Medical Officers, and Phyllis was later appointed a Consultant. Phyllis became a Justice of the Peace, and a Governor of a local school. Douglas was an active member of many NHS management committees.

There were various alterations to the Wimpole Road premises as new partners came and went after Uncle Ryland eventually retired. The first of these was Charles Bigger, Douglas's old friend from Emmanuel days, with his second wife Dorothy, also a doctor. After they died Douglas and Phyllis moved over into an Upper Flat, that they created above the surgeries, at No 52.

They lived there after they had retired and it was there that Douglas died in 1970, of cancer of the lung. At his request Phyllis looked after him at home to the end. She was joined for the last month or so by my wife, Susan, herself a UCH trained nurse, taking turns round the clock with Phyllis to nurse him. He died on July 10th 1970 at the age of 72.

The following tribute was published in the 'Essex County Standard' – the local newspaper.

Dr D CLENDON
An Appreciation

FOR 40 years or so Douglas Clendon was one of the outstanding medical men of Colchester. Not only was he Anaesthetist to the Essex County Hospital but he ran a large and busy practice in the town. He served on both the Colchester and Severalls Hospital Management Committees and he took a very active interest in British Red Cross and in District Nursing affairs. Yet it was not in these hard facts that lay the real worth of Douglas Clendon, but in the solid and sterling qualities of his character.

A sound and shrewd doctor he certainly was, but he brought to his practice a humanity, a love of people in their troubles, that gave many households a wonderful affection and deep trust of the man they knew to be their friend, their counsel, and their guide. My own home was no exception.

He was I suppose, a quiet and reserved man, yet this heightened the power of his words when he spoke. In medical circles he was listened to with respect and we all knew that he had an honesty, an uprightness that doubled the value of his guidance.

Always one felt that he put the good cause before his own personal feelings. This in turn lead him to be regarded with trust and affection by those who knew him. No doctor that I know was more thoroughly respected by colleagues, friends, acquaintances and patients alike.

He did not say the unkind word when it often seemed justified. Of one man I know who treated him unkindly Douglas always managed to speak of the good work he had done. This was the measure of the man.

All this did not mean he was without spirit. He could be raised to wrath but I suspect he often felt sorry for it.

He could be most excellent company, for he enjoyed a joke and was rather fond of telling stories against himself. He was not easily put out by embarrassing circumstances and had a sangfroid that is valuable in any man, but in particular a doctor.

I sought his company and companionship for I was happy in it. We shared many interests in common, not least a love of old churches in East Anglia, and when we could we would slip away and spend a day just looking and discussing churches in Suffolk or elsewhere. These were among the happiest days of my life.
JBP

That tribute was written by his friend John Penfold. John was the Consultant Pathologist at the Essex County Hospital, and was not alone among the Consultants in having Douglas as their family doctor.

One of Douglas's interests had been the history of the Hospital, and he had been its historian for many years. John Penfold took over this role and in 1984 wrote and published a book entitled "The History of the Essex County Hospital, Colchester 1820-1948". The book was dedicated to Douglas, and its later chapters give an interesting insight into the circumstances in which he worked during much of his professional life in Colchester.

Phyllis lived on in the Upper Flat for nearly twenty years after Douglas died. As she gradually developed her own tastes and style of life, it became obvious how much she had suppressed her interests to support Douglas during their marriage. In 1990 she moved into a retirement home in Oxford Road. It had been a nurses home, and was close to the hospital where she and Douglas had worked.

She died on 31st December 1991, aged 90.

Her ashes were buried, alongside Douglas's in a grave at Colchester Cemetery.

CHAPTER TEN

JOHN SIDNEY CLENDON
(1913-1996) ('Jack')

Jack's funeral was held at St Stephen's Presbyterian Church, Lower Hutt on 12th July 1996. As part of the service, his four children – John, Ross, Graham and Alison – expressed their appreciation of his life in the following words.

John

"Good morning relatives, neighbours and friends of Jack.

For those who don't know me, my name is John and, as if you can't tell, I'm Jack's oldest son. Together, my brothers and sister and I would like to spend a few minutes to tell you a little about our father and his life.

Dad was born in Lower Hutt in February 1913 at the Clendon family home in Queens Road, apparently arriving too early for his mother to make it to the nearby maternity home. For those of you who knew Jack well this may come as a surprise and I know you will be pleased to learn that there was this one occasion in his life when Jack was early.

The actual site of the Clendon family home and Jack's birthplace is now difficult to identify – Graham may tell you more about this but as far as I can tell it is now part of the Queensgate supermarket carpark. This is I think a typical reflection of the huge changes Dad saw take place in Lower Hutt during his lifetime.

Eighty-three years later, when Dad died last Saturday, it was not at 10 Norton Park Avenue, his home of almost fifty years, as he had hoped and expected. Still, as I am sure Dad would have agreed, Ward 23 at Hutt Hospital was the next best thing. There he received the very best and most compassionate care for which we are all very grateful. When the time came, Jack said his good-byes and died peacefully and comfortably in his sleep.

And in a larger sense he did die at home – home in Lower Hutt where he lived out the greater part of what was a long and full life.

Funerals mean different things to different people. During the past twenty years, when I have lived for the most part in South-East Asia, I have attended quite a number of funerals – mostly Muslim, Buddhist and Hindu but also one or two Christian. There are certain themes that they all have in common – grief, mourning, thanks to God for such a life, celebration of what has been and what is yet to come.

On this occasion today I have no doubt that Dad would want it to be a thanksgiving and a celebration. Above all, a chance for reunion of family and friends – something he himself always enjoyed so much.

Jack was a great talker, a very great talker indeed. To a greater or lesser degree we his children have inherited that gene. So I shall say no more except to introduce you to Graham, Ross and Alison who will in turn tell you more about the father we all loved, and about his life.

Over to you Graham."

Graham

"My father was born just a short walk from here – in the family home at 16 Queens Road – since swallowed up by the Queensgate complex.

The phone number was 58. Lower Hutt was at that time a rural village – paddocks, long straight dusty roads, meandering boggy creeks. "Everyone knew everyone else" as my Dad used to say. A small boy's paradise.

And this small boy was lucky enough to have been born into a "good" family. His father and his Uncle Vye owned Clendon Brothers, grain and coal merchants, just over the old bridge from here.

His mother, Anna Orr, was from a modestly respectable Irish family; a lively and interesting family, a talkative family, a family mainly of women, apart from Dad's namesake, his uncle Jack and his cousin Ralph Orr.

And Dad's own immediate family was mostly female too. He was the son long waited for – both his parents were over 40. Was he spoiled? I think perhaps he was.

Sister Kelsey, eight years older than Dad and a stepdaughter to Dad's mother, was by all accounts a bit of a handful. Dad's father remained aloof from this family friction. Despite this, cousin Molly Leathem recently described the Queen's Road household as a basically happy muddle – a safe and happy home full of noise and activity.

Weekends might be spent traveling by horse and gig, either to the batch at Point Howard or to visit the Orr relatives in Thorndon.

Dad had an abiding interest in animals – his father's horses, his own pet donkey, injured birds and his beloved dog, Bob, a faithful companion through many years. Dad once said Bob's death affected him like no other. Dad had a soft hearted and sentimental streak. Strangely he couldn't abide people who regarded themselves as animal lovers – SPCA cranks he sometimes called them. I guess it's a question of balance. Dad was quite a good shot with a 22 and could bag a rabbit with ease.

Dad attended Eastern Hutt primary school – very different in some respects from the school of today – class sizes of 60-70+. Many of the pupils bedraggled urchins with no shoes. Dad's mother saw to it that her boy always wore shoes. She had ambitions for her son and the newly opened Hutt Valley High didn't measure up. Jack was sent by train and tram all the way to Wellington College. And so began the ritual of travel between Hutt and Wellington which became a continuing and constant feature of most of Dad's working life – running for the tram.

A vital part of Dad's boyhood years were the camping expeditions – adventures really – he made with his father and Uncle Vye and cousins Arthur and Tom to the central North Island – rugged remote territory then. Rough roads, primus stoves, boiling radiators and punctures. Tins of benzene, and bowsers few and far between.

Dad was proud of the fact that even as a youngster he was a far more capable driver than his father. Sadly the magic of that period is gone, but sometimes on our family holidays in the old blue Consul in the late 50's we, his children, could catch glimpses of it. I am grateful for that.

Sport played an important part in Dad's college and Varsity years. Especially rugby, and perhaps surprisingly, he was a middle-weight boxer. He's kept press clippings of his schoolboy bouts all these years.

Dad's school reports show he was a capable all rounder – not overly brilliant but good enough to gain entry to Law School – studying part time and working as a clerk in a legal firm for 25 shillings per week.

The onset of the Depression brought many troubles to what had been up to then a happy and untroubled life. The grain and coal business went bust. Dad's mother, aged 60, sickened and died of cancer. The lovely house, so recently built in Penrose Street, had to be sold up. A job – any job – for a law student, was hard to find. Dad was considered lucky to get a cadetship in the Government Land Transfer Office. Dad and his father were reduced to living in his mother's Tinakori Road flats. Studying, working and returning each night to cramped digs with an aging father. These were difficult years for my father.

There were bright spots – Tom's marriage to Sheila, Arthur's marriage to Joyce, his graduation in 1935, the birth of Noela to his sister Nell (the sweet-natured one, he always said), the progress of his sister Nancy in her career and her marriage to Johnnie Walker.

Things were coming right, but the war was to intervene."

Ross

"Dad spent the years 1941-1946 serving overseas with the 6th Field Ambulance, first in North Africa and then in Italy. After the war in Europe was over, he spent six months in England before returning home.

For many of those who lived through it, the Second World War was the most intense and dynamic time of their lives. Certainly in Dad's case I think the memories of those years, both good and bad, were never far away for the remainder of his life. This is not to say he relived them constantly. On the contrary, after his return to civilian life he in many respects put those years firmly behind him, never, for instance, becoming an active member of the RSA until, in his later years – well after I had left home – he took to going to the occasional reunions of his wartime comrades – events he looked forward to and thoroughly enjoyed.

Shortly before he died, Dad gave to John three slim albums of black and white photographs he brought back from the war – photos which will serve as reminders of those many and various war stories we children, and many others of you here today too I suspect, heard from Dad over the years. These photos do not ignore or disguise the horrors of war. But what comes through most strongly – for me at least – is that here were men in the prime of life whose lives ever after would be shaped by what they suffered and shared and celebrated together – and especially by the foreign places and people, so far removed from Lower Hutt, that they saw and met in those years away.

I experienced first hand some of the intensity of those war years in 1979 when Dad and I together went on a short pilgrimage to one or two places which for Dad had been highlights of the Italian campaign. I particularly remember the day we visited the Commonwealth War Cemetery near Monte Cassino. Dad was normally a man who kept his emotions under fairly tight rein, notwithstanding the fact that he was a sensitive even sentimental man. But on this particular day – we had begun it seeking out the grave of Bob Corser, one of his boyhood freinds from Point Howard – he was totally overcome when he come upon so many gravestones bearing names he remembered well.

To balance that rather somber story, I will also always recall how we finished that day – staying at a small Italian inn with Dad brushing up his rusty war-time Italian on the locals, and by the end of the evening persuading all those present in the bar to join in some opera arias and popular war-time tunes, some of which I suspect had become unfashionable after Mussolini fell. Dad at times like this was on his best form – sociable, friendly, without airs or graces, and with a contagious even impish sense of humour.

Once the war was over, Dad returned to the friends and familiar surroundings of Lower Hutt and resumed work with the Lands and Survey Department which he had first joined in 1933.

It was around this time that undoubtedly the most important event of Dad's life occurred – his meeting with our mother. Dad has imbued in all his children a great pride in being Clendons. But, in addition, through his marriage to Loris, he had the good judgment to ensure that his children would be half Sullivan as well, something which has stood us in good stead and given us another huge support network of cousins, aunts and uncles and many other friends and family members besides.

The precise circumstances of Dad's first meeting with Mum are in dispute. According to the Sullivan side – and I consulted Aunty Joan and Aunty Jean on this yesterday – Mum and Dad were introduced a few yards from here at a St. Stephen's social – given in honour of returning servicemen. According to the Clendon side – and here I produce Aunty Nancy as my expert witness – the match between my parents was arranged by former leading parishioners of St. Stephen's at a dinner given in their Woburn home. Irrespective of the exact circumstances of that first meeting, what is not in dispute is that St. Stephen's – both the church and the tennis club in Dad's case – played an important role in Mum and Dad's lives at this time and for long after.

Dad married Mum next door in the old St. Stephen's church in May 1947. For a few months following their marriage they lived in a flat in Berhampore. From there they moved to 10 Norton Park Avenue in Epuni, Dad's home for the rest of his life. We, his children, will always be grateful for the happy, nurturing and stable environment that he and our mother provided for us there. John came first, born in 1948. I followed in 1951, Graham exactly two years afterwards, and later – in fact, quite a bit later – Alison followed.

In 1952 Dad was appointed officer-in-charge of the Department of Internal Affairs local government branch. On reflection, this was another pivotal event in Dad's life, at least from our point of view, because through his regular attendance at county clerks' conferences, he and Mum became life-long friends of Morland and Mary Fox in Tauranga. Throughout our childhood we seemed to go almost annually on a summer holiday to Tauranga or one of the beaches surrounding it. I also remember once being told by Morland Fox that it was not insignificant that exactly nine months after one of those fondly remembered holidays Alison was born.

By 1960 Dad had become a senior group executive officer in the Internal Affairs Department. In that capacity he had responsibility for areas as diverse as wildlife, firearms and explosives, lotteries, film censorship and local government.

In 1964 he was to leave Internal Affairs upon being appointed Treasury Solicitor, a position he filled until 1973.

At an age when most other men his age were retiring, Dad embarked on a final ten years of service in varying capacities on different Royal and Government Commissions. In particular, he was Chairman of the Trade

Practices Commission from 1974-75 and a Member of the Commerce Commission from 1978-1984. He was 71 when he finally retired for good.

What Dad was first and foremost was a public servant. He was proud to be so. The civil service was an organisation he held in the highest regard, and over the years he served a number of different Ministries and Ministers ably and loyally. Although he displayed a keen interest in politics, in the best traditions of a professional civil service he was always apolitical. Throughout his life he never indicated to my brothers, my sister or me how he voted.

We, his children, were particularly grateful for the comradeship and intellectual challenges offered by these various government jobs in the decade following what was surely the greatest tragedy of Dad's life, the early death in 1977 of his wife, Loris, from a brain tumour at the age of 60. Despite that blow, Dad had much to be grateful for in the years remaining. There were, for instance, the overseas trips, including the one to Britain and Europe that he and Mum had long planned but which sadly Dad now had to undertake alone. During that period Carol and I were living in London and some of my fondest memories of Dad are associated with that visit – a visit I was recalling yesterday as being of three or four weeks, but which was – according to Carol – closer to four months.

During these last few years there have been three key figures in Dad's life: his sister Nancy; his beloved daughter Alison, and Graham – to all of you I am grateful – especially you, Graham, who helped ensure that Dad could continue living an independent life at Norton Park Avenue virtually until the end.

I have talked too long – a failing I have probably inherited from you, Dad. But, failings or not, you were proud of us all, Dad, and we were proud of you."

Alison

When you are sorrowful, look again in your heart, and you shall see that in truth you are all weeping for something that has been your delight.

"We all know you were never short of a word or two Dad.

Today it's my turn !

From our sorrow we want to thank you for all of your uniqueness as our Dad, Grandpa Jack and our friend.

You wore your Clendon heritage with great pride and kept us informed so that we too can tell our children of SOME of the Clendons' exploits.

Thank you for that !

Thank you too for choosing Mum as your partner in life. You were never the same after you lost her. But Dad you continued to do so much for our family over those sometimes hard nineteen years. Your thoughtful interest, pride and generosity in our wider family has helped us all.

Undoubtedly, most of our own basic values have sprung from the heritage which you and Mum in a unique partnership gave us.

Dad there is so much more we will always remember with pride.

Kahlil Gibran put it this way:"

> *Go back to the joy of your dwellings and you will find there*
> *That which Death cannot remove from you and me.*
> *Close your eyes and you will see me with you forever more.*

(The Treasury of Kahlil Gibran)

CHAPTER ELEVEN
TOM CLENDON
(1907-1997)

Tom died shortly before this book went to press and it seemed fitting to include a brief, albeit inadequate, tribute to him.

He was born on September 28th 1907 in Lower Hutt, the first son of Vivian and Rose Clendon who had been married the year before.

He and his wife Sheila met at school and were married in January 1930 when he was 22 and she was 19. The engagement ring had been bought by Tom's Uncle Sidney on a visit to England in 1928.

They lived initially with Tom's parents, and were living there at the back of the house with three children in 1933 when his Uncle Arthur and Aunt Elsie visited them from England.

Tom was a Civil Engineer. He had just qualified when the 1931 earthquake devastated the town of Napier. He was working for the local authority in Wellington, where he had trained, and was assigned immediately to survey a large number of the buildings in Wellington to determine whether they would be safe in the event of an earthquake. Many were not, and were condemned. As a result a great deal of reconstruction was required. Tom was involved with the Council in developing the structural requirements and designing buildings that would withstand earthquakes. As a result he gained a wealth of experience in this field. After 19 years with the Council, and 5 years with a building firm, he set up his own business in 1950 as a Consulting Engineer. The business flourished, was highly successful, and continued as Clendon Burns & Park Ltd after Tom retired.

For 26 years Tom and Sheila lived in Lower Hutt, but Tom then bought 40 acres of land in Eastbourne that was considered inaccessible. It was situated up a steep hill, so steep that it would be impossible to build a road up there. The land was sold for a bargain price to Tom, who had worked out how to build the access road. Although notoriously steep, the road is safe and passable. Tom built a house for himself up there with glorious views over Wellington harbour, and developed the site. Several of the family live there. Latterly Tom and Sheila moved down near the sea.

"When we got married we thought it would be nice to have two boys and two girls" Tom said at age 87 on his 65th wedding anniversary in January 1995. Tom reckoned that the reason he and his wife Sheila were still going strong after 65 years of marriage was self defence – against the 10 children, 40 grandchildren and 40 great-grandchildren that made up the family. "The eldest daughter was married with her own children when my last one came along" said Sheila, then aged 84.

In their retirement both Tom and Sheila said that the secret of keeping going was to keep active. Until recently both played golf, with Sheila enjoying yoga and eurythmics and swimming in the sea when the weather is warm, and Tom playing bowls. Known as "Pop" by his children, grandchildren and great-grandchildren, Tom was much loved and respected by his family. One son and five daughters live in Eastbourne and hardly a day passed without one dropping in to see him.

Tom died in his ninetieth year, on May 23rd 1997, peacefully in his sleep at home. He had no fear of death and said of it "Death . . . it's part of life, no good worrying about it. It's just a niggle shall we say"

A service was held in St Alban's Anglican Church, Ngaio Street, Eastbourne, on May 28th. Sheila wrote: "Tom was well known and had friends in many walks of life and his funeral showed it. There was a tremendous crowd, & many couldn't get in the church, so a loud speaker was installed and a tape taken. All the girls spoke, & several people afterwards said "It was the best, happiest, funeral I've ever been to". Many of the crowd followed the hearse to the Akatarawa Cemetery."

Ryland Clendon. June 1997.

CHAPTER TWELVE

GOODBYE, MR CHITTY

by Alistair Cooke

In 1977, soon after Eric Chitty died at age 70, Alistair Cooke wrote an affectionate "Letter from America" which was published in the TV Times. At that time Erik was well known to the viewing public as the irascible schoolteacher Smiffy in the popular TV series 'Please Sir!' – but to the Clendons he was the family genealogist whose life-time hobby had been researching and recording the Chitty and Clendon ancestry. To the distinguished journalist Alistair Cooke, Erik Chitty was a friend . . . right from the time they first met at Cambridge.

"Erik Chitty was the first friend I ever made at Cambridge and remained the closest throughout our time there. Just before he died we checked our memories of the first meeting, and they matched. We met on a dank October morning almost fifty years ago, in the study of the man, one Eustace Tillyard, who was to supervise our work in English literature throughout the first year. Up to that moment I – a boy raw from the north country – had been pretty nervous in the presence of so many nonchalant public schoolboys and bouncing country accents. But once inside the study of Mr. Tillyard with Chitty teetering on the edge of an armchair, I felt as blithe as Noel Coward.

If Tilly was the shyest teacher I ever knew, Chitty was the most trembly human being in the presence of any stranger. He literally sweated anxiety, mopping his forehead and hands with a handkerchief.

But once he took to you the anxiety fell away like a dead skin, and from the first week on I recognised in this grave little man who at first looked like an amiable bullfrog in a brown plus four suit, that I had discovered an original.

On our way back to our college that first day, we found we had many tastes in common, chief of which was a burning desire to become famous actors. He took me to his rooms and opened up his scrapbooks. He kept the scrapbooks all his life and they were as meticulously indexed and filed as the FBI's most wanted list.

We had both acted in school plays, but Chitty had the photographs and reviews, and even then , it seemed he always played old men – from King Lear to the butler in You never can tell. In fact, he struck me then as a born old man, and you could say of him – as Oscar Wilde said of Max Beerbolhm

– that he had the secret of perpetual old age.

The university dramatic societies of those days were entirely male – men played the women's parts, and there was some pretty squealing competition, I can tell you, to collar the parts of Ophelia or Desdemona. Chitty and I shared the rude, premature idea that this was weird, if not embarrassing. Out of this was born the notion of the first mixed dramatic society at Cambridge.

We mobilized a few other sympathizers and founded the Cambridge University Mummers, of which I became first president and Chitty, with his neat accounting habits, the first treasurer. We had a tussle getting it going.

The Vice Chancellor thought that by having women (from the two women's colleges) play women's parts was "somehow unnatural". But he gave in, and most of our second term was given over to rehearsing our first show — a performance of Henry Fielding's burlesque tragedy, Tom Thumb the Great.

The older societies bitterly resented any squatters moving in on their territory, and sent one of their stalwarts (I guess stalwarts is not quite the right word) to review our performance. The Cambridge Review came out with a blasting notice, which said – among other dreadful things – "Mr. Cooke knows all the tricks but I regret to say can perform none of them. If Mr. Chitty could be removed to one of the older societies, the Mummers could confidently cease to exist."

Well, I understand that it has staggered along with some confidence for 50 years, recruiting along the way such talents as James Mason and John Clements, and – till the day he left to got to the Royal Academy of Dramatic Art to play balky old men and querulous old men, and lovable old men in repertory and in society play houses and at home and abroad throughout the war, and on into television and movies till the last year of his life – Erik Chitty.

In all those years, he surely grew and mellowed, but he never changed one iota of his character. At Cambridge in 1927 and at his house in Harrow, where I had tea with him five days before he died last July, he was the same sweet, unfooled, affectionate, sceptical man, with a sharp humour that mocked nobody but the pompous and the affected. He had read a great deal in literature and law (he took a Law Degree) and what he knew he knew with great accuracy. But he was impervious to fashions in literature or ideas – totally without pretension at a time when it was very square not to swoon over T. S. Eliot and Ezra Pound or at the German expressionists.

Anybody who worked with him under a testy or fancy director must have felt grateful for the relief of his pawky humour. Those to whom he gave his friendship, were luckier still: they had found, for life, a sheet-anchor in a man of unswerving loyalty and unshakable common sense."

CHAPTER THIRTEEN
LINKS WITH EMMANUEL COLLEGE
CAMBRIDGE

Introduction

There are two reasons for describing the links between the family and the College.

Firstly, the family association with Emmanuel dates back to 1620, when the first Clendon was admitted as an undergraduate, and has continued in each century thereafter.

Secondly, it was the details of these early Clendons at Emmanuel, as reported in Verr's "Alumni Cantabridgienses", that provided the original researchers with the first recorded information about the Northamptonshire Clendons. Within a few weeks of each other in 1929, Erik Chitty and Arthur Clendon learnt of the references to these Emmanuel Clendons in "Alumni Cantabridgienses" quite independently – Arthur, from the Master of Emmanuel College itself, and Erik from a volume in the Library at the Society of Genealogists. This ancient link with Emmanuel thus provided the foundation for the research into the Northamptonshire Clendons pursued over many years by Erik Chitty, and Arthur's son Douglas Clendon.

The College

Emmanuel College was founded in 1584 by Sir Walter Mildmay. He was Chancellor of the Exchequer to Queen Elizabeth I and came from Northamptonshire, as did the Clendons of that time. He bought the site, formerly a Dominican friary, for £550. Some of the old buildings still remain, notably the friary chapel now the dining hall, and the refectory which served initially as the College chapel. The present chapel and cloisters constitute the most outstanding architectural feature of the College. Completed in 1667, they were built to designs by Sir Christopher Wren. The gardens are also renowned for their beauty; the pond in the Paddock was formerly the Dominican monk's fishpond.

Established originally for the education of Puritan parsons, "a seed-plot of men for the new Protestant Church", a third of the first hundred British graduates who settled in New England were products of this regime. Among these was John Harvard who, when he died in 1638, left half his estate and 320 books to found a "schoale at Newetowne". This was named after him and became America's first University. Many of the early Clendons to graduate from Emmanuel were parsons, although the puritanical influence diminished after 1660 when Charles II ascended the throne.

The pattern of growth of the College since then can be traced by reference to the Clendon archives. A photocopy of the page in the admissions book, for the year when our first direct ancestor William Clendon (4), see below, was admitted, shows that 28 men entered the College during the year from May 5th 1659 to May 2nd 1660. It also shows that the men joined the College individually on different dates, scattered throughout the year.

230 years later the numbers were much the same, although the curriculum had broadened to include a range of academic disciplines, and new undergraduates entered together as "freshmen" at the start of the academic year. 30 entrants are shown in the freshers photograph for October 1887, when Arthur Clendon was admitted to read an honours degree in Classics. However by 1953/54, the year of entry of the most recent family member, David Clendon (13), 144 men were admitted – a 480% increase in 65 years. Since then women have been admitted and the number of men have declined; a total of 183 matriculated in 1995/96, about a third of whom were women.

The Clendons

When Erik Chitty discovered the entry in "Alumni Cantabridgienses", he wrote a letter dated 27th December 1929 to his cousin Marion Chitty in Glens Falls, USA telling her so and listing the eight he had found as follows:

1.   CLENDON . . . Admitted sizar 1620.

2.   CLENDON Thomas. Admitted sizar 1620. Matric Easter 1620. BA 1623/4. MA 1627. Incorporated at Oxford 1627. Sequestered to All Hallows, Barking 1643. Doubtless Rector of Radwinter 1667-77. d.1677. [Buried there 1677 June 3rd].

3.   CLENDON Henry. Admitted sizar 1623. Matric 1623/4

4.   CLENDON William. Admitted sizar at Clare Dec 1 1658 of Wellingborough Northants. Matric 1659 as "Clendar". Migrated to

Emmanuel Jan 18 1659/60. BA 1662. MA 1664. His father was master at Wellingborough School. Rector of Draughton Northants 1665-70. V of Weekley 1670-5. Rector of Scaldwell 1675-1722. Buried there 1722 Sep 14.

5.   CLENDON Thomas. Adm. sizar at Emmanuel July 19 1681 of Northants. son of William (4). Bapt. at Draughton Mar 27 1665. Matric 1683. BA 1685/6. MA 1689. Ord. priest (Lincoln) Mar 11 1687/8. R of Fenny Drayton, Leicestershire 1708. V of Kilsby Northants 1702-10. d 1710.
[There is an error here in "Alumni Cantabridgienses" – it was later proved that he was Rector of Fenny Drayton 1708-1737, and buried there on September 6th 1737.]

6.   CLENDON William. Adm. sizar at Emmanuel Mar 5 1689/90, of Northants. son of William (4). Matric 1691. BA 1693/4. Ord. deacon (Peterborough) Jun 6 1696, priest Jun 3 1699. Clerk of Scaldwell, R of Creaton, Northants. 1708-54. d. Jan 4 1754.

7.   CLENDON Thomas. Adm. pensioner at Emmanuel Jun 25 1713, of Northants. Matric 1713. BA 1716/17. MA 1720. Ord. deacon (Lincoln) Jul 14 1717, priest (London) Mar 13 1719/20. Curate of Fenny Drayton 1717 (to his father, see 5). V of Reculver 1729- & Sturry 1734-57. d.1757.

8.   CLENDON John. Adm. sizar at Emmanuel Jan 22 1740/1 son of William (6) Clerk, of Creaton, Northants. School, Guilsborough. Matric 1740/1. BA 1744/5. MA 1748, Fellow 1747. Ord. deacon (Norwich) Dec 1746, priest (Ely) Jun 5 1748. V. of Brompton Regis, Somerset 1751-1802.

In addition there is a further early Clendon not mentioned by Erik Chitty in the letter, but recorded in a later edition of Alumni Cantabridgienses and in the 1974 edition of the Clendon family history. The following is an amalgamation from both sources.

9.   CLENDON Beveridge. Adm. pensioner (age 19) at Emmanuel as Pauline Exhibitioner Mar 19 1757, Matric 1757, left 1760. b. 1737? at Boxley, Kent. St Paul's School 1749, aged 12. Apparently the son of Rev John Clendon 1699 1772, Vicar of Desborough, Northants who was the son of Thomas (5).

There is then a gap of 130 years until Arthur Clendon (10) was admitted in 1887. Arthur was the great great great grandson of Thomas (7), whose father was Thomas (5) and grandfather was William (4). However, Arthur did not know until 1929 that his forebears had been at Emmanuel. This is confirmed by the correspondence (traced in both the Emmanuel Archives and in Clendon papers) that he had with Peter Giles the then Master of the College. They had met at a Dinner in Birmingham of the Cambridge Graduates Club and Arthur brought up the subject of his ancestry. Arthur followed this up with a letter dated October 19th 1929, in which he says:

> . . . my Grandfather's grandfather* was Thomas Clendon A.M. Vicar of Sturry and Reculvers [sic] Kent . . . I wonder whether you have any particulars of him. He is the earliest ancestor I have any certain knowledge of and the family tradition is that he came from Northamptonshire. I did not know of which University he was. All the Club very much appreciated your kindness in coming to our Dinner and not least the Emmanuel men present.

Peter Giles consulted "Alumni Cantabridgienses" and sent Arthur the information on a post card. In a letter to his son Douglas dated Oct 24th Arthur expressed his excitement about this discovery in the following words:

> I have had some most interesting letters from Giles, Master of Emmanuel. He has discovered that Thomas Clendon, my grandfather's grandfather* Vicar of Sturry was at Emmanuel as well as his father & grandfather & perhaps 2 generations earlier. I give on the back the tree as sent by Giles . . .

It thus seems clear that the family connection did not influence Arthur or his parents in their choice of College in 1887. Nevertheless it was Arthur's own connection that caused his son Douglas (11) to choose Emmanuel in 1919. In 1948, when the full history was known, Ryland (12) applied. At his selection interview he was told that the family connection tipped the balance in favour of an offer of a place. David (13) followed in 1953.

Details of these four later Clendons are given below. Arthur's are taken from Alumni Cantabridgienses, and the remainder from College and family records.

> 10. CLENDON Arthur. Adm sizar at Emmanuel Oct 5 1887 Son of J. Esq of 199 Monument Road, Edgbaston Birmingham. School, King Edwards

---

* Arthur made an error here. The Vicar of Sturry is his grandfather's grandfather's father.

High Birmingham. Matric Michs 1887; Exhibitioner; Prizeman; BA
1890; MA 1894. MA (London) 1897 . . .

Arthur's career details have been omitted as they are covered earlier in the
book. His father's initial is erroneously given as 'J' instead of 'T', and the
address is that of the Hickinbotham family, his father having emigrated to
New Zealand.

11. *CLENDON Douglas Ryland Thomas. Adm. Oct 1 1919. Matric Oct 22*
1919. Son of Arthur Clendon (10) schoolmaster of Edgbaston
Birmingham. School, King Edwards High, Birmingham 1909-1916. Also
at Royal Military College, Sandhurst, Berkshire 1916; exempt from
Previous examination for military service. BA 1922. MA 1961.

12. *CLENDON Thomas Ryland. Adm. Oct 1948. Matric Oct 1948. Son of*
Douglas Clendon (11) medical practitioner of 53 Wimpole Road
Colchester. School, Epsom College. BA 1951. MB BChir 1954/55. MA
1957.

13. *CLENDON David Arthur. Adm. Oct 1953. Matric Oct 1953. Son of*
Douglas Clendon (11) medical practitioner of 53 Wimpole Road
Colchester. School, Epsom College. BA 1956. Ord. deacon (St Albans) Jun
1 1958, priest (St Albans) May 24 1959. MA 1961.

Links with the College have continued by Ryland and David, through
attending the formal re-unions, and informally. Members of the 1956 Third
boat, coxed by David, (reported then as "A lively Third boat did very well
to win its oars and brought the boat up to the third division"), subsequently
clubbed together and bought a shell coxless four for the College Boat Club.
David attended its launch, and has recently been invited by the Master to
the dedication of its successor, a coxed four.

In 1993, Ryland was greatly assisted by Dr Sarah Bendall, then the
College archivist, who searched the College archives for records of the early
Clendons. This included a visit on 25th January 1993 to study the archives
and have lunch with the Fellows at High Table. He was given photocopies
of records concerning early Clendons, and donated some photographs and
other Clendon papers to the College. One of these, a letter from Douglas to
his mother, was subsequently published with a pen and ink illustration, in
the Emmanuel College Magazine (Vol LXXV) under the Title "Letter from a
Freshman, 1919'. It is reproduced below.

Letter from a Freshman, 1919

"21 Earl Street
Cambridge
28-10-19

Dear Mother,
> *You ask about my rooms. They are about 12x15 ft and contain at present*

Tables 3 (Two I am having cleared out)
Desks, Writing, very splendid 1 (just arrived)
Pictures, enormous. 7
Ditto small innumerable.
Wall attachments, useless, with shelves 2
Ornaments to hide them 500000
Chairs, large comfortable 2
ditto small, uncomfortable 4
ditto, ditto, ditto, cane for piano 1
Pianos, good, 1
China on mantlepiece, etc about 50 pieces
Ditto on wall, about 20 pieces
Edward VII, photo of, complete with Minoru and trainer, in frame 1
Family, Landladie's and friends, photos of 9
Matches, holders for, stone, 2 Ash trays, large brass 1 Mantle piece, attachment
for, complete with nine mirrors and many nick nacks 1
Brackets, gas, good, 1
Brackets, gas, bad, 1
Cushions 4
Settee 1
Also carpets (several layers) rugs, five irons coal scuttle clock cupboards shelves
and oddities.

The desk is a splendid affair. Everyone spots it as soon as they get in the room.
It is the only bit of furniture which is pleasing to the eye. The rest of the room is
so very 'Furnished apartments'. The wallpaper I imagine was put on as a
celebration of Evlyn's second birthday. Have I told you about Evlyn? She is the
only child of the house. Everything happened 'When Evlyn was two'. They have
kept house ever since Evlyn was two. When Evlyn was two Mrs Porter made her
only excursion out of Cambridge. She went to Southport for a week. I have heard
Evlyn's life history from her second birthday (I don't think she was ever any
younger) until the present day. She married last vac and lives in the country. I

get it in episodes. Episode one was related to me while the tea things were being cleared away half-an-hour after I arrived here. If I am skilful I only get two episodes per meal – one for laying & one for clearing away. At breakfast I generally manage to get away at the end of the current events. Its very like the pictures. Continuous performance. I have now reached the stage when the spool has wound itself round and I am recognising the opening scenes. There are other serials. The college porter is engaged to what will be his fourth wife. This is called *Money for nothing or the financial status of the Porter's wives with notes on the current romance*. There is also 'The man upstairs' on 'How to live on potted meat and fish paste', 'Daily report on hubby's views on life', 'Talks with Miss Beale' or 'Spicy selections from Cambridge scandals' and so on. All this fails to depress me at all.

I have written to thank for the desk which is a beauty. It has given a tremendous spurt to my letter writing. So far I have spent £43-0-0 which includes Matric fee Caution money Amal clubs and a blazer. It seems a lot.

Good by
Best love
Douglas"

CHAPTER FIFTEEN

A RUBY RHYME

Peter Clendon wrote this for his speech at Ryland and Susan's Ruby
Wedding celebration on January 9th 1994.

When Ry first met Sue, it was love at first sight
But to win her fair heart he sure had to fight
Her head was turned by a number of beaus
But she was quietly waiting for Ry to propose.

He got down on one knee and said "Marry me Sue"
She said "Yes of course, let's have a big do".
And so they got wed on a cold January day
And started a family without much delay.

Sally was born in March the next year
It was on Sue's birthday, two reasons to cheer,
Caroline followed and then Judith too
Three girls in a row what were they to do.

Three children were born, yet no 'son and heir'
But it wasn't long after that Peter was there,
A son at last after all of these years
But "Look at him Sue, he's got my big ears"!

The biggest was next, of course I mean Tom
They thought he was twins, but out came just one
The family was growing and filling the nest
So they decided to give having children a rest.

Then eight years later, while on a week-end
In Amsterdam, Sue got pregnant again;
Nine months later when out popped the 'pest'
Ry and Sue had six of the best!

Now all six have left home and are all fully grown
Five have got wed and have kids of their own
So Granny and Gramps have time on their hands
And spend it all travelling to far away lands.

From New Zealand to China and back again home
Year after year they continue to roam
All over the world on their various sorties
But always returning to stay "Trusthouse Forte's"!

Forty years on we are all gathered here
So raise up your glasses and give them a cheer
They've come a long way since Jan '54
Let's hope they're together for many years more.